GOODNESS TO GO

A Handbook for Humanitarians

Fran I. Hamilton, M.D.

Goodness To Go

A Handbook for Humanitarians

by Fran I. Hamilton, M.D.

Copyright © 2013 by Fran I. Hamilton, M.D.
Goodness to Go
Printed in the United States of America
ISBN 978-0-9889388-9-2

Publisher's Cataloging-in-Publication Data
Hamilton, Fran I., 1955 -
Goodness to Go: A Handbook for Humanitarians
by Fran I. Hamilton.
     p. cm.
     includes index

Dedicated to Grace Shanti

with gratitude, respect and love

Contents

Section Three: Mobilize Integral Service

Section Four: Integrate Heart, Head, and Hands

Author's Note

Goodness To Go is a handbook for humanitarians dedicated to the spirit of service that lives within us all. Proceeds benefit the missions of the Goodness To Go social enterprise, including support of girl empowerment programs developed by the Child In Need Institute (CINI) in Calcutta, India. For decades, CINI's programs have uplifted the lives of millions of impoverished people in the birthplace of my daughter, Grace Shanti.

A special focus of the Goodness To Go enterprise is joining the twenty-first century's global abolitionist movement and emancipation networks to end involuntary servitude, especially that of children. Every form of human trafficking must end. It's been 150 years since the U.S. Civil War, and as slavery was ending in the United States, the Thirteenth Amendment to the Constitution was drafted. It states that "involuntary servitude shall not exist going forward." May that be so in our lifetimes.

My life journey leading to the writing of *Goodness To Go* has circled our home planet. I was born into a medical family in Canada and taught at a Jamaican girls' school in the West Indies in my mid-twenties. In Boulder, Colorado I worked as the co-director of an alternative high school for several years before starting medical school. For a third year elective, I volunteered on a mobile hospital bus in rural India with the PRASAD (Philanthropic Relief Altruistic Service and Development) Project. This profound opportunity deepened my global citizenship and awareness of integral service as a flow of goodness between equals.

After residency, I worked as a family physician and attending faculty member in poverty-stricken areas of upstate New York, which included serving as the medical director for nursing homes caring for disabled adults. Back in Colorado, I worked at the People's Clinic for uninsured patients before joining Boulder Family Practice in 1995. In the marvelous juggle of life, I'm grateful for the ongoing opportunity to practice integrative medicine in the foothills of the Rocky Mountains.

On Christmas Eve of 2000, Mark Sherman and I returned from Calcutta with our adopted daughter, Grace Shanti. Ten years later, we flew back to India for Grace's first visit to the land of her birth. This challenging and transformative threshold in our lives was chronicled in a blog that is contained in Goodness To Go's website (www.goodnesstogo.org).

The highlight of the journey for me was meeting Samir Chaudhuri, M.D., the pediatrician and public health physician who has served as the founding director of CINI since 1975. Dr. Chaudhuri is a humanitarian of great integrity who has developed more than 100 sustainable grassroots programs that uplift five million lives with a relatively small annual budget. In 2011, the World Health Organization awarded CINI's remarkable effectiveness. The Goodness To Go social enterprise works in partnership with CINI to augment programs that empower "the girl child at risk for the flesh trade" to have expanded educational and occupational opportunities.

Throughout my life, calls to the path of service have engaged me, including professional work in the fields of education, health care, and wellness coaching. Although event planning and fund-raising for nonprofits have been woven throughout ongoing explorations of what ignites and sustains my social conscience, I haven't worked as a professional activist or community organizer. Each one of us brings all of who we are and the totality of our life experiences to our involvements. For me, decades of daily spiritual practice and creative endeavors, in addition to ongoing formal education, parenting, and professional disciplines, have been integrated into all aspects of my life.

Although most religious traditions recognize the value of engaging in compassionate, humanitarian service, this handbook does not come from a religious point of view. While the word "God" is not used in the four sections of *Goodness To Go*, a spiritual quality infuses them in much the same way that it infuses genuine gratitude, humility, and the cultivation of an open heart and mind. There are countless names for the unconditional spirit of goodness. In Sanskrit, for example, the power of good-heartedness is *suhrdaya shakti* or *shubha*. This auspicious goodness is beyond the dualities of good and bad based on relative value judgments.

For millennia, spiritual traditions have invoked the vision that mutually beneficial human actions connect heaven and earth. Ralph Waldo Emerson wrote, "Go put your creed into your deed." If you choose not to include the mystery of the sacred in your worldview, you may be able to overlook occasional references to it throughout *Goodness To Go*.

The cultivation of faith in a mystery or intelligence beyond the full comprehension of the mind is important to many people. Alice Walker calls this creative intelligence "The One Big Life shared by us all." Some people refer to it as the Presence or Sacred Source. David James Duncan calls it "the Creator, the One who loves us all in such a huge way". Each one of us is living today as a result of the love of thousands, even millions before us and all around us. Lynne McTaggart refers to our all-embracing, interconnected resonance as "the Bond." Whatever your personal perspective, hold your preferred name for what many experience as a higher power or supreme consciousness when it is referred to in this book.

There is an elegance and generosity in our intention to find the goodness in us and invite it to come forth. Each individual's path manifests uniquely. During a doctor's visit, we may want a single prescription or magic pill to deliver the goal of complete wellness. Most often, this is a misguided illusion or simply wishful thinking. In addition to grace, it is the self-care, resources, and environments, both internal and external, that each person brings to the healing process that are key. In much the same way, the process that unfolds throughout this book offers guidance and perspective, not right answers or magic bullets. You'll discover your own values, truths, and create supportive communities as you articulate and act on your callings, commitments, and intentions to expand your service to life.

As the creative process of refining your gifts, skills, and integral service unfolds, remember that developing the internal motivation and resilience to change one's behavior is an ongoing process. Rekindle your heart and listen to your body. As a physician and educator, I spend much of my workday attempting to inspire and motivate patients to discover their own capacities to release fears and unhealthy choices as they incorporate more beneficial behaviors into their daily lives. Optimal personal and global wellness is not achieved by fear of negative consequences but by keeping love and respect for life shining in each moment.

Practice *does* make progress. Active engagement with the content and inquires within this book is key to imbibing what it has to offer. If you want to digest a delicious meal, it's not enough to simply read a cookbook. Gathering your resources, cooking the food, and ingesting your creation are required. Remember that the integration of new behaviors into daily life often takes at least four to six weeks. Metamorphosis may take a little longer. Specific stories and particular experiences may become portals for you to experience the emotional inspiration of your ethical values. While integral service is grounded in everyday experience, the ongoing refinement of your intentions and the effective mobilization of your inherent goodness is a great multi-dimensional adventure.

A treasure trove of multifaceted jewels from around the globe awaits you. As you engage with *Goodness To Go*, listen for your call to action. The incorporation into your life of even one idea from this book may be enough to kindle and sustain inspiration as you mobilize compassion through your integral service.

Acknowledgments

Everyone and everything that has ever come into being is a result of untold evolutionary forces, astonishing synchronicities, and unfathomable mysteries. Creation is inter-being. At least a lifetime of relationships and opportunities has contributed to the writing of *Goodness To Go*. Gratitude flows to each person who has shared goodness with me in any way, who has fed or befriended me, taught or challenged me, supported or mended me, forgiven or inspired me, or who has been open to receiving these gifts from me. For every opportunity to learn and expand my understanding, for every moment of compassion and kindness, wisdom and love, for the magnificent beauty and bounty of life on planet Earth and the happiness at the heart of things, I give thanks.

My mother loves language and my father revels in the quest for knowledge and skillful means. My Aunt Fran's enthusiasm for life was spirited and Uncle Dave's creative wisdom was healing. The generosity of several teachers has been particularly potent in my life: Sheila Paterson, David Marsh, Jim Crosby, M.D., Stan Erney, M.D., Max Regan, and Dr. Clarissa Pinkola Estes. The exemplary lives of many humanitarians, writers, and visionaries, including Dr. Jean Houston, Lynne Twist, Mahatma Gandhi, and Martin Luther King, Jr., continue to motivate the missions of Goodness To Go. The teachings of the Siddha Yoga meditation path and Swami Chidvilasananda guide me daily with their wisdom and grace. May my deep respect, gratitude, and love know no bounds.

I'm grateful for every teacher, student, and patient who has engaged with me in reciprocal learning, and for every encounter that has enriched my compassion and strengthened my resilience. Many thanks to Mark Sherman for building my dream writing studio and for his tremendous support of our social enterprise, Goodness To Go. During early stages of writing of this book, Claudia Murray offered encouragement as well childcare on that Sunday afternoon five years ago during which I scribed seven initial chapter titles. In many ways, serving as Grace Shanti's mother is the essential inspiration and motivation that keeps the fires of Goodness To Go burning bright.

Goodness To Go

The generosity, steadfast support, interior book design, and cheerful equanimity of Dina Carson at Iron Gate Publishing made it possible to launch *Goodness To Go* into the world. I appreciate Jody Berman's skillful editorial counsel and the generosity of every reader, underwriter, volunteer, publicist, printer, and distributor who contributed to making this vision tangible. The power of love of many people is needed to create and manifest almost any meaningful endeavor. Angie Francis reviewed the raw manuscript, and her contributions to the Goodness To Go social enterprise have been invaluable. Megan Yalkut at Hamsa Designs developed many versions of the logo, blog, and book cover designs, and continues to update our social enterprise's website and social media presence.

Ongoing thanks to Boulder Community Hospital, medical colleagues, and the patients I'm honored to serve. Their support of a flexible work schedule allows me to embrace callings in addition to medicine, including the missions of Goodness To Go and Child In Need Institute. To mobilize the spirit of giving, Goodness To Go is committed to developing an integrated K–12 service learning curriculum, to inspiring interconnected communities of Goodness To Go groups internationally, and to expanding programs that prevent girls from being sold into Calcutta brothels. Please contact us if you have ideas or skills you'd like to contribute. We are also deeply honored and grateful to partner with Dr. Samir Chaudhuri who has served as the founding director of Calcutta's Child In Need Institute for forty years.

Bountiful thanksgiving to beloved Grace Shanti Sherman, who was seven years old when this book began to take form. I am blessed beyond my ken to serve as your mother, amazing Grace; your love, compassion, and wisdom inspire me in all ways. May this book be an offering to you, to all children and their families, to this and future generations, to everyone everywhere. May it inspire the creation of untold legacies of compassion in action. May our goodness be on the go so that all life can thrive in vibrant health, loving harmony, and deep peace.

Fran I. Hamilton, M.D.

Mother's Day 2013

Boulder, Colorado

Introduction

Welcome to *Goodness To Go*. This book is a resource to support, encourage, and mobilize the spirit of service that yearns to be expressed in our world. You are on planet earth at this time for a reason. Whether your integral service is called volunteerism, civic participation, or sacred activism, you are needed

Utilize this handbook for humanitarians to translate your natural compassion into beneficial actions that are sustainable and enjoyable. Your generosity includes wisdom, discernment, and remembrance that self-care is essential. The paradigm of integral service presented in *Goodness To Go* is free of judgment and guilt about adding more "shoulds" to your to-do lists. Start where you are. A depleted caregiver needs rejuvenation while those with vibrant health may be eager to explore new ways to express their compassion in action.

The dynamic integration of self-care and sustainable service is a key principle throughout *Goodness To Go*. Woven throughout each section is a process of self-inquiry that unfolds as you pause to reflect on questions, quotes, and ideas. The practice of articulating insights, ideas, and actions steps is valuable for clarifying the evolving vision of your integral service. As you engage with the material, you'll clarify service intentions, practices for self-care, community or global issues that especially call you, and specific action steps that are mutually beneficial.

Our lives have many periods of transition. No matter what life stage or generation we belong to, we yearn to be free to create a life that is meaningful for us. Our noble hearts want goodness to expand on planet earth, and the expression of this natural goodness is the ground and heart of *Goodness To Go*. Its focus is the expression of our innate goodness in unconditional service that honors both recipient and giver, free of attachment to a particular outcome.

Compassion in Action

For many healthcare practitioners, the natural inclination for life to heal itself, for people to be whole, is readily apparent. I share the trust that healthy people empowered with the knowledge of their goodness will naturally utilize this power for the welfare of all. Allow yourself to be open to the process offered in *Goodness To Go* and to aligning with a worldview that sees everyone as a potential expression of our basic human goodness.

You may have been disheartened in the past when initial flames of inspiration felt smothered by the busyness of everyday life. Trust that the embers of inspiration do not extinguish completely. Often the sheer magnitude and multiplicity of global concerns constrict our heart with a sense of overwhelm. With compassion, we can bring spaciousness to contracted states of mind and harmonize needs for care of our soul with sustainable service to our world.

Human beings serve social networks that are becoming global and expanding exponentially. Many of us want to move beyond modern-day culture wars and polarized political extremism that demonize the "other side." We yearn for the wisdom of humility and clarity to be free from the fury of our own resentments, wrote theologian-philosopher Reinhold Niebuhr, longing to be free from imprisonment in fears of each other.

Despite the ambivalence and ambiguity of the human condition, and the moral challenges of integrating idealism and realism, there is delight in being alive. The worldview of *Goodness To Go* includes this realistic idealism, celebrating our magnificence as it acknowledges human frailty and our capacity to inflict brutal harm. Constructive contention vitalizes actions based on democratic values; an enforced or apathetic consensus is meaningless. Keeping our spirit and hope alive requires inspiring stories, supportive communities, and sustainable approaches to reigniting our courage and resilience.

Each one of us is travelling in our own way on the path of life serving life. In every moment, let's move at our own pace consciously and deliberately. It's helpful to relax our grip on any attachments to beliefs or habitual patterns that no longer serve us. Sometimes we need to go into old blockages and constrictions to release them. Although this book honors our inherent goodness, it's not about naïve hopefulness, being a "do-gooder," or being so heavenly minded that we're no earthly good. Rather than a top-down paradigm where provisions are handed out to under-resourced people, integral service is a flow of mutual empowerment between equals.

Explore choices for living in the world with moral engagement, creating new stories of *us* living *now*. In many ways, *Goodness To Go* springs from conservatism of shared values that give meaning to our collective narrative, such as mutual respect, justice, and environmental health. When we're motivated to conserve something essential that we value, we're willing to transform alienation to empathy. We mobilize the skills of our heart, head, and hands so that our legacy flourishes beyond our lifetimes. This is the tradition of conservation and activism from which *Goodness To Go* emerges.

Intrinsic to a life well lived is alignment with our ethics and values. Another essential element in our pursuit of happiness is giving back. *Paying it forward* or offering our integral service is not merely an add-on to a meaningful life. Caring for life gives meaning to life. Multiple global issues around the world are calling us. European nations are negotiating relationships and solutions to their debt crises, civil wars are raging as other wars draw to a close, and glaciers are melting at alarming rates. We can adjust skillfully and creatively, not merely adapt to toxic, dysfunctional situations. Every challenge and transition offers opportunities for new perspectives, increased wisdom, and the gift of caring for life.

Change is an inside job. Many people have found that commitment to an ongoing process of self-inquiry through life coaching, therapy, or regular spiritual practice supports lasting change. Learning is experiential—you feel it in your body, your heart, and in the opening of doors of your mind. Our quests lead us deeper into our hearts as well as to the edges—more frontiers than fringes—of what we think we know. It's valuable to resource our resiliency. Trust in our capacity to engage in this transformative process of expanding our perceptions, opening our hearts and minds, and serving the world in mutually beneficial ways.

Integrity is the essence of everything that is meaningful. With heart, head, and hands aligned with core values, be a *go-giver*. For decades, a social psychologist and priest named Steve Lawler studied a powerful pattern followed by people around the world who enjoy life fully. These go-givers express their vitality in ways that create good news for and with others. Lawler describes this pattern as: "Know yourself. Be yourself. Give yourself away." Giving ourselves includes offering our goodness in generative, sustainable interchanges. "The caldron of compassion," wrote deep ecologist Joanna Macy, "can reconnect us with our power. We are interwoven threads in the intricate tapestry of life."

Goodness To Go

How to Use This Book

Living mindfully and serving with kindness are important for life to flourish on earth. This handbook offers guidance and perspective as you recognize what is true for you. From an inner well-spring of enthusiasm and compassion, your path of community or global service unfolds as you clarify and act on your callings, commitments, and intentions.

No one else, including parents, high-end consultants, psychologists, politicians, or psychic astrologers, can tell you your purpose or what forms the expression of your gifts will take over your lifetime. However, as you work with the tools offered in this book, you'll create a context and process that will enable you to clarify your own vision and insight about what you want to offer, the enthusiasm to take the next step, and ways to sustain your compassionate heart.

Many themes are explored in *Goodness To Go*. Although you may choose to read it front to back, reflecting on the questions at the end of each chapter, you may simply want to open to a page at random and explore its content for a day or a year. The inquiries woven throughout the book provoke creative thought and action, helping to translate your dreams into new life designs. As your vision of integral service evolves, an invaluable practice is to keep a companion journal of emerging insights, questions, ideas, and action steps. This journal might also include space for sketches, images, and articles of interest.

Goodness To Go is divided into four sections. The first section focuses on the inspiration of the heart, and the next on empowering the mind. The third section serves to clarify your integral service and mobilize your helping hands; the final section integrates heart, head, and hands as you launch your goodness to go. After each of the four sections, take time to pause and look back over your notes and reflections. This is an opportunity to distill and describe the essence of your explorations and discoveries. Look for patterns of interest and energy in your responses to various inquires posed. Contemplate an element, insight, or question that stood out for you in some way. A useful approach is outlined in the A*B*C*D Self-Inquiry Process following this Introduction.

As you engage with the self-inquiries throughout *Goodness To Go*, may your heart and mind be open to compassion and wonder. Allow your hands to be open to receive as well as to extend in fellowship and goodwill. "Trust yourself and you'll know how to live," wrote Goethe. Remember that the assimilation of new behaviors into daily life takes at least four to six weeks, and ongoing clarification and incorporation of our intentions and action plans is revitalizing. Flashes of insight can fade away if not tended with care and writing brief daily assessments in a notebook is illuminating, even exhilarating. As you tread lightly on the earth, recognize that there are infinite paths leading to the heart of goodness.

Although we may not always see it, everything plays to our greater good as we find enjoyable, sustainable ways to express our natural goodness. Consider inviting friends to meet regularly in small Goodness To Go gatherings or creating an online community to motivate and mobilize compassion in motion. Uplift one another's spirits and support the implementation of specific, scheduled action steps.

Remember two abiding guidelines: be free of guilt and judgment. Honor your interest in engaging with *Goodness To Go* and participating on the path of right action without guarantee of the outcome. Resource your resilience as you cultivate empathy and equanimity, curiosity and enthusiasm. Together in this perilous time we have the opportunity to strengthen ourselves and skillfully contribute to a transformative global shift. "We can do it," wrote the champion of civil rights Cesar Chavez, "Yes we can." Compassion for self and others is our guide. Let's begin.

A*B*C*D* Self-Inquiry Process

A process of *appreciative inquiry* that employs our guiding principles of compassion and nonjudgment is outlined below. Active engagement with questions woven throughout *Goodness To Go* helps to clarify what is true for you and makes the adventure of manifesting your integral service more meaningful and fruitful.

The A*B*C*D* self-inquiry process is a suggested framework for easeful, in-depth exploration of topics or questions in which you're interested. As ideas and questions present themselves and you actively engage with the process outlined below, additional insights and inquiries that can serve to focus ongoing contemplations will be generated. Experiment with this process and modify it to suit your nature as you engage with *Goodness To Go*.

Let your whole body relax as you feel the chair beneath you. Bring your attention to sensations in the present moment. Be aware of the sound of your breath and the expansion of your chest. Rest in the pause between inhalations and exhalations. Observe the space in which the breath dissolves and arises. The power to turn within is in this pause.

A—Attention. Gather any supplies needed for a period of uninterrupted reflection and writing. Prepare yourself inside and out by focusing your attention on your topic of reflection. Do what is necessary to be at ease and undistracted in this moment.

B—Balanced Breath. Breathe evenly as you let go of thoughts and other mental activity. Follow the flow of your balanced breath into your heart. Formulate and optimize a question about your topic. Repeat this question silently to yourself.

C—Connect and Contemplate. Respectfully ask your heart for insights and wisdom related to your question, with the intent of aligning with your heart's attributes. Silently listen with gratitude for the voice of the heart. A response may come quickly or appear weeks later. Practice remaining open and attuned as you cultivate the power of patience.

D—Download and Describe. Use free writing to record your uncensored ideas, insights, thoughts, images, connections, related inquiries, and resources. Develop small, specific, scheduled steps to implement your action plan.

Take time to pause, reflect, and enjoy this process of self-inquiry and self-knowledge, noticing what you feel, think, and perceive, and making note of patterns of personal interest. Listen for the subtle voice of intuition and insight. Articulate and record your initial thoughts and questions as well as evolving inspirations and action steps.

Deeper self-knowledge and integrative understanding extend the power of opportunity to be ourselves fully and give ourselves in beneficial ways. The process of self-inquiry can be remarkably illuminating and useful. The examined life is worth living—enjoy your journey.

Section One

Summon Your Heart

A human being is part of the whole

called by us "universe."...

We experience ourselves ... as something

separate from the rest –

a kind of optical delusion of consciousness.

This delusion is a kind of prison for us,

restricting us to our personal desires and to

affections for a few persons

nearest to us.

Our task must be to free ourselves from this prison by

widening our circle of compassion

to embrace all living creatures and

the whole of nature in its beauty.

—Albert Einstein

1

We're All in This Together

Within is the fountain of good,
and it will ever bubble up,
if thou wilt ever dig.

—Marcus Aurelius

Now is the time for us to join together for our mutual benefit. We live on one small jewel of a planet with the astonishing ability to support life. We're needed, and our wake-up call is sounding. With compassionate hearts, open minds, and hands ready to act with benevolence, we're called to create a better world for ourselves and for all life.

We're stewards of this unfathomable gift of life on earth. Our home has not been inherited from our ancestors; it is borrowed from our children. Each one of us has unique gifts to offer to our world, and life is most meaningful when we're able to share our gifts with our communities and future generations. Gifts take many forms, and some have profoundly transformative effects for humanity. What we're giving informs where we're going.

The stories we tell about the world and our place in it change as our experience and understanding change. Some societies live their stories of mutual cooperation. Others focus on dominator worldviews. Stories can be cultural, personal, and archetypal. The myth of Prometheus, an archetypal tale of the hero's journey, recognizes the generosity of the heart and the unity of all life.

Prometheus saw that the transformative energy of fire was not meant to be controlled by the few and so he shared it with humanity for the benefit of all. With epic courage, Prometheus stole fire from gods who were often petty with greed, jealousy, and pride. These humanlike Olympians could be crudely dominating or, in some circumstances, generous with compassion and wisdom. Fortunately, Prometheus chose to be free of the hoarding mentality that tempts many monopolies. By mobilizing his goodness, Prometheus gifted humanity with the element of fire.

Fire power can be used to cook food, forge steel, or turn cities into infernos. Fire also symbolizes other transformative powers, including expanded knowledge and the inspiration to create, serve, or discover new tools of technology. The wise use of any powerful energy requires compassion and intelligent wisdom. We have the freedom to choose how we'll use power. Harnessing the transformative fire of nuclear energy, for example, might light our homes or poison our home planet. The fires of cravings in our senses and minds can wreak havoc, whereas gentle flames of love are life affirming. Because transformative powers can be destructive as well as creative, it's important to keep the heart of mutual respect and kindness in mind.

There are several variations of the mythic adventure of Prometheus. In one telling of the tale, the mighty Zeus played the role of a benevolent teacher celebrating Prometheus's expanded capacities rather than punishing him for a perceived hubris and disruption of the status quo. After learning that humans had achieved new levels of power in the form of fire, Zeus met with Prometheus to discuss its wise use in the new paradigm.

With compassion and insight, Zeus informed the intrepid pioneer that the nature of fire is to transform all it touches, and that this mighty force could be used for good or ill. The ability to tame and train the power of fire, as well as to discipline any egotistical attachment to that power, would be paramount. Zeus then promised to share ancient knowledge with humanity about two specific qualities that are required to wield any power with wisdom and skill. In this teaching story, the key values for right use of power are *reverence* and *merciful justice*. If we forget or ignore this, our new powers will be our undoing.

Justice with mercy and reverence for life are mighty callings. Both require self-knowledge and the empathic imagination to enter into someone else's perspective. Compassion, the generous willingness to make a place for another in one's heart and mind, informs reverence and justice. Both are elements of the universal Golden Rule. Merciful justice is born from the recognition of our deep interdependence and takes into account the needs of the whole. Reverence implies respect and awareness of sacredness. Honoring our oneness with the miracle of life in all of its diversity is an expression of reverence.

Reverence and justice are transformative inspirations essential to the discovery and expression of our goodness to go. Dr. Martin Luther King, Jr., who recognized that injustice destroys societies, wrote, "The arc of the moral Universe is long, but it bends toward justice." Reverent justice is not about lofty idealism or dichotomies such as good versus bad. Rather, the expression of our inherent goodness involves staying open with clarity and kindness to acknowledging all that is.

Like Prometheus and many humanitarians before us, we're able to mobilize our goodness and offer our abilities, energy, time, and other gifts as our integral service. The compassion inherent to both justice and reverence also informs service. As our empathy awakens and deepens, we practice cultivating that which benefits all beings. We're embarking on a great adventure that will uplift our lives and live on as our legacy. Let's clarify what mobilizing our goodness to go means.

What Is *Goodness*?

Goodness is a profound inner resource that can be transmitted to others. That which is genuinely beneficial to others and ourselves is goodness. The deep compassion and authenticity of goodness are free of judgments of what we "should" do or rigidly adhere to moralistic expectations to "do the right thing." The heart of goodness is within us. Like flowers opening in sunlight, we naturally benefit from the inherent goodness of justice and reverence. Does our sense of justice arise from respect for the dignity of each living being? Do we feel reverence for life in all of its expressions? Being reverent is not merely acting reverential on the outside. Simply "being nice" will not suffice.

Although language is a valuable tool in the expression of our intent, it has significant limitations. As we consider what it means to be good and true, we recognize that many people were raised in family cultures where they strove to be "good" and not "bad." As a result of early conditioning (including punishments for not being "good enough"), personal reactions to the word *good* have been affected by arbitrary rules and authoritative injunctions. In the context of this book, however, goodness is beyond dualities such as good–bad or right–wrong.

The beneficial element of something is its goodness. Healthy, nutritious food is good for us, yet to assimilate its nutrition we need to chew, swallow, digest, and fully imbibe it. A good-natured person often has a cheerful, cooperative disposition that is inspired to render loving service. A good-hearted soul is naturally kind and generous, free of the guilt or aggressive power-seeking of do-gooders.

Our egos can be critical, even vicious judges of ourselves or others. Ego-mind often thinks we're "better" than others because of what we do or don't do. It insists on taking credit for any good that our actions may bring. It may deem itself superior or "holier than thou" if we're able to resist temptations and indulgence in excess. In the movie *Chocolat*, a character says, "I think we can't go around measuring our goodness by what we don't do, by what we deny ourselves, what we resist, and who we exclude. I think we've got to measure goodness by what we embrace, what we create, and who we include."

All children are born with basic goodness. Even as adults, if we look for the good in ourselves and others, we'll usually find it. Our goodness is our natural capacity for generosity, loving kindness, compassion, and happiness. Our inherent goodness is grounded in the intent and effort to express this goodness in the form of integral service. "Sometimes we forget," writes Nobel Peace laureate Archbishop Desmond Tutu, "that human beings are fundamentally good! This is a world that is part of a moral universe."

Humans are complex, multifaceted, and multidimensional beings and character is formed through our responses to countless experiences. Environments, internal as well as external, shape our development. Our values may be unclear or change, and our motives may be mixed. Nevertheless, it's realistic to have deep trust in the goodness of the human heart. This handbook for humanitarians is written from the perspective that each one of us has the capacity to experience and express this innate goodness.

What Is Goodness to Go?

Goodness to go is integral service, mutually empowering, beneficial contributions to the welfare of others that can be enjoyable, even thrilling, as well as sustainable. "Thrillionaires" light up when they give. Goodness as compassion-in-motion creates and sustains cultures of giving. It arises from the intention to be wholly integrated with one's deepest values, visions, and life commitments.

The ongoing commitment to live for the common good requires all of one's resources, including patience, intelligence, and compassion. We can create lives that are both good *and* "successful." As the intention to weave integral service into the fabric of life is refreshed on a daily basis, practice makes progress. This kind of service is *incorporated*—literally united with our corpus, the body of our lives—and so is naturally sustainable. It recognizes our oneness with all life, and from this awareness emerges the natural impulse to be of service. Our goodness to go is radically sustainable because it is rooted in the ever-present source of one's inner self. It is the flowing and flowering outward of the compassion dwelling within the heart of being.

The meaning of other words used throughout this book may need to be refreshed, updated, or returned to their original intent. *Altruism* is unselfish regard for the welfare of others. *Conscience* is not merely a generator of guilt but rather "the consciousness of the moral goodness of one's own conduct, intentions, or character together with a feeling of obligation to do right or be good."

As we are, such are the times. Centuries ago, St. Augustine reflected on the themes of altruism and conscience, and noted that as we live good lives, the times are also good. Although human beings have different capacities, the potential for humanism lives in every heart. The degree to which we nurture and manifest our potential is up to us.

A humanitarian is a philanthropic person who promotes human well-being. A friend told me that when she was a college student, she wandered around campus saying to herself, "I want to be a humanitarian." Perhaps you're holding this book because you've felt a similar call to express gratitude, to share resources, or to uplift spirit when it suffers.

Although a humanitarian is first a human being, what does it mean to be human? It may be that our essential spiritual being has taken human birth for the opportunities it offers for our soul's maturation. Others believe that biology and survival strategies tell our whole story. We share most of our coded genetic information with other species of life on earth. There are many opinions about what determines and constitutes human nature. We may be a paradoxical mix of genetic coding for both compassion and competition, but is that all we are?

Decades ago, Ram Dass's book *How Can I Help?* inspired many people. Those with years of philanthropic experience suggest that a more useful question to ask is, "What do you need?" Implicit in this question is a respect that people know what they need and are willing to utilize resources to help meet that need. In this vein, any sentiments of paternalism, colonialism, or fostering dependence are replaced by mutual respect between partners creating solutions together.

Although helping those suffering or in need can be benevolent and charitable, it is this aspect of "aiding the needy" that taints the word *charity* for those who regard it as a Band-Aid. If we define charity as aid to another person who is perceived to be less resourced and more needy than ourselves, judgmental dualism and separation are implied. The charity of true service, however, is a mutually respectful and empowering relationship between equals.

It's true that people suffering from systemic injustice need more than temporary fixes. An integrated systems approach that addresses underlying causes of disparities is essential to transforming inequitable socioeconomic structures. The "teach them to fish" metaphor reminds us that distributing fish, no matter how kindly, does not end hunger. Solar panels are not helpful if the community doesn't have the skills to repair malfunctions or the resources to replace broken parts. Building schools does not guarantee that children will receive an education.

Nevertheless, there are times when people do have an immediate need to be bandaged with tender loving care to help their wounds heal. That is why both approaches—the transformation of dysfunctional systems as well as direct aid—are needed. Some call this "giving with both left and right hands." Integral service arises from an inclusive awareness of both the left hand of immediate care and the right hand of systems transformation.

The word *philanthropy* comes from the Greek *philanthropia*, to love humankind. Love, it's been said, is what we are. A philanthropist or humanitarian whose goodwill promotes human welfare engages in love in action. The inherent goodness and beauty of our soul want to be expressed through actions emerging from a vibrant, inner discipline. This disciplined awareness supports the freedom to choose beneficial intentions and actions. If we bring only a semiconscious, laissez-faire approach to our actions, they can be harmful. "Oh, sorry, I didn't mean to hurt you" frequently follows unconscious or inattentive behaviors.

To be of integral, philanthropic service, first do no harm. This includes not disempowering self-sufficient people or misleading them with claims that imported infant formula is better than breast milk. Ignoring local systems of medical care or dropping off limited supplies of expensive, unavailable medicines is disempowering. Despite our best intentions, our actions can cause harm if they raise hopes with temporary social programs or create dependence on water or energy supplies that are not sustainable. Our commitment to ensuring the recipient's self-sufficiency needs to be long-term.

There are many examples of good intentions gone awry within the field of international development. All stake-holders affected must be involved in creating solutions for their problems as well as in acquiring necessary skills for ongoing problem solving. Dysfunctional socioeconomic paradigms can sometimes be modified through systemic collaboration. In other instances, toxic weeds need to be pulled out by their roots to make space for healthy gardens to flourish. Apartheid needed to be abolished, not merely reformed.

What Is *Integral Service*?

Integral service is compassion in action that serves our interconnected wholeness. Life naturally serves life. Rather than seeing something as broken that needs to be fixed or helping someone we judge as less powerful, integral service is a relationship between equals. It is mutually beneficial action that is so integrated with our core values that it's a natural expression of who we are.

Integral service is an offering of one's heart, mind, body, and soul. This offering honors everyone involved in the natural cycles of giving and receiving, and has nothing to do with paying lip service to superficial ideals. Beneficial actions that transform the world are offered by "evolutionaries" who understand that transformation of our world is integrated with our commitment to evolve ourselves. Personal evolution brings planetary transformation. Participating in this evolving, dynamic balance of giving and receiving brings meaning, happiness, and a state of deep contentment.

Marian Wright Edelman, a celebrated African American activist, is a life-long advocate for the rights of children. Edelman is the founder and president of the Children's Defense Fund and has described service as the very purpose of life. "It is the rent we pay for living on the planet," Edelman declares as she continues through her seventies to offer integral service to disadvantaged and vulnerable young people.

Throughout *Goodness To Go*, we'll honor the original, basic goodness of words such as *charitable* and *service*. Our in-breath reminds us of our need for self-care. Flowing out with the exhalation is our natural impulse to care for others. Offering service integrated with values such as compassion and generosity is central to most religious and spiritual paths. Integral service doesn't have a bleeding heart or polished egotistical pride; it's an act of love that diminishes the ego's hold on the self. Its unconditional offering is "selfless" in that it diminishes ego absorption in our small selves. As it gives of itself, integral service reveals our natural sacredness.

Global wisdom traditions recognize the divinity in all, honor the natural cycles of giving and receiving, and encourage the compassionate expression of our gratitude in concrete ways. Ralph Waldo Emerson wrote, "It's one of the most beautiful compensations of this life that no man can sincerely try to help another without helping himself. ... Serve and thou shall be served." That which is given from the spirit of service allows lives to flourish.

Volunteerism is important in the lives of countless individuals. Some activists call their service *informed action* to distinguish their efforts to transform root causes of social problems from *direct aid*. Others refer to their goodness to go as *creative* or *sacred activism*, regarding their social justice, energy equity, or environmental activism as engaged, practical compassion. Today's volunteers have been called the new humanitarians whose giving is "citizen generosity."

Cultivating goodness to go is a choice that calls for flexible perseverance and creative skill-building. Destructive criticism, pessimism, and defeatism require no particular skill to tear down hopes and dreams. "No pessimists ever discovered the secret of the stars, or sailed to an uncharted land, or opened a new heaven to the human spirit," wrote Helen Keller in celebration of integral optimism.

Negative connotations are sometimes projected onto words like *selfless service*. The mind can distort just about anything, and at times seems incapable of trusting that anyone intends to offer unconditional service. Viewing service as merely a Band-Aid given by self-righteous do-gooders can taint the lens through which we see the intent to give. More problematic is doubting every philanthropic act simply because some tricksters have siphoned off financial contributions intended to help vulnerable people.

Not every culture has a positive connotation of the word *service*. Although global spiritual traditions value compassionate service to humanity, various cultures express service differently. Also, the notion of service has been poisoned for some people by association with servitude and the abuse of servants and slaves serving "masters" who used ignoble, abusive force. It is the spirit of giving, not the words labeling the offering, that is the essence of integral service.

True service is not servitude. It is the mutual empowerment of equals, the upliftment of giver and receiver into a state of oneness. Acts of true philanthropy reflecting love of humanity have a simple, natural quality. The intuitive eye of the heart notices a need and responds with clarity and kindness. The light of generosity purifies and expands our heart and isn't sullied by ego's shadowed misunderstanding equating vastness with grandiosity. Humility doesn't proclaim itself humble; generosity doesn't trumpet its magnanimity.

A Taste of Integral Service

Near the end of my surgical rotation as an intern, an experience of integral service graced my life. It was a glorious summer day, and I was about to head out of the hospital on a much-anticipated adventure. Just before I turned off my pager, its unwelcomed beeping sounded. Although I was tempted not to answer, responsibility tapped on my conscience and I returned the call of the attending surgeon.

As I listened to his directions, I winced. Sinews of resistance began to constrict my heart as it became obvious that my plans to leave town would be delayed. The bowels of a woman with metastatic ovarian cancer were obstructed, and I was to write a preoperative physical examination in her hospital chart. Thinking that I could do my duty swiftly and efficiently, I swung my stethoscope around my neck. As the elevator ascended to her floor, I hoped that I could leave in time to join some portion of the festivities I'd been anticipating for weeks.

Entering the patient's room, I saw loved ones surrounding her. Below the bandana around the woman's bald head, luminous, pale blue eyes and her warm smile gently welcomed me. My heart relaxed in her kindness and I no longer felt like rushing my task. As I listened to her story as well as her heart sounds, I sensed subtle light permeating the room. The blessings of compassion warmed me from the inside out.

We were not strangers; a timeless sense of connected oneness was palpable. At one point the woman asked with some intensity, "You'll be there in the surgery, won't you?" My heart immediately answered, "*Yes.*" Yes is so much more than a word; it is an opening to a new world. Giving the woman a hug, I left her bedside to write the preoperative report.

Goodness To Go

When I called my attending surgeon, he asked me to assist with the palliative surgery. My response affirmed this moment of destiny.

Because it takes time for operating teams to prepare for unexpected surgeries, I went to my apartment to meditate. My restless mind found it challenging to be still and free of thoughts. Reverie and rumination were entrenched habits. However, this meditation was different. A profound stillness enveloped my mind. Its expansion was vast and its silence rested in the resonant space of the heart.

When I returned to my usual state of consciousness, an exquisite tranquility pulsed through me. It was difficult to imagine the agitating attachment that had gripped me earlier. As I walked back to the hospital, the world was illumined with soft light, inside and out. This state of grace and transformative experience of compassion continued for hours throughout the surgery. Since then, I've explored many ways to foster this inner state.

Our essential nature has been described as unbounded consciousness and we can choose to serve this ocean of compassion. The study of compassion has spread to scientific fields such as affective neuroscience, and evidence is growing for the beneficial effects on the mental and physical health of those who practice compassion.

As we commit to the practice of seeing and honoring each person we meet with kind regard, our offerings of integral service are continually refreshed. From this expanded perception, we call forth the highest and best in each other and ourselves. Staying small doesn't help anyone. If we defend our imagined limitations, they'll shrink our lives. Our greatness serves the greatness in others. As we live in kindness from our own strength and worthiness, we help to create an equitable, sustainable, and peaceful world.

Service to society and the global village is expressed in the Golden Rule. This transcultural value of reciprocity holds that we do unto others as we would have them do unto us—and as we do for ourselves. As we learn what is important for us personally, such as healthy food and environments, safety, shelter, education, work opportunities, freedom of faith, medical care, and merciful kindness, we realize that is what we're also to give to others. As we expand our concern to include the needs of the community as well as personal fulfillment, innovative and life-sustaining solutions are born.

What Is Sustainability?

If offering your goodness to go is to be more than a flash in the pan, it's important to find healthy, enjoyable ways to maintain your inspiration and motivation. Sustainability is a dynamic, committed, conscious response to changing needs. Sustainable service is integrated with our deepest values and becomes a natural expression of our compassion and generosity. This kind of service arises from a harmonious integration of our wholeness and is not merely another item on endless to-do lists.

Integral sustainability arises from an expanded awareness of life's interconnectedness. It lets go of dualistic perceptions that have polarized, either-or qualities, such as loss or gain, right or wrong, and praise or blame. Opposition and even antagonism prevail in dualistic thinking: *It's us or them. If you're not for me, you're against me.*

To perceive the whole, we must include not exclude. True integration is not merely tolerance but a deeply democratic process that invites and nurtures all energies to harmonize as one whole. To experience the whole, we need to open our intelligence to understanding its myriad facets and holding the creative tension of paradox and different perspectives.

As our hearts and minds open, we recognize our wholeness. A healthy mind requires the integration of two functional brain hemispheres with different abilities and orientations. The whole is more than the sum of its individual parts. Think of the contributions made by individuals such as Leonardo da Vinci and Albert Einstein. Both integrated the logic of left brain hemispheres with the pattern recognition and creative imagination of the right hemispheres. Consider the potential of billions of empowered whole brain–whole heart human beings to make the world a better place.

Sustainability was defined by the United Nations in 1987 as the ability of current generations to meet their needs without compromising the ability of future generations to meet theirs. This awareness recognizes that all life has a right to be here but, tragically, entire species are rapidly becoming extinct. Our minds can feel and our hearts think as we integrate formidable inner and outer resources to support healthier ecosystems for all life.

Life on earth is interconnected across time and space. This interconnection is an external manifestation of our internal integrity, our oneness. It is not sustainable or ethical for any person or group to disregard or compromise the integral well-being of others or of the whole.

Goodness To Go

The sense of entitlement that accompanies elitism is dangerous to life on earth. "All are expressions of one love," wrote environmentalist John Muir. "When one tugs at a single thing in nature, he finds it attached to the rest of the world."

Incorporating integral service into your life in a sustainable way does not imply the achievement of a static balance. The state of being unbalanced is a natural consequence of being alive. As a child, you may have stood in the middle of a teeter-totter making adjustments to maintain that simple balancing act. A sense of imbalance gives us messages about how to reorient as a harmonious whole. Feeling unbalanced or ungrounded may be telling us it's time for an adjustment or to turn the page to a new chapter in our lives. On the other hand, feeling groundless may be a state that we learn to live with.

In many ways, our lives are more like mobiles than balance beams. A mobile has a particular beauty when the balance of the suspended elements is harmonious. These elements may be different sizes, colors, and textures whose relationship to each other is constantly changing as they respond to currents of air. Together, however, their continuous dance creates a work of art. This balance is inherent to a well-designed mobile. Its harmony is sustainable. In much the same way, service can be a beautiful, integral, and naturally joyful current throughout our lives.

The Balanced Breath of Integral Service

As we give, so we receive. The in-breath of self-care naturally flows into the out-breath of service. We inhale divine inspiration and exhale our offering, letting it go into the world without judgment or expectation. Hippocrates wrote, "There is one common flow, one common breathing. All things are in sympathy." This common air, Walt Whitman wrote centuries later, bathes the globe. One cycle of breath balances our exhalation and inhalation with spaces between. Throughout *Goodness To Go*, all of the elements of one breath remind us to integrate self-interest and other-interest, receptive self-care and active service.

As we breathe in deep and breathe out long, we dynamically balance the rhythms and harmonies of our life's energy. Inhalation focuses on feeling and being, drawing in vital energy that flows to every cell in our body. To inspire is to be infused and enlivened with spirit. When we allow ourselves to exhale fully, we're able to extend life energy to the world with our thinking and doing functions as we make space once again for deep inspiration to occur.

A daily practice of breath meditation may enrich your engagement with *Goodness To Go*. With deep inhalations, refresh your self-care, and as you breathe out long, honor your commitment to integral service. Within each round of breath are pauses where the breath dissolves. Pay attention to the stillness and stability of the timeless moment in which the breath subsides and arises. These dissolving spaces are potent with resonate stillness, and their vitality is accessible throughout your day. Some call this eternal space the heart or still point.

Exhale service, inhale self-care. An essential element of the in-breath of self-care is regular physical exercise. Although you may have little time to go to a gym and little patience for exercise machines, find ways to include enjoyable physical movement in your life. When it's integrated with valued activities such as being in nature, walking children to school, or dancing, it takes less effort to incorporate exercise into daily schedules. Likewise, offering service can be naturally sustainable when it aligns with guiding principles and priorities of your life.

Self-care includes more than healthy food and regular exercise. Contemplative reading, time in nature, creative expression, life coaching, emotional clearing, centering prayer, and meditation are also elements of self-care that sustain integral service. As inner work brings about maturation and evolution, inner transformations illumine your world. Personal evolution is a generous, not selfish, priority that affects the legacy you leave.

Self-absorption is not the revitalizing self-care that is integral to cycles of giving and receiving. We have to have something to give before we can give. Guilt about needing time for ourselves is useless and disempowering. We need clear awareness about our values, which may evolve over time, as well as vigilance about the integrity of our alignment with those values.

An eleventh-century Persian philosopher and mathematician named Omar Khayyam described a pivotal awareness to practice: "Be happy. For this moment, this moment ... is your life." Most healthy humans want to experience happiness, not merely fleeting pleasure. Genuine happiness comes from integral alignment with our core values, generosity, and freedom—including freedom from attachment, greed, and intolerance. Integral service increases opportunities to experience our inherent joy and peace. In what ways has happiness been related to compassion in action in your life?

Goodness To Go

Together on Spaceship Earth

The beauty and mystery of life on earth is profound. If we're to be responsible stewards conserving the wonder of life, our integral service is essential. Wherever we're going, we're going together. The 14th Dalai Lama, a globally respected spiritual leader forced by military aggression from his Tibetan homeland, reminds us that, ultimately, the decision to save the environment must come from the human heart.

First, let's do no more harm. Physicians take the Hippocratic oath, vowing, "First, do no harm" and this intent is important for all professions or individuals seeking to live in conserving, benevolent ways. Since tremendous harm has been done, let's strive to heal the damage as best we can and rejuvenate wholeness so that the earth and our children's children can thrive.

Consider the complexity of events spanning eons that have contributed to being alive in this moment. The diversity of life's beauty is astonishing, and reverent appreciation of our differences is vital. Let us express our gratitude in our actions. Caring for life on planet earth is not a way to get rich; it is a way to be rich. Our home planet needs both our loving attention and the wisdom of all cultures if it is to remain a healthful environment for everyone. Global thinkers and leaders including former president Bill Clinton describe three key challenges for our interdependent world: inequality, instability, and unsustainability.

For hundreds of years, our approach to globalization has been based on economic profit. Trade in spices, gold, and other resources enticed us more than the wisdom, beauty, and cultural enrichment of other peoples. The United States and European governments have long supported oppressive dictators and tyrants around the world, including in the Middle East, Africa, and South America, because of desire for commodities such as oil. For centuries, corrupt regimes that have been kept in power by more prosperous nations have crippled the potential and consciousness of millions of people. Corruption has poisoned hearts and minds in virtually every country. The son of an African dictator purchased a yacht that cost ten times more than is spent on health care for his entire country.

Oppression is being challenged around the world. Uprisings with immense bloodshed in Syria, Egypt, Yemen, and Libya are recent examples of a decisive No to oppression. Protestors want the fall of autocratic regimes and demand revolutionary democratic change, as witnessed in the Arab Spring of 2011 followed by the sobering "summer of autocrats."

Movements to abolish all forms of slavery, to legislate women's equality, and to increase transparency in financial sectors are ongoing.

Social inequality as well as political and economic instability lead to increased conflict within homes and between nations. Arab women are courageously speaking up and pioneering new styles of leadership, despite fragmentation, prolonged anarchy, stricter reinstatement of emergency law, and postponed elections. However, the vision of what could be takes time to clarify and actualize and the support of Western nations is needed during these transition periods to democracy. Digital testimony received from cell phones may inform us, but those images are also used by brutal regimes to identify and seize demonstrators from their beds to be tortured and often murdered. Like almost any tool, technology can be used to heal or harm.

Some commentators in democratic countries have said, "We don't have to do that much; we just have to do the right thing." Of course, determining the wisest response is subtle and complex. Nothing great comes easily and without support, fledgling democratic movements often fall prey to aggressive dominators taking advantage of regional and societal instability. Although the Libyan people's desire for dignity and justice was great, it proved to be very difficult to dislodge a mentally unstable despot who had stolen nearly 150 tons of gold before ordering the military to bomb and torture civilians. There are tremendous challenges inherent in building any new system, especially when the self-interest of those in power resists reform or structural transformation.

Ibrahim Abouleish is the founder of Sekem, an Egyptian company that aims to contribute to the comprehensive development of the individual, society, and environment. In an interview, he observed, "If a society loses its spiritual capital, it could result in the inability to cope with transformations such as these. ... I think the only thing to do now is to be very optimistic, to be connected with others and to serve the spiritual world." Investing in green economies and clean energy technologies is an optimistic, practical, and sustainable way to contribute constructively to our energy destiny.

In our interconnected world, nearly everything we own, wear, or listen to is from another land. Mutual respect and gratitude, merciful justice, and reverence for all life are positive potentials for this grand experiment of globalization. However, we all lose if globalization diminishes the esteem of indigenous peoples, increases economic and educational disparities, and flattens cultural diversity into a monoculture trending to the lowest common denominator.

Consumer cultures based on waste and greed foul our only home and are not sustainable for life on earth. Single-use plastic packaging pollutes our oceans and destroys marine life eating the toxic, almost indestructible plastic and Styrofoam. Water is our life's blood. Oil extraction methods that poison water also poison life. Our lives are inextricably linked with the health of earth's biosphere, and it's not possible to shop our way out of current global crises. Simple awareness of what is enough can decrease overconsumption and redefine what is true progress.

It is imperative that we effectively address the issue of the population explosion. Millions of families lack access to birth control, which limits their ability to be responsible about the number of children they have. Reducing birth rates is by far the most effective way to decrease humans' carbon impact on our global environment. Research consistently proves that educating girls decreases birth rates and increases health outcomes.

Promoting population growth to maintain economic growth is a Ponzi scheme that will ultimately collapse. Already, the earth's natural systems are no longer able to replenish the resources that we spend. Hopefully, we're not past the point of no return and we'll make it a priority to empower all people to be able to control their reproductive rate.

"Every step we make has the power to heal and transform," says the renowned global activist and spiritual teacher Thich Nhat Hanh. A mature consciousness and wise heart help to discern which beneficial steps are ours to take. Conscious alliances committed to benevolence toward all beings are especially imperative at this time. A "developed" nation may be financially rich but not culturally wealthy in compassion and wisdom. Nations like the United States cannot promote the notion to "grow like us" because the resulting environmental degradation would devastate life on earth. We must be less wasteful, less harmful, and much wiser.

India, Brazil, and China, for example, have the benefit of ancient, sophisticated cultures as well as growing technological innovation to inform their industrialization. Our planet cannot maintain its health if nations refuse or neglect to integrate wise governance with recent scientific understanding and technological capacities to reduce the pollution of our magnificent planet. There are now regions in China where the environment is so polluted with toxins that the bees have died. Farmers are trying to hand-pollinate plants because bees pollinated 90 percent of food crops. We all benefit when governments choose not to follow the environmentally devastating Western approaches to "progress" throughout the industrial and then electronic ages.

We'd be wise to regularly refresh our sense of astonishment and gratitude for the profound opportunity of life. The geneticist and mathematician J.B.S. Haldane has written, "The world will not perish for want of wonders, but for want of wonder." For many reasons, millions of children are missing the opportunity to develop a wonder-filled relationship with the natural environment. How can we renew our sense of awe for the gift of life and pass on that revitalization to future generations?

The future waiting to be born needs us. "Only a life lived for others is a life worthwhile," observed Albert Einstein. As we serve the global common good, our lives grow rich with meaning, wisdom, deep peace, and happiness. By recognizing our oneness with others and genuinely welcoming their goodness, we practice expanding our generosity.

Positive transformation is sustained from the inside out. As we learn how to skillfully navigate our personal evolution and expand the understanding of our unique gifts, we'll bring fresh perspectives to global change. Seeds of creative altruism sprouting nourishing roots support the positive transformation of our world. Our increasing global interconnectivity compounds the impact of our actions. Let's begin.

Pause, Reflect, and Record

- "Everything is interdependent. Everything is interconnected. ... Our survival and our future are very much linked to one another," wrote the 14th Dalai Lama. What does this mean in your life?

- What are you deeply concerned about? What holds the most meaning for you in this moment?

- What are essential themes for your future? To what extent do you value inner peace, authenticity, connectedness, self-expression, adventure, creativity, expanding your horizons, service to life, or leaving a meaningful legacy?

- What are the gifts that you came here to share? What simple, specific, scheduled steps could you take to explore what your integral service is to be?

2

There is No Other

I have come into this world to see this:
Men so true to love / they would rather die
before speaking an unkind word. ...
The sword drop from men's hands even at the height
of their arc of rage / because we have finally realized
there is just one flesh / we can wound.

—Hafiz

In every culture and age, mystics have pointed to the existence of one life energy, and have maintained that the world is one. Unus mundus. As we begin the exploration of our goodness to go, it's helpful to recognize that there is no *other*. Recently, my twelve year old daughter exclaimed, "Oh, I get it! We're not just interconnected. Everyone *is* everyone."

As we summon the heart that recognizes our unity, integral service free of judgments about apparent differences is mobilized. When we welcome another, we welcome ourselves. In the ancient Sanskrit language, the word for welcome literally means, "I have arrived." This Indian greeting of *namaste* acknowledges the One who dwells in all. As we free ourselves from judgments that divide us, we're united by our mutual commitment to justice, freedom, and respect for each human being.

The light of a single rainbow is a continuum of every color. Many colors, textures, and life forms are required to create natural wilderness and magnificent gardens. Both need room to grow. While diversity colors our communities with beauty, underlying the paradox of diversity is our oneness. There is just one that we can wound, just one that heals.

Our diversity needs to be fully included in our worldview. "Beware the differences that blind us to the unity that binds us," wrote Huston Smith, the renowned history of religions professor. Dichotomous thinking splits the whole into mutually exclusive, opposed, or contradictory pa though we're one interconnected life, dualism insists on identifying with individual differences. It differentiates attributes in ways that make us feel separate from others: "I am tall, short, black, white, rich, poor, man or woman."

This old habit of dividing the world into "us versus them" has ingrained prejudices and class distinctions. Power and resources have accumulated in the hands of a few who feel superior to or more entitled than "others." It takes One to know One. A twentieth-century Trappist monk, Thomas Merton, who practiced recovering the awareness of our original unity, wrote, "We are already one. But we imagine that we are not."

With unity of spirit, it's possible to respect and embrace a diversity of beliefs. Genetically, we all emerged from DNA that migrated from Africa. We share our gene pool with trees, fish, and many other species. In addition to our genetic codes, our breath is interconnected. Within one atmosphere surrounding our home planet, our out-breath is transformed by trees into oxygen for another's inhalation.

The life force or spirit within us is known in some cultures as *prana*. In 1852, a legendary Native American leader known as Chief Seattle expressed his understanding of the pranic life force: "The air shares its spirit with all it supports. The wind that gives us our first breath also receives our final sigh." Chief Seattle also recognized, "No man can be apart. We are brothers, after all."

There are more than seven billion human beings on planet earth, and it is in our collective self-interest to recognize the interconnectedness of our shared journey. Truly, we're all in this together. The wisdom of Howard Thurman, the African American theologian who inspired many civil rights leaders, transcended any particular era of history or religious tradition. Like many, he experienced pure Being as the embodiment of wisdom, light, and truth. Thurman recognized that mystical experiences of unity with eternal Spirit naturally find expression in humanitarian service.

In what ways can we widen our circle of compassion and experience our essential unity with the whole of creation? This question is vital to the maturation of our heart of service and we benefit by revisiting it often throughout our lives.

Beyond the Veil of Duality

One facet of the inherent inquiry into our unity is a direct experience of the whole. The "felt-sense" of a personal experience of oneness transcends delusions of duality. Direct experience is virtually impossible to articulate clearly; try to describe the precise taste of a strawberry. For millennia, many people around the world have sought peak experiences of transcendence and several have attempted to articulate their knowledge of radiant space and the profound energy of Consciousness.

During these sublime moments, a taste of pure, unconditioned awareness is experienced as a sensory veil parts to reveal the manifestation of the One. The apparent multiplicity of the phenomenal world drops away. Familiar levels of everyday awareness expand into a spacious wisdom that is experienced as more true than anything the mind is capable of conceiving.

Inexplicably, one summer day years ago, I experienced what Thomas Merton referred to as the hidden wholeness in all visible things. Its occurrence was a mysterious gift of grace that revealed the underlying oneness of existence. I was eighteen years old and didn't think that life could get much better. Happily, I played music and shared food with friends by a gorgeous jade river flowing between rounded banks of white granite.

At one point, like numerous other times that sunny afternoon, I stood on the warm bank and dove into the clear river. Suddenly and unexpectedly, my world changed. Within me a deep, ancient voice intoned *ONE. ONE. ONE.* Awe flooded my awareness. As I came up from the dive, my head broke through the surface of the water and I looked around in astonished wonder.

Although the world looked familiar in one sense—pine boughs were green, friends laughed—I could literally see that everything was a manifestation of one energy: one sacred, infinitely creative energy. Everything in the world, just as it was, was the manifested creativity of one Consciousness. One radiance shone through all things. In silent glory, I marveled, and at the same time, felt delightfully at home in this experience of unity awareness.

My sense of identity also expanded. I was not merely my adolescent self. I was also the pure awareness looking through my eyes and feeling through my skin. Although I was studying empiric sciences at the time, the inner knowing that I experienced was far beyond conceptual belief, doubt, or explanations generated by the deductive reasoning of an egocentric brain. It was a recognition, a taste of knowledge of the one sacred Self. To this day, I yearn to be in that state of nondual awareness and inexplicable beauty once and for all.

31

Goodness To Go

Our interconnected globe requires only a few flights to circumnavigate. During medical school, I flew to India for an elective on a mobile hospital bus. Afterward, as I continued on a one-way ticket around the world, a tender, visceral experience of our home as one small planet enveloped me. *We are one. We are the circle and the circle is All* is an understanding familiar to many people.

The circle is a universal symbol or archetype of our interconnected wholeness. Native peoples ask us to reflect on where we begin and others end. A visionary leader of the Sioux Nation named Black Elk taught, "There can never be peace between nations until we know the true peace which is in the souls of men. This comes when men realize their oneness with the universe and all its powers, and that the Great Spirit is at its center."

Allow archetypal questions to penetrate deeply. Ask yourself: Who am I? What is essential to that which I am? Our inner speech, our thoughts, can affect us in many ways. Thoughts are not necessarily true so don't believe everything you think. Teachers implore us to THINK before we speak. Five conditions to consider: T—Is it truthful? Is this the right time? H—Is it helpful? I—Inspiring? N—Necessary? K—Kind?

Be conscious of Consciousness. Let your heart expand. Rejoice in the potential to be free of suffering. Take several deep breaths and pause in the space where the exhalation dissolves. Remove your attention from agitating thoughts and place your awareness in your heart or on a benevolent thought, prayer, or mantra. With gentle mindfulness, work with feelings and emotions as well as inner and outer speech. Experience the natural flow of your integrity, the aligned integration of your thoughts, speech, and actions.

In an ancient wisdom text it is said, "The wise say that the all-knowing state is that in which the embodied soul becomes one with everything. ... The powers accruing from this should not be used for selfish gains but for the welfare of people." As you practice being one with each moment, you'll begin to sense that there is no other. Experience the power of One. It may happen feeding your child in the middle of the night, at a board meeting in which mutual accord sparks collaborative synergy, during prayer, on a hike, or through another gift of daily grace.

Life Is Relationship—United We Stand

We're all connected within one web of life. When we see ourselves in each other, it's natural to nurture and support one another. The recognition of our interrelatedness in known as *ubuntu* throughout the African continent. In 1965, Dr. Martin Luther King, Jr. summarized the essence of ubuntu philosophy. He wrote, "All mankind is tied together; all life is interrelated and we are all caught in an inescapable network of mutuality, tied in a single garment of destiny. Whatever affects one directly, affects all indirectly. For some strange reason I can never be what I ought to be until you are what you ought to be. And you can never be what you ought to be until I am what I ought to be – this is the interrelated structure of reality. And by believing this, by living out this fact, we will be able to remain awake through a great revolution."

Each living creature is a microcosm, a small universe. Individual cells join together to form inter-dependent organ systems sustaining increasingly complex life forms. Creation is always making more from less. Human beings are composed of trillions of cells, most of them not uniquely human, and every cell functions within multiple related systems. Every stage and level of life involves trillions of inter-relationships. The universe is in a ceaseless process of becoming and an evolutionary impulse to make the world a better place lives within us.

We can create societies that oppress human potential or civilizations that support generative processes and opportunities to release the great gems of our creativity. The jewel of creativity—combined with kindness, wisdom, knowledge, talents, and skills—allows us to contribute to the betterment of planet earth and our human family. We all value clean air and water, safe bridges, efficient transportation systems, and government integrity.

Consider the upliftment to your life of your favorite works of art, dance, musical composition, poetry, and architecture as well as the opportunities that digital technologies make available to us. How sublime it is when we have the time, health, enthusiasm, educational and mentoring opportunities to express our natural creative energies. Mahatma Gandhi had a profound commitment to the right of freedom for everyone so that their unique potential and distinct service could be contributed to the world.

The Jewish philosopher Martin Buber believed that humans were created for relationships of mutuality. He celebrated the value of respectful, dignified exchanges in subject-to-subject relationships. In the reciprocity of I-Thou encounters, neither participant is dualistically objectified, which typifies I-It relationships. Ralph Waldo Emerson wrote in the mid-1800s, "The heart and soul of all men being one, this bitterness of 'His' and 'Mine' ceases. His is mine. I am my brother, and my brother is me."

There can be no lasting peace while current levels of inequity and deprivation exist on our small planet. It is not sustainable, equitable, or just that we are divided into "haves" and "have-nots." Our zero-sum thinking—for someone to win, someone else has to lose—needs to change. It is simply not true that for our needs to be met, someone else has to suffer or receive less. For centuries, we've grown sufficient food, and the earth has supplied enough resources to meet the needs of all. The real issues have been the distribution of those resources as well as human values and political will.

Beyond the Illusion of Security

Although we want to be safe from harm, a permanent state of security is not possible. Sickness, old age, and death are inevitable. Genuinely stable systems integrate natural laws, order, and chaos and anticipate transitions and transformations. Life requires adaptation and letting go of many old structures.

In her book *Insecure at Last*, Eve Ensler describes how cultural prejudices, economic policies, and traditions of injustice create an environment of global despair and rage that, until balanced, will inevitably lead to hatred and violence. On September 11, 2001, millions watched with shocked horror and despair as the Twin Towers collapsed, sensing that the attack was a vengeful reaction to America's global military, financial, and resource dominance. Seismic economic and power shifts occurred in the years following those terrorist attacks.

Creating conditions that sustain global freedom and justice is inspired by respect and love, not fear or blame. At the same time, it is urgent that we're responsible about our reproductive rate, otherwise our social justice and environmental activism will be for naught. The population explosion is a critical global concern. It took many millions of years for *Homo sapiens* to reach one billion in 1804. Adding the next billion took 123 years. In only eighty-four years, those two billion more than tripled. By the end of 2011, there were more than seven billion human beings on earth.

It's not prudent for rich countries to blame the world's woes on the overpopulation of less resourced countries or for impoverished nations to lay the blame on the inequity of overconsumption by wealthier countries. One child in America typically uses the lifetime resources and creates much more pollution than 180 children living in Bangladesh. Both overpopulation and overconsumption are key dilemmas that require comprehensive, equitable, sustainable solutions.

More of us than ever before know in our bones that we are interdependent. Unique individuals are forms of one creative life energy. Personal autonomy and safety are ultimately delusions, and an individual's "net worth" cannot be determined by accumulations of capital. Regardless of how high end our financial resources may be, illness or disaster may strike at any time and we'll need life to care for life in the form of integral service.

It's ultimately unsustainable to isolate ourselves, intending to "take care of number one". We can't safeguard our own children's lives without consideration of all children, including those to come in future generations. We have the choice to live in ways that don't jeopardize *any* child's opportunity to live a healthy and happy life on this astonishingly beautiful, irreplaceable, singular planet. When we acknowledge our interdependence with our fellow travelers on spaceship Earth, an attitude of gratitude and the responsible commitment to stewardship naturally develop.

Impulses of the heart can be clouded by thoughts. The mind can be our best friend or our worst enemy, leading to bondage or liberation. It serves as a vehicle for both profound contentment and untold suffering. Paul Hawken, a prolific eco-economist and steward of planet earth, writes, "We can just as easily have an economy that is based on healing the future instead of stealing it. We can either create assets for the future or take the assets of the future. One is called restoration and the other exploitation. ... Inspiration resides in humanity's willingness to restore, redress, reform, rebuild, recover."

Pause, Reflect, and Record

• In 1855 Chief Seattle wrote, "Humankind has not woven the web of life. We are but one thread within it. Whatever we do to the web, we do to ourselves. All things are bound together." In what ways do you experience being one with life?

• How could you expand your perception of the connections between all living beings? How do our differences contribute to our strength?

• List some ways that you feel separate, disconnected, or judgmental. Are there any judgments about yourself or others that you would like to release? Describe.

• The global humanitarian Margaret Wheatley has written, "It's not the differences that divide us. It's our judgments about each other that do." Write your insights and questions in response to her comment.

3

Interconnectedness

All things are connected....
Whatever we do to the web of life,
we do to ourselves.
Whatever befalls the Earth,
befalls all the children of the Earth.

—Chief Seattle

The interconnected waters around the globe are essentially one ocean whose waves continuously arise and subside. In the life span of a wave, it swells, crests, and merges back into its source. While the transitory form of any wave is relatively brief, its true nature is water and it returns to the ocean. In much the same way, our human form takes birth and eventually dies as our life forces merges with Life. When we're aware that the ground of our being is one ocean of consciousness, it is possible to be peaceful, free, and happy even in the midst of great storms.

In the decades since the publication of Albert Einstein's theories about the relativity of time and space, physicists and cosmologists have explored both subatomic and intergalactic mysteries. One intriguing discovery is that if the direction of spin of an atomic particle is changed, the spin of a distant charged particle is *immediately* affected. How are we to account for this immediacy? Isn't time required for the transfer of information across space and the process of cause-and-effect to then occur?

The heart of goodness knows that our connectivity is our unity. The number of intermediate links between any two people in the world (better known as degrees of separation) is fewer than we thought. A friend of your friend knowing a friend of their friend creates a net of connectivity. Social media data suggest that in only five steps of inter-relatedness, we could connect with just about any other person on the planet. When we summon our hearts together, we can be a powerful force of goodness in the world.

Goodness To Go

In the ancient Sanskrit language of India, a potent phrase expresses the understanding that the whole world is one single family: *Vasudhaiva Kutumbakam*. Perennial wisdom and spiritual texts have described ways of being, knowing, and living from this awareness for millennia. Scientists are now recognizing that everything is connected at very deep levels, speaking of fields of universal energy and quantumentanglement.

The net of our interdependent connectivity spreads information and affects behaviors of all kinds, negative as well as positive. The First World War was a global war triggered by the assassination of one heir to a throne, Archduke Ferdinand of Austria. Ultimately, more than nine million combatants were killed. In the summer of 2012, billions of people around the globe witnessed the lighting of the Olympic torch in London and were inspired by images transmitted through satellite telecommunications systems.

Our essential underlying interconnectedness is recognized in every culture. One definition of the South African philosophy known as *ubuntu* is *I am what I am because of who we all are*. Archbishop Desmond Tutu wrote, "A person with Ubuntu is open and available to others, affirming of others ... you are connected and what you do affects the whole World. When you do well, it spreads out; it is for the whole of humanity."

Everything causes everything else. One significant contribution to scientific understanding of the quantum level was made by the 1945 Nobel laureate in physics, Wolfgang Pauli. His exclusion principle of mathematical symmetry proved the existence of *nonlocal causality*. As strange as it may seem, an invisible, abstract pattern beneath the surface of atomic matter appears to determine its behavior in a noncausal way. This vast, interconnected substratum, or field of energy, affects matter in ways that are not linear. In other words, a relatively simple cause-and-effect function is not the dominant force operating in the universe.

We live in a vast ecology of interdependence. The sun, our closest star, dies at the rate of 40,000 tons of helium per second. One billionth of that light and warmth reaches earth, making life possible. Plants transform sunlight into food through photosynthesis. We exchange respirations with trees, inhaling their oxygen as they cleanse the atmosphere of carbon dioxide emissions. Every millisecond, six septillion interconnected biologic processes serve to maintain our astonishingly complex human bodies.

The DNA in each one of our cells contains the genetic information that creates the whole of our being. "Everything is connected to everything else," comments physicist David Bohm. "We are not sure how this connectedness works, but there is a certainty, there is a 'separateness without separateness.' ... Yourself is the whole of mankind. That's the idea of the implicate order—that everything is unfolding in everything. The entire past is unfolded in each one of us in a very subtle way." Bohm has also commented that the very act of studying and interpreting the universe changes and even creates it.

Many people have experienced moments of the transformative awareness that we are as one. Several years ago a fireman shared with me one such experience of his interconnection with everyone and everything. While he was sitting in his backyard studio, engaged in a session of centering prayer, the man's focus shifted to the seemingly infinite levels of reality that supported his session of mindfulness practice. First, he noted that the floor supporting the cushion on which he sat was supported by the foundation of the building. His wonder, humility, and gratitude expanded as he sensed interconnected support systems continuing down to the center of the earth and then flowing around the globe.

All of us inhale oxygen from oceans and our exhalations flow around the earth. We actually are made of stardust, and the generous service of countless beings and levels of support makes our lives possible. More is being done with less as life is created and sustained by trillions of tiny miracles. It's our good fortune to live in a dancing universe, as quantum physicist Wolfgang Pauli marveled, where everything is unfolding in everything.

Life, including consciousness, evolves in ways that increase potentials for wisdom, beauty, complexity, and goodness. It's possible to move from a binary "either-or" way of seeing to more expanded, inclusive "both-and," I-Thou perceptions. Envision the evolution from a dog-eat-dog worldview to a global commitment to mutually beneficial, equitable, win-win solutions. Like Chief Seattle, the naturalist John Muir experienced that we live in an omnicentric world united with all life. "When one tugs at a single thing in nature, he finds it attached to the rest of the world," Muir observed.

One with Life

You are not lone. The understanding that we are all one is transformative and evolutionary. In his book *A New World*, Eckhart Tolle writes that three words—"One with Life"—are the secret to the art of living.

When we live in this experience, we're one with the now and can develop a spiritual relationship with the universe. Love is the new currency.

Scintillating holograms are one metaphor that cultural creatives have used to depict how each part of the universe contains its wholeness. Buckminster Fuller's architectural perspective designed the geodesic dome, and ancient Hindus described the universe as a multidimensional, jeweled net. In this vast web, each joint is a gem that reflects every jewel in the net. From our individual point in this web of oneness, we embrace the full measure of our lives and do our part in the pattern of life.

Universal needs of human beings, ranging from physical needs for air, food, water, warmth, and sleep to needs for protection, belongingness, meaning, and fulfillment, have been described by psychologist Abraham Maslow. Maslow describes the highest human needs as transcending the exclusive focus on realizing one's potential, helping others realize their potential, and connecting with others beyond the ego-mind. When we want our lives to make a beneficial contribution, these highest needs are met through integral service. What or whom do you serve?

The notion that we are separate entities is a persistent illusion. Philosopher Martin Buber believed that human beings are a part of a moral universe in which nonduality is rich with mystery. Buber's writings on the reverence and respect inherent in I-Thou relationships reflect the understanding that we are wholly one. We disregard our I-Thou relationships and buy into the illusion of other to our mutual peril. It is a fundamental misconception that we exist disconnected and separate.

On the deepest levels, there really is no other. Neurophysiologists at the University of Missouri scanned the brains of individuals who reported experiences described as spiritual, such as transcendence, a sense of universal unity, or complete selflessness. Independent of cultural or religious backgrounds, these experiences were associated with decreased brain activity in the right parietal lobe. Although the finding is an association and not an assertion of causation, this decreased brain activity can occur through meditation, prayer, or by making a conscious intention.

Healthy brains appear to have the same neuropsychological capacity to experience nondual human and spiritual connections. Perception extends beyond the dualisms and retinal reflections of binary vision. When your partner or child experiences a difficult emotion, you've probably felt agitated "vibes" before they spoke. Many sensitive people are finely tuned to their environments, including that of our shared home planet. One woman woke in desperate sobs on the morning of September 11,

2001 before she consciously knew anything about the thousands of people who had died in terrorist attacks.

Spiritually attuned individuals in every culture have sought to express our underlying oneness, and there are those who tease and deride these individuals, calling them "fringe folks" or "one-worlders." Hostile sarcasm and cynical criticism can be thinly veiled as the intellectual rigor of skepticism. The world is as we see it. We are all part of one being, one body, one planet. Ancient Vedantic scriptures tell us "thou art that," *tat tvam asi*. There is no difference between the observer and that which is being observed.

All cultures respect the loving goodness that contributes in meaningful ways to the world beyond personal desires. Ancient laws of hospitality remind us to welcome strangers as well as friends and family. Genuine welcoming is an integral part of what makes us human and honors our inherent goodness. At its heart is a recognition of the One who dwells within us all. Our hopeful imperative is to expand our affection to include all of life, not only the few persons nearest to us.

Thich Nhat Hanh eloquently describes the experience of interconnectedness as hundreds of thousands of stems linking us to everything in the cosmos, supporting us, and making it possible for us to be. This metaphor of the vine of human connectivity shows up in every culture around the globe. As we perceive our interdependence, or inter-being, empathy grows. When we understand that we are one with nature, we're in allegiance with Mother Earth and protect her wilderness and natural environments. We all live downstream.

Awareness of our deep, genuine interconnections can restore the world to wholeness. We are society. Society is us. How do we integrate this into our lives and perceive our interconnectivity on a continuous basis? The experience of our oneness is both a celebration and a call to action for our benevolence to ripple through the web of life. Live your life on purpose.

It takes tremendous courage, resilience, and mindfulness to awaken a perception of our interconnectivity in the midst of frenetic, complex societies where attention spans seem to be dwindling at alarming rates. Air pollution and environmental toxins affecting the brains of fetuses may be contributing to increased rates of attention deficit disorders. The ability to focus attention even for those with normal brain anatomy and chemistry is diminished by some kinds of repeated computer use. The design of virtual games and social media platforms stimulates reward centers in our brains, leading to computer addiction behaviors in millions of people. It's difficult to think critically, digest an entire book, or evaluate and integrate complex streams of information with only a Twitter attention span.

What We Resist Persists

In a polarized age, many of us feel divided by race, class, gender, faith, rigid opinions, media distortion, and partisan politics. All members of our global family are descendants of our original African ancestors; Muslims, Jews, and Christians alike are children of Abraham and Sarah. Yet, ungodly tyranny and injustice have been perpetrated by illusory beliefs about religious superiority or differences, from the horrors of the Crusades to modern-day terrorist attacks. Many people question whether religious fundamentalism actually *decreases* human morality.

With so much pain and suffering around the globe, it's understandable that sensitive individuals sometimes try to close their hearts or defend themselves in any way they can. When we refuse to know, we're practicing and fixating ignorance. Some of us claim compassion fatigue but are unwilling to engage in self-care or do the growth work that expands our circle of caring. We have the choice the summon our courage and release the goodness in our heart as we acknowledge and address difficult issues.

In the face of atrocities and grievous injustices, desperate efforts to escape or protect ourselves are understandable. However, turning a blind eye, sticking our head in the sand, or contracting our heart ultimately protects and serves no one, especially ourselves. Without ready access to unbiased public information, it's tempting to cling to our own segregated source of opinion, ignore or resist facts that challenge our limited knowledge, and passionately believe whatever we think. Ironically, what we resist persists and even gains strength as resistance digs in its heels.

The price of hating others is loving ourselves less. Is it possible to genuinely love ourselves when we loathe another? Resistance, including denial of our interconnectedness, has a contracted, dark quality whereas spreading the light of love has an expansive quality. New ways of thinking lead to new ways of being. To spread love on this planet spiraling within a galaxy circling in an expanding universe may be the purpose of human birth.

Hope allows more life-affirming, expanded perspectives to take hold. Although this is the moment to stand as one, how are we to do this? How are we to love our enemies? Tribal warfare continues to run rampant. Old cultural hatreds, bigotries, and exclusive religious doctrines fuel ancient animosities. Economic systems lacking both reverence and justice have forced millions into grueling poverty; the resulting anger breeds violence, which makes the world less safe for us all.

However, we'll create paradigm shifts as we open doors in peace with the fullest love of which we're capable. The practice of peace is the practice of love. Love is inclusionary; it is not passionate infatuation or exclusionary affection. Awaken to your ability to lead and serve from the peace and love in your heart.

Reverberations of Kindness

Recall some of the wonderfully true stories about one person or committed group whose positive actions transformed many lives. The multiplier effect, like compound interest, often invokes a sense of wonder. How might we accomplish our work in this chaotic time of unprecedented global transformation? Margaret Wheatley is a leadership consultant whose response to this question is, "When we seek for connection, we restore the world to wholeness. Our seemingly separate lives become meaningful as we discover how truly necessary we are to each other."

The thread of a single human tale of interconnection through generations reveals the uplifting impact that one person can have on humankind. One such story begins in Missouri when it was still a slave state. Two women, Mary Washington and Susan Carver, were good friends. Mary was an African American woman who had recently given birth to her son George. Susan and her husband Moses were white farmers who would not participate in slavery and thus became targets of a group of racists known as Quantrill's Raiders. With flour sacks over their heads and holes cut out for their eyes, the Raiders terrorized rural Missouri with arson and murder.

One winter night, the Raiders attacked and burned the Carver farm and shot several people. Mary was killed as she clung desperately to her infant son George. When Moses Carver learned of the fate of his wife's best friend and that her baby had been kidnapped, he arranged a meeting with the Quantrill's Raiders a few days later.

On his only remaining horse, Moses rode hours north to meet four of the Raiders at a crossroads in Kansas. They were carrying torches and their faces were hidden in flour sacks as they threw Moses a burlap bag in trade for his horse. As they rode off, Moses pulled the cold, nearly dead baby out of the bag and put the child inside his coat on his chest. Walking home through the bitter night, Moses spoke softly to the child. He promised to honor George's mother, raise George as his son, educate him, and give him his name.

George Washington Carver went on to study agriculture at Iowa State University and eventually became famous for his research with peanuts and sweet potatoes. One of the students he mentored was a six-year-old boy named Henry Wallace who was the son of a dairy science professor. Carver instilled in the boy a love for plants and a vision of what agriculture could do for humanity.

Henry Wallace went on to become the secretary of agriculture and then vice president of the United States during Franklin Roosevelt's first term. Wallace used the power of the vice presidency to create an agricultural research station in Mexico whose goal was to hybridize corn and wheat for dry climates.

To run this research station, Vice President Wallace hired a young scientist named Norman Borlaug. After successfully hybridizing corn and wheat, Borlaug went on to win the Nobel Prize for pioneering the Green Revolution in agriculture. He hoped that the additional food would give humanity a few decades to discover effective ways to control the population explosion. The types of corn and wheat that Borlaug and his team developed are credited with saving two billion people in arid climates around the world.

Mary, Susan, Moses, George, Henry, and Norman are all players in this true tale of goodness to go. The integral service of one individual after another gradually led to changing the course of human life on planet earth. So many uplifting stories continue. How many lives will depend on the choices and actions we make? Each one of us matters and our actions matter. Choose to celebrate diversity, embrace inclusiveness, and create a healthier world. As we live and create our future now, recognize the power that one person has to make a difference for generations to come.

Pause, Reflect, and Record

- Have you experienced the sense that life is the dancer and you are the dance? Have you felt that *life lives you*, relaxed and open to the flow of life rather than trying to force it, control it, or cling to the past? Describe.

- Family members, teachers, safe environments, and personal health are a few of the stems of support that empower us. Reading has been described as a uniquely human privilege. What are at least three sources of support that made it possible for you to read this sentence in this moment?

- Who or what supports you in taking action when you're stuck, overwhelmed, or afraid? Describe your feelings about these sources of support in your life.

- How do you support yourself emotionally, physically, psychologically, and spiritually? How might you enhance this until radical self-care is an ongoing practice?

4

Natural Compassion

Compassion and love are not mere luxuries.
As the source of both inner and external peace,
they are fundamental to the continual
survival of our species.

—The 14th Dalai Lama

We can become a shelter of compassion for one another. Through our compassion, we connect with others and offer our goodness to go. Compassion springs from awareness of the interdependence of all things and is an inherent aspect of our nature that we can develop and embody. Our brains are hardwired with neurons that fire with empathy when we experience someone's suffering. Engagement with our innate goodness increases our compassion for human mistakes and suffering. The philosopher Huston Smith writes that we become compassionate from the insight that one is the other.

As we allow our natural compassion to expand, we become messengers of peace. The word *compassion* comes from the Latin roots *com*, meaning "with," and *pati*, meaning "to suffer." Compassion is the heart's awareness of another's pain as well as unselfish tenderness directed to the one in pain. The healing elixir of compassion is the function of wisdom in our everyday life. Some call expressions of compassionate *practical* or *engaged compassion*. Many have experienced that compassion becomes real when we recognize our shared humanity and see through the eyes of others.

Goodness to go is more about compassion in motion than sympathy in service. Bleeding hearts see others as helpless and in need of rescue. Some kinds of sympathy disempower those in pain, disconnect everyone involved, and magnify suffering. The warmth and equanimity of compassion fully present in the face of human anguish is much more helpful. When misery is met with compassion from within and without, despair and anger begin to dissolve. Compassion grows. Without compassion, suffering can lead to bitterness and spawn brittle anger and resentment.

Millennia ago, the sage Confucius described compassion as tsu, or "likening to the self." Through self-inquiry, we discover what is hurtful to ourselves and then commit wholeheartedly to refusing to inflict that harm on others. The core teachings of religions and spiritual paths emphasize the profound, universal practice of compassion. True compassion, the healing waters of the heart, is much more inclusive than simple tolerance that turns a blind eye as it ignores apparent differences or disagreements. The path of compassion and deep peace emerges as we develop a disposition for benevolence and justice, practice moving from reactivity to creativity, and transform fear and greed to respect and generosity.

Radical Compassion

"Compassion is the radicalism of our time," the Dalai Lama states. This radical compassion embraces diversity with respect and kindness. It sees that our hands are the hands with which compassion goes about doing good. When we see life as a journey of awakening for the benefit of all beings, the many faces of compassion begin to reveal themselves.

Compassionate action is the highest ideal of world religions. Hadith are narrative records of the sayings or customs of Muhammad and his companions. One traditions says, "Feed the hungry and visit the sick, and free the captive, if he be unjustly confined. Assist the person oppressed whether Muslim or non-Muslim." The Sufi poet Rumi wrote, "Love is the religion and the Universe is the book." The essence of the Torah, the Five Books of Moses of the Hebrew Bible which is the source of the Ten Commandments, is to *love your neighbor as yourself.*

It's been said that compassion, feeling and even suffering with another, is the basis of morality. This is radical compassion. *Radical* is a powerful, multifaceted word which means a root part, a basic principle or foundation. Being radical also implies a departure from traditional ways with a disposition toward transforming existing views, habits, or conditions. The status quo is rarely radical. A counterculture in the 1960s that valued peace over materialism challenged the Establishment. Its radical commitments helped to empower women as well as end racial segregation and the Vietnam War.

Authentic compassion is radical in that it is rooted in unconditional loving acceptance of ourselves and others. This genuine compassion for all beings is one of the noble goals of humanity. If everyone who is able offers one benevolent action toward the fulfillment of this noble promise, what kinds of healing and restorative justice could we see? Mobilizing our radical compassion is a key task of our times.

One example of radical compassion is evident in the growing numbers of eco-justice ministries whose members serve in many impoverished regions around the world. Being acutely aware of the relationship between expanding populations and increased poverty, many priests serving in these regions no longer support the Catholic Church's suppression of most birth control methods. We need to keep alive conversations about the reproductive rights of all people. Families need to be able to responsibly limit their size for their own healthy survival as well as that of life on earth.

Compassion has been described as the opposite of injustice. Its merciful wisdom brings a responsive and just balance that includes forgiveness and reconciliation. Creating societies with radical compassion at their foundation will be met with many challenges. There is a facet of human ego that is irrationally attached to the notion that life can be without problems and that is doesn't matter who suffers to support our comfort.

This illusion and its self-centeredness waste precious time and energy. Life involves change, challenge, adaptation, and evolution, and we can be the change we wish to see in the world. Being fully alive includes experiences of fear, sadness, and anger. Conditions that cry for help are often uncomfortable, even horrific, situations of abuse, violence, hunger, pain, or injustice that are best met with the heart and hand of compassion.

Mercy and tenderness arise when we no longer shield ourselves from uncertainty and vulnerability. We have the courage to be warriors of kindness, to offer our open, strong hearts to the world. There is a basic fragility of existence as well as a basic goodness. When we practice being open to what is, we're able take in the pain of the world and allow our hearts to transform it with compassion. This loving kindness is willing to remain present in the face of suffering and naturally brings goodness to everyone it meets.

The perception of goodness has a sacred quality and opens channels of illumination in our hearts. As our compassion shines, we're more able to perceive the light of goodness within everyone. For centuries, people have resonated with the prayer of the physician Maimonides: "Inspire me with love for all of thy creatures. May I see in all who suffer only the fellow human being." In the heart of compassion, suffering is released and transformed.

The renowned medical missionary Dr. Albert Schweitzer learned to bear the mighty beams of love. He believed that people cannot find peace until they extend their circle of compassion to include all living things. As we offer our compassionate patience and strength to bearing the world's suffering, that love in action transforms the situation from the inside out.

We're Wired for Empathy

Expanding our circle of empathic caring is at the heart of goodness to go. Scientific research is beginning to penetrate the mystery of the neurobiology of empathy. Functional magnetic resonance imaging (MRI) lights up when the right prefrontal cortex of the brain detects that another being seems to be in pain. Mirror neurons in the brain help us to emulate and learn on many levels, including the development of empathy in childhood. Modern physics has come to understand what nurturing, compassionate people have long known: there is at root no distinction between self and other. Every photon's spin is affected by another's, regardless of the distance between.

On some level we're affected by the misery suffered by others, even on the other side of the globe. Modern-day abolitionist movements are working to free the 27 million people worldwide who are enslaved. Every year more than one million children are forced into the multibillion-dollar sex trade. Children as young as three years of age are sold by impoverished parents to traffickers promising employment. As a result of brutal exploitation, young girls attempt suicide or die after contracting HIV. Millions of children are orphaned by disease or violence every year, and about 1.2 billion people don't have access to safe drinking water. More than 25,000 children under the age of five die from preventable causes related to poverty and disease each day.

In March of 2008, religious scholar and former Catholic nun Karen Armstrong launched her dream of a global Charter for Compassion as the winner of the innovative TED (Technology, Entertainment, and Design) prize. For Armstrong, compassion is not just a sentiment but also an expression of care in action. The Charter for Compassion is a document whose intentions are both to promote tolerance so that all people can live together in peace and to serve as an antidote to exclusionary, fundamentalist interpretations of religion.

E-mail invitations were sent to millions of Muslims, Christians, Jews, and others to create this global charter of the world for the world. The global community responded, and eighteen religious leaders crafted the final wording. Thirty partner organizations, including the UN Alliance of Civilizations and the World Council of Religious Leaders, planned hundreds of related events.

The global, interfaith process leading to the Charter of Compassion focused on *how* not on what we believe, as well as our natural predisposition and impulses toward compassion and commonality. After studying the message of all major world religions, Armstrong wrote, "Compassion was the major test of any true spirituality. ... Religion is really an art form and a struggle to find value and meaning." Armstrong went on to say that practicing the virtue of compassion is a form of ethical artistry that requires the dethroning of ego. Like any artistic endeavor, dedication to practicing compassion requires strong aspiration, discipline, and resilience.

Mature compassion, strength, and gentleness that is manifested as kindness toward oneself and others produces nonaggression. Aggression is harmful and unstable. The gentleness of nonaggression gives rise to compassion for oneself and for every aspect of creation. It makes possible a lasting peace for all. Our world needs the strength and gentleness of our heart, mind, and character. Let yourself experience gentleness in your own being as you engage in transformative service. Departing from old paradigms requires patience, strength, courage, and loving kindness as we bring genuine compassion to personal failures, family conflicts, political systems, and all areas of our lives.

The Persian theologian known as Rumi wrote centuries ago, "In compassion and grace, be like the sun." Such unconditional giving and acceptance is not easy. It's uncomfortable to acknowledge the weakness or ignorance in ourselves and others. We may resist having compassion for offenders as well as victims. Often, we're tempted to avoid these and other discomforts. Yet, as ecopsychologist Joanna Macy notes, avoidance produces psychic numbing, which resists experiencing our pain for the world and other beings. Both the conditions that need compassion and our defensive resistance are uncomfortable. Simply put, we're uncomfortable feeling uncomfortable. Nevertheless, numbness is not a condition for empathy or happiness.

Since peace of mind can be our natural state, agitated avoidance and confusion are clues that we're off course. Compassion, our capacity for caring concern, is a compass that senses our alignment with the wisdom of our heart. When we're feeling confused or resistant, we're able to mindfully explore those feelings with kindness. As we adjust our course with the compass of compassion, our minds settle, become clearer, and accept what is. Then, with a peaceful heart and powerful resolve, we learn to mobilize skillful action that reflects our intention to create positive change.

Opening to pain is often the beginning of compassion. Recall how mirror neurons wire us for empathy. Certainly there are times when we're not able to fully process another influx of painful information or experience. However, much of the time, it may be that a cause or condition of this compassion fatigue is resistance. It's exhausting to resist opening our heart to our interconnectedness and intersubjectivity with the entire world. What we resist not only persists, it exhausts us.

Goodness to go is compassion in action. Integral service is engaged empathy. When we cultivate an open heart saturated with compassion, we ride the waves of change with resilience and equanimity, finding meaning in everything that happens.

Practicing the Breath of Compassion

Compassion exists in the wellspring of everyone's heart. How do we learn to drink this nectar and become the embodiments of compassion? Practices that cultivate our "compassion channel" are good medicine for the world and for ourselves. One classic Buddhist practice is called *tonglen*, a contemplative practice of exchanging self for other. Practices that involve centering breath often involve exhaling tension and inhaling fresh energy, yet in *tonglen* this cycle is reversed.

We begin this practice by consciously breathing in the hot, contracted energy of a painful emotion or situation. Within the space of our heart, this suffocating energy is transformed before being exhaled as cool, expansive energy flowing to the world. Relaxation and openness are encouraged as participants experience their gentle, vulnerable hearts. Sensitive or wounded "soft spots" are allowed to simply be within our spacious compassion.

The breath of compassion is a method for dissolving constrictions in our heart-mind, connecting with our natural compassion, and overcoming our fear of suffering. The core of *tonglen* is to breathe in someone's pain so that the person in pain has more space to open, relax, and find well-being. Then, with the out-breath, whatever is felt to be beneficial is sent to that person. For example, if someone is ill or in pain of any kind, or a child is suffering, breathe in your wish to dissolve the sadness, fear, and pain, and then send to that person with your exhalation whatever you feel would relieve their suffering.

The Buddhist nun Pema Chodron encourages us to practice *tonglen* as a way to dissolve perceived barriers between us. We have involuntary tendencies that push pain away, build walls, and cling to pleasure or safety. Whenever we feel stuck, when our heart feels numb or tight for any of a thousand reasons, we have a choice. We can shift our attention and clarify our intention. Choosing to breathe in suffering, we intend to completely feel and accept it for ourselves and for all people stuck in the same way. Pain then transforms into compassion, which is offered with our exhalation. Compassion breathes compassion.

Acts of kindness, including practices that cultivate compassion, ignite the powerful love abiding in the human heart. Love is the light of goodness to go that extends our kindness to others. It takes real courage to be present with compassion, to stand in our light, and not be enslaved by our genetics, our automatic nervous systems, our belief systems, or the opinions of others. The natural sage that we are comes forth as we choose the good again and again. When fear is experienced, approach it with loving kindness rather that fighting, fleeing, freezing, constricting, or denying.

Fear can mean Go—challenging us to move into adversity with curiosity and kindness. Every challenge is a living opportunity to strengthen our ability to be fully present with whatever is. Over time we learn to accept everything that happens as an opportunity to cultivate our capacity to hold all the world in a heart grown strong with courage, compassion, and love. As we practice compassion, fear dissolves, and we learn to *be the compassion*.

Pause, Reflect, and Record

- Make space in the next few days to experiment with practicing the breath of compassion.

  1. Breathe in the contracted, hot energy of a painful situation.

  2. Allow this energy to release agitation and rest in the heart.

  3. Breathe out your calm, expansive offering of goodwill.

  What do you notice from this practice?

- During what phases of your life has compassion for self and others, or from others, been particularly important? To what extent do you agree that compassion is necessary in your personal life and the world at large? Describe.

- What are some thoughts and questions that arise when you consider the invitation to serve the ocean of compassion? How is radical compassion related to goodness to go?

5

Ethical Artistry

Caring is everything.

—Friedrich von Hugel

Ethical artistry takes form when our inherent inclination toward compassion come to life in integral service. Around the world, ethical artistry often expresses three key principles: giving without expectation; loving unconditionally; and living without judgment. The principles by which we conduct our lives inform our ethical standards which in turn motivate our actions in the world. Our goodness to go expresses virtues including compassion and respect as well as reasonable, well-founded standards, such as the rights of all people to life, liberty, and freedom from intentional harm.

As we perceive our goodness and resourcefulness, compassion ripples out from an open heart. Karen Armstrong is an ethical artist and religious scholar, as mentioned in Chapter 4, who initiated a global, interfaith process leading to the Charter of Compassion. Central themes in her work included a focus on how, not what, we believe, as well as our natural predisposition toward compassion. How do we believe? Is our faith blind or constantly refreshed? Are we vigilant in our examination of our moral beliefs and ethical standards, ensuring that we consistently live up to those standards?

The translation of religious or spiritual values into beneficial actions for others is a practical manifestation of compassion. The ethical artistry of compassionate action is highly regarded by all spiritual traditions. Like other artistic or ethical endeavors, dedication to the ongoing practice of virtues such as compassion requires daily renewal of our creative inspiration, commitment, and discipline.

Goodness To Go

Around the globe, inspired change-agents of all ages are part of the largest social movement in history. "You really can change the world if you care enough," states Marian Wright Edelman, founder of the Children's Defense Fund. Ours is a time when empathy, creativity, and courage are needed at its foundation. When our caring is integral to our core values, we're naturally inspired to act with beneficence. As agents of positive change, we don't get stuck in numbness, avoidance, or resistance. When the light of our unconditional compassion is offered for the highest benefit of everyone involved, it brings out the best in each situation that we encounter.

It's understandable that most people don't seek to add more stress or pain to their lives. However, refusing to move outside comfort zones can reinforce tendencies to get stuck in habits of armoring and numbing the heart. The prophet Ezekiel addressed this attachment to avoidance of life's difficulties when he said, "I will break your heart of stone and give you a heart of flesh." Nearly all humans experience suffering at some point in their lives. Although it can feel utterly intimate and personal, suffering is shared by humanity. It's an experience that connects us.

There are examples in every culture of how empathy can ripen in the heart. Centuries ago, Francis of Assisi grew up as the privileged son of a wealthy Italian merchant. When he recognized that revulsion and fear of leprosy prevented his heart from being fully open to those ostracized by this disfiguring, infectious disease, he chose to live in a leper colony until his "heart was flesh." Rather than flagellating himself for ego's judgmentalism, he extended mercy to himself. Very naturally, that mercy expanded to include all beings. The simplicity lived by St. Francis was that of a heart-centered life radically open to all of life. His "poverty" was the expansive wealth of freedom from attachment.

Like ethical artists in every generation, Francis recognized that the present moment is a doorway into the compassionate stillness of inner Presence. The courage of Francis's commitment to living each moment with an undefended heart can be inspiring. Nevertheless, many of us feel depleted by what has been referred to as compassion fatigue. We perceive ourselves to be overwhelmed by the atrocities and inequities in our world. They hurt. We hurt. Understandably, in the face of pain and suffering, some element of our humanness is afraid. It contracts away and tries to avoid relating to any pain, whether it's that of others or ourselves. Wise discernment clarifies what we can control and what we can't, and reveals the kindest, most skillful response of which we're capable.

When you feel weakened by dwelling on what is outside your reach or cannot yet be, extend compassion to yourself as well as others. The support of others, wisdom teachings, and the resilience to work skillfully with painful sensations, emotions, and situations are resources available to us. Consider that our one true Self is sacred. This unified identity has been described as the light of pure love and for thousands of years our mystical union with the source of this light has been celebrated. In the fourteenth century, the Persian poet Hafiz, known as *the tongue of the invisible*, gave voice to this invisible realm when he wrote, "There is a bridge between you and anything. It is love."

Tend and Befriend

In his book *The Age of Empathy: Nature's Lessons for a Kinder Society*, research psychologist Frans de Waal observed that mammals, including humans, congregate in social groups that have evolved to be cooperative and empathic. Evolutionary forces move us toward ever-widening realizations of our inter-connectedness and goodness. Integral philosophers describe how we're driven by our creative purpose to make the world a better place.

Human nature is essentially social. Rarely does long-term survival of a community or a species depend on survival of the fittest or on a dominant, isolated alpha leader. The tendency to physically fight our way out of a conflict is often regarded as an element of male energy; the tending instinct has been seen as more inherent to the female domain. However, both aggressive and nurturing energies exist within all human beings. Our "tend and befriend" instinct is hardwired into our genes and chemistry as much as the fight, flight, freeze, or "freak-out" reactions to distress.

One way that we befriend one another is through genuine hospitality. Welcoming strangers, friends, and family is at the heart of spiritual paths around the world. A gracious welcome acknowledges and honors our connectivity, the one living energy within us, and invites the best in all parties to come forward. Most cultures have recognized that the character of their community is revealed by how respectfully the poor, the young, the elderly, and the sick, as well as the animals and the earth, are tended and befriended. Do stronger members empower or exploit vulnerable members of society?

Participatory development emphasizes the full inclusion and involvement of the recipients in development initiatives. Rarely is it beneficial to distribute handouts or dictate solutions for the problems of others. Handing out fish for a day doesn't provide food security. Ongoing experiential education and systemic reform is usually required for useful, even life-saving changes to be sustainably integrated into people's lives. An age-old Chinese proverb reminds us, "Tell me, and I will forget. Show me, and I may remember. Involve me and I will understand – and take ownership and responsibility for the solution's sustainability."

It's worthwhile to extend our circles of compassion to include all living things. When we befriend someone, we begin to demystify the notion of "other." Cultural exchange and other relationship-building programs are built on this understanding. When we engage in mutually respectful friendships, we see that this befriending is the basis for any relationship that goes beyond the conditional nature of many business and political interactions. Friendship based on mutual respect reaches across aisles, walls, borders, and even across centuries of cultural conflict. One example is the coalition of Israeli and Palestinian women that builds friendships to keep alive dialogue and other lines of communication between their polarized governments.

Collaboration and care-giving are hardwired into our neurology and are essential traits of twenty-first century servant leadership. In *The Tending Instinct*, Shelley E. Taylor describes how care-giving initially evolved for the protection of children. Early loving attachments resource our resilience throughout our lifetimes, and facets of nurturing behaviors remain evident in countless everyday acts of kindness and altruism.

Tending to others and being tended to in egalitarian social groups regulates our stress systems, helps us to recover from illness more quickly, and shapes our growth and development toward greater resilience. Millions of caregivers around the world reveal that humans have evolved in ways that make it natural to be empathic ethical artists. Although the heart of ethical artistry is not gender-based, it naturally supports cultural and political gender equity.

In every culture over thousands of years, our tending instinct is evident in our willingness to open our hearts to care for the children of others. From Guatemala to the Congo, millions of orphans are being raised by various family and community members ravaged by poverty, illness, and violence. Thousands of volunteers have traveled to assist in regions devastated by natural disasters, and many philanthropic organizations serve in war zones.

At the same time, our empathy can feel paralyzed by the scale and complexity of problems today. The population of the capital of Bangladesh, for example, has increased fiftyfold in fifty years. Climate change and global warming are documented in photographic surveys of melting and receding glaciers. Rising oceans could lead to as many as 100 million people becoming eco-refugees by the end of this century. Between 1990 and 2005, we destroyed an average of 50,000 acres of forest a day. In 2011, 1.5 million acres of the Amazon rainforest, home to nearly a third of the world's biodiversity, were slashed and burned.

Girls in Afghanistan are brutally attacked on their way to and from school. Terrorists continue to thwart children's opportunities to learn to read, throw acid to disfigure girls' faces, murder their courageous teachers, and have beheaded young people for socializing together. Millions of land mines continue to desecrate the land, mutilating and killing long after militaries have officially departed. Courageous individuals are putting themselves in harm's way to rid the earth of this abomination.

Treacherous dictators terrorize millions. Genocide continues to rage. Half the world lives on two dollars a day and over a billion people struggle to survive on less than a dollar a day. As they spend hours collecting water and firewood for their families, thousands of girls in developing nations are raped in addition to being deprived of education opportunities. A groundbreaking documentary called *Girl Rising* was released in 2013. It spotlights the resilient spirit of nine girls subjected to grave injustices and the power of education to transform their lives and uplift their communities.

In Pakistan in October of 2012, a courageous fifteen year old advocate for the education of girls was shot in the head and neck two days before the inaugural International Day of the Girl. Miraculously, Malala Yousafzai's heroic voice will be able to rejoin the global movement to educate the 500 million adolescent girls in developing nations who are desperate to be educated. Educate a girl—change the world.

Years ago the great humanitarian and physician Albert Schweitzer described feelings of helplessness in the face of grave concern, a crisis of confidence among the wealthy nations. He lamented, "It will ever remain incomprehensible that our generation, which has shown itself so great by its achievements in discovery and invention, could fall so low spiritually as to give up thinking." When our hearts and minds are stunned by anguish, we need to be able to revitalize ourselves and encourage creative thinking to discover skillful, wise solutions to global crises.

Goodness To Go

David Edwards is a contemporary writer who has reflected on our complex, accelerating times where many people ask, "The world's problems are so big and so numerous, what can one person do?" Edwards responds, "Once you realize that helping others is also helping yourself, the size of the overall problems becomes irrelevant. You're not a one-man or one-woman army out to save the whole world. You help simply because it does good and it feels good. ... Once you start to see through the myth of status, possessions, and unlimited consumption as a path to happiness, you'll find that you have all kinds of freedom and time. It's like a deal you can make with the universe: *I'll give up greed for freedom*. Then you can start putting your time to good use."

Everyone encounters pain and fear, passion, aggression, and ignorance. Although there are situations where a calculated retreat is the course of greatest wisdom, to flee in an attempt to escape or ignore painful situations is usually the way of fear. To blindly fight or suppress the situation and the feelings engendered is the way of anger, ignorance, and aggression. To befriend what is, whether it's inside or out, is the way of compassion. When you're tempted to flee or fight a difficult person or situation, take a deep breath, remember the power of the pause, and consciously ask yourself whether you'd be willing to befriend the situation. Consider the wisdom of no escape, having the freedom to stay, and the wisdom to serve what is.

The Power of One

Karen Cunningham Marx is a powerful example of the positive impact made by one heart open to tending and befriending those in need. As a single mother and owner of an interior design business, Marx joined her African drumming teacher, Abdoul Doumbia, in 1998 to travel to Mali with some of his students.

This cultural adventure included a visit to her teacher's rural home of Foutaka Zambougou, a remote, sub-Saharan village of mud huts and hand-dug wells. Zambougou was without roads, electricity, or cell phones and is an eight-hour journey from Bamako, the capital of Mali. Although the villagers' survival was perilous at the best of times, and half of the children under the age of five had been dying of dysentery and malaria, their kind hospitality was profoundly generous.

The following year, Marx returned to Zambougou, not knowing that years of drought had nearly depleted the village's grain supplies as well as those of neighboring villages. Near the end of her stay, Marx climbed the stilts of a round, mud-brick granary and lifted the pointed, thatched roof. Seeing very low supplies of millet, she asked her drumming teacher, "Where's the food?" Eventually, she learned that the village had been unable to sell its two cows to buy more seeds. With rationing, the 2,000 villagers had only about five weeks of food left and no solutions in sight to ward off their starvation. Understandably distressed, Marx felt there must be something that could be done to help, but initially she didn't know what that was.

On the plane ride back to the United States, she asked herself, "What in the world can one person do to help? Maybe the Malian government could help? Or Oxfam? U.S.A.I.D.? The Peace Corps? Maybe the World Bank?" Despite tremendous efforts, she had no response to entreaties made after she arrived home. Marx ultimately realized she was possibly the only person cognizant of the plight of this village who was willing and able to do something to help. She came to accept that this service was hers to offer.

A remarkable story of ethical artistry unfolded over the following decade. Initially, Karen Marx founded the Mali Assistance Project, raised enough money in a few weeks to purchase 67,000 pounds of millet, peanuts, and beans in Mali, rented four large trucks, and returned just a few days after the villagers had run out of food. Due to the lack of communication systems, they had no idea that their guardian angel was on her way with needed sustenance and so much more.

Marx went on to involve not only the Malian government but also the Peace Corps and Engineers Without Borders in Zambougou's aid and development. She empowered the villagers to voice their needs and participate actively in the process. As Marx met with the elders and young mothers, she became a deeply respected friend. Negotiations to hire oil rigs led to the drilling of 300-foot wells that provided the village with its first dependable, safe water supply.

The power of one is mighty and often mobilizes others. This single mother with personal health issues went on to participate in the building and ongoing support of a school and maternity clinic as well as a water collection system for a community garden. Karen Marx's journey is one of countless remarkable stories that reflect the power of one to tend, befriend, and uplift the human spirit.

The Ethics of Empathy

The ethics of empathy were embodied in the life of Mohandas "Mahatma" Gandhi. In the 1940s, this attorney-philosopher inspired a nonviolent, egalitarian movement that led to India's independence from England. Reflecting on the powerful resonance of Gandhi's example, Albert Einstein wrote, "Generations to come, it may be, will scarce believe that such a one as this ever in flesh and blood walked upon this earth."

Gandhi's phrase "Be the change you wish to see in the world" has galvanized renewed interest in the ethic of service. Gandhi grew up in a home that practiced social and religious harmony, giving equal honor to sacred texts of various faiths. His empathic ability to unite millions in nonviolent service of their collective well-being was rooted in his natural respect for the dignity and sacred interconnectedness of all life.

Gandhi believed that rights and duties are inseparable, like two sides of a coin. Great freedom demands great responsibility. With tremendous courage and integrity, Gandhi put into action his understanding that freedom, including personal and political autonomy, is an essential right for every being to manifest his or her true nature. This freedom also allows people to dutifully contribute their distinct service in a socially responsible manner.

The integrity with which Gandhi lived his ethic of empathy and service has been deeply respected for generations. One admirer is William Drayton, founder of Ashoka, the largest network of social entrepreneurs worldwide. Drayton believed that one of Gandhi's greatest insights was that a new type of ethics grounded in empathy, not in rules, was emerging early in the twentieth century. Gandhi recognized that empathy had become a powerful, paradigm-shifting force in the world. People were responding more to the call of their heart's compassion than to the heavy hand of "thou shalts"—*thou shalt give, thou shalt comply, thou shalt do what's expected.*

As human society became interconnected and faster paced, rule-based ethics that had developed in homogenous communities in which people tended to stay for life were no longer adequate to govern new levels of complexities in diverse human relations and interactions. Empathic understanding involves imagination and cognition, and is necessary to manage behavior wisely and ethically.

In his book *How to Change the World*, David Bornstein explained, "The new circumstances demanded that people become more ethically self-guiding. People had to be able to put themselves in the shoes of those around them." Our ability to imagine ourselves in another's shoes is a capacity that appears to involve areas of the brain's frontal lobes. Under healthy conditions, it usually begins to manifest in children about the age of four.

Do unto others as you would have them do unto you. Nearly every culture teaches children to live by the Golden Rule. "Hurt not others in ways that you yourself would find hurtful," the Buddha reminded his devotees. "And if thine eyes be turned towards justice," the Baha'i faith teaches, "choose thou for thy neighbor that which thou choosest for thyself."

Every civilization has respected integration of core values into daily life where deeds are aligned with thoughts and words. This integrity makes self-respect and mutual trust possible. If we grow up in a reasonably healthy, life-affirming culture where universal ethics are valued, we tend to act in ways that are congruent with our values in order to respect ourselves. In many families, kindness, honesty, and trust are highly valued, and children imbibe the value of their words being "golden."

Many people yearn for a world of peace with merciful justice and equality for all. As a girl, Jody Williams empathized with the pain and injustice experienced by her deaf, schizophrenic brother. This future Nobel laureate had also been distressed as a teenager by the horrors of the U.S. war in Vietnam, and later helped to end U.S. intervention in El Salvador's civil war. Williams recognized that when the hearts of citizens change, the culture changes. Weapons can be reforged into instruments of peace, guns into plowshares.

Jody Williams went on to coordinate education, medical aid, and humanitarian relief projects in Central America. In 1992, she was instrumental in launching the International Campaign to Ban Landmines (ICBL). Five years later, Williams and ICBL were co-recipients of the Nobel Peace Prize, and more than 156 countries have signed the land mine ban treaty.

Williams's compassionate advocacy continues with various UN human rights councils and with countless other initiatives of positive change. One is an experiential, social justice organization called Peace-Jam, whose mission is to create a new generation of global citizens committed to compassion and equity. In collaborate with Nobel Peace Prize laureates, young activists around the world are engaged in creating one billion peacemaking initiatives by 2018.

Goodness To Go

In the 1940s, while Gandhi's nonviolent campaign for India's freedom was waged, the horrors of World War II that were occurring on another monumental battleground revealed the profound importance of the ethics of empathy. A totalitarian regime in Germany showed the world once again how lack of regard, respect, and empathy could brutalize millions of innocent men, women, and children.

During World War II, an American diplomat in France, Hiram "Harry" Bingham, could not ignore the suffering of the Jewish people at the hands of the Nazis. To do what he felt was right, Bingham challenged indifference and anti-Semitism in the State Department and disobeyed orders from Washington. By doing so, he provided aid and travel documents to at least 2,500 Jewish refugees, including Max Ernst and Marc Chagall.

Although Bingham's humanitarian service angered many colleagues, ended his career, and led to financial hardship, he had no regrets. Bingham's children did not learn of their father's noble deeds until going through his papers after his death. The U.S. Postal Service released a stamp honoring Harry Bingham in 2006, and his daughter has shared a hymn that the Bingham family often sang:

> *Once to every man and nation,*
> *comes the moment to decide,*
> *In the strife of truth with falsehood,*
> *for the good or evil side;*
> *Some great cause, some great decision,*
> *offering each the bloom or blight,*
> *And the choice goes by forever,*
> *'twixt that darkness and that light.*

After World War II, a vision of the inherent rights of all people was articulated. The Universal Declaration of Human Rights was adopted in 1948 by the General Assembly of the United Nations. It affirmed that the inherent dignity and the equal, inalienable rights of all people were the foundation of freedom, justice, and peace.

Although there are many examples of the horror that results when ethical artistry is forsaken, untold individuals in every country express their commitment to acting with integrity. Take a moment to allow your attention to follow three deep breaths into your heart region. Relax your mind and body as you inhale deeply and breathe out long. Bring your focus to the pause between breaths. In rich detail, begin to imagine with strong intention the kind of future that you would create for the children of today's children. Nurture optimism. This positive intent has far more power than wishful thinking. Live the future now.

Three Types of Empathy

Let's explore three facets of empathy: imagination, spontaneous communication, and emotional empathy.

1. *Imagination.* When have you allowed your creative cognition to imagine walking in someone else's shoes? How did it feel to make a place inside yourself for another's pain as you put yourself in their shoes? What did you learn? How did it grow and nurture your compassion?

2. *Spontaneous communication.* The facet of empathy that neuropsychologists Benson Ginsberg and Ross Buck at the University of Connecticut call *spontaneous communication* is usually just below the conscious level. This communication channel appears to rely on subtle energies and chemical signals called pheromones and may provide the matrix for organisms to maintain an ongoing dialogue about the world around and within them. Some examples of spontaneous communication are the effect of looking deeply into the eyes of an infant peaceful in your arms or stroking a beloved animal companion. When two beings are empathically in tune with one another, their autonomous nervous systems become synchronized as measured by their heart rates and blood pressure. When have you been aware of the subtle energies at this level of empathic resonance?

3. *Emotional empathy.* We tend to be more aware of *emotional empathy* in which we resonate with the energetic vibrations of feelings. Notice how different *glad* and *sad* feel. Emotion is *e-motion*, or energy-in-motion. Our body-mind experiences a wide spectrum of feelings, from deep peace, heartache, and "butterflies" in our stomach to subtle appreciation and awe for the flow of love as well as artistic and natural beauty. Adding our thoughts to the basic energies of "mad, sad, glad, or scared" creates nearly endless variations of emotional themes. When have you truly rejoiced with the good fortune of a friend? If a beloved friend is suffering or a child is crying in pain, how does your body feel? Where does it feel most heavy or constricted? Instead of escaping from the discomfort, when have you moved closer to suffering with an open heart?

Widening our circles of compassion and empathic caring is a key element of integral service that we can help children integrate into their lives. Cycles of violence often begin with bullying in school and cyberspace. Children need to understand that there is no such thing as an "innocent" bystander. Barbara Coloroso is an internationally renowned educator who recognizes that dehumanization and contempt underlie spectrums of aggression from bullying and prejudice to genocide. There are many useful tools that can release us from cycles of violence. The ethical artistry of expanding our circle of caring is at the heart of them.

Pause, Reflect, and Record

- For each of the three facets of emotional empathy listed above, record some of your experiences.

- Recall people whose lives have manifested ethical artistry. Who in particular inspires you? Why?

- Describe a time when you "walked your talk" and the power of integrity coursed through your thoughts, speech, and actions. How did it feel in your body, heart, and mind? What inspired and sustained this integration of heart, head, and hands?

- You may be concerned about many pressing issues and feel overwhelmed at times. List at least eight community or world problems that particularly call forth your empathy. Offer blessings to each problem as you hold it in your heart. Then ask yourself, "What are the three problems that call me most strongly?"

6

Altruism

When you do something good for another person,
do it wholeheartedly, expecting nothing in return.
When you give the light of your own heart to another person,
you bring out the best in him; you give him
the power to be what he has the ability to be.

—Swami Chidvilasananda

Altruistic generosity is at the heart of goodness to go. Recall some of the astounding stories of altruism you've heard throughout your life: people diving into torrential rivers to save a stranger, donating a kidney anonymously, and firefighters running into infernos to save lives. In Hawaii, a depressed young man was preparing to jump from a windy promontory when a policeman ran to grab his hand. Both started to fall into the abyss. Without hesitation, the policeman's partner pulled both men to safety. When the first policeman was asked why he hadn't let go of the young man's hand, why he'd been willing to sacrifice commitments to his family as well as his life, the policeman replied, "I couldn't have lived with myself another day if I'd let that man die."

How is it that we can participate in the peril and pain of another to the extent that we're willing to spontaneously sacrifice our lives for someone else? Experiences of danger, pain, and even horror can put us in touch with the depths of being alive. Studies have shown that individuals are willing to risk themselves for the good of those living in close proximity, regardless of how closely related they are. The courage of life and the realization of our interconnectedness break through everyday awareness in many different circumstances. As we remain awake and listen for the gift or teaching within our life experiences, our wisdom and altruism grow.

The astonishing complexity of life on earth is due to cooperation, from single cells joining to form higher organisms to people collaborating in the creation of cities, computer chips, and civilizations. Martin Nowak is a biologist and mathematician who directs Harvard University's Program for Evolutionary Dynamics. In his 2011 book entitled *SuperCooperators: Altruism, Evolution, and Why We Need Each Other to Succeed*, Nowak explores five crucial mechanisms that drove cooperation in highly social species like ours. He also discusses how the survival advantage of social interactions drove our need for language which created alphabets and languages, which in turn led to larger, more powerful brains. It's truly remarkable that human beings agreeing to associate particular sets of vocal tones with consistent identifications and meanings.

Human cognition and memory expanded to monitor group interactions, understand complex motive and intentions, and communicate with one another. For millennia, compassionate, altruistic, and cooperative behaviors have been at work in the lives of human beings, and our innate morality has been systematically explored since Plato's time.

The French philosopher Auguste Comte developed the word altruism in the nineteenth century. It can be defined as unselfish devotion to the welfare of others. This does not necessarily mean that we deny ourselves for the sake of the other. Rather, we act altruistically from personal insight and the often subliminal experience of our interdependence.

Why are we willing to die for our beliefs? In *The Foundation of Morality* written centuries ago, philosopher Arthur Schopenhauer's response was that acts of radical altruism are moments where there is a breakthrough of metaphysical realization of our oneness. With experiences of our interconnectedness, moral courage arises naturally. The truth of our unity becomes spontaneously realized and our inherent nobility shines forth.

There are many other expressions, facets, and degrees of altruism. Think of the sacrifices made by billions of parents around the world to give their children a better life than the one they had. Risking personal safety on behalf of principles that we value calls us to various battlefields, whether as a soldier, fireman, or activist. Compassion for strangers as well as loved ones is familiar. More difficult is compassionate altruism for our tormentors. We may be able to love our neighbors as ourselves but how are we to love our enemies? Many spiritual leaders emphasize the importance of expanding our kindness until we experience as much compassion for the abuser as we do for the abused.

This depth of altruism can be a profound challenge, needless to say. Inspiring stories abound. One is set amid the atrocities committed by

Chinese soldiers ordered to destroy Tibet's ancient Buddhist monasteries. Thousands of monks and nuns have been imprisoned, tortured, and murdered during this continuing genocide. One monk who'd been repeatedly tortured for over twenty years was eventually released from prison. When asked what he feared most during his imprisonment, he replied quietly, "That I would lose compassion for my torturers." This is the power of deeply committed spiritual practice, compassion, and resolute altruism.

All for one and one for all is hardwired into our DNA. Evolutionary biologists study the intrinsic motivation driving impulses toward cooperation and altruism. Charles Darwin wrote much more about cooperation than survival of the fittest. Our capacity to cooperate has been key to human evolution, and altruistic behaviors are observed in many other species as well. Creatures living in social groups develop altruism as an evolutionary genetic advantage. When we all get along, each one of us is more likely to thrive.

This is one of the key mechanisms driving the evolution of cooperation: the increased survival advantage of individuals belonging to groups with tighter bonds and more cooperative members. Elephants, bees, ant colonies, and other social species demonstrate amazing cooperation. Whales, dolphins, wolves, and birds cooperate for their mutual advantage and have evolved complex communication patterns.

The urge toward getting along together and supercooperation lies at the heart of life's complexity, from multicellular creatures to human language. Altruistic sharing confers survival advantage from the ground up. Biologists from McMaster University in Canada have observed complex communal cooperation even in plants. Some plant species demonstrate altruistic behavior toward their kin at the root level. To share precious sunlight, roots that recognize their kin's roots will change the behavior of the plant they nourish by decreasing the number of leaves it produces. Together, all for one and one for all, they flourish.

Every culture has an expression of the ethic of reciprocity, such as the Golden Rule, and altruists in every age have renewed our faith in the goodness of which human beings are capable. Many initiatives have been undertaken so that the courage and commitment of altruistic individuals will be remembered to ennoble future generations. School curricula, museums, and monuments around the world commemorating altruism inspire and mobilize us. The courage and integrity of those who saved endangered Jews during the Holocaust is legendary. In addition to sacrificing their own lives, these people risked the lives of their loved ones. The Nazis' "kith and kin" policies often dictated the murder of all family members of anyone aiding Jews.

Documentary and feature films have featured Jewish survivors of World War II and their altruistic protectors. Many books inspire us anew, including Diane Ackerman's *The Zookeeper's Wife* about a Polish woman who hid Jews among the animals in her family's well-known zoo. The Dutch woman Miep Gies, who risked her life to hide, feed, and support Anne Frank's family, also slipped Anne a small journal. Gies found the diary after the Nazis sent Anne's family to concentration camps and gave it to Anne's father when he returned as his family's sole survivor. Miep Gies died in 2010 and Anne Frank's diary lives on as a testament to the human spirit in the face of unfathomable evil.

Despite the horrors of the Holocaust, Anne Frank experienced the courage and compassion of her benefactors. She wrote, "I still believe that people are really good at heart." There are many empowering stories about people's goodness and the strength, courage, compassion, and generosity of the heart. One collection of inspirational stories is *Stone Soup for the World* by Marianne Larned. The fable of cooperation and individuals' small contributions leading to the creation of soup that nourishes the entire community reminds us that the whole is more that the sum of its parts.

Although narratives about altruists are inspiring, we can't give what we don't have available to us. We're told to put on our oxygen mask before assisting another. We inhale with attention to self-care before we exhale our integral service. To embark on the transformative journey of healing our planet, we must be able to release our own suffering. Otherwise, we may resist or avoid full participation in life, burn out, or repeatedly sabotage our best intentions. How many times have you seen the ways that old physical injuries limit current functioning? In much the same way, psychological wounds need to be healed or they can stunt our development and distort or limit the full expression of our goodness to go.

The Economics of Altruism

The 1970s saw the expansion of the research field of behavioral economics which explores factors affecting financial decision making. It's become clear that altruism is a significant element in human motivation and that our ethics and hearts affect how we utilize the energy of money. Indeed, altruism is the rule rather than the exception. One of the leading economists studying altruism is Herbert Gintis, an emeritus professor at the University of Massachusetts. Gintis is the lead author of *Moral Sentiments and Material Interests*. He observes that human beings are motivated by morality and believes that ethical behavior may inspire a renaissance of economic theory.

For 200 years, standard economic theory has ignored human empathy, courage, and generosity and slandered human motivation. What trickles down from its negativity is cynicism and greed. Since the time of Adam Smith, the eighteenth-century Scottish philosopher who wrote *The Wealth of Nations*, and later John Stuart Mill, traditional economic models have insisted that people are motivated solely by avarice and personal interests.

Although Adam Smith lived in a time when a one-sided economic model was being developed, he was aware that our interests are not solely self-centered or malicious. Smith celebrated our altruistic instincts in *The Theory of Moral Sentiments*: "How selfish so ever man may be supposed, there are evidently some principles in his nature, which interest him in the fortune of others and render their happiness necessary to him, though he derives nothing from it except the pleasure of seeing it." It's time to correct the traditional economic model with the awareness that altruism, not avarice, is a primary motivation for our behaviors.

The impulse of altruism finds endless ways to serve. More than four billion people lack access to socioeconomic participation and even to the most basic legal protections. Without the primary building blocks of participation in civil society, such as identity documents, property and labor rights, as well as legal status for small enterprises, people are forced to live on the margins of society. Due to violence or environmental upheavals, millions of refugees have had to flee their homes without their identity documents. This exponentially compounds their difficulties in rebuilding their lives.

Altruistic problem solvers collaborated to create the Microjustice Initiative that empowers people directly at the grassroots level. Like microcredit, microjustice delivers a needed service economically to the world's poorest populations. In 2006, Dutch lawyer and legal activist Patricia van Nispen tot Sevenaer moved to La Paz to start Microjustice Bolivia, and the United Nations is sponsoring microjustice projects in several impoverished countries to address legal empowerment issues.

Access to justice services is an issue around the globe. Poverty and homelessness continue to exist in developed as well as third and fourth world nations. Eviction and unemployment issues, domestic and medical matters, and obtaining welfare benefits are just some of the legal needs of the indigent. Mental illness and other disabilities exacerbate all of these issues.

In Salt Lake City, Jensie Anderson, a University of Utah law professor and soccer mom, coordinates legal outreach efforts for homeless people. Under a highway viaduct, she sets up a card table and offers free legal advice and referrals, saying, "It's not all altruistic. I have to do it or I don't think I'd sleep at night."

Like microjustice, microcredit is a crucial factor in reducing poverty. Melinda Gates, co-chair of the Bill & Melinda Gates Foundation, has recognized that savings accounts for safeguarding these loans and the resulting earnings are also important to break the cycle of poverty. The Gates Foundation has committed more than $350 million to make safe financial services widely accessible to the poor so that they can weather unexpected events, accumulate money to invest in education, increase their productivity and income, and build their financial security.

Mobile phones are useful in virtual financial systems and their use is expanding exponentially. A 2010 UN study found that cell phones are one of the most effective advancements in history to lift people out of poverty. Micro-enterprises and web-based businesses are beginning to flourish in developing nations. Cell phones enable a school-based business in rural Uganda to generate needed operational funds.

Innovative mobile phone cash-transfer services are opening markets and transforming lives. Workers removed from financial institutions now have safe ways to manage and transfer money. Also, agent banking, in which small stores and post offices serve as banking outlets, is an innovative trend to expand financial services in areas of the world without a banking infrastructure. Countless individuals contribute to the rivers of innovation, compassion, and altruism that help the human spirit soar.

Adoption—Expanding Global Families

The commitment to adopt a child often leads to unforeseen opportunities to expand our heart of compassion. The word *adoption* comes from the Latin root *adoptare*, "to choose." Families are formed and blended together in many ways. The biblical Moses is one of countless "chosen ones" who was adopted as an infant. Adoption widens our circle of caring beyond our local tribe.

Every person needs to be in relationship with others in order to thrive, yet more than 140 million orphans worldwide are without families. Unfortunately, government administrations are growing more, not less, reluctant to facilitate international adoption policies. Orphans require advocates to champion their needs. In some regions in sub-Saharan Africa, 40 percent of all children are orphaned.

Orphaned children have access to fewer resources, including education, which is key to breaking the cycle of poverty. Uneducated, unemployed youth are easy targets to be drawn into violent gangs, tribal wars, and terrorist groups. The Nyaka AIDS Orphans Project is one of many organizations working to free orphans from the cycle of systemic deprivation and poverty. Its remarkable founder, T. Jackson Kaguri, is in partnership with the Stephen Lewis Foundation. After serving in Canadian politics, Lewis became deeply engaged in global humanitarian efforts. *It takes a village to raise a child* is a familiar saying, and Kaguri, the 2012 CNN hero from Uganda, adds, "It takes children to raise a village."

A documentary by Jane Gillooly called *Today the Hawk Takes One Chick* explores some of the issues of Africa's AIDS orphans from the perspective of the grandmothers. These elders have committed to adopting the children without parents, including those to whom they are not related by family or tribe. As many as fifteen orphans are cared for by one grandmother.

The film records some of the tremendous misery rampant in the rural drought of Swaziland, a country whose 40 percent HIV infection rate is the highest in Africa. The grandmothers and countless others are unsung heroes of self-sacrifice and human dignity. It is a testament to the human spirit that compassion and the tending impulse are alive and well in so many areas of extreme poverty.

The acclaimed actress Isabella Rossellini is an adoptive parent. She wrote, "Adoption feels like a genetic connection because it links us directly, not only to our own gene pool, but to the genes of all humanity. ... Adoption carries the added dimension of connection, widening the scope of what constitutes love, ties, and family." This experience is alive in adoptive families, including those attending the summer Heritage Camps held annually in the mountains of Colorado.

There are various levels of readiness for every step we take in life. Although my heart knew that I was meant to be a mother, I was not ready or willing to consider adoption until it was clear that my body would not sustain a pregnancy. All sorts of desires, fears, and attachments closed my heart to the adoption option for some time. Letting go of those attachments was a transformative and often painful process.

Eventually, I was blessed beyond my ken to adopt a healthy baby girl from Calcutta, India. How perfect it was that modern medicine could not jump-start a pregnancy for me. Who could know what a match Grace and I would be? When she was seven, Grace Shanti said, "When you're an orphan, it's as if you live in a dim world. Then you tear through a veil into a brightly lit world with a new mommy. ... My soul couldn't have chosen a better mommy for me." I give thanks every day for the profound opportunity to serve as her mother and for the power of love that dissolved my fears.

Some people have questioned why we adopted from India. Many adoptive parents meet similar challenges, especially when they're called to the other side of the globe. Upon reflection, it was clear that India is my backyard. My life path, including volunteer medical service in rural India and decades of study of Indian philosophy, led to the natural choice of adopting a Bengali daughter. Your journey of integration will reveal what is calling you.

Like most families, adoptive parents and their children often encounter unexpected challenges. One older couple adopted six children, all of whom eventually manifested a degree of physical or mental handicap. For many reasons, girls are much more likely to be orphaned. A couple with two biological children learned that teenage girls were the most difficult orphans for which to find placements. After arranging to adopt an African adolescent, they discovered that the girl had a sister with AIDS living in another orphanage who she hadn't seen for years. This couple opened their hearts even further and adopted both sisters.

Kari Grady Grossman, award-winning author of *Bones That Float: A Story of Adopting Cambodia*, is an adoptive mother and co-founder of Sustainable Schools International (SSI). During the process of adopting their son from Cambodia, Grossman and her husband were inspired to develop a school in their son's name. All children benefit from education, mentoring, and various training opportunities. Even basic literacy skills may lift a child out of the exploitable class and income-generating life skills can lift them out of poverty.

As the programs of SSI expanded beyond school scholarships, the empowered communities have experienced additional advantages. Parents' employment opportunities increased as they learned to manufacture fuel briquettes made from waste. Community members rescued some of the girls from their villages who were trafficked into the sex trade. As we cultivate our innate capacities, our integral service in turn uplifts communities locally or on the other side of the globe.

"In any dark time," writes archetypal psychologist Clarissa Pinkola Estes, Ph.D., "there is a tendency to veer toward fainting over how much is wrong or unmended in the world. Do not focus on that. There is a tendency, too, to fall into being weakened by dwelling on what is outside your reach, by what cannot yet be. Do not focus there. That is spending the wind without raising the sails. We are needed, that is all we can know."

The consciousness of our interconnectedness, our compassion, and our altruism are the alpha and omega—as well as the heart—of goodness to go. Integral service includes transformative action that creates changes within and without. Increased awareness, clarity about our values, and inner strength support altruism, allowing our compassion in action to benefit others.

Pause, Reflect, and Record

- What examples of altruism or community volunteerism have inspired you?

- Living anonymous organ donors are examples of radical empathy and altruism. What might contribute to their deep trust in the inexhaustible flow of goodness in the world?

- What obstacles stifle your altruism? How might you go beyond blocks, resistance, or impediments, both internal and external?

- It has been said that "what matters most is doing what matters." What really matters to you at this point in your life? Why?

7

Summon the Power
of Your Heart

*If one completes the journey to one's own heart,
one will find oneself in the heart of everyone else.*

—Father Thomas Keating

Wise beings throughout the ages have taught that generosity opens our eyes, including the inner eye of wisdom, the eye of the heart. The heart is not only a physical pump of our life's blood, it is a wellspring of creativity and compassion. The heart is literally an organ of feeling, sensation, and perception with ways of seeing that connect us with others. The adventure of integrating mind and heart as we create the story of our lives is remarkable. Some describe the journey from the head to the heart as the longest to take. Our integral service begins in the heart and is fueled by its goodness.

Overreliance on logic and reason often leads to analysis paralysis and prevents us from experiencing the wonder and mystery of life. Meaningful coincidence, or synchronicity, is one of those mysteries. Carl Jung, a pioneering Swiss psychiatrist, was open to synchronicity and spiritual mystery as well as rational thought. He wrote, "The more that critical reason dominates, the more impoverished life becomes. Overvalued reason has this in common with political absolutism: under its domination, the individual is pauperized."

Our heart is an astonishing organ of neural cells and nearly tireless muscle fibers. Its four chambers serve as metaphors for some of its attributes: courage, flexibility, inspiration, and openness. The heart is courageous and strong, adapting to changing conditions with clarity and precision. The heart also inspires curiosity and creativity, and is open to receiving the delight and wonder of life. We feel love and heartache in the center of our chest. Often the heart knows what intellect alone cannot. To experience pure love and the rapture of being alive, we need the creative interplay of heart and mind.

The heart is nourished by experiential knowledge of our true nature and finds meaning beyond apparent facts. The brilliant mathematician and seventeenth-century philosopher Blaise Pascal was a strong proponent of the scientific method who also recognized that the heart has its reasons of which the mind knows nothing. In the eye of the heart, all life matters. An awakened heart longs to express its gratitude, generosity, and goodness. This generosity in turn expands and purifies our hearts and minds, allowing great qualities to abide in us. What we give from such a heart flowers in beneficial ways and the lives that it touches flourish.

The Greek word for unconditional love is *agape*. In a collection of Dr. Martin Luther King, Jr.'s, writings entitled *A Testament of Hope*, he explored the generosity and power of this love. "The only way to change humanity is to keep love at the center of our lives. ... Everybody can be great ... because everybody can serve. ... You only need a heart full of grace ... a soul generated by love."

The power of love is a divine force uniting all life; its wisdom knows life's underlying goodness and its generosity extends goodwill to all. We begin by cultivating respect for ourselves and then extending it to others. This practice of honoring one another is mutually empowering. The kind of power we need is an energy that *powers with*, not over, another. Dr. King goes on to describe this *powering with* as the ability to achieve purpose with a vigilant awareness of its manifestations and effects on others.

Attributes of the Heart

For millennia, the heart has been a universal symbol of the wellspring of goodness within us. The qualities of the heart, such as reverence and courage, are doorways to the recognition of our oneness with the light of consciousness animating everyone and everything. In healthy human beings, the transcultural attributes of the heart give rise to our deepest values, which in turn inform our belief systems.

An ancient Indian spiritual text called the Bhagavad Gita describes dozens of virtues that are our natural inner wealth. Some of these inner treasures are generosity, courage, forgiveness, serenity, fortitude, compassion, and freedom from greed, pride, and anger. They form a four-chambered heart, or wheel of goodness with gratitude at its hub. The four chambers are:

Love: compassion, reverence, devotion, tenderness, purity of being, goodwill, harmony, benevolence.

Respect: truthfulness, uprightness, absence of slander, self-discipline, modesty, honor.

Peace: patience, serenity, kindness, acceptance, nonviolence, merciful justice, forgiveness.

Courage: enthusiasm, perseverance, vigor, joy, concentration, determination.

Attributes of the heart are inherent human potentials. With healthy development, these innate qualities naturally unfold and enrich our lives. Values are held on many levels, including individual and cultural, and it's easy to misunderstand the deepest values motivating our behavior. Although they may change over time, values are like maps that help to guide ethical behavior in social interactions, serving as standards to evaluate issues, behaviors, and events.

In the Western Hemisphere, especially after the financial debacle in 2008, the value of transparency has been touted. Are we now walking our talk? Are we creating economic systems and oversight regulations that make it possible to evaluate the honesty, integrity, and transparency of all banking and business transactions? How will trust be developed with trading partners who value inscrutability more than transparency? What happens to human relationships and interactions if mutual trust is not a shared value?

As with value systems, we develop elaborate sets of beliefs over time as a result of complex socialization processes involving family, peers, education, environment, work, religion, and ethnic and national affiliations. Beliefs and values often change as a result of experience, deep self-inquiry, and increased awareness. As we clarify our values, our behaviors, beliefs, and sense of identity are refined.

Most people have a hierarchy of values, with some standards or beliefs held as more important than others. Priorities, including inner ways of being as well as outer actions, may not equate with principles. If forced to make a choice within our hierarchy of values, we usually choose to satisfy the more important value and compromise the one deemed less important. At this point in your life, where is integral service in your worldview? If you grew up with adults modeling service as a natural part of their lives, that value may rank higher for you than it would for someone traumatized in a war-torn country.

Aside from needs for safety, love, and nourishment, our deepest core values often have a moral quality: reverence for life, fairness, equality, truthfulness, and integrity. Amoral values, such as the desire to control large sums of money, can lead to immoral actions. As we've seen repeatedly, power without love can be used to horrific ends.

Values may be held at three levels—core identity, deep beliefs, and daily standards of behaviors. Self-respect often rests on our commitment and ability to live our values, to walk our talk daily. From enduring principles come deep beliefs that guide our behavior. Beliefs inform the next level of everyday attitudes, standards, and norms of how we expect people to act.

Kindness is an example of a value a person may hold at all three levels: I *know* my heart is kind (core identity); I *believe* in the power of kindness (deep belief); and I *value* kindness in action (standard of daily behavior). Many people have experienced that walking their talk, living aligned with their core values, contributes to their happiness. What are values to which you are committed on all three levels—identity, beliefs, and behaviors? Take a moment to gratefully acknowledge yourself, your intent, your goodness, and your efforts.

Our rational mind determines the limit of what it thinks is possible while our unbounded heart simply dissolves those impositions. It is joyful and empowering to experience breakthroughs, the unfolding of freedom from long-held limitations. Ralph Waldo Emerson encourages us to act from our wise and courageous heart: "We are very near greatness: one step and we are safe; can we not take the leap?" When we summon the power of the heart, we can.

Cultivate a Limitless Heart

The living waters of the heart contain many noble attributes. Social artists and warriors of the twenty-first century speak their hearts' truth and act with mutual respect and responsibility. They're not hooked by the fear that fuels dualism and poverty mentality. Unconditional love that harmonizes and illumines life is able to release the constriction of fear and turn enemies into friends. Love is the new currency and sharing its light can be the purpose of our lives. We take a stand to spread our love as we work together to protect our environment, prevent the extinction of species, and empower those who are suffering around the world and in our communities.

Our calling to integral service can be our life's passion. Like our heart, our stance as warriors of kindness needs to be grounded, stable, flexible, and strong, inside and out. Compassion includes passion, the powerful, vital energy in motion when human beings feel deeply. Passionate feelings are often intense, ranging from almost uncontrollable rage to inextinguishable flames of love. When strong emotional reactions arise, taking balanced breaths is one of many practices that support our return to equanimity of heart.

In the face of great darkness, the heart seeks to act with loving-kindness. Like the sun, there are hearts whose compassion shines on everything and everyone in the same way. If it's possible for them, it's possible for us, however challenging the path. Just as sunlight is free from attachment to who and what it will shine on, compassion is free from attachment to ideologies or recipients' identities. While empathic kindness does not condone hurtful behavior, it has unconditional qualities, such as respectful regard for the basic goodness within everyone's heart.

How are we to translate and incorporate noble practices into daily life? How do we cultivate compassion in action, especially when we're feeling distressed, impatient, injured, or betrayed? Wisdom traditions in cultures throughout the world have many approaches to the development of kind and skillful means. Shantideva, an ancient yoga master, gave many teachings about cultivating compassion that involve self-inquiry into why we wish to relieve the suffering of others. As we contemplate compassion, we might explore the effect of daily remembrance and repetition of a Buddhist teaching—*cultivate a limitless heart.*

One of the reasons that humans value reverence, mercy, and related attributes is that these qualities are the best of who we are. We cherish love and compassion and the happiness they bring. "If you want others to be happy, practice compassion," writes the 14th Dalai Lama. "If you want to be happy, practice compassion." Many people practice random acts of kindness every day, such as putting coins in a parking meter for the next person. A simple smile or word of thanks can start a chain reaction of goodness on the go. Be kind. Everyone is carrying an invisible burden of some sort; we simply don't have enough information to judge.

A woman shared that wants no regrets at the end of her life. Therefore, she's chosen to live in such a way that her answer to death's question "Were you kind?" will be a resounding *YES!* The Dalai Lama declares that his religion is kindness and encourages us to practice loving kindness in every moment. Remember to offer this genuine friendliness to yourself as well as others. Love is gratitude. Gratitude is love.

At the start of each day, refresh your intention to cultivate a limitless heart and become a shelter of supreme compassion for yourself and others. When you notice thoughts and actions that are not aligned with your heart's intention, make adjustments to realign with your integrity. Variations of timeless centering practices include relaxation breathing, replacing negative thoughts with uplifting images or teachings, slowly drinking a glass of water, repeating empowering affirmations or prayers, or walking in nature.

When we're committed to lifelong learning, growth, and evolution, we'll challenge unexamined beliefs in old paradigms with gentle curiosity. Our allegiance shifts to more conscious, uplifting worldviews. A light touch is helpful; there is no need to "should" on ourselves. More useful than criticizing our human tendency to forget and make mistakes is to celebrate when we've remembered our commitments.

What frees us from fear's bondage and mind's attachments to temporary possessions? The teachings of St. Francis and others describe that when one lets go of the self-centered desire to save oneself first at all costs, the delusion of separateness begins to dissolve. Although in our interconnected world separateness is an illusion, the fear it generates is our greatest bondage.

A being who has long exemplified the cultivation of a limitless heart has been venerated in the form of Kuan Yin, the Goddess of Mercy. Millions honor her as a holy mother who embodies the power of divine compassion and forgiveness. By remembering Kuan Yin, legend says, her blessings are felt as a softening of the heart and a cooling of the mind. Just as gentle rains soften the earth and allow the soil to bring forth nourishing goodness, compassion softens and opens our heart.

Merciful Kuan Yin took the vow of a bodhisattva to stay in the world until all sentient beings were free from suffering. In branches of Buddhist philosophy, the path of the bodhisattva evolved as the highest ideal. The bodhisattva is an enlightened one who chooses to sacrifice final absorption in the Absolute until the salvation of all living beings is assured. Bodhisattvas choose to take birth wholly for the upliftment of humanity. This willingness to delay one's own salvation until everyone else's is attained is the generosity of a limitless heart.

There are many ways to enhance qualities such as mindfulness, compassion, and patience. The Buddha described one such practice: "Bring virtue to whatever you are doing. When you sew, make garments with the thought of compassion. When you cook, make food with patience. When you play music, offer it with generosity. Let whatever you are doing become your meditation."

The Chinese sage Confucius focused on the virtues of benevolence, righteousness, respect, and wisdom. These qualities are alive in every wisdom tradition. Although ego-mind may flare with anger or greed and try to avoid, deny, or suppress uncomfortable emotions, we're able to gently and steadily overcome any habit that ignores pain. Pablo Casals, a twentieth-century Spaniard and one of the greatest cellists of all time, felt that the capacity to care is the thing that gives life its deepest significance. Our hearts are naturally open to caring for life. How might we strengthen our aspiration and ability to be open to each moment, no matter what it brings?

Pause, Reflect, and Record

- What capacities of your heart, such as love, respect, peace, and courage, would you like to strengthen? How might you do this?

- What steps could you take to cultivate a limitless heart? How could you become a shelter of compassion for yourself and others?

- We all have aspects of our psyches, personalities, and subconscious minds that we dislike, ignore, avoid, or reject; these aspects are sometimes referred to as our shadow. What are some aspects of your shadow that you haven't fully embraced or that call for transformation? What aspects of your shadow could be seen as a gift that needs to be listened to or protected?

- What constricts your heart? How might you practice bringing the light of compassion to your shadow places?

8

The Rays of Gratitude

What is love?
Gratitude.

—Rumi

The gratitude of the heart finds expression in our goodness to go. Centuries ago, the Roman philosopher Cicero wrote that gratitude is not only the greatest of virtues but the parent of all the others. "Gratitude bestows reverence," wrote John Milton, "allowing us to encounter everyday epiphanies, those transcendent moments of awe that change forever how we experience life and the world."

Gratitude is also remembrance with thanksgiving, a moistening and softening of our hearts that awakens us to respect and love. In the Christian tradition, St. Paul encouraged the practice of gratitude: "In all things, give thanks." Thankfulness is a garden whose grace takes form as integral service. Like two branches growing from the trunk of gratitude, the giver and receiver are connected in a mutual exchange of generosity.

With gratefulness, we acknowledge life's blessings, in times rich with challenge as well as contentment. Awareness of our connection with all of life expands as we reflect on the countless beings that contribute to our lives. Whose service contributed to life-saving immunizations and the advantages of modern dentistry? Consider the people who make possible each meal we eat. Many of us consume food grown by farmers working at great distances from our communities. Who transported our food to local markets and who, other than Prometheus, harnessed the energy sources that cook our meals? How do we thank all of the individuals who developed the infrastructure that supplies clean water flowing from our taps?

Gratefulness is a universal ethic that reveals life's fullness. Its spirit of trust and generosity that turns strangers into friends is shared by all cultures and religious traditions. Transcending divisive dogmas, gratitude brings a sense of sufficiency, that what we have is enough. Choosing to be grateful and to cherish each moment is a life-affirming habit that provides a common language and cross-cultural bridge between us.

Gratefulness is where active recognition and healing of our relationships with ourselves, with all beings, and with the earth begin. It is the great turning from ego attachments toward living with freedom and joy. It's been said that happiness is evidence of a grateful heart shifting its focus from regrets about the past and worries about the future to appreciation of the resonant presence and deep peace available now.

Gratitude is a seed that blossoms into many virtues. In Chapter 7, attributes of the heart, such as peace, love, respect, and courage, were mentioned. Consider why Cicero and others have said that gratitude is the source of human virtues. When we're young, we often think we're grateful because something on the outside made us happy. Later, we learn that inner practices of gratitude and compassion contribute to being happy.

On the spot, in the middle of a conflict, it's easy to forget our best intentions and our regard for gratitude. When anger flares and stress hormones surge through our body, it's difficult to be fully present with our heart and mind open in the moment. How do we develop gratefulness on the spot for unwanted learning opportunities? Even when we trust that petty tyrants can be powerful teachers and provide motivation for our personal growth, we often begin with fledgling appreciation for that possibility rather than full-fledged gratitude.

As we develop an unconditional attitude of gratitude, we learn to appreciate the valleys of life as well as the sunny grandeur of the peaks. "Thanks for everything" we may have said more than once in our lives. However, appreciating the value of *everything* that happens in our lives usually takes time as our understanding and perspective expand. Practicing gratitude includes ongoing efforts to be free of selfishness and the petty fickleness of the mind so that the eye of the heart can perceive the light of goodness in every moment.

We're fortunate to be alive as members of the global family. Many indigenous peoples have long believed that to be human is an honor and a gift that requires mindful gratitude. The Iroquois' thanksgiving address called Greetings to the Natural World concludes with: "Everything we need to live a good life is here on this Mother Earth. For all the love that is still around us, we gather our minds together as one and send our choicest words of greetings and thanks to the Great Spirit. Now our minds are one." For all that we have received and for all that we are able to give, may we be truly grateful.

Cultivating Gratitude

In the garden of gratitude, our hearts and minds become one as virtues thrive and love grows. Early in the 1900s, an American educator and clergyman named Henry van Dyke wrote, "Gratitude is the inward feeling of kindness received. Thankfulness is the natural impulse to express that feeling. Thanksgiving is the following of that impulse."

Gratefulness is an emotional and psychological wealth that turns a meal into a feast, even when our financial resources are meager. It contributes to experiences of sufficiency that allow us to live contentedly with relatively small means. It's being truly wealthy although not necessarily rich financially. Practicing gratitude and recognizing sufficiency in our lives enrich each other in spirals of positive feedback. Many people explore gratefulness as a global ethic. Brother David Steindl-Rast, a Benedictine monk born in Vienna in 1926, contemplated gratitude deeply, describing its two great branches as gratefulness and thanksgiving.

A grateful person experiences his or her bowl of life as full to the brim with interconnectedness. This is enough. I am enough. Sufficiency is the wealth of knowing that you have, and are, enough. From this fulfillment, heart's bounty spills over into thanksgiving, the second great branch of gratitude. As the cup of gratitude flows over, thanksgiving takes form, including that of integral service. Offerings of thanksgiving are born of twin recognitions: our interconnected oneness and that our basic needs are met by the sufficiency of life.

Brother Steindl-Rast is a spokesman for A Network for Gratefulness and he challenges us to expand our gratefulness to embrace all the difficulties of the world. We live with different perspectives, almost in different worlds. Each of these worlds has its own vocabulary, concerns, values, needs, and skill sets. Our grateful hearts embrace it all with arms grown strong with love.

Sharing our gratitude affects others in positive ways, which tend to ripple out in the ocean of life. Acts of kindness support cultures of giving inside and out, and never go to waste. Generosity has spawned generations of philanthropy. The importance of philanthropies having effective, sustainable programs with policies of transparency is recognized. In the past few years, an American investor named Warren Buffet developed the Giving Pledge to inspire billionaires to donate half of their riches to charity.

Nipun Mehta moved from India to Silicon Valley when he was a boy. In 1999, this young computer programmer and three friends offered an act of pure giving as an experiment to discover if giving could lead to meaningful happiness. After they built a website for a homeless shelter and then for over 4,500 other nonprofit organizations at no charge, ripples of goodness extended to a loosely knit, evolving global organization. Their CharityFocus initiative has given rise to HelpOthers, DailyGood, KarmaTube, iJourney, Karma Clinic, Service-eXchange, Karma Kitchen, ProPoor, and other inspirational efforts. As Mehta gave money, then time, then himself, he enjoyed offering integral "frictionless service" that expressed his innate generosity, happiness, and compassion.

New behaviors wake us out of old habits and complacencies. Consider responding to familiar inquiries of "How are you?" with the somewhat unexpected, "I'm grateful!" It's an old habit to be "me and more" centered; thankfully, there are many ways to become free of such tendencies. We can give back or pay it forward, expressing gratitude through daily acts that acknowledge life's bounty. Before their meals, families around the world offer prayers of thanksgiving. Some prayers include what they're grateful for receiving and, at times, for what they've not been given to endure.

Many people make daily entries in gratitude journals and find the practice to be a powerful way to make an attitude of gratitude more steadfast. Throughout the day, they note moments to cherish—difficult lessons as well as beautiful gifts—and include them in that evening's journal entry. This affirming habit of cultivating gratitude is an "inside job" that develops a life of its own. Thankfulness grows for having resources that one can give as well as for a heart that aspires to give.

A pioneer in the deep ecology movement, Joanna Macy wrote: "Gratitude for the gift of life is the primary wellspring of all religions, the hallmark of the mystic, and the source of all true art. Yet we so easily take this gift for granted. That is why so many spiritual traditions begin with thanksgiving, to remind us that for all our woes and worries, our existence itself is an unearned benefaction, which we could never of ourselves create. ... To us is granted the privilege of being on hand: to take part, if we choose, in the Great Turning to a just and sustainable society. We can let life work through us, enlisting all our strength, wisdom, and courage, so that life itself can continue." When we experience the gift of life as a blessing, we are blessed and naturally extend our blessing. If we are thankful for life on this planet, we will care for it.

Pause, Reflect, and Record

- For what are you most grateful? What is a learning made possible by a difficult experience for which you are now thankful?

- How might cultivating gratitude help mobilize your goodness to go?

- Consider keeping a gratitude journal. You may want to keep it by your bed and list memorable moments, people, places in nature, interactions, or lessons learned before sleep. Remind yourself of all that is good in the world. Take time on a regular basis to contemplate your experience of this practice of gratefulness.

- Write a poem, song, or prayer of gratitude.

9

Courage—
Freedom from Fear

Courage is not simply one of the virtues,
but the form of every virtue at the testing point.

—C. S. Lewis

Courage makes possible our goodness to go. The impulse to express our gratitude as integral service can be constricted by many types of fear. If we haven't summoned the courage of our heart, it's easy to get caught in a state where what we fear is fear itself. Have you ever avoided something because of fear? Fear can derail and defer dreams or be a wake-up call. It can trigger us to resist life challenges or remind us of opportunities to strengthen our courage and freedom.

Courage is not only required on the battlefield, in extreme sporting conditions, or when taking a stand against corruption and injustice. Developing courage, whether physical or moral, in the face of fear is a habit to be patiently cultivated step by step every day. Moral courage support us in the maintenance and exercising of other virtues of the heart, such as equanimity, resilience, and forgiveness.

"Courage lies in being oneself," wrote French architect Fernand Pouillon. When the going gets tough, courage makes possible other virtues; nearly everything we do requires courage. It takes courage to face each new day, give voice to our truth, accept death, and to make peace. "Peace is the healing and elevating influence of the world," wrote former president Woodrow Wilson. Even in the midst of misery, courage allows us to lift our hearts and minds toward understanding. If we listen carefully, we often discover insights and gifts of goodness in even the most difficult circumstances. Peacemaking and courage manifest as small choices and steps made with a big heart.

Goodness To Go

Many wisdom traditions explore the essential virtue of fearlessness. Rabindranath Tagore, the Bengali poet who in 1913 was awarded the Nobel Prize in Literature, wrote, "Where the mind is without fear ... where words come out from the depth of truth ... where the clear stream of reason has not lost its way into the dreary desert sand of dead habit ... into that heaven of freedom, my Father, let my country awake."

Homer wrote, "Go on with a spirit that fears nothing." Nourish that spirit and fear not. Our spirit of service needs resiliency but it does not require thick psychological skin as we care for the environment or act to reduce suffering. Even very sensitive people serving in traumatic situations are replenished by sufficient self-care and therapeutic support. Our minds, hearts, and spirits can be fiercely vulnerable, open, and strong as they connect with the matrix of life's vitality.

Courage and Resilience

Courage is evident in our very first actions. We taste our courage during the incredible journey of birth and as our fledgling steps launch us into the world. Later, as we face physical decline or endure great despair, the power of resilience and courage sustains us. In our own ways, each of us works with fear and summons courage into our daily lives. With nobility and grace, sadness and fear are released on wings of courage.

Resilient natives near the North Pole have a saying that if you're going to walk on thin ice, you might as well dance. To be courageous does not mean the absence of fear. Fearlessness is the willingness to experience our fears and continue to make the next best, even graceful, move. It is summoning the power of one's heart in the face of fear. We choose to act with love in spite of fear because we value love more than succumbing to fear. Consciously, we choose to *give no fear* in our imperiled world. We decide that moving toward a more openhearted life, acting with compassion on behalf of equity and wholesomeness, is our legacy for future generations.

Millions of people around the world are burdened with fear on a daily basis. Many struggle to live with honor and integrity in an atmosphere of terror generated by abusive spouses or brutal dictators. Fear also kindles through millions of brains due to a genetic shortage of the neurotransmitter serotonin. Anxiety and attention disorders are on the rise. Moment by moment, we come face-to-face with how we'll react or respond to fear. As we meet the challenges of working with fear, courage and compassion grow.

Courage—Freedom from Fear

The dignity of Rosa Parks was steeped in courage when she kept her seat on a segregated bus and thereby took a stand for civil rights. That courage was a beacon for the movement for racial equality—and indeed for the rights of all people—across the United States and around the world. More than fifty years later, Mrs. Parks's actions and words continue to encourage people around the world. She said, "You must never be fearful about what you are doing when it is right."

One of the leaders of the civil rights movement, Dr. Martin Luther King, Jr., sought to inspire volunteers of the movement when he said that the time is always right to do what is right. Courageous truth-tellers are often unsung heroes who act when the right thing to do is theirs to do. In 2002, Cynthia Cooper was named one of *Time Magazine's* Persons of the Year for her role as a whistle-blower who unraveled the WorldCom fraud, the largest corporate fraud in history at that time.

We can choose courage over fear. When my daughter was five years old, we flew to the jungles of Costa Rica. Although Grace had been looking forward to riding the zip line in Monteverde, she began to freeze with fear when faced with the immediate prospect. For a few minutes, she reflected on the option of not experiencing the zip line and how she might feel afterward if she opted for that choice. Then she gently shook her little body as if she was sloughing off the fear and went for it. After the adventure of flying solo 100 feet up in the jungle canopy, Grace's smile lit the sky and she joyously exclaimed, "There was some fear, but mostly it was exciting!"

Fear and excitement are experienced as physiologic equivalents by our bodies, and unprocessed fear is often held in our bodies. Traumatic flashbacks haunt millions of people. Many everyday experiences trigger fearful feelings, emotions, and energy patterns such as frustration, isolation, overwhelm, and confusion. Sometimes, a diagnosis, an accident, a false accusation, or an arrest initiates an ongoing series of profound difficulties that require tremendous courage to cope with.

In 1947, General Aung San, the leader of the Burmese independence movement, was assassinated in Rangoon. After forming the National League for Democracy, his daughter, Aung San Suu Kyi, was put under house arrest in 1988, where she remained for fifteen years. In 1991, she was awarded the Nobel Peace Prize. World awareness about the Burmese military regime's ongoing genocide of ethnics continues to grow, especially after witnessing its inhumane repression of international aid following the 2008 cyclone that devastated the region. The rape and slaughter of Burmese refugees continues, and organizations such as Burmese Lifeline are courageously trying to protect potential victims of this ethnic genocide.

Aung San Suu Kyi survived an assassination attempt in 2003. She was aware that torture and death could have met her at any time. Unexpectedly, she was released in November of 2010. Profoundly gentle and strong, Aung San says, "The only real prison is fear, and the only real freedom is freedom from fear."

Psychological prisons are made of fear, guilt, and dysfunctional beliefs. Rather than remaining trapped by disempowering thoughts and feelings, we're able to shift our focus to the spacious sky between and beyond limitations. Why do we stay in prison when the door is so wide open? With tenderness, we again ask ourselves this question that the Persian poet Rumi implored us to contemplate centuries ago. As challenging as it may be, it's possible to be free of fear-based thinking. Instead, we choose to be aware of the consciousness that is the source of our thoughts.

It's a waste of life energy to let fear hijack our imagination and create something we don't want. Instead of getting stuck in agitated eddies of worry, experiment with the notion that the edge of your comfort zone is actually your path. Challenge and release the content of fearful thoughts and experience the substratum of unencumbered energy without doing anything to change the fear or get rid of it. What is your experience?

Fear and discomfort are clear indicators that you're at your edge. Try moving closer with curiosity. The next time fear arises, see if you can feel the energy of fear in your body and actually befriend it as you drop the storyline that seems to be its trigger. Living on purpose requires the strengthening of our ability to re-direct attention and reminded ourselves that we are agents of change and not victims carried along by vicissitudes of the mind. Currents of our personal and global history are shaped by our moral convictions creativity, and resilient courage.

Redesigning Your Life Course

As we strengthen our courage and clarify our calling, creative energy reinvents and redirects the trajectory of our lives. George Eliot wrote, "Our deeds determine us, as much as we determine our deeds." At various times throughout our lives, we're called to summon our courage and give birth to another expression of ourselves, a sort of rebirth in the most unencumbered sense of that word.

Adolescence and midlife are classic times in our personal evolution when we long to find our life's purpose and its unique expression. At times of transition or uncertainty, we often delve deeply into the archetypal question "Who am I?" When a marriage or career dissolves, when we recognize that old ways of being are no longer aligned with who we are or want to be now. it's time to redesign our life's course. Transitions usually begin with some sort of ending or letting go of a behavior, belief, or way of being that is followed by a reorientation period that summons our courage. Fresh action begins the next cycle of change.

Life is a constant, cyclical process of change, self-renewal, and revitalization. There are several compelling books about adult developmental transitions, including Frederic M. Hudson's *Mastering the Art of Self-Renewal* and Angeles Arrien's *The Second Half of Life*. Reaching the "fabulous fiftieth" birthday can be a time of reinvention, one that is still relatively rare in countries with lower life expectancies. In 1900, the average North American lived only forty-seven years, which is still the case in many parts of the world.

A longevity revolution is beginning in most industrialized nations, and small cultural regions of extraordinary longevity are being studied. Human beings have made greater gains in average life expectancy in the past century than in the preceding 5,000 years. Two-thirds of all human who've reached the age of sixty-five are alive today. These changes in our health and longevity provide us with great opportunities to reinvent, instead of retire, ourselves.

Longevity and vital health are not ends in themselves but means to manifest our goodness to go. We've come to see that retirement as a permanent vacation without purpose is early death. A retired teacher voiced the heart of many vibrant, talented retirees, saying, "I want more meaning in my life." We can grow whole *and* grow old.

Reinventing ourselves takes courage and often includes re-examining our paradigm or worldview. A paradigm is a lens through which we filter our perceptions of the world. It's the way we make sense of things, the set of assumptions, beliefs, concepts, values, and practices that form our view of "reality." In her powerful book, *Your Money or Your Life*, Vicki Robin challenges an old, greed-based paradigm that "more is better." She explores how individuals, as well as local and global communities, could create lives rich in justice and joy based on core values rather than excessive consumption.

What is enough? Lynne Twist in *Soul of Money* describes how fixating on the toxic myth that *there's never enough* becomes a justification for an unfulfilled life. Our beliefs literally determine our perception. What we think is what we see; what we perceive is what we get. If our mind thinks that a stick is a snake, it often floods us with stress hormones. Also, early conditioning as well as explanations, conclusions, and interpretations of experiences contribute to our outlook on the world. Pessimism, mistrust, fear, and cynicism often make our world smaller and less friendly.

Thankfully, the prescription of our lenses can be changed! So-called common sense can be a surprisingly uncommon sensibility. At times, it's a misused term for simplistic judgments within an unquestioned paradigm. Unexamined assumptions and beliefs can become "life sentences" that limit our possibilities indefinitely. It's useful to regularly question assumptions and limited knowledge, both personal and cultural.

Let Your Life Speak—The Power of Intention

"Established in Being, take action," says an ancient Buddhist text. In the early 1700s, the English Quaker John Woolman, best known for his lifelong crusade against slavery, walked his talk to let his life speak. As the inhumane institution of slavery has demonstrated, it takes many generations to begin the process of restitution for injustices. Tragically, human trafficking and many other forms of slavery continue today.

Surely, now is the time for our lives to speak. Courageous, compassionate action and merciful justice have been topics of philosophical and spiritual inquiry for millennia. In *The Republic*, Plato inquired into the nature of justice and goodness. In this Socratic dialogue, he asks: What are the right relationships between the elements or structures within the human organism as well as in external society?

What determines various levels of *right relationship*? Plato wrote that only when there is justice and goodness within the human being could there be justice and goodness in the external world. For moral courage, compassionate reason, and merciful justice to live in society, we need to let our life-affirming qualities speak from the inside out. Our creative intelligence is nourished by the energy of awareness and informed by the discernment of virtues such as gratitude, justice, and goodness.

Integral philosophers in our post-Platonic world describe how evolution progresses toward ever-widening realizations of beauty, truth, and goodness. In his book, *Evolution's Purpose*, Steve McIntosh discusses how evolutionary impulses and choices based on our values drive our sense of moral obligation to share our gifts with the world. As the realization of our inherent goodness grows, we're naturally motivated to give back to the world with creativity and generosity.

Let your life speak. Mahatma Gandhi fully lived his belief that "a small group of determined spirits, with an unquenchable thirst for their mission, can alter the course of history." He wrote, "Let our first act every morning be the following resolve: 'I shall not fear anyone on earth. ... I shall bear ill-will towards no one. I shall not submit to injustice from anyone."

Many tales throughout the ages have described courageous souls going forth with the shield of virtue and the sword of truth. In ancient Indian scriptures, this conscious, intelligent energy at the heart of goodness is called *dharma*. Dharma means "that which holds together" as well as truthfulness, or right action. It is the power of righteous intent that is free of ego judgments, fears, and desires and which offers both protection and a path to genuine happiness. In India's Bhagavad Gita, Arjuna is an archer and spiritual seeker who aspired to be a warrior of dharma. In Plato's *Republic*, the Warriors symbolize dharma.

For centuries, nurses have been at the frontlines of human suffering, and thousands of these caregivers include social activism in their daily lives. Recognizing that reinstituting a small tax on financial transactions could generate billions of dollars, a nurses' union is speaking out and acting up. The revenue from this tax could be directed to generating jobs lost in the recession as well as to education, housing, and medical care for the needy.

As we find our true voices and let our lives speak, we learn about the power of intention. "Intent precedes the ability to do," wrote the cognitive psychologist Jerome Bruner. When we create an intention, we are shaping a lens or context through which to view and respond to virtually any situation in our lives. Reflecting on our inner priorities and clarifying our intentions are powerful ways to feel more grounded, authentic, and "on purpose." We stop dithering and flailing around, scattering our energies. We refuse to submit to resignation and truancy from life.

Some aspects of acting with purpose are clarifying why we desire or need a change to take place and identifying what resources and abilities we can access to effect that change. Articulating our inner motivation and intention fuels our commitment toward a specific, informed action. When we act with purpose while recognizing that we cannot control the outcome, our empowered life does not feel out of hand.

Henry David Thoreau, who died at forty-four of tuberculosis, made a conscious choice to live intentionally. Thoreau deliberately sought a new self-definition, a new way to live, and a new understanding of what is essential. His decision to live on Walden Pond reflects three qualities that Quakers, St. Francis, and many others value highly: simplicity, integrity, and peace.

Simplify. Simplify. Simplify. It is deeply empowering to practice living with simplicity, integrity, and peace. Simplicity is knowing when we have enough and being willing to be stripped to what is essential. We are not seduced by consumerism. We avoid excess and waste, using our creative energies to reuse, recycle, resource, repurpose, and reinvent. Integrity implies wholeness, at-oneness. We are consistent in our trustworthiness and deliberate in our harmony of intention and action. Our thoughts, words, and actions are aligned and integrated with our core values. Goodness is on the go.

Living in peace with courage includes practicing gentleness, patience, and having a respectful approach to ourselves and others. If we would have peace, we practice forgiveness. We are open and attentive in the present moment, less driven by fears, frustrations, impatience, or a desire to control outcomes. We may not agree with someone's behavior but we can remember that we never know enough to judge, not even ourselves.

"Don't judge each day by the harvest you reap, but by the seeds you plant," wrote Robert Louis Stevenson. It may take many decades of development for us to appreciate the seeds that we plant. Our lives include the in-breath of gathering and cherishing and the out-breath of sharing and service. In his classic poem entitled *If*, British writer Rudyard Kipling encouraged us to maintain equanimity in the face of life's challenges. Kipling also reminded us to contribute in ways that our "heart and nerve and sinew serve ... long after they are gone." The strength of our gratitude and courage frees us to manifest benevolent, meaningful purpose in the world unattached to the fruits of our service.

Pause, Reflect, and Record

- There is a saying: "Life starts beyond our comfort zone." Is there an element of truth for you in the challenge that this phrase holds? Describe a time when you summoned the courage to go beyond your comfort zone.

- What experience of a breakthrough—where you freed yourself from an old belief, where the impossible seemed possible—have you had in your life?

- What factors contributed to your breakthrough? What did you let go of, accept, or understand more deeply that allowed this breakthrough to occur? What beneficial change or creative energy was released by this shift in perception?

- What qualities of character (courage, integrity, commitment to service, etc.) are you called to develop at this point in your life? How could they support your goodness to go?

10

Forgiveness—
The Power of Peace

Do you want peace? Forgiveness offers it.
Do you want happiness, a quiet mind,
a certainty of purpose, a sense of worth? ...
All this forgiveness offers you.

—Author unknown

An important element of our goodness to go is the co-creation of a healthy, peaceful future. At the same time, we're reminded by South African Nobel Peace laureate Archbishop Desmond Tutu that there is no future without forgiveness. *Let there be peace and let it begin with me.* For thousands of years, abuses of power around the world have fueled countless atrocities in which the power of peace seemed remote and almost inaccessible. Yet the inner peace that leads to forgiveness and the forgiveness that leads to inner peace is the way to let a new life begin.

Forgiveness and compassion invoke one another; both take the thread of our lives through the eye of the heart, allowing us to heal and serve once again. Although forgiveness does not require reconciliation or condone hurtful behavior, it is necessary for the possible reconciliation that leads to deep peace. A woman known as the Peace Pilgrim walked for years across America sharing her message of peace. "Do all the good you can each day," she said. "No one finds inner peace who avoids doing his or her share in the solving of collective problems." Our integral service contributes to the peace that is the greatest good.

"Peace cannot be kept by force," wrote Albert Einstein. "It can only be achieved by understanding." Forgiveness, letting go of our attachment to a grievance with another, is known as *kshama* in Sanskrit. The verb root *ksham* means "to be patient, to forgive." Both patience and forgiveness have a quality of spacious equanimity, a gentle letting go of attachments, and forbearance. Recall a time when you immersed yourself in the power of peace, fully present in the moment as it is without multi-tasking or compelled to rush on to what's next? How could you expand those moments of peace and patience in your life? How do you keep caom and carry on?

Social activism and other forms of integral service often require the capacity to endure and forgive as well as to accept the validity of diverse points of view. Root meanings of the word *forgiveness* include "to release the grip," "to let go," and "to lift up." When we're forgiven, there's a natural tendency to pass on our gratitude by forgiving someone else's hurtful, confused behavior. Developing a benevolent disposition and cultivating forgiveness require deep inner work. It's not easy to grant pardon without harboring resentment, but as we practice being the love that is capable of forgiveness, we access our nobility and willingness to reengage with life.

Psychologist Paul Coleman wrote, "Forgiveness is more than a moral imperative, more than a theological dictum. It is the only means, giving our humanness and imperfections, to overcome hate and condemnation and proceed with the business of growing and loving." Elise Boulding, a Quaker sociologist who died in 2010, was known for her holistic approach to peace research. She wrote, "There is no time left for anything but to make peace work a dimension of our every waking activity."

As within, so without. Exploring the path of peace requires strength, courage, and patience. Practicing peace is far from passive, and gentleness is the greatest strength. The renowned violinist Yehudi Menuhin said: "Peace may sound simple, one simple word. But it requires everything we have, every quality, every strength, every dream, every high ideal."

Opening our heart to forgiveness is one way to *be peace*. We can learn to forgive for good and allow our peace to ripple out to every person and situation we encounter. "Forgive them, for they know not what they do," implored Jesus as his body suffered agony. The mature compassion and radical generosity of this plea for the forgiveness of torturers has engendered respect and awe for millennia. As we resolve to mobilize our compassion in action, it's valuable to cultivate the patience and strength required to receive and work with whatever comes our way.

Understandably, many victims of brutal injustice have difficulty accessing the power of peace. They may find it nearly impossible to engage in the process of forgiveness and to allow life's loving energies to flow freely again. Every day we see the consequences of this knot in the heart. It requires patience to abide with things as they are and great effort to open in tolerance and forgiveness. A release or letting go of any attachment to pain is important, as is a willingness to hurt less and live with more peace. Hopefully, this commitment to releasing attachments and embracing the power of peace will inform peace talks around the world.

The philosopher Spinoza taught that reality is one substance with an infinite number of attributes. The capacity for peace is one such attribute. He wrote, "Peace is not the absence of war; it is a virtue; a state of mind; a disposition for benevolence, confidence, and justice." Deep peace is peace for everyone. Synonyms for the peace that is its own reward are harmony, accord, amity, calm, concord, serenity, stability, and tranquility. The practice of happiness is also the practice of peace, and forgiveness is foundational to both. Peace is not a point of arrival or a final destination. Peace is the way.

Empowered Forgiveness

Commitment to the practice of forgiveness is a gift that keeps on giving to ourselves and others. In 1994, Robert D. Enright, Ph.D., established the International Forgiveness Institute to learn more about the process of forgiveness. Dr. Enright, an educational psychologist at the University of Wisconsin–Madison, is known as the father of forgiveness research. His books include the seminal *Forgiveness Is a Choice* and his book for children, *Rising Above the Storm Clouds: What It's Like to Forgive.*

Forgiveness is about personal power and the power of love. We choose to no longer be a victim, blaming others or the times for a loss of power or self-efficacy. The process of forgiveness sets us free from imprisoning bitterness, anger, revenge, and resentment. It is not forgetting, excusing, condoning, or reconciling oneself to a wrong done. Releasing the grip of suffocating anger leads to increased hope and self-esteem and more peaceful behavior. There is a peace and understanding that comes from blaming less, taking life experiences less personally, and being less attached to, even reframing, our grievance stories.

The quality of our awareness is a key determinant in the quality of our lives. Where we focus our attention contributes to the creation and maintenance of both negative and positive emotional states. Deliberate attention, which occurs in our prefrontal cortex, affects neural pathways connected with older, primal emotion brain centers. If we focus on, rehearse, and ruminate on wrongs done, it fuels the hurt, resentment, and aggression. If we focus on practices that foster love, love is what we'll experience. When we love profoundly, we help others to live vibrantly. Goodness is naturally on the go.

Letting go of painful ruminations is good for the body as well as the soul. It reduces blood pressure, psychological distress, and depression and leads to increased optimism, physical vitality, and compassion. Resisting or refusing to practice forgiveness fixates the distressing situation in the mind and body. Our bloodstream is flooded with stress hormones such as cortisol, which compromises the immune system and increases the inflammation underlying most chronic diseases.

Acknowledging or confessing our unforgiveness, asking for help with anger, and actively participating in forgiveness training, such as writing about the painful experience for twenty minutes a day, support both our immune system and our inner state of peace. It's human to make mistakes. Remorse about a behavior is very different from shame that condemns us.

Practicing forgiveness for a hurtful behavior that we regret arises from our strength and goodness, not from blame or shame. It includes accepting responsibility for the behavior and its harmful consequences, as well as our commitment to refrain from similar behavior in the future. Our natural remorse then takes the form of remedial action undertaken with resolve to strengthen our skillful alignment with the values of our heart.

Both the acknowledgment of our unforgiveness and participation in the process of forgiveness take considerable compassion, resilience, and resolve. In the Quran (42:43), it is said that to be patient and forgive is surely an affair of great resolution. People describe a state of grace when they make the heroic choice to release pain into forgiveness. Rather than being stuck in a web of unforgiveness, energy is freed up to create a happier, more peaceful life. It takes generosity, discipline, and vitality to be light of heart.

The practice of peace and happiness is a revolutionary art. Knowing that our service may alter and even transform difficult circumstances contributes to our happiness. Allowing the light of happiness to illumine our lives often includes forgiveness of people or situations that have hurt us. "I will be of good will to all men," Mahatma Gandhi repeated each morning, despite repeated imprisonment and brutal treatment for his commitment to justice. Acceptance and the illumination of love transform shadow aspects of human psyches and behaviors.

Human beings have endless opportunities to choose forgiveness. In July of 2008, a misguided man opened fire in a Unitarian Universalist Church in Tennessee, slaughtering members of the congregation. In chapel services, the children had declared, "Ours is the church of the loving heart, open mind, and helping hands." The assailant's handwritten manifesto described his hatred for "liberals" who were vilified as unpatriotic, evil, and treasonous in books by media personalities he'd been reading.

The church chose not to meet hatred with hatred, and after the attack many local townspeople declared that the children of this church were their children. Neighbors of all faiths and convictions offered ongoing support. A sign saying everybody welcome hangs at the church's entrance. In a 2009 *Newsweek* interview, the church's minister, Chris Bruce, wrote that members of his congregation had "been healed by the feeling that there is a love greater than our theological differences, a compassion that is not limited by the boundaries of any creed. I firmly believe, now more than ever, that love is stronger than death. Love is more powerful than hate."

Let Peace Begin with Me

Forgiveness is a process that utilizes personal power to calmly care for our wounded feelings and lives. One technique involves breathing forgiveness in through the heart and out through the solar plexus. Another directs the *tonglen* breath of compassion to experiences that would benefit from the practice of forgiveness. A forgiveness tonglen is outlined at the end of this chapter. Forgiveness is the commitment to focus on the kindness and beauty in our lives and to release our attachment to blame, no matter how justifiable it may be. Radical forgiveness is a choice and ongoing practice.

Archbishop Oscar Romero, a twentieth-century champion of world democracy, served amid widespread and injustice and violence in El Salvador. The archbishop lived his commitment to forgiveness, to peace, and to speaking one's truth to power. He wrote, "Peace is the generous, tranquil contribution of all to the good of all." Outer peace begins as a benevolent state within our hearts and minds.

There is no future without the peace of forgiveness. Violent conflict, human trafficking and slavery, genocide, and apartheid have brutalized untold human beings, and we cannot change the past. Archbishop Desmond Tutu asserts, "There can be no peace without reconciliation, no reconciliation without forgiveness, and no forgiveness without giving up all hope for a better past." There is wisdom in the recognition and radical acceptance of what has been and what is present now. This acknowledgment allows our energy and wisdom to be utilized to create a more positive future. Releasing our futile insistence on changing the past allows space for reconciliation and a possible peace.

A forgiveness researcher, Fred Luskin, Ph.D., conducts studies at the Stanford Forgiveness Project and the Fetzer Institute's Campaign for Love and Forgiveness. His research shows that the beneficial choice and learnable skill of forgiveness can reduce anger and malice in individuals as well as increase the ability to manage emotion, grievance, and interpersonal hurt.

Our inner states as well as actions affect others. Native Americans of the Iroquois Confederacy created the Great Law of Peace based on the premise that the Giver of Life did not intend for people to abuse one another. Many indigenous peoples and others trust that all people with intact emotional pathways and reasoning ability desire peace and have the power to create it.

Inner work such as therapeutic interactions and self-inquiry is healing and frees up life energy that can be directed to serving our communities and our world. Dr. Martin Luther King, Jr., emphasized, "It is not enough to say we will not wage war. It is necessary to love peace and sacrifice for it." Both inner evolution as well as action aligned with our integrity is required. The peace of forgiveness is an inside job.

"Peace is the only battle worth waging," wrote Albert Camus. Peace is an inner state, a path to rigorously explore, and the battle that must be fought. Civil rights activist A. J. Muste cultivated the strength of both heart and backbone. He wrote, "We cannot have peace if we are only concerned with peace. War is not an accident. It is the logical outcome of a certain way of life. If we want to attack war, we have to attack that way of life." This "attack" is skillful and compassionate, not aggressive.

To be a peacemaker, we first have to live our own inner peace. In much the same way, for authentic transformation of the world to be sustained, there needs to be an ongoing effort of self-transformation on the part of those engaged. If you'd like empathy to be more evident in society, cultivate a daily practice of empathy. As you change yourself, you change the world. Be the change.

Utilizing the Power of an Awakened Heart

"Today, peace means the ascent from simple coexistence to cooperation and common creativity among counties and nations," wrote Mikhail Gorbachev, a former Soviet president. Will we commit to creative cooperation and collaboration or cling to the accumulation of power? The choice to go good or ill with power is an aspect of the utilization of our intelligence and free will. Cognitive, emotional, and creative intelligence are forms of power; people may or may not choose to *do good* with the power available to them.

There are many ways to use or abuse the various kinds of power available to us. Power can be a physical source of energy, such as hydroelectric, nuclear, geothermal, or solar power, or the ability to produce some sort of effect, including the power of a reaction. Another aspect of power involves forcefully exerting *control over* others. Many in positions of leadership and governance can be distinguished by their commitment to *powering with* their constituents as opposed to brandishing force as they *power over* others.

The efficacy of evolving cultures, whether social, economic, or philanthropic, is affected by their relationship with power. The ways that we orient ourselves around power are distinguishing points of reference. Do we value cooperation or competition more highly? Do we want to power over others or share power with them? A person's gender is relevant in social policy because equity is still an issue in many parts of the world. Women of the world hold up more than half the sky, do the majority of work on our planet, and yet have access to a fraction of the resources. Reconciliation need to be ongoing.

Although the Golden Rule's value of treating others with the respect and generosity with which you want to be treated is universally recognized, it is not consistently practiced. We often choose to ignore this moral currency of reciprocity and cynically retort that *those who have the gold make the rules.* Accumulation of money is often associated with accumulation of power. Many financially resourced people are dedicated to collaboration and community, and many are not.

Some players of financial "games" are adamant that they win at all costs, regardless of the harm done, succumbing to destructive behaviors associated with addiction to money. Moral behavior opposing a "greed is good" mentality is disregarded or disdained. The oil corporation Exxon-

Mobile regards itself as a separate sovereign entity and has directed funds to African dictators who cooperate with Exxon's oil extraction practices.

In realms of political power or in killing fields, weapons and brutal corruption often dominate and oppress. What is needed for deep democracy to flourish for all citizens longing for freedom? For there to be a healthy future for our children, it is imperative that we make peace within and between ourselves. How do we begin the to waken the heart of forgiveness and create new paradigms of sustainable health and peace?

Strong commitment to acting from an authentic alignment with our core values brings both peace and progress to our relationship to power. Our loving hearts, open minds, and helping hands sustain our integral service Progressive, egalitarian policies invite respectful discourse between countries that have maintained a frosty regard for decades. The beliefs of Islam, Judaism, Christianity, and other religions honor forgiveness and peacemaking. An Islamic prayer asks: "Shall I not inform you of a better act than fasting, alms, and prayers? Making peace between one another: enmity and malice tear up heavenly rewards by the roots."

King Abdullah is the elderly monarch of Saudi Arabia who took the throne in 2005. In a country without a democratically elected parliament, he appointed the first female assistant deputy minister, is modernizing schools, and investing in science and technology. Steps toward gender equity and reform are still regarded as progressive in many societies. These reforms renegotiate relationships to power, showing respect for women's abilities and their right to participate in governance.

At the same time, a desperate regression in citizens' relationship to power has occurred in many nations, including Pakistan. After its historic 2008 election, a democratically elected civilian government replaced a dictator. The secular party honored women's rights and supported schools for girls. Extremist Taliban terrorists retaliated, brutalizing young women, murdering officials, and bombing more than two hundred girls' schools. Eventually, a half million citizens fled their homes as the government fought to displace the terrorists.

Social commentators have referred to groups like the Taliban as religious exclusivists rather than fundamentalists. Exclusivists of any religion diminish the role of women, tend to believe that their divinity is "on high"—exclusive, distant, separate, and superior—and insist that only the controlling force of their ideology is true and righteous. Brutal terror, torture, and flagrant disregard for human rights, and even life itself, continue to be inflicted across the globe in the name of religious ideology. Understandably, it's very challenging to begin the process of understanding and forgiving perpetrators of egregious harm.

People committed to the power of peace often sense that a sacred energy lives in everything. They're inspired to explore the dual mystery—the transcendence and immanence—of this sacredness. The respected author of *From Aging to Saging*, Rabbi Zalman Schachter-Shalomi, has been a holder of the World Wisdom chair at Naropa University in Boulder, Colorado. Reb Zalman, as he is affectionately called, regularly engaged in interfaith dialogues that focused on peace and forgiveness. A section of his translation of a Jewish prayer of forgiveness says:

You, my Eternal Friend, witness now
that I forgive anyone who hurt
or upset me or who offended me—
with words, deeds, thoughts, or attitudes... .

Let me forgive others, let me forgive myself,
but also let me change in ways
that make it easy for me to avoid
paths of hurtfulness to others.

I seek peace, let me be peace.
I seek justice, let me be just.
I seek a world of kindness, let me be kind... .
Source of goodness and love in the universe,
Let me be alive to all
the goodness that surrounds me.

If we are to have a future, forgiveness is essential. Like compassion and loving kindness, forgiveness is an act of radical goodwill. Practice cultivating a commitment and capacity for recognizing your goodness as well as the goodness in each person you meet. Explore the path of peace. Inspire, support, and empower yourself and others to be alive to the goodness within and around them. This is the great service of goodness to go.

A Forgiveness Tonglen

- The practice of forgiveness enhances well-being as it releases constrictions of the heart. The goodness of courage, hope, trust, and gratitude can flow again. Consider setting aside time for sessions of forgiveness *tonglen*, during which you can practice the breath of compassion described near the end of Chapter 4.

- Start with a relatively minor irritation and move to a more painful experience. Forgive yourself for a mistake made, a lapse of kindness, or a hurt you may have caused. Then extend this practice to include a friend or family member with whom you're having a difficult time. Gradually, expand your heart to include all beings who have injured you in some way.

  1. Recall a situation that would benefit from forgiveness, for yourself and another.

  2. Breathe in any suffering, hardness, bitter negativity, or reactive defensiveness.

  3. In the light and spaciousness of your heart, allow heavy feelings of being wronged or unjustly treated to be transformed.

  4. Free of judgment, breathe out trust, forgiveness, healing, openness, and compassion.

Pause, Reflect, and Record

- Describe a personal experience of forgiveness.

- What does contracted or frozen resentment, anger, or outrage feel like? Are there broken places in your relationships with others that you can mend? From whom do you need to forgive or seek forgiveness?

- What grievance or injustice have you experienced that seems to stifle your offering of integral service? How might you acknowledge this painful experience in your life and even *accept what is*?

- *There is a heart that forgives everyone and everything.* The longing to forgive and be forgiven is an invocation of our compassion. What would your prayer or invocation of forgiveness include? Write a draft.

11

Integral Optimism—
Hope and Trust

Hope is a dimension of the soul ... an orientation of the spirit,
and orientation of the heart.
Hope is ... an ability to work for something because
it is good, not just because it stands a chance to succeed.
It is not the conviction that something will turn out well,
but the certainty that something makes sense
regardless of how it turns out.

—Vaclav Havel

With each sunrise, life begins anew. Hope recognizes and trusts that life offers countless opportunities to make a fresh start. The world needs our hope. Sometimes hope whispers; at other times it cheers us on. The promise of new life is entrusted to every pregnant woman. A toddler trusts that Mother Earth will rise up to receive his next step. Blessed with the opportunity to receive an education, disciplined students send forth college applications with hope. Every new promise or endeavor to which we commit, including integral service, has some element of trust at its core.

Trust, hope, and faith have an element of sacred mystery. In one of his Epistles, St. Paul says, "I have fought a Good Fight; I have kept the faith." It's been said that faith goes up the stairs that love built and looks out of the windows that hope opened. To fight the Good Fight with a joyful hope inspiriting the adventure, it's helpful to trust the goodness of our dreams. This trust has hope and faith at its heart—it is not the simplistic, superstitious habit of wishful thinking that was bemoaned by Eleanor Roosevelt.

Goodness to go is rich with trust and hope. Trust implies a steady resolve that springs from a mature relationship with one's thoughts and feelings. This maturity is not necessarily related to chronological age. Recall Anne Frank's trust and fortitude in the midst of persecution when she wrote that people are good at heart. Positive emotions and states of mind like trust, confidence, hope, and optimism can be learned. They strengthen our psychological immune system as well as the resilience to sustain our integral service. "Hope dies last," a Spanish phrase reminds us.

Many irrepressible optimists insist that they are the true realists. Vaclav Havel, poet, playwright, and former president of the Czech Republic, reminds us that the gift of hope is as big as life itself and includes the ability to work for something simply because it is good. As he led Czechoslovakia to freedom from Soviet rule, Havel recognized that hope is a dimension of basic human goodness that does not depend on external accomplishment. Our best intentions and efforts may fail or even achieve results contrary to what we've intended. We have a right to our actions but not to their fruits.

There are political and cultural regions in which it is especially challenging to sustain integral optimism. More that 80,000 citizens have died during the Syrian civil war and brutal regimes terrorize many nations around the globe. In Afghanistan, the vast majority live outside of urban areas and are controlled by the shadow government of fundamentalist Taliban extremists. Hundreds of terrorist attacks occur daily that are not mentioned in news reports, and tens of thousands of civilians, soldiers, and aid workers have died during the war in Afghanistan.

The NATO coalition's invasion of Afghanistan began on October 7, 2001 following the Al Qaeda organization's September 11th attacks in the United States. The war was intended to dismantle Al Qaeda and remove the Taliban regime that protected Al Qaeda, objectives which proved to be virtually impossible to accomplish fully. Millions of girls and women fear increasingly violent repression of their human rights by insurgencies of Taliban's dark forces when the United States completes its withdrawal from Afghanistan.

How do we keep hope alive as we learn to accept all that is? In times fraught with uncertainty and risk, it's helpful to orient the compass of our soul, spirit, and heart with the magnetic dimension of hope. Living with this spirit of the possible supports our goodness to go. "Every heart that has beat strong and cheerfully has left a hopeful impulse behind it in the world," wrote Robert Louis Stevenson.

Other facets of the virtue of hope are the desire for positive interconnectedness and the willingness to act for a future good. At least three motives fuel hope: we want to survive; we want positive relationships and experiences of belonging; and we are motivated to achieve mastery and to be accomplished people whose communications are effective and respected. Survival. Connection. Mastery.

The hope to survive motivates us to ensure that basic needs like food and shelter are met. Practical life skills and resiliency enhance our chances of survival, as do supportive communities. Our hope for emotional fulfillment, intimate relationships, and safety lead us to find ways to trust and be connected. Mastery-motivated hope supports our discipline as we learn new information and skills that in turn enrich our communities and uplift our world.

A Latin proverb simply says, "While I breathe, I hope." (*Durn spiro, spero.*) To keep hope alive and well, self-care is essential. Often, initial inspirations for projects fade or take on an obsessively driven quality that depletes our emotional and physical resources. As our integral service increases, our radical self-care needs to keep pace. We can't go faster than the speed of life for very long or serve "tirelessly" without being rejuvenated. Burnout has been described as a disorder of hope, not only as a condition of emotional exhaustion and physical depletion.

Physical and psychological depletion is especially familiar to those in helping professions, in the trenches of combat or philanthropic service, to caregivers of chronically ill family members, and to anyone who doesn't tend to personal needs on a regular basis. It's possible to become so depleted that we cannot truly "see" another, making integral service virtually impossible. Despondency, cynicism, or compassion fatigue may result, as well as a loss of functionality that looks like depression. Burnout makes us brittle. Yet the soul's hope springs eternal when we take care of our needs, clearing the path to the wellspring of our heart.

Integral optimism serves as a trustworthy antidote for many kinds of challenges and is accessible to people in all cultures and of all ages. Illness and disability present themselves at any age and provide endless opportunities to let go and carry on. Michael J. Fox is an actor, producer, father, author, and activist who meets the debilitating effects of Parkinson's disease with grace and optimism. In his book *Always Looking Up: The Adventures of an Incurable Optimist,* Fox writes about this hard-earned perspective that expands possibilities. Integral optimists summon the courage to see all experiences as additional opportunities for learning, maturing, and giving back to life.

We're encouraged to commit to a "hope-centered way of life" by the authors of *Hope in the Age of Anxiety*. Anthony Scioli and Henry Biller contend that a spiritual belief system serves as a foundational wellspring of hope across cultures. Having even one thread of hope has helped generations of people live through trials and tribulations, captivities and cruelties. Resilient individuals who've been traumatized find ways to resocialize and reinspire themselves as they overcome adversity. For decades, to help keep hope alive, Amnesty International volunteers have written to individuals imprisoned for challenging the status quo and voicing their hopes for a more equitable, prosperous future. Letters and petitions are also sent to people in positions of leadership with trust in their goodness and willingness to restore justice.

Roshi Joan Halifax is a Zen Buddhist teacher who wrote, "Trust and patience combined with openness and acceptance enable us to sustain ourselves. ... With equanimity and compassion as inseparable companions in our work we are also less judgmental and less attached to outcomes." Whether we're raising children or leading a nation, the temptation to try to control others or make them agree with our perspective is significant. It's an ongoing practice to flow with trust and be unattached to outcomes. Millennia ago, the Taoist philosopher Lao Tzu asked, "Can you lead people without imposing your will?" Can we do our best and let it go?

Around the world, calls are sounding for leadership that empowers participatory democracy as well as global health and prosperity. If we turn a blind eye, "business as usual" will prevail. A prominent German activist, Rudolf Bahro, has said, "When the forms of an old culture are dying, the new culture is created by a few people who are not afraid to be insecure." The transition time before a new paradigm has become fully functional can be very challenging for individuals as well as cultures. Vacillations of hope and fear are evident in many countries, including Egypt, Syria, Afghanistan, and Libya, as hopeful citizens envision and restructure new forms of governance.

Beyond Hope and Fear

Hope seems like a mixed bag or double-edged sword at times. Why, in addition to striving with diligence, did the Buddha exhort us to be free from hope and fear? Fear often constricts our life's energy, creativity,

116

and intelligence. But why let go of hope? Is there a problem with a desire for positive outcomes such as global health, peace, and justice? Is it that we're to be free of attachment and expectation?

Webster's dictionary defines hope as "desire accompanied by expectation of fulfillment." According to the wisdom of the ages, attachments and hopeful expectation create a perfect storm of inner torments such as fear of failure, frustration, anger, and despair. Latching onto hope for pleasure and gain includes the fear of their polarity, loss, and pain. Beyond the vacillations of hope and hear, it's possible to smile at and befriend fear in a state of equanimity. Rather than being an attachment, hope inspired by life's miraculous mystery is a form of emotional prosperity.

The renowned psychologist Erich Fromm recognized the inner wisdom from which hope springs: "Those whose hope is weak settle for comfort or for violence; those whose hope is strong see and cherish signs of new life and are ready every moment to help the birth of that which is ready to be born." Rather than lamenting and fearing changes in the status quo, choosing to birth a new paradigm brings hope. It takes courage and trust to commit to the freedom that is a root of happiness and supports our choice to live in accord with our deepest values.

True to our values, grounded in who we are, we cherish each moment free of attachments to hope and fear. Our lives flow with the energizing clarity of beneficial action that is beyond judgments of good or bad. We may even feel guided in some way. Some trust the "rightness" of an action intuitively; others recognize it as the most harmonizing, appropriate action for the particular time and circumstance.

Hopefully, twenty-first century leadership will focus on the common good and move beyond ideological constraints. Valuable time and energy is wasted by petty politics obsessed with partisan or personal advantage. Although visionary leaders, volunteers, and people of every persuasion formulate plans to address complex problems, it's helpful to see plans as experiments, not certainties. The Christian mystic Thomas Merton emphasized that it is relationships, not outcomes, that give meaning to our efforts. He wrote, "Concentrate not on the results, but on the value, the rightness, the truth of the work itself."

As hope is rekindled, we also acknowledge that suffering and fear have increased around the world with wild oscillations. T-shirts boast NO FEAR. Bumper stickers tell us to KEEP HOPE ALIVE. Since hope and fear often flip back and forth, we need to be careful not to get caught in this trap. If we allow it, fear can sour our life's energy and our hope for life-affirming change. Both fear and attachment to having our hopes met can lead to disappointment, hopelessness and anger. Anger follows our chain of desires, especially when our desires and expectations are thwarted and unfulfilled. In dreams there is truth. What happens to a dream deferred? Does it dry up or explode? Hope and trust in ourselves creates infinite possibilities. How do we prevent our hope from becoming a victim of disappointment or a casualty of fear?

Emotions are human, and although fear is not the enemy, our reaction to fear can choke our enthusiasm for life. Some experiences of hope emerge from the lens of joy and trust in life, while others are a reaction to fear. For example, if we fear that we'll be fired for speaking up about a workplace breach of ethics, we may "hope" to hang onto our job by keeping our mouth shut. Of course, compromising our integrity does not generate true hope.

What do you hope for? How do you generate and sustain hope? Sir Walter Scott wrote, "Hope is brightest when it dawns from fears." Hope is greater and far more luminous than fear. Nevertheless, in the face of overwhelming fear, it can be very difficult to smile, let it go, or summon our courage to act in spite of our fears. Attached to directing our lives even as our spirits sink in fear, ego-mind undermines our positive hope with discouraging thoughts and emotions. It often takes a long time to move beyond the hope-fear dichotomy.

One who has hope has everything states an Arabic proverb. Exercising the power of hope strengthens it. Fear-based attachments, whether to people or possession, bring suffering. Attachments, even hopeful ones, can become real problems and expectations often become heavy, sticky burdens. Attached to our desires (even the desire to alleviate suffering), we hope and wish they'd come true. Trust and gratitude become conditional: *"If* funding comes through for this service project, *then* I'll trust that I'm supposed to stay involved." However, we can have confidence that there are valuable lessons for us in *whatever* happens and trust that we're exactly here we're meant to be.

Living Hope

The song of hope may fade but it never stops completely. Living hope is acting with courage and the knowledge that there are things more important than fear. Our right actions or skillful means feel light and flowing with a choiceless choice that we *know* is meant to unfold. Instead of falling prey to cynicism or hopelessness, or rocking between hope and demoralizing fear, we experience a place beyond hope and fear.

This state of equanimity includes a trust that is beyond rational knowledge. St. Clement of Alexandria wrote, "If you do not hope, you will not find what is beyond your hopes." Somewhat paradoxically, enthusiastic participation in life is necessary in the process of becoming freedom from all attachments. Perhaps on the other side of hope lies the transcendence of hope, of being free from fear even in the presence of fear.

Hope has wings and includes the courage of innovative ideas and the holding of creative visions that have been called "crazy wisdom." Thinking outside the status quo is an element of crazy wisdom. Steve Jobs, the visionary Macintosh computer entrepreneur, revived his faltering company, Apple, in the 1990s with fresh design concept and a powerful advertising campaign. With one small Apple logo, the ad's slogan that was accompanied at times by the face of the Dalai Lama was simply "Think different." Designs multiplied, sales soared, and Apple is now one of the most innovative and prosperous corporations in the world.

Keeping hope alive includes this courage to think outside the box of conventional wisdom. "The ones who are crazy enough to think that they can change the world are the ones who do," Jobs said. Now is our time to track emergent forms of hope and embody these new forms. Some people experience new expressions of faith and hope as a postmodern spirituality. Intentional communities, barter and alternative currency systems, and cooperative housing initiatives are increasing in many countries. Hope broadens our range of goals, helps us to see challenges as normal, expected parts of life, and fuel the resiliency of our goodness to go.

When the spirit of service is invoked, a relationship with something bigger than ourselves, perhaps even beyond our comprehension, is involved. With faith, we are encouraged and energized to learn as we go, to figure out what works, and to let go of fear of failure. Patience, endurance, and forbearance grow. T. S. Eliot noted that in our patient, steady effort and waiting are held our hope, love, and faith.

"In all things it is better to hope than to despair," wrote Johann Wolfgang von Goethe. Modern playwrights in every genre explore the duality of hope and despair. Tony Kushner, author of the theatrical epic *Angels in America* and the screenplay for the acclaimed film *Lincoln*, writes: "Despair is cheap. Anyone can do that on their own. Hope is the thing you generate in yourself by recognizing that despair is a luxury. ... Most of us ... have an ethical obligation to look for hope and to find it."

Lisel Mueller, in her collection of poems entitled *Alive Together*, describes hope as the singular gift that invents the future. To achieve or become something in the future, we hold it in our creative imagination now. Winston Churchill reminded us that optimists see opportunity in difficulty and Abraham Lincoln wrote that the best thing about the future is that it only comes one day at a time.

The future that is waiting to be born is somehow present in hope. Yet some brands of hope have a quality of dependence on a desired future. That kind of dependent hope doesn't usually accept what is now. When we acknowledge and accept what is, we disengage from futile struggles that are fixated on making the world change. We wake up, dream a new dream of what could be, and clearly discern what are the wise and skillful steps that are ours to take.

An Australian proverb says that those who lose dreaming are lost. Hope in our dreams for the future is a creative, life-affirming stance. Our individual lives are transitory and it's futile to resist the flow of change. Trying to swim against the currents of change is exhausting and frustrating. Instead, we develop trust our ability to meet challenges and cultivate a hopefulness that is not attached to a particular outcome. Be patient as you nurture the flame of hope. Hold fast to the trust that love is greater than fear. Don't let the strength or size of your hope limit you. Within the invincible summer of hope, pursue your dreams.

Trust—A Living *Yes*

Trust in yourself; that is the beginning. Strengthening our heart's attributes, including trust, allows us to live with courage, discernment, and resilience. As we develop an unconditional affirmation to life as it is and deepen our confidence in our ability to take care of ourselves, we carry within us a flexible resourcefulness wherever we go. With the confidence and enthusiasm of trust's living yes, we act in ways that benefit the present and create a positive future. Trusting our integrity and ability to learn from mistakes builds dreams one step at a time.

Trust is one of the synonyms of hope and the power of this hope creates the future. Optimism. Patience. Confidence. Responsibility. All are facets of trust. From a root word that means faithful and true, trust is an assured reliance on the truth of something. Within a charitable or financial trust, a duty is imposed in faith as a condition of a relationship. Our daughter was committed into our trust by the adoption agency. A trustee of a philanthropic organization is committed to the sacred duty of caring for the resources of the organization for the current and future upliftment of the beneficiaries.

Trust is an element of the enduring patience that is an expression of inner strength and freedom. Such patience can be an antidote to anger. Trust is accepting and saying yes to yourself, acknowledging your mistakes as well as merits. This grounded confidence is the beginning of any act of service. Fortitude is then required so that we don't get bogged down in pettiness and disappointments or trapped in anger or horror. Our trust muscle strengthens with careful attention. We choose not to be a quitter and trust ourselves to follow through with our resolve. Commitment and trust enrich one another.

It's a subtle practice to be fully present in the timeless moment with unconditioned trust, doing our best and letting it go. If we avoid the present and rush into the future, we leapfrog over valuable lessons available only in this moment. Sometimes we give a wink to the present moment while looking ahead to the future, expectantly wishing for good things to come. Our awareness is one step ahead of our body, full steam ahead.

A more grounded kind of hope that is incorporated into our bodies and moves at the speed of life focuses on what we can be and do in the present. If pessimistic thoughts arise, we recognize the distraction and decide when and if we'll actively dispute them. Another approach is to unhook and re-direct our attention to the spaciousness between breaths or onto a positive image or thought. Persevere resolutely as you bring mindfulness to the quality of your thoughts. Thoughts become habits, influence your perception, and create your world. *As we think, so we become.*

There is much to be optimistic about in our interdependent world. Former president Bill Clinton brings global optimists together every year for the Clinton Global Initiative (CGI). Concrete, measureable, and reproducible progress is being made in at least five key areas: technology, health, green energy economies, gender equality, and sustainable planetary justice. Cell phone technology is lifting people out of poverty in many ways, including through access to online banking services. Global communication networks also democratize charitable giving, allowing people of modest means to contribute to service organizations by texting their favorite philanthropy.

Other key areas of innovation include increased effectiveness of health programs developed through the collaboration of governments, private sectors, and foundations. Safe, sustainable energy is essential, and investing in clean energy technology is good for business as well as the planet. Gender equity is increasing. Women's social, political, and economic gains are expanding opportunities for their families, communities, and countries. The fifth area is justice for our planet as well as its inhabitants. A growing interdependence revolution is spreading a new *communitarian* mindset to help a healthy, equitable future be born.

The infinite shines through the finite. Actions aligned with our deepest intent create a new world. Eleanor Roosevelt's irrepressible optimism was apparent in her trust that the future belongs to those who believe in the beauty of their dreams. As you listen to and heed your inner wisdom, align your posture, breath, mind, and intention with your attention. With clarity and steadfastness, imbibe and manifest your insights. Trust your courage, fortitude, and integral optimism. Connect with the goodness of your heart and contribute your gifts in service of a purpose that is enjoyable and meaningful for you.

Pause, Reflect, and Record

- Recall moments richly resourced with genuine hope and trust; recognize and acknowledge the attributes of your heart that you brought to bear on these situations.

- Set aside time to contemplate integral optimism and compassion-in-action using the A*B*C*D* Self-Inquiry Process. How could regular self-care deepen your trust in your ability to sustain integral service in your life? List three small, specific, scheduled steps that would revitalize your enthusiasm to serve life.

- Which one of the five ways that the world is getting better (technology, health, green energy economies, gender equity, or planetary justice) draws your integral optimism the most strongly? How might you contribute your goodness to go to this area?

- You've completed Section One of *Goodness To Go: Summon Your Heart*. Record questions, insights, inquiries, and action steps from this section with which you'd like to engage further.

Section Two

Empower the Mind

12

Don't My Ducks
Have to Be in a Row?

If you do not dare, you do not live.

—Spanish Proverb

In Section One of *Goodness To Go*, we explored approaches to summoning the heart of integral service. Let's keep the heart in mind as we turn our attention to the power of the mind to help us clarify our unique gifts, awaken to our life's purpose, and activate our service with integrity.

Inside our heads is an astonishing organ that consciousness utilizes for its human expression. Our brains have 100 billion neurons and each of these nerve cells makes 1,000 connections, or synapses, with other neurons. In many ways, the brain is a microcosm of the vast interconnectedness of planetary systems and the macrocosm of the universe through which we travel.

There are many different styles of thinking: some rely more on feelings and others value factual precision. Many people are committed to understanding root causes of problems, and others prefer to "fix" what's on the surface in front of them. Some people's thoughts move in spirals and others in linear sequences with varying degrees of internal logic.

One thinking style insists that pragmatism equates with personal matters being optimally managed before all else. This dualistic thinking is adamant that *all of one's ducks have to be in a row* before offering beneficial actions to anyone or anything else. It's useful to challenge our thoughts and consider hybrid approaches to redefining success. Goodness to go isn't about being the best in the world but creating what's best *for* the world.

Positive Impact is Our Objective

"First do well and then do good" is a stance promoted by old paradigms. Inherent within this linear thinking is the belief that there is a distinct separation or disconnect between *doing well* and *doing good*. However, with our values focused on positively impacting our communities and the world, we create work that is both meaningful and financially sustainable. With *impact investing*, economic profit and social good flow in a dynamic interplay.

The definition of *doing well* need not be confined to the accumulation of money. It can be understood in terms of the "return" on the community, not only on our invested capital, and as meeting basic needs through fulfilling work that doesn't negatively impact, and preferably enhances, others' opportunities. Engaged citizenship and integral service are important elements of every type of work, and it's possible for capitalism to be conscious and creative, not merely competitive. Street sweepers and presidents alike can uplift the environments in which we all live.

There is a global awakening and surging of the human spirit to empower individuals and communities and create social systems that are wise, just, and inclusive. As we forge the path ahead together, both mind and heart are required to address resistance or fear of change, to awaken our dreams, and to deepen our commitment to integrating service into our lives.

Being willing to journey on this path is opening ourselves to a daring adventure. There are people who dive into challenges, trusting that wings will grow on their way down. Some, depending on their relationship with risk, regard such leaps as confident expressions of spontaneity. Others dismiss them as naïve or foolish acts of impulsivity.

Our thoughts affect our goodness to go. When we feel overwhelmed with current duties, desires, and responsibilities, when we're running as fast as we can, we often feel like we're falling behind. Fearfully, we project our current state into the future and can't imagine how we could do more. Rather than considering radical self-care, working smarter not harder, or letting go of involvements that are no longer deeply meaningful, we tend to constrict. At these times, thoughts often mislead, mesmerize, or weaken us. We tell ourselves, "Maybe when I get a few more parts of my life sorted out, or when this recession ends, I could think about volunteering somewhere."

Rather than justify our inertia, we could challenge fear-based thoughts and find ways to revitalize our enthusiasm for integral service. Self-care is an ongoing requirement for the rejuvenation of life enthusiasm and meaning. Exhausted caregivers grow tired of being tired, not of giving. Comfort food, fantasies of escaping to a tropical island, or illusions of being in full control of our lives might seem to offer temporary relief. However, it's wise not to believe everything we think. A familiar rationalization is that our current situation may not be comfortable, but at least it's familiar. Attachment to our comfort zone leads to resistance when life asks us to move beyond it. We forget that if we do not dare, we do not live.

"Evolve ... or die," states Eckhart Tolle, the author of *The Power of Now*. Our commitment to break free of limiting belief systems and old patterns of resistance and deception challenges old fears. When we experience the great goodness within ourselves and share it with others, the ripple effect uplifts our world. Centuries ago, the illumined Indian poet Kabir wrote, "The river that flows in you also flows in me." Take a moment to recall a time when you welcomed your greatness and shared your gifts with others, even when all of your ducks weren't polished and lined up in a row.

Survival of the Wisest

Good planets are hard to find. The combination of synchronous elements that allow life to exist on earth is almost inconceivable. Our home planet is the right distance from a star, orbiting in the proverbial "Goldilocks" sweet spot, where temperatures are not too hot and not too cold for life to exist. We're at the right degree of tilt, with magnetic poles and sufficient mass to hold an atmosphere that can create water vapor. Organic molecules have enough protection from solar electromagnetic storms, and the huge planet Jupiter is in a stable orbit that shields earth from bombardment by large meteors.

Recently, it's been discovered that the laws of physics are not precisely the same throughout the universe. Our planet's neighborhood at the edge of the Milky Way galaxy is an astonishing and rare pro-life zone. Despite recent astronomical discoveries of planets orbiting other stars, earth may well be the only place in the entire universe where conditions are conducive to creating a biosphere that can support the wonders of life. She is rare, indeed, and we are not merely inhabitants but stewards who are responsible for evolving our awareness sufficiently to preserve a healthy home for children and all living things.

Goodness To Go

The seventeenth-century philosopher Sir Thomas Browne wrote, "Life is a pure flame, and we live by an invisible sun within us." To be alive is an inestimable gift and every moment of life is a miracle. Our home planet is staggering in the rich diversity of its beauty. Professor Thomas Berry, a cosmologist and cultural historian, writes, "To tell the story of anything, you have to tell the story of Everything." Cosmology, the scientific study of the creation of this universe, tells us that we all came from the same source.

The eminent physicist Stephen Hawking calls that point from which space and time are born "the singularity." Professor Hawking suggests that creation occurs as the "event horizon" on which all objects appear. Many billions of years ago, vast energy compressed as a single point exploded outward in an event called the Big Bang. Astonishingly, this explosion occurred with just the right amount of power and speed to allow the creation of galaxies and solar systems.

Much, much later, about four billion years ago, initial life forms began and a mere 150,000 years ago our ancestors in Africa used their marvelous minds to create tools, language, and the concept of time. We all emerged from that original human gene pool and share a profoundly inclusive kinship. We come from starlight that became single-cell organisms that evolved and adapted into the nearly incomprehensible diversity of life on earth. From our common source of life, we're all together on one small planet. "We are all wanderers on this earth," says a Gypsy proverb. "Our hearts are full of wonder and our souls are deep with dreams."

As Without So Within

We are cosmological beings, the universe in human form. Our body is composed of 100 trillion (a quadrillion) cells, 90 percent of which are nonhuman, such as yeast, fungi, and bacterial cells. There are 100 times more microbial than human genes within our metagenome. In 2002, Nobel laureate Joshua Lederberg coined the term superorganism to describe this ensemble of human and nonhuman cells that constitute our body.

Each human cell within our superorganism has 400 billion molecules conducting millions of processes between trillions of atoms. In each millisecond, six *septillion* events occur within each individual's body to preserve the balance and homeostasis required for life to continue. That is ten times the number of stars in the universe. Within each of us is the story of infinite miracles and wonder reaching back to the first cell with the very first gene holding the message and promise of life.

It's the nature of our body and Mother Earth to serve us in more ways than we'll ever know. Our inheritance is the rare and complex gift of life on this planet of infinite beauty and potentially sustainable abundance. It doesn't take long to circle the jewel of planet earth. With a few relatively short flights, we can circumnavigate the globe. She is small and precious, and feelings of wanting to care for her generous bounty naturally arise.

As within so without. Just as our body is composed of trillions of interconnected ecosystems, so is planet earth. Many have begun to call our living planet Gaia, after the ancient Greek goddess of the earth, Gaea. In *The Living Universe*, Duane Elgin asserts that when we perceive that we exist in a living universe, we shift from isolation and greed to gratitude. He writes, "We are ourselves participants in a cosmic garden of life that the universe has been patiently nurturing over billions of years. ... Feelings of subtle connection, curiosity, and gratitude are understandable. ... A living-universe perspective invites us to shift from indifference, fear, and cynicism to curiosity, love, and awe."

When we love, we naturally want to care for the beloved in tangible ways. One measurable aspect of caring for our living planet is reducing the amount of excess carbon dioxide that we emit into our atmosphere. If we love this planet, the carbon dioxide level for life as we know it needs to be 350 parts per million (ppm) or less. Three hundred and fifty parts per million is our planetary safety zone. It is estimated that two degrees Celsius is the maximum temperature increase that the globe can sustain without causing runaway climate change. If we want a healthy planet for our children, further investment in fossil fuels is socially reprehensible. If we burn available coal and gas reserves, human life will not be sustainable on earth.

Many people continue to deny, dispute, or ignore the fact of global warming even when presented with decades of photographic evidence, as presented in James Balog's award-winning documentary *Chasing Ice*. Climate "skeptics" contest that no one can know if the consequences of climate change will be disastrous or not. Some believe they won't be affected personally and can't be bothered with the plight of future generations. Balog, a scientist and photographer, had been a climate skeptic until his Extreme Ice Survey collected thousands of images of massive glaciers receding and deflating at unprecedented rates over the past few years. The evidence for climate change in Balog's powerful documentary is indisputable.

In 2009, at the University of Colorado's annual Conference on World Affairs, the grandfather of global warming, James Hansen, Ph.D., gave the keynote speech. This National Aeronautics and Space Administration scientist was the first to warn us about climate change back in the 1980s. "If humanity wishes to preserve a planet similar to that on which civilization developed and to which life on earth is adapted," Hansen explained, "paleo-climate evidence and ongoing climate change suggest that carbon dioxide will need to be reduced from its current 385 ppm to, at most, 350 ppm." If we want to preserve our planet, we no longer have time to waste.

After seeing *Chasing Ice*, my young daughter said with quiet conviction, "If we want to live, we need to learn to do things differently." Usually, to do things differently, we need to think differently. Planetary patriots, including activists John Muir and Julia Butterfly Hill; politicians who've supported environmental protection legislation; visual artists; parents; children; educators; and writers continue to serve earth and her inhabitants. In 2012, the renowned environmentalist Bill McKibben ignited a "Do the Math" divestment campaign to send shockwaves through the fossil fuel industry, the most profitable corporations "in the history of money."

The earth needs global citizens who care about corporate and institutional investments and can do the math. School campuses are important places to educate, organize, and translate new understanding and ideals into action. Tens of thousands of students at more than 150 colleges and universities are demanding that their schools' endowments divest of fossil fuel investments. Climate activists from all walks of life, including former oil executives, are committed to creating a healthy planet for future generations. We're intelligent, creative beings who are all stakeholders in the environmental health of our home. We live on one evolving earth with one evolving future.

Evolutionaries

Wise adaptation to change is the game now as it has and always will be. "Here in the impermanent and yet continuously flowing world, let us stand together for future generations," writes Vietnamese Zen master Thich Nhat Hanh. Let us stand together in celebration and evolution of compassionate wisdom, not merely survival of the physically fittest. As

Don't My Ducks Have to Be in a Row?

Charles Darwin noted, "It is not the strongest of the species that survive, nor the most intelligent, but the ones most responsive to change."

Human beings have many capacities, from appreciating the majestic mystery of a peacock's tail to resilient adaptability in harsh desert or polar environments. Intelligent wisdom doesn't merely bemoan problems and describe symptoms of failing systems. It identifies primary causes, acknowledges what they are, and creates mutually beneficial responses and solutions. As we collaborate to develop new paradigms and social systems, we are resourced with great strength, wisdom, and creativity.

The renowned cultural anthropologist Margaret Mead wrote: "Never doubt that a small group of thoughtful committed individuals can change the world. Indeed it's the only thing that ever has." Evolutionaries are those who acknowledge responsibility for their personal evolution as well as for creating our collective future. Who are evolutionaries whose goodness to go you particularly respect? In what ways are you an evolutionary?

One recent example of human adaptability is evident in Bangladesh, which is now less dependent on international aid after the introduction of microcredit loans and flood-resistant rice crops. Although its citizens are still too impoverished to have contributed much to global carbon emissions, they are victims of global warming, nevertheless. Bangladesh is at sea level, and every meter that the sea rises will create 35 million more climate refugees. Flooded rivers also prevent children from getting to school. Innovative adaptation and design by a Bangladeshi architect led to the creation of fleets of floating classrooms and climate shelters fueled by solar panels on their roofs.

Human adaptability is apparent in many inspiring examples of international cooperation. Satellite flood forecasts analyzed at Georgia Tech in the southern United States assist villagers in Bangladesh. Symbols representing flood predictions are sent to cell phones supplied to rural farmers. These local citizens then raise the appropriate number of flags to alert their communities, thereby saving resources and lives. There are many other examples of participatory development being created by evolutionaries who recognize essential elements of sustainable change. Useful evolution happens from the inside out, engages the voices and skills of all involved, meets genuine needs, and is mutually equitable.

A. J. Muste was an evolutionary peace activist who was also a wise, committed leader of the civil rights and labor movements. He wrote, "There is no way to peace, peace is the way." Although history is plagued by aggression, violence, and war, we're learning from our mistakes and can choose to act anywhere along the spectrum from competition to collaboration and cooperation. We have the capacity to be resilient and benevolent and the ability to choose the path of reconciliation rather than retaliation. Practical, holistic approaches to peacemaking and restorative justice are urgently needed throughout our global community.

One of many communities that is choosing the path of peace is the American Jewish World Service (AJWS). Despite centuries of strife and recurrent genocide of Jewish people, this international development organization continues to pursue global justice through grassroots change. Motivated by Judaism's imperative to work for social justice, AJWS is dedicated to alleviating poverty, hunger, and disease among the people of the developing world, regardless of race, religion, or nationality. Through volunteer service, grants, advocacy, and education, AJWS fosters civil society, sustainable development, and human rights for all people.

Peace is every step. The Quaker tradition also focuses on the common good of peace and social justice. In 1920, as England was struggling to build peace from the ashes of war, Quakers gathered in London. For centuries, the Quakers' vision of true peace included cultural and financial security with respect for human rights and dignity, not merely the absence of violence. At the beginning of the twentieth century, the Quaker peacemakers wrote, "The world today is in sore need. Does it not rest in part with us whether its pains are to be the agonizing of a dying civilization or the birth pangs of a new and fairer life in which justice shall dwell?"

Although it takes courage and stamina to protest an inequity that affects one personally, depths of benevolence and compassion are also required to change unjust social behaviors that affect others. Throughout history, prolonged, difficult campaigns seeking to end racism and slavery have been mounted. Decades of noble, evolutionary integral service by abolitionist movements made it possible in 1863 for President Abraham Lincoln to ratify legislation that ended slavery in the United States. It is our task to end involuntary servitude for every man, woman, and child around the globe. There are more than 27 million slaves today and sites like Slave Footprint and Slave Tracker are increasing awareness about this global atrocity.

Understandably, agents of protest and change usually work to end an injustice that harms them personally. The tremendous efforts of those who sought an end to the abomination of human slavery were some of the first to act on behalf of others. William Wilberforce devoted his life and political service to changing Britain's economic attachments to, and attitudes toward, slavery. One of his greatest supporters was the former captain of a slave ship who wrote *Amazing Grace* from the depths of his profound remorse. This hymn has been sung for centuries around the world in celebration of the evolution of human consciousness: "I was blind but now I see."

There were several movements in the United States that gradually contributed to cultural shifts in awareness about social justice. In the 1880s, the social gospel tradition was a force changing New York's social and political structures so that justice was a more legally sanctioned possibility for everyone in society. Catholic social values and ideals influenced liberal democratic thought and President Franklin Delano Roosevelt's advisors. Social justice principles and advocacy contributed to the development of the New Deal in the United States, which revitalized millions of lives devastated by the Great Depression in the 1930s. This is one example of how a society can shift from an I-*conomy* to a *We-conomy* through citizenship based on values of equity and sustainability.

Nearly a hundred years after the Quaker peacemakers articulated their message following the First World War, it is more relevant than ever. Now is the time to support the birth of a "new and fairer life in which justice shall dwell." If we wait until "one of these days" to serve life, it may be "none of these days." The beauty and astonishing variety of life on earth that has evolved over hundreds of millions of years is at risk of being destroyed forever by choices that we have made and are making right now. In 2011 alone, poachers slaughtered more than 25,000 elephants in order to sell their ivory tusks. If consumers refused to purchase ivory, elephants may be saved from extinction.

Every day, 85,000 acres of invaluable rainforests are slashed and burned. In a recent twelve-month period, more than six million acres of this irreplaceable habitat, home to nearly a third of the world's biodiversity, were clear-cut and destroyed. These complex, magnificent ecosystems cannot be restored, and more than half of the tropical rainforests on earth have already been lost forever. In addition to the destruction of natural beauty, habitats, and entire species of life, we're losing the potential discoveries of life-sustaining biologic pharmaceuticals. The climate change summit held in Copenhagen in December of 2009 had a veneer of political agreement on some issues, but we need more cohesive, committed action from our international community.

We are defined not only by what we create but also by what we refuse to destroy. The creative wisdom and love of each one of us is needed now, not only to survive as a species and a planet but also to thrive. We can choose to make peace and preserve the rare opportunity to live and love. A Shenandoah Native American saying states, "It is no longer good enough to cry peace, we must act peace, live peace, and live in peace." When we live our lives as prayers of peace, creating deep peace within and without, we will not merely decry war. We will make life sacred by our sacrifice of love.

Opportunity Calls

Mahatma Gandhi was a remarkable example of service-oriented leadership. He insisted that people not wait until they are free of selfish motives or have all of their ducks in a row before contributing to society. In 1926, Gandhi wrote in a letter to a friend: "If we all refuse to serve until we attain perfection, there will be no service. The fact is that perfection is attained through service." The Bhagavad Gita, an ancient Indian text studied by Gandhi, emphasizes service: "Keep performing good actions. Never wonder what kind of fruit you are going to attain and when." Dr. Martin Luther, Jr., applied many of Gandhi's principles of nonviolence and service-oriented leadership. He once said, "Life's most persistent and urgent question is: What are you doing for others?"

The expression of our goodness ripples through our interconnected world and has countless beneficial impacts in addition to inspiring people, touching our hearts, and offering mutual support. Accelerated change has brought humanity to a crossroads, and the next ten years may be the most important to creating quality of life for the next ten thousand years. Although currently there is enough for all, the resource strains created by more than seven billion people seeking a life of equity, justice, and sufficiency require tremendous collective shifts. Responsible, humane solutions to population control need to be implemented without delay.

We're facing urgent global issues and most people don't want to hide their heads in the sand. At this pivotal time in history, it's important to remember that all of us are crewmates on planet Earth and all hands are being called on deck. Regenesis and healthy evolution are required on many levels. We still have time to embrace great opportunities to collaborate in personal, societal, and global change. Wherever we're going, we're going there together. We're called to a new kind of shared leadership and stewardship in which the talents of each individual are essential for humanity and planet Earth to heal and thrive.

It's been said that because we live in physical bodies capable of independent movement, we have a right to act, but not to claim the fruits of our actions. This can seem somewhat paradoxical. Most actions, including integral service, have inner as well as outer fruits. However, attachment to the ambitious achievement of our external goals, even noble, altruistic ones, is usually problematic.

What is helpful is to do our best and let it go without expectations. The state of our mind and heart affects how we approach each moment. When the main character in the film *Like Water for Chocolate* prepared a meal for her guests with love, they thrived. When she was angry or sad, her offering made people suffer. Like every worthwhile endeavor, integral service requires compassionate self-inquiry and ongoing rejuvenation. It's essential to nurture the state of our mind, our heart, our compassion, and our health. Like protection of our external environment, inner conservation of vitality and goodwill is an act of peace.

There are many approaches to the nurturance of our empathy and understanding. Since we have to digest everything we take into ourselves, from fast food and violent films to gossip and pornography, discernment is essential. What we expose our heart, mind, body, and senses to can increase or deaden our empathy. Self-care enhances our compassion for self and others; self-inquiry and journaling, sufficient sleep, nourishing food, regular exercise, and time in nature are nurturing ways to revitalize.

We are the ones that we've been waiting for. If we're alive, we have a role to play. As we nurture our highest aspirations to share our unique gifts, our goodness to go is naturally activated. People everywhere are stepping into action. "Everybody can be great, because anybody can serve," declared Dr. King. This is the eleventh hour of the imperative to focus our creative intelligence and heart's wisdom on the development of a sustainable, just world. It is a time rich with crises, with both danger and opportunity.

Jean Houston, Ph.D., is a principal founder of the human potential movement whose global goodness to go has spanned more than half a century. In these times of unsettling darkness, Houston writes, we observe the shadows of human existence more deeply. With resilience, compassion, and deep conviction, we can create together the call for a higher vision for our world. Houston encourages, "In our time, it is for each of us ... to become the light so that our families grow stronger, our communities knit tighter, and anything that divides us from each other and our earth is transcended."

It's important to nourish and replenish our energy every day. An element of skillful energy management is learning ways to conserve and not leak our strength. In turn, our vitality is refreshed as we receive from our inner spring of inspiration and allow it to flow forth with benevolent intent and skillful means. If we rise to the occasion, the exciting challenge of completely redesigning the ways in which our cultures, sciences, and technologies interact with nature is ours. The decisions that we make in the next few years will affect more generations than ever before. We have the great good fortune to live at a time when our lives can be far more meaningful than merely lining up a few ducks in a row.

Pause, Reflect, and Record

- "If you're not part of the solution, you're part of the problem." To what extent do you agree with this statement?

- Are there ways that you're postponing your integral service until *your ducks are all in a row*? Describe. How could you free yourself from beliefs, illusions, or excuses that stifle the expression of your natural goodness and generosity?

- What are you doing for others at this point in your life? What do you feel called to do?

- To what extent do you feel responsible for creating the future?

- What are the values and responsibilities of global citizenship?

13

Our Heart-Mind Intelligence

Watch what you think.
Thoughts become words.
Words become actions.
Actions become character.
Character becomes destiny.

—Buddha

"As a man thinketh in his heart, so is he," one translation of Proverbs 23:7 says. The heart and mind are an integrated whole with a subtle, unified energy field. Some cultures don't differentiate heart and mind and recognize that both are used in decision-making processes. Many of us live in a digital information age, but we're infinitely more than binary beings. Although the brain is usually regarded as the center of consciousness, the mind is more than convoluted brain tissue and the wisdom of the heart is not confined to an organ of contracting muscle fibers.

The field of neurocardiology indicates that a neural center is located in the heart. The emerging field of energy cardiology explores how the heart's intelligence not only produces hormones and neurotransmitters that affect cognitive functioning, it contributes to immunity regulation, contains stored information in cellular memories, and communicates with other hearts. Have you ever experienced a sense of intuition, inner guidance, or knowing what another person is feeling, even at a distance?

A growing body of research suggests that the tone of our parasympathetic nervous system's vagus nerve represents an important mechanism underlying emotional, self-regulatory, and behavioral processes. One function of the vagus nerve is inhibitory control over our heart rate. Neuroscientists at the University of Arizona believe that cardiac vagal tone may be a biomarker for our ability to sustain attention and regulate our emotions. They found that decreased modulation of vagal tone was associated with increased social anxiety and defensiveness.

While the sympathetic nervous system floods us with fight-or-flight hormones when we perceive or even think about a threatening situation, the balancing rest-and-digest effects of our parasympathetic nervous system help to return us to a state of calm homeostasis. Trauma therapy, walking in nature, breath meditation, and other related practices enhance vagal tone and our ability to self-regulate our thoughts, emotions, and behaviors. What is your body's capacity to regain calm after you've been in a stressful situation?

Medical researchers estimate that at least half of the cells of the heart are neural cells like those that form our brain. There are direct neural connections between the heart and brain that may be the biological underpinning of mirror neurons and of our instinct to care for others, to tend and befriend. Neuroscientist Bruce Lipton believes that the human brain is establishing neuropathways that allow us to perceive in new ways. The neural blueprint of the human spirit is discussed in Joseph Chilton Pearce's pioneering book *The Biology of Transcendence*. It may be that we're preparing neurologically for a quantum leap in understanding our interconnected heart-mind intelligence.

Living Life's Goodness

Many spiritual traditions are aware of the unified intelligence of our heart-mind, recognizing that the heart contributes a sense of connectedness with a higher calling that the brain alone cannot provide. Several wisdom traditions believe that actions directed by the mind without the counsel of the heart are dangerous and frequently destructive. We're reminded to allow the mind to rest in the heart, to respect its wisdom, and to act with clarity and compassion.

For centuries, meditators have experienced that there is essentially one heart-mind, a universal function expressing its unity through each of us in all of our diversity. In ancient times, physicians and theologians saw the heart as the "thinking organ," the dwelling place of the soul. More recently, the success of heart transplants lends support to this notion. Many transplant recipients have reported inheriting attributes, cravings, and knowledge from their donor. In *The Heart's Code*, Paul Pearsall, M.D., makes a strong case for the heart as the seat of the mind as well as the altruistic soul.

Both the mind and the heart know the importance of calmness, strength, and flexibility, of letting go as well as receiving, and of moving at an optimal pace. In the normal rhythmical contractions of the heart, freshly oxygenated blood is pumped out to make space to receive the incoming, oxygen-depleted return of blood. To make room for new ideas and behaviors, our minds often need to let go of old patterns and beliefs, including cynicism and habitual criticism of the world. Meaningless distractions and vapid entertainment waste our time and energy. We have the power to engage in the real world in ways that enhance our cognitive, physical, psychological, and community well-being.

Our experience of life depends on the quality of our perception: the world is as we see it. Since nearly everything is impermanent, especially our fleeting thoughts, it's wise not to believe everything our minds think. The awakened one known as the Buddha also reminded us to *watch what we think*. "Train yourself in doing good that lasts and brings happiness," Buddha taught. "Cultivate generosity, the life of peace, and a mind of boundless love."

When we're awake in the present moment, we're able to witness the creations of our minds. Habitual, mistaken thoughts frequently become our reality, and it makes sense to use our discernment and choose uplifting thoughts. With peaceful thoughts, we see more goodness in the world than if the prescription of our glasses is clouded with anger. When we practice gratitude for life's wonders, opportunities, and lessons, goodness grows in and around us. Personal integrity, accurate perceptions, and beneficial actions are paramount. St. Augustine noted, "As we live good lives, the times are also good. As we are, such are the times."

When we offer our compassionate service with love, love is what we'll experience. If we fear that there's not enough to go around, then fear is what we'll get, and opportunities to mobilize our goodness are missed. When we free ourselves from fear and its manifestations as guilt, anger, insecurity, or seeming indifference, we're present to experience the moment and to access our full power. Alberto Villoldo, psychologist and author of *Power Up Your Brain*, believes that everyone is born to make a difference.

Good thoughts are good company; toxic thoughts contaminate and misguide us. Thankfully, both the "hardware" of the brain and the "software" of the mind can change; we're not as hardwired as we've been led to believe. Neuroplasticity is a real phenomenon and with patience and regular practice, we can perceive, literally see the world, differently. Although we know that waves merging back into the ocean aren't separate entities, the experience of recognizing that there really is no "other" is often a radical change of perception. The heart-mind intelligence of a twentieth-century sage from India, Meher Baba, experienced that we are *love and love* must love. He taught that spiritual union is nothing other than knowledge of oneself as the Only One. Love merges into Love.

Frontiers of Heart-Mind Leadership

Nearly 2,000 years ago, the Roman emperor and philosopher Marcus Aurelius implored, "Stop philosophizing about what a good man is and be one." The wise mentor known as Yoda in the Star Wars films said, "There is no *trying*, only doing." Mark Twain encouraged us to explore, dream, and discover our goodness and courage. He wrote: "Twenty years from now you will be more disappointed by the things you didn't do than by the ones you did do. So throw off the bowlines, sail away from the safe harbor. Catch the trade winds in your sails."

Rather than outer space, it seems that inner space—the heart-mind and its awakening consciousness—is the next frontier. In the first half of the twentieth century, visionary philosopher and geologist Pierre Teilhard de Chardin wrote extensively about the increasing complexity and sublety of human consciousness. He believed that the universe is a "living host" in which our consciousness made a leap from instinct to thought. In this evolution of consciousness, our minds became capable of reflection, of mirroring or coiling back on themselves. Teilhard de Chardin believed that we're "collaborators in creation of the Universe" and that a "thinking layer" of mind, or noosphere, stretches around the earth's biosphere.

What we think and do now will affect the future of life on earth. This is not the time to wait passively for someone else to assume the mantle or hoard the power of leadership. We're involved in great experiments in consciousness and in how effectively we'll get along with each other in creative collaboration. Sharing with others what we've learned about incorporating inner frontiers into our daily lives inspires and sustains us as we manifest our paths of integral service.

Playing out in the global arena is the clash between old territorial paradigms that are dying and new collaborative ones that need our help to take birth. The new world that is being born offers new ways to participate consciously in our evolution. Walt Whitman wrote, "You shall scatter / With a lavish hand / All that you have / Learned and / Achieved, / And those who love you / Shall rise to your example / And be inspired."

We're be the leaders we've been waiting for. The creative intelligence and collaboration of interconnected, conscious individuals generate more innovative ideas than solitary leaders isolated in hierarchies. In this time of great flux, three prominent developments are converging. The visionary psychologist and futurist Peter Russell describes these as:

- **accelerating crises**—environmental degradation, overpopulation, financial inequity, and terrorism;

- **increasing technological connectivity**—the World Wide Web is creating a global community;

- **growing spiritual awakening**—a collective awareness, being, or soul is emerging.

The reinvention of humanity is upon us. The healing of humankind and our planet needs to be evolutionary, not merely redemptive. An emerging concept about a conscious earth ecology is known as Gaia. This subtle and wise awareness has evolved over eons and has been described by eco-philosopher Peter Russell, environmentalist Paul Hawken, and many others. For millennia, every culture has had diverse communities sharing this common ground of Gaia awareness. Spiritual communities—whether they're called monasteries or ashrams, congregations or sanghas—serve as crucibles of inspiration, protection, and support of evolving consciousness.

In *Friends on the Path*, Thich Nhat Hanh spoke about the importance of spiritual community in this new millennium. He described the three refuges of the spiritual aspirant: the awakened teacher within us; the *dharma*, or wisdom teachings; and the *sangha*, or spiritual community. Hanh teaches that Buddha-nature is not only within one enlightened being from the past and that "the next Buddha will be a Sangha." Basic goodness lives within every person and community. We're advised not to assign the beacon of leadership to one person or group when it actually resides within each one of us.

The light of transformative awareness is growing as human beings free themselves from the tyranny of greed and suspicious small-mindedness. This is happening on the outside as well as the inside. Two million Iranian people rose up against brutal repression in 2009. During the Arab Spring of 2011, civilians in North Africa and the Middle East battled autocracies. By 2013, the death toll from the Syrian uprising exceeded 60,000 people, with many thousands more refugees seeking safe haven in neighboring countries.

Many traditions teach that we can heal our deepest psychological wounds and develop the ability to reconcile, hold, and live with mystery, paradoxes, and apparent opposites. As the effects of trauma transform, we're able to more freely access our deepest wisdoms and greatest gifts. We can develop the capacity to be as the great prophets, saints, and bodhisattvas. We are the ones we have been waiting for. As we expand our identity to include all of creation, we are truly the Awakened Ones.

Speaking Truth to Power

Thoughts become words, which seem so innocent on the pages of dictionaries. Yet, "how potent for good or evil they become in the hands of one who knows how to combine them," wrote nineteenth century novelist Nathaniel Hawthorne. Words become actions. Beneficial action arising from the strength of courageous hearts and resilient minds manifests our goodness to go. It takes gutsiness to speak our truth, as well as a flexible spine aligned with our core values. "Nothing that I can do will change the structure of the universe," wrote Albert Einstein. "But maybe, by raising my voice I can help the greatest of all causes—goodwill among men and peace on earth."

Dr. Martin Luther King, Jr. warned that our lives begin to end the day we become silent about things that matter. Understandably, many of us are conflict avoidant and wiggle out of taking a stand. We fear humiliation, confrontation, offending others, and loss of our livelihood if we're truth-tellers. At the same time, we have innate capacities for courage, goodness, and authentic, respectful communication.

The quality of the thoughts that we communicate to ourselves, referred to as self-talk, affect the way we feel and act. While continuously repeating sacred mantras to himself, Mahatma Gandhi spoke his truth of nonviolence to the formidable power of the British Empire. Throughout decades of intense challenge and frequent imprisonment, he sustained himself with the remembrance of goodness: "When I despair, I remember that all through history, the ways of truth and love have always won. There have been tyrants and murderers, and for a long time they can seem invincible, but in the end they always fall. Think of it—always."

We can be the kind of leaders who care for others, take a stand for what is important to us, and commit to making our voices heard. Whenever possible, servant leaders attend to their needs while serving others, and recognize that often the needs of others need to be met first. Parents the world over go without so that their children are fed. The duty of captains is to be the last to leave their ships. There's an old teaching story about the difference between heavenly and hellish states of mind. In both places, bowls of food line banquet tables with very long-handled spoons. In hell, people starved because the spoons were too long to feed themselves. In heaven, people reached across the table to feed their neighbor and in turn were fed. Serve and thou shall be served.

To articulate our truth to any facet of power, most of us don't need to be nicer. It's the backbone of mental fortitude that needs to be exercised and strengthened as we cultivate moral courage. To offer our integral service, we need a clear mind, a compassionate heart, and a strong, supple spine. Entrenched beliefs and opinions usually take time to change. To slowly erode old barriers and pursue the building of new, equitable structures in the face of adversities requires the staying power of resilience and persistence.

Summoning Our Voice of Courage

The integrated intelligence of our mind and heart has tremendous power. During the Vietnam War, a pivotal figure in American history acted with integrity once he understood that his conscience was calling him to speak truth to power. Daniel Ellsberg, Ph.D., was a former Marine and Vietnam War hawk who worked as a high-level Pentagon official. Gradually, he learned about the decades of deliberate distortion, especially surrounding war escalations, that a succession of U.S. presidents had presented to the world.

The Vietnam War, a war that the Vietnamese call "The American War," was not a "just war" in Dr. Ellsberg's estimation. He discovered top-secret reports detailing the lies of generations of presidents and Pentagon officials. Although Ellsberg initially attempted neutrality, a crisis of conscience and culpability swept over him as he listened to the conviction of fine young men who courageously chose jail instead of military time. Ellsberg wept for over an hour during this dark night of the soul. In a documentary film about his transformative integral service, Ellsberg described how the process of determining his response to this crisis of conscience cleaved his life in two.

What did he do once he knew? Through painful reflection, analysis, and discernment, Ellsberg emerged with a new paradigm of awareness and action. When he recognized that he was willing to go to jail to help end the war, Ellsberg's goodness to go was mobilized. Like many who have raised their voices for freedom and justice, Ellsberg trusted that if people understood the deception, hypocrisy, and horrors of war, they would do more to end it.

Henry Kissinger called this warrior of the human spirit the "most dangerous man in America," and the documentary film by that name (*The Most Dangerous Man in America: Daniel Ellsberg and the Pentagon Papers*) was nominated for a 2010 Academy Award. The *New Yorker* magazine wrote: "So many people risked their livelihoods to put the 7,000 page Pentagon Papers out there—we have not celebrated Daniel Ellsberg enough. Let's begin."

For three decades near the end of the twentieth century, a vicious military government in Guatemala tortured, murdered, and "disappeared" hundreds of thousands of civilians and created a million refugees by destroying 450 villages. Many impoverished family members of a girl named Rigoberta Menchu Tum were among the victims of these gross human rights abuses. Despite extreme danger, Menchu became the world's spokesperson for these Mayan people, and in 1992 she was awarded the Nobel Peace Prize for her nonviolent work on behalf of the rights of indigenous people worldwide. She was the youngest woman and first indigenous person to receive the prestigious prize.

Menchu's integral service and truth-telling contributed to the 1996 peace accords in Guatemala, ending thirty-six years of civil war and returning many rights to the Mayan people. Throughout the decade leading up to the end of the 5,000-year Mayan calendar on December 21, 2012, Menchu taught about the importance of not succumbing to fear and of environmental restitution to Mother Earth. The Mayans believe that the new age offers many opportunities for the reinvention of humanity.

"Every person must choose how much truth he can stand," wrote Irvin Yalom, the author of *When Nietzsche Wept*. We have the opportunity to strengthen our capacity to hold the multifaceted truths of our age. Like never before, we have access to accurate knowledge of issues affecting our world and are thereby empowered if we have the will to act on behalf of global health and equity. We need not wring our hands, dithering with impotence. With the mobilization of our heart-mind intelligence, new paradigms of peace and justice will be created.

Although education is vital in today's marketplace, university tuition is prohibitive for the majority of young people. All children with sufficient intellectual capacity need to be able to graduate with critical think-ing skills and have more affordable access to excellent university edu-cation. Access to quality education empowers citizens to summon their voices, contribute their gifts, and strengthen democratic communities.

What supports us as we summon our voice of courage? A study re-ported in 2006 in *Science* looked at societal factors that facilitate cou-rageous cooperation. The senior author, Bettina Rockenbach, observed that groups with few rules attract exploiters who quickly undermine cooperation. Successful societies, on the other hand, have socially em-powered people with shared standards who exercise their moral cour-age to enforce consequences, both formally and informally, for hurtful behaviors. Rights such as individuals' freedom of speech are tempered with conditions that protect the rights of others. Citizens may have the right to voice their opinion but not to libel others with impunity or shout "Fire!" in a crowded auditorium.

Successful societies are neither tyrannical nor complacent and have an organic tempering of justice and mercy. Human societies need both the structure of equitable standards of behavior and citizens willing to put their moral courage into action when the behavior of a person, cor-poration, or government is unjust or dangerous. Although citizens may have the right to own a handgun for personal protection in their homes, this does not extend to semiautomatic assault weapons with ammunition clips that can murder dozens of innocent people in minutes.

When citizens and governments uphold equitable codes of behavior, the importance of structural changes of dysfunctional or harmful systems and regulations is recognized. For example, oversight is needed to effec-tively regulate workers in financial sectors. Foxes are poor guardians of hen houses. Despite the protests of some bankers and CEOs, many finan-cial workers are still not able to resist the temptation to acquire fortunes at the expense of others. The purpose of laws is to protect and support people's goodness and resources as well as to provide consequences for ethically wrong behavior.

In addition to equitable standards of behavior, another structural el-ement of society that calls forth our courage and intelligence is the dis-tribution of power. Is power confined to a few or is it widely dispersed? Those who live in societies with a narrow dispersion of power, and con-sequently limited social power, tend to feel little accountability or in-spiration to innovate. Although one-party systems in many totalitarian regimes are obvious examples, democracies are also hurt when power is concentrated and middle classes dwindle. When big money buys politicians' votes aligned with the donors' personal agendas or corporate interests, democracy is damaged.

A 2010 U.S. Supreme Court ruling known as *Citizens United* removed restrictions on political donations from corporations and unions. In response, Justice John Paul Stevens and millions of others have protested that *corporations are not people and money is not speech.* Corporate money is not equivalent to a citizen who has the right to a single vote. "A democracy cannot function effectively when its constituent members believe laws are being bought and sold," Stevens wrote.

When the power of money is concentrated in the hands of a few, laws like *Citizens United* reinforce the concentration of political power. Injustice is far less likely to run rampant when power is distributed equally because people are more likely to act responsibly to uphold shared values of honesty and fairness.

The intelligence of our minds and hearts understands that power must be dispersed through all economic sectors if citizens are to feel responsible, accountable, and engaged, allowing their empowered voices and actions to counter ego's greed. As we co-create a positive future, we'll advocate for equity and fortify the true grit of our perseverance and resilience. We'll also raise our voices in dissent about unlimited political donations from anonymous sources and bring all forms of corruption to the light of day.

When we recognize the importance to a democracy of empowered individuals, regardless of their age, race, or economic status, we'll reward our children for speaking out against injustice. When someone is being bullied, our children do not have to simply watch. There are no innocent bystanders. We'll challenge tendencies to go along with what we should not and choose not to put up with injustice, disrespect, disregard, and dishonesty. We'll recognize and declare when enough is enough.

In the wider culture, we'll publicly protect, reward, and honor the so-called whistle-blowers, the incredibly courageous truth-tellers among us. Malalai Joya is an Afghani woman who stood amidst government officials in 2003, denouncing many as vicious warlords who should be on trial for crimes against humanity. Willing to risk her life, she survived at least five assassination attempts.

In 2003, an assistant U.S. attorney, Melanie Sloan, left her position to run a new government watchdog group in Washington, Citizens for Responsibility and Ethics. As a student in a Quaker high school, Sloan took their values of social justice to heart and has continued to honor them in tangible ways. Although the work of speaking truth to power can be very wearing, Sloan and countless others choose not to succumb to cynicism or fear. These heroic social artists remind us that true power comes not from us but through us.

Even Hollywood celebrates truth-tellers in films like *Erin Brokovich and Norma Rae*. A Hallmark movie honored the profound heroism of Irena Sendler, who was nominated for the Nobel Peace Prize in 2007 just before her death. Sendler was a young social worker in Warsaw during World War II who saved 2,500 Jewish children from death camps. The backbone of her fierce goodness and moral courage inspired others to protect innocent children in the face of extreme danger.

Being free of fear does not mean being without fear. It means that something is more important than fear. Cultivate gutsiness. With the intelligence of your heart and mind, summon forth the power of your inner courage to create a world where all beings can thrive.

Pause, Reflect, and Record

• The Academy Award–winning screenwriter Thomas Schulman wrote, "No matter what anybody tells you, words and ideas can change the world." Describe a word, a book, an idea, an image, or a story that has changed your life.

• What do you know now about your integral service? What do you need to cultivate to start being what you know?

• With compassion and without judgment, describe any disempowering resentments, thoughts, or beliefs that have become habitual for you.

• If you haven't clarified a way to get your goodness on the go, don't wait any longer. What is one small, simple, scheduled step that you could take this week?

14

Mindfulness—Being One
with Each Moment

Realize deeply that the present moment
is all you ever have.... The Now is the only point
that can take you beyond the limited confines of the mind.

—Eckhart Tolle

The power to mobilize our goodness to go is in the present moment. If our thoughts are fixated on the past or the future, our attention is not available to engage fully with what we're doing now. The practice of mindfulness is an enduring discipline that leads to inner freedom. Mindful moments create a mindful life as we put present decisions into a long-term context. Being mindful diminishes regret about a life not lived meaningfully. Dr. Martin Luther King, Jr. reminded us, "The time is always right to do what is right." Genuine self-effort and the abundant gifts of grace are available in this moment.

"Now is the time, and we are the ones we have been waiting for," the Hopi elders remind us. Our awareness of the underlying unity of creation is expanded by mindfulness. Living mindfully, at one with our deepest values, strengthens our personal integrity and health as well as that of our home planet. Our integral service benefits from having a clear mind with the strength to watch our thoughts, choose our words, and speak with good purpose. With steady resolve and practice, we can purify our mind, consciously think what we choose, and act with benevolent intent.

An unencumbered mind lives in the power of now. However, we often delude ourselves into waiting for some mythical perfect moment to respond to a calling or to allow ourselves the time to listen for one. There is an aspect of the human psyche that many refer to as the ego or inner gremlin. This trickster has an insatiable appetite for control and to keep us under its command. It may crush us with belittling criticism or whip us to do and get *more*.

Far too often we're seduced by and believe the distortions generated by ego. One falsehood is that we don't have enough. How sensible and convincing ego sounds when it tells us that once we have enough, we can act upon our deep life forces, yearnings, and callings: *Good things come to those who wait. Someday your ship will come in and then you'll have enough to start on those dreams.* This broken record spins in the illusory groove of current lack, promising milk and honey in future abundance.

Fantasies of having enough of the right combination of time, money, emotional intelligence, energy, education, experience, psychological and spiritual maturity, good karma, and auspicious astrological omens mesmerize us. As evolutionary thinker Jean Houston, Ph.D., founder of the International Institute for Social Artistry and global trainer of leaders for the twenty-first century, says, "Now is the time and we are the people."

When we're aware that waiting games waste the time of our lives, we begin to see that meaning and power are found in the present moment. The quality of mindfulness, of caring attention, allows us to truly connect with the moment, the people around us, and our environment so that we don't space out or rush by, busy and distracted.

In 2007, *The Washington Post* participated in a social experiment about urban Americans' perceptions, tastes, and priorities. The questions raised were: In a commonplace environment at an "inappropriate" hour, do we perceive beauty? Do we stop to appreciate it? Do we recognize talent in an unexpected context?

At rush hour in a metro subway station, few commuters at noticed one of the world's finest musicians, Joshua Bell, playing intricate Bach compositions on a violin worth $3.5 million. When my young daughter heard this story, she responded, "We're missing so much." With the fragmentation that is so common in our time-pressured societies, how are we to focus our attention in the present moment and truly appreciate the beauty and goodness around and within us?

Wisdom traditions in every culture have emphasized the importance of being present. When we practice mindfulness, we not only hear the sounds around us but also become aware of our conscious power to listen deeply. We touch into a source that empowers our ability to choose how we want to live our lives, moment by moment.

Mindfulness—Being One with Each Moment

Be Here Now

Be here now. This clarion call to be mindfully present has sounded through the ages. When we forget, we become mindless—tangled in worries about the future, regrets about the past, and perceptions of apparent differences. Wisdom teachings encourage us to wake up. They describe ways to stay present and attentive to the relationship of union between apparently distinct subjects and objects.

Tibet is the homeland of many globally respected Buddhist teachers known as *rinpoches*. With elegant graciousness, Kyabje Dilgo Khyentse Rinpoche served as an example and translator of ancient wisdoms for modern times. He wrote, "Do not encumber your mind with useless thoughts. What good is it to brood over the past and fret about the future? Dwell in the simplicity of the present moment." Unencumbered minds are free to envision their integral service and to create new paradigms based on equity, innovation, and nonviolence.

The power of mindful awareness is like a mirror in that it clearly reflects what is happening without judgment, interference, or commentary. We make friends with the now and include all that it offers, difficult as well as delightful. If our mind wanders, we use techniques that train it to return to the present moment. For example, we may notice bodily sensations or place our attention on each element of a full cycle of breath.

With concentrated attention, we learn to work skillfully with thoughts and emotions. This is useful as we consider how to include integral service in our daily lives and encounter habitual fears that frequently arise when changes and new behaviors are considered. When we pause consciously, we have the power to choose our response rather than mindlessly react from anger or fear.

With mindfulness, we also strengthen our perseverance and discipline to offer integral service on a regular basis. Laissez-faire approaches to life often entrench habits of being distracted, asleep, aloof, and less than fully engaged. Reasonably good physical and mental health supports the development of any positive habit, whereas poverty, hunger, disease, and abuse understandably make it more difficult to practice mindfulness. The state of our internal and external environments also affects this practice. In digital age cultures, both the increasing speed of life and information overload can stress human adaptability to the point of distress.

Goodness To Go

It's often tempting to tweet our way through the day rather than develop the discipline of sustained attention. However, if our attention span is brief or shallow, it's difficult to think clearly, imbibe complex or subtle teachings, or contemplate ideas deeply. The term *pancake people* has been coined to describe this broad shallowness of information and insight. Aldous Huxley's *Brave New World* dystopia comes to mind. The legalization of marijuana in some areas has made it more convenient for people to disengage from life stresses. Distraction and mediocrity numb us to opportunities to strengthen our mind and take responsibility for manifesting our goodness.

It's easy to practice ignorance, attached to our entertainments or oblivious to what's happening in our communities and around the globe. Nevertheless, the quality of our choices has far-reaching consequences. A Native American proverb reminds us that we will be known forever by the tracks we leave. Many traditions teach that every thought, word, and action continues to vibrate in eternity. Our responsibility is great, and the beauty and benefit of those reverberations are up to us. Since all of life is interconnected, being mindful about our thoughts and actions increases the likelihood that their ongoing effects will be uplifting to ourselves and others.

"Yesterday is history, tomorrow is a mystery, this moment is a present," we've been told. Unconditional presence includes both focused attention and spacious awareness. Research reveals that "efficient" multitasking is an illusion and that the quality of all tasks that require focused attention decreases when we try to do more than one thing at a time. Years ago, Mahatma Gandhi reminded us that there is more to life than going faster.

Most of us have experienced moments when our relationship with time feels frenzied or frustrating. We're almost anywhere but present and in our power. In these moments, it's helpful to slow down, breathe, notice our state, remember our goodness, and let go so that the new life of a new moment can be experienced. Granted, some moments are easier to cherish than others. However, the valleys of our lives hold as much richness as the sunny grandeur of the peaks.

Although it is wise to accept and honor each moment as we give ourselves completely to whatever we've chosen to do, we're often taskmasters at avoiding the present moment. Some people drive while talking on a cell phone with the radio on. Others add text messaging or reading as they negotiate traffic. Of course, tragic injuries and deaths have resulted when the quality of our attention is diluted and distracted.

Sometimes, dreams of escape may simply be more fun than being stuck in traffic on a hot polluted day. Bumper stickers bemoaning "I'd rather be golfing" (or sailing or anywhere else) abound, while others counter with "I'd rather be here now." What are some ways that you avoid, space out, or slip away from the power of the present?

To alter uncomfortable states of mind, many people use alcohol and other recreational or prescription drugs for "attitude adjustments." Repercussions of the drug trade agitate our interconnected world; heroin sales fund Taliban terrorists, and thousands of people continue to be murdered throughout Central America by organized crime and drug cartels. Many users of recreational drugs in more affluent countries are beginning to consider their role in this carnage.

The reward centers in our brains can be hooked in many ways other than by recreational, dietary, and medicinal substances. The minds of millions of people, especially children in strongly digital cultures, are addicted to technological distractions. In addition to spectator sports around the world, there are now large gatherings of people watching others play virtual reality video games. Adolescents, who need sufficient sleep to cope with complex developmental challenges, frequently text friends or play video games late into the night; often, homework is left by the wayside. Many young people are receiving therapy to reduce cravings for technological stimulation and recover socialization skills. Although entertainment and escape may be understandable desires, they also devour time and energy available for developing our gifts and talents.

Being Mindful with Emotions

When fear or any other emotion arises, pause and rest your attention on the flow of your breath. Consider taking an active interest in discovering the nature of the emotion. What is the quality of the energy that has arisen in the form of the emotion? Remind yourself, "Fear (or sadness or anger, etc.) is like that," and return your attention to your breath. After a sustained period of redirecting your attention, what is your experience?

Goodness To Go

Foundations of Mindfulness

According to Buddhism, there are four foundations of mindfulness: body; feelings or the "felt sense" of experiences; mind; and wisdom teachings.

- **Body:** Focusing attention on the body and breath keeps us grounded in the present moment.

- **Feelings:** Being mindful of the impermanence of feelings and sensations of experience can free us from reactive conditioning. Perceived sensations and feelings are primal, preceding the cognitive reaction of emotions that they may spawn. By opening ourselves directly to felt experience, we can become free of resistance created by past conditioning. With steady practice, we can learn to experience pure happiness without attachment, as well as pure pain free of aversion.

- **Mind:** With the subtle awareness of conscious intellect, we are mindful of our mind. We notice its attachments and habitual thoughts, including dualistic judgments. Both judgment and attachment are limiting habits. We practice letting go of identification with a religion, country, gender, or particular professional or economic class that blinds us to the humanity of those we regard as belonging to a different group. We choose where to place our attention.

- **Wisdom:** We know our inter-being. Perennial wisdoms such as compassion, nonattachment, and impermanence are based on the recognition that everything on the physical level changes. Sometimes waking up and being mindful includes inquiry and letting go. Blind obedience to tradition is not an element of conscious living. Be aware of awareness.

To be fully alive, it's essential to engage skillfully in whatever we choose to do at any given moment. There are many effective practices that move us beyond impulsive reactivity, fearful avoidance, or mindlessly spacing out. At times, the practice of mindfulness seems paradoxical. As we learn to focus our attention, our mind also develops the capacity to be more spacious, clear, empty, and free of thoughts. With fewer unfocused thoughts and random ruminations, we have access to more mind. Gradually, our mindfulness grows more subtle, vast, and steady.

154

Mindfulness—Being One with Each Moment

While writing this book, I woke from a vivid dream with a taste of the vast freedom of consciousness. At that time, two close friends were undergoing difficult cancer treatments and I'd also been concerned about a patient who'd been recently diagnosed with breast cancer. In the dream, I was in a medical facility and was informed I had a carcinoma of the pancreas. I knew that the prognosis for this kind of cancer was grim. In the dream, I strongly identified with my role as a mother who loves life profoundly. In primal anguish, the marrow of my bones and the heart of every cell screamed in silent agony, resisting the prospect of an early death after an agonizing battle with cancer.

Then my state shifted dramatically from this painful contraction of anguished fear. Instead of focusing on the future, my awareness expanded in the timeless present. I was boundless, living the peace and joy that surpasses understanding. It was not that I ignored, denied, or forgot that I had cancer cells in my physical body but rather that including this awareness did not affect my steadfast joy and gratitude. In the limitless sphere of consciousness, my acknowledgment of cancer was somehow a minute detail in the midst of vast glory. I woke in wonder, marveling at the gift of this revelation.

There are many practices from every culture around the world that serve to open our minds and hearts, and mindfulness is an especially effective way to inquire into the workings of our minds. In essence, mindfulness is becoming one with the dynamic stillness of our consciousness as well as with every action in this present moment. Prayer and meditation support our ability to access and abide in that nourishing silence. Steadfast mindfulness ultimately means being free of identification with our body, mind, ego, and emotions, liberated in awareness that our true identity is with Consciousness.

Thousands of years ago, an Indian sage named Patanjali taught that we could change depleting mental habits by replacing negative thoughts with true, positive thoughts. This practice is more involved than repetition of new age affirmations. Experiment with heart-mind practices that are meaningful for you, including prayer, visualizations, and mantra repetition. Practice regularly. In every situation, we can choose to constrict our experience of our heart-mind or to expand the clarity and compassion of our perceptions.

As a scholar, teacher, and peace activist, Thich Nhat Hanh's profound dedication to peace and his compassionate understanding of the human condition make him one of the world's most admired spiritual leaders.

Hanh teaches about the practices of mindfulness and peaceful living. "Most of us believe that there are a few more conditions that need to be met before we can be happy. ... If we keep running away into the future, we cannot be ... in the present moment where there is ... transformation," he writes. To care for his own soul so that pain and anger don't harden his heart, Thich Nhat Hanh cherishes the present moment.

Welcoming Each Moment

Things don't always go the way we want them to. Yet as we engage with life and offer our integral service, it's possible to continuously let go and welcome what each moment brings. Jalaluddin Rumi was a poet in ancient Persia who wrote about living in this spirit of welcoming whatever comes. In his poem "The Guest House," he encourages us to welcome all visitors—a joy, a crowd of sorrows, the dark thought—and "be grateful for whoever comes, because each has been sent as a guide from beyond."

It's often difficult to welcome whatever comes and be aware of the thoughts, including beliefs, opinions, and ideas, to which we have attachment or aversion. As I learned more about the trafficking of children, for example, my habitual reaction was to cling to judgment about men who purchase sex with young girls. It was a challenging process to examine my aversion and to consider the social factors that contributed to an innocent boy's development into a man who pimped and raped girls. It is compassion, not rage, that I want to fuel my ongoing commitment to abolishing all forms of slavery.

Although reminders abound that profound love, joy, and wisdom are fully available in each moment, most of us experience that the shadowed, unclaimed, even rejected aspects of our individual selves cloud the light of wisdom. Our shadow contains potentially beneficial power. We have been gifted with the capacity and skill to bring the benevolent light of consciousness to the dark places within and without.

In many ways, this integration of all aspects of ourselves is not about diluting or mixing the dark and light into shades of gray in a weakened integrity or compromise. Rather, minds strong with love can hold creative tension and paradox: at the heart of each member of a pair of opposites is the other. The two are one whole. We've sought to represent this dynamism for millennia and the ying-yang symbol is one familiar representation of the integrated dynamism of masculine and feminine principles.

When we accept whatever comes in each moment and give ourselves to working with it as skillfully as we can, we experience the greatness of our own heart-mind. Being fully present allows us to be generous with our time, even if only a moment is available. Offering our full attention and presence to each person with whom we interact is respectful integral service. The gift of listening honors the one listening as well as the one speaking in the timeless present moment.

Breaking Free of Dualism

Mind caught in dualistic thinking is forever trying to tear wholeness apart. The pioneering psychiatrist Carl Jung used the term *the devil* to describe this tendency of ego-mind. He wrote, "The devil is a dualist. He's forever trying to make two out of one." Dualism sees disconnection, and this separation creates fear. When dualistic mind projects a "self" and "other," a cycle of deepening fear and reactive dualism often becomes entrenched.

Attachment to dualism can be dehumanizing, which is seen in prejudicial judgments and behaviors of all sorts. Dehumanizing prejudices have been prevalent throughout history in every social class, from underprivileged to aristocratic and ruling classes. We've seen the road to hell and suffering that results from not tending to our shadow selves. Slavery and genocide are grotesque expressions of dualism.

The dangers of dualistic thinking have profound consequences. We have only to recall that Nazi officers played with their children during midday meals after killing Jewish children with impunity. The dualistic thinking of terrorists and psychopaths denies the enemy or "infidel" basic human regard or respect. Perhaps it is ego's rigid, arrogant exclusion of the "other" that is the true infidel. The "holy war" with ego is a battle to be waged within us; what is truly holy is our interconnected oneness.

The new paradigm of goodness to go emerges from our recognition of our interconnected unity. As we act with the clearest intention for benevolence of which we're capable in any given moment, we cultivate discernment. Discernment is more subtle than insistence on distinctions. We're vigilant about dualistic tendencies to judge, criticize, or condemn ourselves or others, which can lead to comparison and feelings of fear, anger, hatred, or superiority. As good and bad swirl around us, we have the ability to align with the strength, stillness, and compassion resonating in our center.

Goodness To Go

Of course, when we're ill or sleep-deprived, it's easy to forget that frustration and fatigue are temporary states. Remembering the strength available in the present moment frees us from habitual loops of obsessing about the past or fretting about the future. Ego-generated thoughts may hook our attention with fear about including service in our lives, fueling anxiety that we'll burn out or become overwhelmed. The inner dualist tries to convince us, "I need to take care of number one. I can only take care of me and mine or them but not both." This poverty mentality is far less resourced than a simple lack of money.

Many wise beings have recognized that our power is accessible only when we're awake in a state of nondualism. Spiritual teachers from all traditions exhort us to *wake up now*, including waking up from the fear that traps the mind in dualisms of "black or white," "good or bad," "us or them." A classic 1970s television sitcom character whose fearful mind was stuck in dualism is Archie Bunker. As the blowhard bigot in *All in the Family*, Archie was afraid of anything new, including tomorrow.

We need to be mindful about attachment to personal identities, story lines, and belief patterns with which we construct a separate sense of small self. When we identify ourselves with various roles or descriptors, such as being male or female, black or white, rich or poor, we limit and impoverish ourselves. We're so much more than the roles we play, the color of our skin, or the net worth of our financial assets. A wonderful practice is to silently repeat *I AM* and notice the relaxation and expansion possible when the mind drops distorting attachments to external roles or qualities we may have.

Evolution continues on every level. Buddhists describe the emotional fires of greed, ignorance, and aggression as the three poisons that fuel dualism. Thankfully, the potential exists for taming and transforming these destructive energies, liberating our goodness to go. With self-inquiry and the equanimity developed by practices of mindfulness, greed can become generosity, ignorance can be replaced with wisdom, and anger can transmute into compassion.

Make the Mind Your Friend

Our mind can be one of our best friends or worst enemies. Because it is our nearly constant companion, it makes good sense to develop a friendly relationship with this potentially useful instrument. Great beings have taught us to love this restless friend as we search for meaning in our lives. Being aware of the light of our awareness and consciously redirecting its focus are valuable skills. We notice the states brought on by negative thoughts and direct our attention to more uplifting thoughts, or to the space between thoughts.

It's true that we can assign our keen and discerning minds a task and come to erroneous conclusions. Our neural software has glitches and our thinking can be irrational. Attachments and misperceptions that have caused great suffering prevent us from thinking clearly in the present moment. William James warned us about this impediment to inner freedom of mind: "A great many people think they are thinking when they are merely rearranging their prejudices." Our thoughts, feelings, minds, or bodies do not define who we are.

An empowered mind naturally supports our goodness to go. By enhancing our awareness of where we place our attention, we're able to free ourselves from contracted states of mind and increase access to the vibrant power of life. Patience replaces frustration with setbacks and obstacles encountered in the course of offering our integral service. Used consciously, attention is a bridge that connects our awareness with the powerful freedom and potential of the heart. How we respond from moment to moment, how we maintain our inner world, creates our destiny.

This moment is the only now. With this understanding, we stop procrastinating and begin to engage in our lives wholeheartedly. We slow down and relax, let go of personal agendas, and choose to be present unconditionally with whatever is happening right now. Naturally, we manifest the patience, goodness, and kindness that arise. The timeless adage quoted at the beginning of the previous chapter reminds us to *think good thoughts. Words become actions. Actions become habits. Habits become character. Character becomes destiny.*

The quality of our thoughts and character matter. The miracle of mindfulness frees our minds, expands our hearts, and mobilizes our goodness to go. The incomparable gift of consciousness is accessible right now. Obsessing about the past and fearing the future squanders our time, and energy, and our lives. As Thich Nhat Hanh reminds us, the well of peace and joy is within us, "and if we dig deeply in the present moment, the water will spring forth."

A Mindfulness Practice

1. Wherever you are, bring your attention to the flow of your breath. You could be in a board meeting or chopping wood. Take a deep breath in and allow a long breath to flow out. Pause between the inhalations and the exhalations and rest in these pauses.

2. Notice the space around your heart where the in-breath dissolves and the out-breath has not yet begun. Feel the power of the pause where your out-breath dissolves and your in-breath has not yet begun. Repeat at least three rounds of mindful breathing.

3. Exhale physical and mental stresses. With open receptivity, inhale spaciousness and peace. Exhale effective action. Inhale feeling and being. Exhale thinking and doing. Be present. Relax in gentleness. Smile softly.

4. Let all of your senses experience this moment. If you're walking in your neighborhood, listen to every sound around you. Simply notice the people approaching you, the color of their coats, and the pace of their gait, without comment or judgment. Feel the wind on your cheeks and between relaxed fingers as your soles gently caress the earth.

5. You may want to extend this practice to being aware that you are aware. As you listen to the sounds surrounding you, expand your awareness to include the power of listening itself. Then ask yourself, "Who is listening?" Consciousness unfolds its blossoms further. Notice how your experience of everyday wonder and beauty expands. Be conscious of Consciousness.

Pause, Reflect, and Record

- How might you incorporate the four foundations of mindfulness—body, feelings, mind, and wisdom teachings—into your daily life?

- How could you make the mind your friend and welcome each moment?

- Practice reflecting on your thoughts. Pause between thoughts and consciously choose which thoughts, impulses, and insights to nurture. What do you notice as you think about your thinking and discern which thoughts to release?

- How might being fully present in each moment empower your generosity and sustain your ability to offer integral service?

15

There's Wisdom
Outside of the Box

*The only way of finding the limits of the possible
is by going beyond them into the impossible.*

—**Arthur C. Clarke**

The nature of integral service is to release our goodness and allow it to flow. Our intent is to be free of boxes that confine us, such as assumptions, unexamined beliefs and traditions, judgments, hopelessness, ignorance, and rigid adherence to the status quo. As our minds expand into new possibilities, beware of relying on conventional wisdom. Physicians in the past prescribed tobacco for various maladies, and "realists" insisted that Columbus would sail off the edge of the earth. Humans have walked on the moon. Glass ceilings that limited career opportunities for women and minorities are shattering. What ego-mind thinks is in the realm of the possible may only be the ground floor of what could be.

Challenge and rethink the possible. What are sustainable ways to deliver clean water to rural areas in developing nations? Our creative innovation and compassionate service are needed to envision beyond a ceiling or summit of possibility. We need to see with new eyes. We must think differently and act differently in order to manage and heal our world's web of predicaments. The inventive physician-educator Edward de Bono originated the term *lateral thinking* and invited us to "think sideways." Our scale of thinking has been too narrow and our greed too limitless.

Henry David Thoreau encouraged people to go confidently in the direction of their dreams and spoke about the importance of wildness. Although Thoreau cherished natural wilderness, it was *wildness* that he said was the salvation of the world. To what kinds of inner and outer wildness might he have been referring? Leading life by your own moral compass may necessitate parting ways with convention. It's said that on

Goodness To Go

Thoreau's deathbed, one of his final comments was, "The only thing I regret is that I was too well behaved." How might you be *wildly good*?

In addition to moral integrity, we need the innovation that often lies outside the box of habitual thinking. Albert Einstein observed that great thinkers encounter opposition from rigid, less creative minds and that problems cannot be solved by the same level of thinking that created them. The poet Emily Dickinson appreciated the kinds of thinking that were outside a strictly linear, rational life: "Tell all the Truth, but tell it slant." We are called to expand our consciousness as well as our creative problem-solving so that we can participate wisely in the evolution of our global human community.

An evolutionary who thought outside boxes and dogmas died in 2011. Steve Jobs was the visionary co-founder of the Apple computer empire who brought personal computers, user-friendly interfaces, mousing of cursors, smartphones, icons, and iPads onto our laps. As the illegitimate son of university students, Jobs was adopted by a middle-class family, dropped out of college, traveled to India, studied Buddhism and calligraphy, and proved that computer functionality could follow forms of elegant design.

In his talks, the avatar of Apple emphasized the importance of following one's heart and intuition. Jobs encouraged young people to not waste their time living someone else's life. Driven by epic ambition to change the world, he encouraged others to be free of dogmatic traps created by the thinking of others.

Each of us responds in our own unique way to invitations and challenges to discover what is possible. Our dreams frequently take us beyond the confines of the conventional. Johann Wolfgang von Goethe wrote centuries ago, "Whatever you can dream you can do, begin it now. Boldness has genius, power, and magic in it."

Boldness requires energy and a degree of daring, and there are times when we don't feel confident and bold. Sometimes we may feel positively weak-kneed and wobbly. Instead of diving into the fray, there are days when we'd rather stay in bed with a pillow over our head, watching movies, and eating comfort food. At times like these, our kindness and patience are reassuring; enthusiasm revives. Rather than sinking into apathy and ignorance or whipping ourselves with guilt, the inspiration and support of encouragement rejuvenate us. For many people, there is no wisdom greater than kindness.

Misbehave with Integrity

In the early 1990s, I attended a conference in Manhattan entitled "Changing from the Inside Out." I'd recently read *Women Who Run with the Wolves* by Clarissa Pinkola Estes, Ph.D., who spoke at the conference. Estes's book is a powerful analysis of mythological tales that had topped the *New York Times* best-seller list for months and was translated into dozens of languages.

For hundreds of years, the wild, instinctual vitality of the wolf has received bad press from ranchers and fairy tales alike. For Dr. Estes, however, the wolf symbolizes the natural force within us that is filled with great wisdom and creativity. In her empowering talks, a key theme was the importance of acknowledging and honoring our natural rhythms as we practice opening to all of life, the painful as well as the sublime. With generosity and kindness, we attune to our needs as well as the needs of others.

At one point during the conference, I asked Dr. Estes if she would sign my copy of *Women Who Run with the Wolves*. Her inscription was a great and unexpected gift: "Misbehave—with integrity" was her invitation and permission to not be overly well behaved. Her words contained the creative fire and encouragement to think and act outside the boxes of convention and status quo.

Dr. Estes also reminded us that it's our choice whether to focus on life's sweetness or its bitterness. Sweetness comes from root words that reflect the nurturance of an open heart, whereas bitterness is constriction away from the fullness of life. Many conference participants felt they lacked vision about their life purpose or felt stuck in their lives, seemingly trapped in unsupportive relationships and excessively stressful work.

Although the institutions of civilization offer humankind many benefits, society often attempts to civilize us into rigid roles, muffling the deep, life-giving messages of our own souls. Wolves in the wild have been demonized and the wild spirit of horses broken and tamed. One of our tasks on planet earth is to awaken and attend to our own true voice rather than endlessly try to conform to the status quo.

When we feel trapped in suffocating environments, the petals of the heart dry out and may curl tight in brittleness. Few want to be overdomesticated, fearful, uncreative, or to crumble in brittleness. If we succumb to fatalism, sarcasm, or egoism, disappointment chokes and blinds us. We're more vulnerable to making short-term choices and forgetting our obligation to others. Our world gets smaller, self-centered, and even corrupted. Some people cynically "laugh out loud" (LOL) all the way to the bank with money they've taken from others.

During recent years, investment bankers hurt millions of people by selling subprime mortgages. There were e-mails circulated with the abbreviation IBGYBG. It means "I'll be gone, you'll be gone," implying *why be concerned about the consequences of our actions since we won't be around to suffer them*? The short-term gain of some privileged people was void of integrity and caused great suffering. Although few of the unethical financial workers were jailed, there are other forms of consequences and imprisonments.

It's invaluable to remember that how we respond to life, how we maintain the state of our mind and heart moment by moment, determines our destiny. Act with compassion and wisdom. Think sideways. Why squeeze and contort ourselves in compliance with anything that is injurious or no longer optimally functional? Why remain stuck in destructive habits or injustices? If others call us unreasonable, so be it. In full integrity, we acknowledge and accept *what is* while using our intelligence to better the world. We attend to our needs as we tend to the needs of others.

Like Steve Jobs, Buckminster Fuller was a visionary who explored the wisdom outside of several kinds of boxes. As a brilliant architect, futurist, and philosopher, he introduced the word *synergy* into our vocabulary. Fuller described himself as a comprehensive, anticipatory design scientist. His multifaceted genius was deeply committed to making the world a better place through intelligent, efficient design of both structures and vehicles.

Buckminster Fuller created a fuel-efficient car called the Dymaxion and many other innovations. However, his most enduring legacy is the eco-friendly geodesic dome that uses a fraction of the building materials required for the same-sized box-shaped structure. This resource-efficient shelter was one example of human beings doing more with less.

Bucky, as he was called, chose to transcend his dark nights of the soul and commit his life to visioning helpful new global paradigms. Tirelessly, he traveled over a million miles a year into his eighties, inspiring people to dream a new dream. Buckminster Fuller enthralled me with his dynamic keynote speech at an Earth Day celebration held at McMaster University in the early 1970s. For millennia, an invisible mythology has limited humanity with stories about our differences and insuffiennt resources. Fuller created new stories that inspired millions of people to envision increased potential and possibility.

What was the essential paradigm shift that Buckminster Fuller articulated? It was awareness of the radical truth of sufficiency—that there is enough on this planet for everyone everywhere to create a fulfilling life. New dreams and stories can move our thinking from a "you *or* me" paradigm to one that sustains both "you *and* me." When myths that hold us separate from one another shatter or dissolve, new structures, institutions, and paradigms emerge. As a key contributor to the *We* paradigm, Fuller knew that humankind was doing so much more with so much less, and that *there is enough.*

There is enough food for all children and their families. There is enough water and sustainable technology for no one to be thirsty or sickened by polluted water. There is enough knowledge and intention to reverse trends that threaten the health of our economies as well as our ecosystems. There is enough awareness about effective communication potentials to heal old conflicts and reduce hostilities. The creative imagination of Buckminster Fuller and many others sees all the people of the world living life in peace.

In the 1970s, Fuller predicted that it would likely take about fifty years for the old "you or me" paradigm to disintegrate as the We paradigm emerged. Close to forty years after his prediction, a global economic shift began the collapse of the old paradigm. As Fuller and many others have known, the economic and industrial age model of endless growth based on depleting natural resources is fundamentally unsustainable ecologically and economically. Forests, hydrocarbons, arable land, fish, and the ozone level are not infinite. It is also not sustainable ethically to use abusive force, slave wages, debt threats, or resource rip-offs to aggressively maintain financial dominance.

The growing need for ecologic sustainability motivated another committed visionary. Dennis Hayes was the Stanford graduate student who co-founded the first Earth Day in 1970. As a result, people's insistence on having legislation for clean air and water increased. With heightened concern about pollution, the Environmental Protection Agency was established, and many environmental policies went into effect. Ecological concern is no longer outside of the box of convention and Earth Da[y] now a planetary celebration. Citizens in more than 170 countri[es] their commitment to a healthy, sustainable environment. O[ne] of the ripple effect from the first Earth Day is a growi[ng] movement inspired by a resourceful Estonian in which hundreds of thousands of citizens volunteer to clean up the rubbish littering their country.

Ecological intelligence is on the rise everywhere. We're learning about the hidden environmental consequences of what we make, what we buy, and what we throw away. More of us are recognizing that there is no *away*, and social justice activists are challenging the status quo of dumping garbage and toxins near underprivileged neighborhoods. Working together to offer good works to communities inspires collective responsibility: pollution decreases and city parks are reclaimed from drug dealers. It's been said that environmental conservation is not simply the will to protect our planet. It's a new vision of the world.

National days of public service are being held in countries around the world. Many envision the expansion of national volunteer days to engage millions more citizens in hands-on service activities. Eventually, there may be an international environmental protection corps caring for the earth's natural systems that people of all ages could join. Be an eco-warrior. Ask not what the earth can do for you but what you can do for the earth.

Pause, Reflect, and Record

- Are there any ways in which you're currently feeling stuck or uninspired in your life? How could you *think sideways* in your approach to problem solving?

- Describe a time when you tapped into unconventional wisdom with an unexpected, positive outcome.

- T⸱⸱⸱⸱⸱⸱⸱e can envision a world where our natural en⸱⸱⸱⸱⸱⸱⸱ honored and all people are treated with deep ⸱⸱⸱⸱⸱⸱⸱will you do to benefit the larger community?

- ⸱⸱⸱⸱⸱⸱⸱l you take to shift more fully into the We ⸱⸱⸱⸱⸱⸱⸱reases freedom for all life on our planet?

167

16

Transforming the
Face of Resistance

*Wisdom is the hidden treasure
that rewards our most fearless and
diligent examination of our own delusions.*

—**Roshi Joan Halifax**

We've been exploring ways to empower the mind of compassion in action. Envisioning and mobilizing our integral service changes our lives and potentially the lives of others. There may be moments or months of resistance as we redesign our lives to include our goodness to go. Bringing new ways of seeing and being to old paradigms or cultures is like bringing a flower and a rock together. In this timeless metaphor, the flower symbolizes our potential for the blossoming of compassion, clarity, wisdom, and joy. Solid rock represents the heavy resistance of mind, habit, and attachment to familiar comforts or structures. When we're addicted to habitual beliefs and lost in illusions, limited perceptions blind us to the goodness within us and the splendor surrounding us.

Flowers prefer rich soil and rarely can sustain the beauty of their colorful presence in unyielding, rocky ground. As hearts moisten with gratitude, respect, and love for life, our minds relax in gentleness. New flowers of creativity and compassion blossom as our minds, hearts, and cultures open to our interconnection with all life. Like saplings, the roots of our goodness grow stronger as they adapt to environmental adversities. An oak tree's resilience and perseverance aren't strengthened by being staked in artificial hothouse conditions but by meeting the play of life's ups and downs.

Creating a meaningful life and discovering the service work that is ours to do requires patience and perseverance. Although our aspiration may be to relieve suffering, there are no guarantees. What sustains commitment and perseverance throughout a lifetime? There is a saying that expectation is premeditated disappointment. If you're attached to expectations that your integral service will make a difference, it's likely that disappointment will be your companion. How might you transform this dynamic?

The ways in which we relate to hope, fear, and disappointment directly affect our goodness to go; on-going self-inquiry is invaluable. Margaret Wheatley is a seasoned management consultant who asks, "How do we replace the hope of creating change with the confidence that we're doing the right work?" Many people with decades of service experience agree that a hope to change the world is rarely sustainable when it includes attachment to desired outcomes. Offering service with hopeful attachment to our success is a recipe for exhaustion and despair, which in turn reinforces resistance to further engagement.

Rather than succumbing to cynicism, our task is to sustain the confidence and commitment required to continue offering the good work that is ours to do. "Never, never, never give up," repeated Prime Minister Winston Churchill as Britain persevered in its battle against Nazism. Enduring commitment honors the meaningful worth of an endeavor. Margaret Wheatley encourages us to serve as warriors of the human spirit armed with compassion and insight. Her personal vow is to refrain from adding to the aggression and fear of this time.

Every day, we have the opportunity to strengthen our perseverance and renew our commitment to offering service that honors our values and embodies our integrity. "We all stand on strong shoulders," Wheatley writes, "and now it is our turn to serve the world." Our integral service needs the resilience and clarity of an empowered mind so that our goodness can bring forth its life-enhancing gifts. This includes the daily practice of mindfulness and the discipline of radical self-care. Regular practice rejuvenates our spirit with peace and contentment. Resistance dissolves. During difficult times of intense pressure, it's especially important to engage in revitalizing practices more frequently.

Shedding Light on Resistance

Resistance hampers our goodness to go. As we cultivate mindfulness, it's not unusual to meet an inner contrarian. Hidden in the human psyche is a reactive naysayer attached to putting up resistance as part of its power play to control our lives. Although many circumstances require boundaries and the power of no, resistance is more of a habitual naysayer. This constricting force has been called the inner critic, ego, or gremlin and tries to keep us anxious and ungrounded, fretting about the past and worrying about the future.

The resistant ego avoids the powerful light of mindfulness. It prefers to whip us with perfectionism or keep us in the dark, caught in the dualism of hope and fear. At times it's tyrannical. This aspect of mind is obsessively attached to avoiding loss, blame, stress, and insignificance. Personal attachments, fear, and disempowering habits weaken our mind by nudging us into mental grooves such as restlessness, reactivity, reverie, or rumination.

These four habits of mind—restlessness, reactivity, reverie, and rumination—reinforce ruts of avoidance, attachment, distraction, and resistance. Instead of acting with a thoughtful response to a situation, we allow agitated reactivity or spacing out in reverie and rumination to fuel resistance. The power of now is missed. In this way, the resistance generated by these *four "r"s* of restlessness, reactivity, reverie, and rumination weakens the development of the big *R* of Resilience.

There are many circumstances that require the setting of limits and the power of *no*. The maintenance of healthy boundaries has a different quality than automatic walls of reactive resistance. Sometimes, we're misled or hooked by limiting thoughts, or we're simply ignorant and don't know that we don't know. We might not have imagined a possibility or may be missing a vital piece of information. Sometimes we ignore wisdom or healthier choices. In countless ways, the practice of ignorance confines the creative energy needed to generate transformative solutions and mobilize goodness to go.

Perfectionism is another ploy by ego-mind to keep us anxious and depleted with its insistence that everything we do must be "perfect." It takes form as procrastination and defensiveness that weaken resilience and reinforce resistance to full engagement with life. When the inner critic of ego tries to whip us into perfection, we might desperately attempt to be too good for our own good. In some ways, perfectionism is the curse of the "too good" person. Ego demands that we be "perfect and pure" and then harshly judges our efforts, paralyzing us with doubt and disappointment. It judges reality to be imperfect and refuses to accept the perfection of *what is*.

Doing one's best is committing to personal excellence free from comparison with others. When we're exhausted or sick, we're not at our best and therefore "doing our best" may look different. It's healthier to accept what we're capable of at any given moment and aim for excellence rather than perfection. Even "ordinary" goodness and brief encounters that generate positive emotions make us feel more alive. What constitutes "the good life" for you?

We've heard that "the perfect is the enemy of the good" and that the road to hell is paved with good intentions. In her book *Moral Clarity: A Guide for Grown-Up Idealists*, philosopher Susan Neiman describes how ordinary, flawed goodness is our domain as humans. She states that moral action is based on the discernment of moral clarity evaluating actions rather than judging a person's character or perceived intentions. This discernment is easier said than done. Legal and justice systems emphasize the importance of intention. However, projecting our assumptions about another's intentions can be as problematic as judging an outcome. A broken leg may seem like a bad thing, but if it prevents us from being forced to fight in an unjust war, it may be a good thing.

On the path of wisdom, the development of a more resilient psychological immune system is helpful. As Dee Hock, the founder of VISA credit cards, commented, "It's far too late, and things are far too bad, for pessimism." Pessimism and despair drain the energy, discipline, and courage needed to offer integral service.

What and how we decide to be moment by moment affects our perceptions and actions. When we know the One in our own mind, we'll recognize that One in others. With this knowing comes tolerance, patience, and love. As we empower our relationship with fear, free ourselves from its clutches, and transform resistance, we'll choose tenacity over timidity.

Adversity comes in many forms. Children scavenge garbage dumps in an effort to survive and corporate professionals encounter unethical behavior. In 2002, Cynthia Cooper led a small team of internal auditors to uncover $3.8 billion in accounting fraud at WorldCom, bringing integrity to a culture of cover-up and corruption. For her courage and perseverance, *Time* magazine honored Cooper as one of their 2002 Persons of the Year. Recall a time when you've overcome adversity. How did this experience strengthen you?

Perseverance is a key element of resiliency, and to offer our integral service in sustained, enjoyable ways, we need emotional, psychological, intellectual, spiritual, and physical fortitude. As we engage in self-inquiry and shed light on our habits of resistance, including restlessness, reactivity, reverie, and rumination, understanding grows and we're inspired to mobilize our life's energy. When the going gets tough, the resilient brush themselves off and start again with a toughness similar to the heartwood of a strong and flexible tree.

Transforming Resistance with Mindfulness

There are many time-honored ways of transforming resistance into compassion, insight, and resilience. Some of these are ongoing practices of self-inquiry, contemplation, prayer, mindfulness, and meditation. Another is the daily refreshment of our intent to strengthen our resilience muscles. Again and again, we pick ourselves up, brush ourselves off, and go through what is in front of us. As our resiliency strengthens, confidence in ourselves grows. We can develop the fortitude to be first responders for ourselves and others in times of need.

Every mindfulness practice in which you engage regularly is an offering of service, not only to yourself but also to everyone with whom you interact. How do you rejuvenate mind, heart, and body so that your light can shine? Think of places, people, or activities that have replenished your energy. Recall a favorite room, song, seashore, or mountainside. Both external and internal environments, including inner states of mind and heart, affect your well-being.

An age-old approach to working with difficult emotions or psychological states such as resistance is to practice being in full unconditional presence with them, bringing a curious, friendly, inquisitive attitude. When you notice the constriction of resistance, take a moment to respectfully ask yourself what is fueling it. What does this state feel like in your body? Listen for what resistance can tell you about the situation. Explore your willingness to release this resistance. What might happen if you did let go?

Sometimes, being reminded of our good fortune, counting our blessings, and expressing our gratitude help to transform resistance. Activating imagination and perspective is also useful. Imagine walking in the world of Maria, a nine-year-old orphaned girl in Mozambique where civil war, HIV/AIDS, drought, and famine made survival a daily struggle. Maria and her older, severely disabled sister lived with their frail grandmother. By herself, Maria farmed their small plot of land, fetched water and firewood, cleaned, cooked, and ensured that their survival needs were met. Millions of resilient children shoulder responsibilities that deprive them of their childhood and formal education. There are countless stories told and untold that serve as reminders to keep respect, gratitude, and service alive.

Becoming Free of Resistance

Like electronic circuits, our goodness to go is impeded by resistance. In my work as a physician, there are many intense stressors, such as pressured schedules, complex patient issues, bureaucratic impedance, office politics, technology malfunctions, insurance denials, and patients' transference of negative psychological states. My preferred work schedule includes sufficient sleep, early morning meditation, exercise, drinking fluids throughout the day, and taking deep cleansing breaths between patients. Sometimes, I need to add mental reminders to slow down and recognize that although I'm doing my best, I cannot be responsible for another's reactions or feelings.

Resistance slows electric currents, and even bolts of lightning take the path of least resistance. With less resistance, including the guilt that we're "not enough," the current of life energy is conducted effectively and efficiently. It's important to commit to daily self-care to sustain the flow of your energy. Consider modifying your schedule, grounding yourself in the present moment by visually scanning your environment, breathing into constricted areas of your body, releasing perfectionistic expectations, and reframing your notion of what is "good enough" as a parent, spouse, or professional.

One method to support the process of freeing ourselves from dysfunctional thoughts and ways of being is described by psychologist Martin Seligman, Ph.D., in his book *Authentic Happiness*. As the leading researcher in the field of positive psychology, which focuses on the strengths evident in mentally healthy people, Seligman suggests the ABCDE model, developed by Albert Ellis, the father of cognitive-behavioral psychology, to change negative perceptions, unhelpful beliefs, or pessimistic thoughts to more productive, empowering ones.

This model includes awareness of adverse events, and the beliefs that automatically arise. Recognizing the consequences that occur, such as painful feelings, judgments, and reactive behaviors, is the third step. The choice to dispute these limiting habits usually leads to energized empowerment when we've freed ourselves from their confinement and have expanded our skillfulness in response to adversity. This ABCDE model is an involved process that you can learn about on the Centre for Confidence website.

Transforming the Face of Resistance

Persevere in your efforts to reclaim your life energy and enthusiasm. Consider questioning everything that you perceive internally and externally. A pessimistic thought that many people have had, especially during economic recessions, is "I'll never have enough or be enough to offer service." Although, fear associated with unemployment and the risk of losing one's home fuels deeply entrenched beliefs that there's "not enough," we can refuse to be victimized by dysfunctional beliefs.

To decrease resistance, we need to develop life-affirming practices. Habits such as perfectionism, restlessness, knee-jerk reactivity, spacing out, or obsessively ruminating about past mistakes and injustices reinforce resistance to change. "There's too much suffering for me to make a difference" is an untrue, constrictive belief. Transforming unhelpful habits and beliefs as you build resilience supports both your experience of energized abundance and your intent to help others.

As we step back and gain perspective, we're free to consciously examine our relationship with money, assess our connection with our core values, and develop action steps to mobilize our goodness to go. In *The Soul of Money*, global activist and fundraiser Lynne Twist illumines how this self-inquiry can transform all aspects of our lives. As we free ourselves from attachment to material possessions, feelings of scarcity and burden are replaced with experiences of sufficiency and purpose.

When we practice releasing negative thoughts and habitual beliefs, life seems bigger and we feel more easeful and energized. The greatest service is to look upon ourselves and others as embodiments of life's sacredness. Free of resistance, our compassion blossoms naturally like a bud opening into a flower.

Pause, Reflect, and Record

• What concerns do you have about expanding your service? What insights arise as you articulate and examine tangles of fear-based thinking?

• Apply the steps of the ABCDE model described in this chapter as you begin the process of reframing, even transforming, a challenging issue, negative perception, or dysfunctional belief in your life.

• What steps could you make to build resilience, transform habits of procrastination, and decrease resistance to integral service?

• How is "the perfect, the enemy of the good?"

17

Empowering Our Relationship with Fear

Fearlessness may be a gift but perhaps more precious
is the courage acquired through endeavor, courage that comes
from cultivating the habit of refusing to let fear dictate
one's actions, courage that could be described as
"grace under pressure"—grace which is renewed repeatedly
in the face of harsh, unremitting pressure.

—Aung San Suu Kyi

We live in challenging times of change and upheaval that include re-markable opportunities as well as dangers. In order not to become im-mobilized by despair or cynicism, it's useful to develop empowered ways to live and work with fear. An inquisitive, friendly relationship with fear builds our resilience, allowing our goodness to shine regardless of our circumstances. Although we live in bodies with prehistoric hard wiring for fear and its reactive instincts to fight, flee, freeze, or "freak out," we don't have to be slaves to that biology. Anxiety-producing situations can be approached with a "meet it and greet it" attitude, with strong commit-ment and capacity to rise above old fears.

It's likely that our goodness to go will encounter periods of unremit-ting pressure and fear-based thoughts. During especially intense sea-sons of our lives, we may doubt our ability to sustain integral service. Yet even during times of disaster and oppression, we have enormous resourc-es to meet the fear that is generated. Within us are resilience, integrity, compassion, and courage. Despite injustice and tyranny, freedom from fear is possible. Like Aung San Suu Kyi, the Nobel Peace Prize laureate who was a prisoner of conscience in Burma for fifteen years, we can re-fuse to be victimized by fear.

Goodness To Go

With conscious intent and functional neural connections between our mind and heart, we have the potential to respond with equanimity and courage, even in dark times. While research shows that reactions driven by our sympathetic nervous system spur us to fight or flee from threatening situations, the balancing calm of our parasympathetic nervous system helps us discern when to befriend our fear and tend to those involved in whatever situations we encounter.

We have the capacity to manifest grace under pressure. With a clear vow to not add more fear or anger to the world, aggression is transformed and our resilient compassion grows stronger. "You gain strength, courage, and confidence by every experience in which you really stop to look fear in the face. You must do the thing which you think you cannot do," wrote Eleanor Roosevelt.

Many of us are conflict-avoidant, thinking that peace and skillfulness in the middle of an argument are inaccessible. We have the free will to rethink assumptions. We can stop, smile, train our attention to follow our breath into our heart, and summon our courage. We can learn to keep calm and carry on, let go on the spot, and engage in conflict without hostility. A great deal has been written about communicating effectively.

When President Franklin D. Roosevelt gave his inaugural address, he said, "The only thing we have to fear is fear itself." These words contain an implicit understanding that it's possible to renegotiate our relationship with fear, practice new behaviors, and grow stronger as a result. Instead of automatically avoiding fear or conflict, we practice being open and inquisitive. Beneficial relationships, including that with fear, are based on respect. Are there messages or opportunities that a particular fear has for you?

Many ancient teaching stories from the East feature Mullah Nasrudin. His confusion and follies are familiar to anyone who's ever been caught in fear, ignorance, and false pride or has suffered as a result of someone's projections or hostilities. In one story about the irrational hostility with which ego's fear can contaminate a situation, Nasrudin is in a sleepy, suspicious state. A kind sage approached him, bringing water that the thirsty Nasrudin himself had requested. Having forgotten what he'd asked for, Nasrudin projected fearful hostility onto his benefactor. When the wise man questioned this reception, Nasrudin insisted aggressively that *fear is multidirectional.* The dervish replied, "It certainly seems to be stronger than thirst or sanity." Nasrudin counters, "And you don't have to have fear yourself in order to suffer from it!" Sadly, it is true that our lives can be harmed very badly by the fear in others' minds.

Imagine for a moment some of the countless beings who have suffered as a result of the fear of others. Although fearful, life-threatening situations affect millions of people, many other fears stem from mistaken beliefs that we're not good enough. Anguished misperceptions often cause tremendous pain. At the same time, pain can be the chisel that shapes us, as C. S. Lewis observed, and it can help us wake up to other ways to be. Both pain and the way of happiness are resources on the path of engaged compassion cultivating grace under pressure.

Cultivating Courage

Frances Moore Lappé is the author of the 1971 best-seller *Diet for a Small Planet,* which she started researching when she was twenty-six years of age. Despite some trepidation, Lappé trusted her common sense and persevered with her aspiration to understand causes of world hunger. One of her findings changed the way people think about food and the use of agricultural land: food scarcity results when nutrient-rich grains that could support large human populations are fed to livestock whose meat yields a fraction of those nutrients.

As a visionary leader, Lappé has gone on to identify other causes of starvation and to empower the "food self-reliance" movement. In 1987, she received the global Right Livelihood Award for her "vision and work healing the planet and uplifting humanity" and founded the Small Planet Institute with her daughter in 2001 to further the worldwide transition toward a living democracy for everyone. Like many others, Lappé recognizes that current social systems aren't designed to nurture our highest aspirations. The Small Planet Institute reframes limiting ideas, supports the remaking of societal norms, and empowers citizens to infuse values of inclusion, fairness, and mutual accountability into all dimensions of public life.

Lappé is deeply committed to the democratic process and believes that every aspect of our lives is, in a sense, a vote for the kind of world we want to live in. She feels that the hearts and minds of current generations have a profound choice: we can choose death or we can support life on this magnificent planet. In a later book, *You Have the Power: Choosing Courage in a Culture of Fear*, Lappé celebrates the option of staying present and moving forward in the face of fear.

One way to do this is to reduce the burden of fear in our inner environment. We have about 66,000 thoughts a day and researchers have determined that about two-thirds of those are negative or fear based. Obviously, it's more difficult to access our courage when we're drowning in a toxic inner burden of fearful thinking. Practices that clear our energy, such as physical exercise, taking deep breaths, and replacing negative thoughts with insight and understanding are useful in many instances.

Lappé's seven empowering understandings about fear are listed below. A limiting fear-based thought is followed in bold print by a brave new understanding of how to approach, smile at, and even befriend fear. As you reflect on the reframings of fear, hold in your heart and mind a concern that you may have about expanding your integral service.

1. Fear means I'm in danger. Something's wrong. I must escape and seek safely.

   Fear is pure energy. It's a signal. It might not mean stop. It could mean go!

2. If I stop what I'm doing, I'll be lost. I'll never start again.

   Sometimes we have to stop in order to find our path.

3. I have to figure it all out before I can do anything.

   We don't have to believe we can do it to do it; the act of showing up, even with our fear, has power.

4. If I act on what I believe, I fear conflict will break out. I'll be humiliated, ineffective, and rejected.

   Conflict means engagement. Something real is in motion. It's an opening, not a closing.

5. Our greatest fears are our worst enemies; they drag us down and hold us back.

   Our worst fears can be our greatest teachers.

6. If I'm really myself, I'll be excluded. If I break connection, I'll be alone forever.

To find genuine connection, we must risk disconnection. The new light we shine draws others toward us, and we become conscious choosers.

7. I'm just a drop in the bucket. My effort might make me feel better, but it can't do much.

   Every time we act, even with our fear, we make room for others to do the same. Courage is contagious.

The process of developing more empowered understanding, skill sets, and response patterns takes time. Many social activists are aware that after pertinent knowledge is gained, our attitudes don't always shift. However, if we consciously cultivate an inquisitive mind and experiment with behavior changes, practice makes progress.

Knowledge changes attitudes that inform new behaviors that strengthen through practice. Some refer to this as the K.A.B.P. model: Knowledge. Attitude. Behavior. Practice. As you experiment with empowering your relationship with fear, work with one of the understandings listed above for a month before incorporating another. As with any change, new attitudes and behaviors are most effectively implemented when steadily practiced over time, usually for at least four to six weeks.

The kind of hope that inspires Frances Moore Lappé's integral service is not the flip-side of fear. This hope is a deep trust and courageous conviction in the wisdom and benevolence of our principles and endeavors. It's something we *become* through our life-affirming actions. Like many others, Lappé feels we're living in extraordinary times in which a revolution in human dignity is emerging on every continent. Witness the democratic uprisings and global movements to empower women, educate girls, protect ecosystems, and abolish all forms of human slavery. Our goodness is on the go and is needed now.

Working with Emotions

Fear often serves as a wake-up call that inspires us to act with courage and integrity. It shows us opportunities to learn, be brave, and take leaps of faith. Fear is also a signal that we're engaged with something that matters to us, or that someone or something we value is threatened. As an ally, fear alerts us to take action to preserve that which we care about.

Goodness To Go

When reactive fear, resistance, or withdrawal is noticed, remember to pause, giving yourself time to chart a new course. Even a temporary attitude adjustment offers the opportunity to choose wiser habits of mind and more beneficial courses of action. As you patiently redirect your attention and listen to inner wisdom, your best response to the situation will become clear. It might be to offer space and silence, or to practice the *tonglen* breath of compassion described in Chapter 4. With self-inquiry, learn to identify aspects of fear in order to work with them with courage and kindness.

Peace is accessible in the pause point, the space between breaths or the gap between thoughts. The ongoing practice of noticing, being fully present, and expanding the space of the pause is empowering, even liberating. Maintaining healthy, flexible boundaries is also important. When we pause in the still point, our hearts and minds open to the flow of creative intelligence and healing energy. In her book *Attitude Reconstruction: A Blueprint for Building a Better Life*, Jude Bijou offers a practical, playful journey to transform sadness, anger, and fear into joy, love, and peace.

If you're feeling down and out and want to lighten up, pause and mindfully make a change. Try splashing your face with water, going for a short walk, dancing, tapping your fingertips lightly above your heart, or breathing mindfully as you shape your lips into a gentle smile. Many people have found that when they clean something on the outside, their insides are cleaned, too. "Pick up a broom and sweep out your heart," a wise teacher said.

Thomas Jefferson noted that it is "tranquility and occupation" that give happiness. At times, the tranquil energy needed to engage in goodness to go gets stuck in frustration and fruitless struggle. To get unstuck, get moving. Challenging habitual patterns of thinking and behaving is a transformative aspect of cognitive-behavior therapy. Create a list or toolbox of ideas that helps you to get unstuck and inspires your capacity to serve in meaningful ways. You might visualize opening a window or being encircled by light, imagine dark mental clouds blowing away, repeat a teaching or mantra, or walk in nature. Work with a life coach or therapist who can support your journey of being in the world in healthier, happier ways.

Other ways to shift your thoughts and attitudes are to sing a favorite song, meditate or pray, reflect on an inspirational book, take a nap, or do something kind for someone else. We have the remarkable freedom to redirect our attention and re-engage our actions in more fulfilling ways. There are many empowering resources to support the transformation of our relationship with fear. In addition to *You Have the Power*, Frances Moore Lappé has written many other pioneering books including *Get a Grip: Clarity, Creativity, and Courage in a World Gone Mad*. Another helpful book is *The Big Leap: Conquer Your Hidden Fear and Take Life to the Next Level* by Gay Hendricks.

An empowered mind supports our self-determination. The neurologist and psychiatrist Viktor Frankl survived the Nazi concentration camps during World War II. He experienced firsthand the power that is accessible for determining what even the most horrific events will mean to us. Dr. Frankl stated: "Man is *not* fully conditioned and determined but rather determines himself whether he gives in to conditions or stands up to them. In other words, man is ultimately self-determining. Man does not simply exist but always decides what his existence will be, what he will become in the next moment."

Ralph Marston is the author and publisher of *The Daily Motivator*, one of the web's most enduring sites of inspiration. He regards excellence as an attitude rather than a skill. "Achievers concern themselves with excellence, but do not obsess over perfection," he writes. "Things get done by doing them in the real world, not by putting them off until conditions are perfect. ... Achievement and excellence are built not by fearing the mistakes, but by confidently handling the mistakes and the surprises that come along. ... Go beyond merely dreaming and planning and speculating about the ideal way to reach your goal. Make use of whatever you have available to get it done."

Do the best you can where you are with what you've got. Emancipate your mind from fear. Collaborate. Move outside the box of conventional thinking and artificial distinctions. Trust your ability to meet obstacles and challenges outside your comfort zone. Lead your life with courage and creativity. Gather available resources, arrange for the support you need, make the first step toward achieving your goal, and actualize your life's vision.

Pause, Reflect, and Record

- For each of the seven empowering understandings about fear articulated by Frances Moore Lappé, describe a current example from your life where you could reframe an anxiety-producing situation in an uplifting way and relate to uncertainty with more confidence.

- "Do the thing and you will have the power." What did Ralph Waldo Emerson mean by this comment? How could you apply this to your integral service?

- "Be lamps unto yourselves. ... Be your own confidence. ... Hold to the truth within yourselves," the Buddha encouraged us. How committed are you to participating in this transformative journey of *being your own confidence*?

- How have you empowered your relationship with fear in the past? When is a time that you befriended uncomfortable feelings or other players in a conflict? What helped you to engage in conflict with more compassion and equanimity?

18

Trusting Yourself

Self-trust is the first secret of success... .
Insist on yourself; never imitate.
Your own gift you can present every moment
with the cumulative force of a whole life's cultivation.

—Ralph Waldo Emerson

In the previous chapter, we explored how the empowerment of our relationship with fear frees us to offer our unique gifts to the world. *Trust in yourself. That is the beginning.* This is a message from great beings of many world wisdom traditions. Beginnings are like seeds carrying blessings that need to be nourished. What is needed for our mind to be able to say *yes* to ourselves and the innate goodness in our hearts? As we develop resilient trust in the goodness that lights up from within, self-confidence grows. How are we to cultivate minds that are clear with compassion and tenderhearted with bravery?

Trust and faith are confidently grounded in the natural goodness of our hearts. The word *confidence* stems from the Latin root meaning "faith." Its deep roots develop the resilience to bend and not be broken by internal and external challenges. When we face and learn from challenges, the peace of self-confidence grows. With resilient trust, we approach our lives with inquisitiveness and gratitude, learning from everything and everyone.

Our gifts, including that of integral service, emerge naturally from who we are, just as we are. Each of us is one of a kind, and so our gifts are unique offerings to our global family. How do we maintain true self-confidence that is not eroded by unhealthy elements in our upbringing, beliefs, media exposure, cultural and societal norms, and outdated systems? It's a creative and often time-consuming endeavor to unwrap our gifts and discover how to share them with integrity. What ongoing practices strengthen self-trust? How do we discover our unique gifts that we acknowledge with gratitude and present with love?

An American mother who became a Buddhist nun has written extensively about nourishing the unconditional confidence that supports the discovery of our gifts. Pema Chodron writes, "The root of true confidence grows out of our ability to be in unconditional friendship with ourselves, to train in gentleness, and to trust in our natural intelligence to navigate life. ... There always is the potential to create an environment ... that is conducive to loving-kindness." Chodron also reminds us to trust the unfolding of our lives and that nothing ever goes away until it teaches us what we need to know.

From the strength of our gentleness, confidence grows. With gentleness, we're careful and merciful with ourselves and others. With loving respect and trust, we move forward. Like anything we cherish, gentleness must be cared for, maintained, protected, and given space to expand. A gentle environment inside and out removes fear, allowing us to appreciate and trust the innate goodness of the universe. Try beginning each day in a calm, unhurried manner, gently embracing and giving full attention to each moment. What might this look like in your life?

Let the Mind Rest in the Heart

As you cultivate inner gentleness, let your mind become more serene and your heart expand. Self-trust can be experienced on many levels. One way to tap into trust and let your whole body relax is by taking deep, easeful breaths. After intense physical exertion or a progressive muscle relaxation exercise, lie still on your back, let go into deep silence, and breathe deeply, focusing on the space between breaths. Following the balanced flow of the breath throughout your day connects mind and heart and calms your nervous system.

Take a moment now to exhale, releasing thinking and doing. Inhale feeling and being. Again, gather your attention in your center, pause, and exhale with a deep sigh. Relax fully. Inhale tranquil *yin* energy and exhale flowing *yang* energy. Our neurology was designed for the regulatory homeostasis of our parasympathetic nervous system to predominate most of the time. It's not optimal to have frequent traumas and unpredictable threats activate the fight-or-flight sympathetic nervous system. Stress is a natural part of life but financial pressures, health issues, work performance demands, and community violence have reached levels of distress for millions of people.

Animals naturally know how to "shake off" and discharge the stress hormones that flood their bodies during threatening events. However, many people have lost touch with those instincts, and live in societies that are chronically overstimulating or are characterized by ongoing trauma. Unfortunately, therapeutic interventions, trauma therapy, and other approaches to self-regulation of unbalanced nervous systems are not available to most victims of violence and catastrophic events.

When we're anxious, adrenalin is released and we tend to take rapid, shallow breaths. To calm our agitated mind, it's helpful to inhale slowly through our nostrils, like filling a pitcher with cool water. Pause. Witness where the in-breath dissolves before the out-breath begins. Place attention in that space of the pause and expand it. Then, through pursed lips, gently and slowly exhale, starting at the top of the chest until the abdomen is emptied. Notice where the out-breath settles into the space between breaths. Trust grows when breath, mind, and nervous system are calm and integrated.

This deep, steady breathing supports the parasympathetic nervous system that balances the sympathetic nervous system. Mind follows breath and gradually rests in the heart. Panic attacks and high blood pressure are reduced. This integration of heart and mind is nourishing and healing on many levels. By simply following your breath as it goes out and dissolves in the space between breaths, you can connect with your heart, let yourself be, and rest in your compassionate nature. Self-trust grows.

Thich Nhat Hanh is the renowned practitioner of socially engaged Buddhism who was nominated for the Nobel Peace Prize by Dr. Martin Luther King, Jr. Although Hanh has witnessed profound horrors and suffering, he trusts the vast power of the heart. "How can I smile when I am filled with so much sorrow?," he asks. "It is natural—you need to smile to your sorrow because you are more than your sorrow." We are so much more than our emotions, thoughts, and difficulties. Through daily practices of breath meditation, compassionate self-inquiry, and integral service, we create vessels large and strong and pure enough to hold the opening of our minds and hearts.

Acknowledge Your Self

Self-acknowledgment is a key to self-trust. When you experience your own loving kindness and recognition of your goodness, self-respect grows. Ralph Waldo Emerson honored our inner greatness when he wrote that what lies behind us and what lies before us are tiny matters compared to what lies within us. Refresh your commitment to being nonjudgmental as you cultivate magnanimity and forbearance. When you acknowledge and share these inner treasures, roots of self-trust that sustain your integral service grow strong and deep.

Self-acknowledgment is not to be confused with rote repetition of positive affirmations. When you practice recognizing and acknowledging your inherent goodness every day, you begin to identify with your true Self rather than with the small ego self. You're less hooked by negative thoughts, knowing that you're *not* your thoughts, feelings, habits, judgments, or even your actions. Let yourself be free of internal judgment and badgering. Allow wounds to heal, knots unfurl, and enthusiasm to spread its wings.

One of the key antidotes to a lack of confidence is love. The nature of love is to spread goodness, and acknowledging the manifestations of goodness is an act of love. Self-acknowledgment is not about brandishing the ego that wants to take credit for nearly everything; it's more about attributing our goodness to its rightful source. A Japanese Zen Buddhist teacher Taizan Maezumi wrote, "Have good trust in yourself, not in the one that you think you should be, but in the One that you are."

The practice of self-appreciation and self-acknowledgment amplify the awareness of our basic goodness. It's difficult for many of us to trust the greatness of the gift of ourselves just as we are. The ego always finds ways to make us feel not good enough. When we identify with its judgments, emotions, or tangled thoughts, we forget the compassionate One that we are. Harsh criticism deriding our inadequacy lashes out when perfectionistic expectations take over. Belittling judgments are toxic. They weaken our spirits when what we yearn to experience is the goodness of everyone, including ourselves.

Understandably, it's difficult for self-trust to grow unshakable roots in an undermining inner environment. Guilt, anger, and fear weaken our ability to perceive the sacred in all aspects of life. When we misperceive ourselves as separate from others, fear and mistrust arise from illusions of isolation and difference. Frank Herbert wrote in the science fiction classic *Dune* that "fear is the mind-killer." When we mindfully practice relating to fear with the courage of our heart, we're able to move forward with the action to which we're committed.

If you begin to doubt yourself, remember that self-trust is the antidote to self-doubt. Install and find trust with all its qualities in your being and in every part of your body. Each morning, welcome yourself and the new day. Practice befriending your shadow places and the traumas and wounds that may contain important gifts and teachings. If you need to work through and transform difficult feelings such as anger and guilt, trust that love is ultimately both the gift and the lesson. Feel the release and relief of being free from the burdens of emotions that constrict your mind and heart.

Sometimes an inner control-monger fuels self-doubt with negative thoughts like *you'll never be good enough or you're not strong enough to meet that challenge.* Ego feels in charge when we allow it to make us feel weak, small, and unworthy. My young daughter referred to the petty tyrants she encountered on playgrounds as "bossy boots" and later acknowledged that they served to strengthen her resilience. Adversity is a natural part of our evolving maturation. In *The Measure of My Days,* Florida Scott-Maxwell wrote, "Life does not accommodate you; it shatters you. Every seed destroys its container, or else there would be no fruition." As we navigate the peaks and valleys of life's changing seasons, we learn to appreciate their lessons, trust ourselves, and to be grateful for our growing efficacy and wisdom.

It's enjoyable to explore the creativity, wisdom, and basic goodness of our original self. Radical acceptance, tolerance, and nonjudgmental appreciation of what is occurring at any given moment spills over into our relationships. We learn not to take things personally and stop projecting our values and perceptions onto others as old lenses are replaced with a new prescription. When we experience ourselves and our world from a fresh perspective, we sense the vast goodness of life.

There are many forms of fear born of fatigue and loneliness and many ways to be light. Sufficient sleep, self-care, and meaningful social engagement are essential. It's illuminating on many levels to bring the light of understanding to shadowed corners of our psyche and society. The flames of inspiration are tended as we refrain from burdening ourselves with harsh judgments or impossible to-do lists. We trust who we are, radiate good humor, enjoy the moment, and laugh in moments of joyful ease. Angels can fly, the saying goes, because they take themselves lightly.

William A. Ward was a well-known optimist writing in the mid-twentieth century. One of his maxims was: "To make mistakes is human; to stumble is commonplace; to be able to laugh at yourself is maturity." When you put forth right effort aligned with your core values, superconductivity makes it an effortless effort. With cheerful lightheartedness, refrain from judgment. Experience that you have all the time and energy that you need.

Flowing with the Rhythms of Life

To everything there is a season. Since change is inevitable, it makes sense to accept the rhythms and honor the transitions of life. Around the world, more goes right than goes wrong. Every day, in each of the sevenbillion human beings on this good earth, vigilant immune systems eliminate nearly every cancerous mutation of a cell. More forces support us than we know and some kinds of optimism are realistic. We can adjust our sails rather than complain about the wind. The glass can be perceived as half full rather than half empty. Trust the wisdom and sacredness of the breath. In the course of one breath, there is a time to inhale and a time to exhale.

We're human beings, not human *doings*. In many cultures, people are distressed when they feel that they're moving faster than the speed of life for too long. Yet as Mahatma Gandhi reminded us, there's more to life than going faster. Time to reflect upon and integrate our experience seems to be vanishing and entire species of life are becoming extinct. Electric lights and graveyard shifts eliminate the restful darkness of night. Telecommunications keep us wired to our work and to each other 24/7 as infomania increases and meaningful knowledge is more difficult to discern.

We deny or ignore that we're contaminating and depleting our Mother Earth. We pretend that we'll live forever but act as if we won't be around to suffer the consequences of our current actions. Illogical or ill-informed thinking are on the rise. Multitasking is an expected norm, although it's been proven to be a virtual illusion. Focused, compassionate attention is a form of energy that integrates the energy of love. Recall or imagine an experience of being listened to with unconditional presence.

Trust your instincts and the rhythms of life, death, and transformation. There is a time to speak and a time to maintain silence, a time to serve and a time to rest. There is a time to inhale and a time to exhale. Many cultures honor the sacred rest of the Sabbath. As you choose to create time and space to listen to your inner voice, ego gently falls away and the power of trust and peace grows.

How can we release our grip, let go of trying to control life, and relax into the flow of trust? Release allows real ease. One approach is to practice equanimity and appreciation for everything that happens; trust grows that an experience comes at the time it is intended (or practice *acting as if* that may be true). Another practice is seeing that everything that happens contains a gift or teaching for us. Trust includes the strength of courage, acceptance, and faith. Helen Keller describes this kind of faith as the strength by which a shattered world shall emerge into light.

Trusting ourselves and honoring life includes acceptance that there will be anguished as well as luminous days. When a great loss or injustice is experienced, intensely painful emotions often arise that are best met with compassion. With gentleness and self-care, we allow our minds to become more serene. Gradually, we begin to ask ourselves how might warriors of kindness respond to this situation. Not only spiritual warriors like Jesus, Buddha, or Gandhi, but how do *we* cultivate openness, trust, and patience in our daily lives to treat all with reverence and merciful justice.

Although inherent goodness is everyone's birthright, most news reports focus on destructive events and negative human behaviors. Taking in such information can fuel a sense of vulnerability, overwhelm, and distrust that breeds anxiety and disregard. We become obsessed trying to control our world or attached to ignoring problems. Although it's not easy to come by, the wisdom to discern what we can change and what we cannot is essential to resilient self-trust.

As you begin to offer integral service, don't *try hard* to make things right. Clenching your teeth with strained effort causes headaches and constricts your heart. In the midst of disturbing events, it's helpful to rest in your essence and release your goodness. Be aware of your state and your intentions. The magnificent power of homeostasis is at work. Its exquisitely intricate balancing processes within your body and all of earth's ecosystems serve you every moment of your life. Know that this dynamic balance is your natural state.

Challenges faced and handled nurture the equanimity that springs from self-trust. Generosity grows as self-doubt subsides. Maya Angelou, a Nobel laureate in literature as well as a former U.S. poet laureate, has experienced many difficult times in her life. She wrote, "I've learned that you shouldn't go through life with a catcher's mitt on both hands. You need to be able to throw something back." Angelou trusts life's cycles of receiving and giving.

As you meet life's changes, allow the daily practice of balanced breath to strengthen your nervous system and your confidence. Another practice is to offer the merit of your actions for the benefit of all beings. Have faith. With trust and integral service, our troubled world will emerge into light. Accept what is as you become the change you want to see in the world. Respect your own personal rhythms; an old proverb tells us, "Slow and steady wins the race." Along your path of goodness to go, move at your own pace. The momentum of small steps of service will uplift the world.

Pause, Reflect, and Record

• How might you acknowledge and celebrate some of the countless resources available to you, such as positive relationships, nature, clean water, fresh air, safe shelter, music, education, health, energy, spiritual practices, uplifting dreams, goals, commitments, and community?

• What are some of your personal gifts, talents, abilities, and resources that could support your integral service?

• As you engage in self-inquiry and nurture self-trust, are you courageous in compassion as well as honesty? What might motivate "brutal honesty?" Describe.

• How could incorporate self-acknowledgment into your daily life?

19

Patience

Be patient with everyone, but above all with yourself.

—St. Francis de Sales

Patience is essential for learning, living, and letting go. With patience we learn what our gifts are and how we to offer them as goodness to go. Integral service is an organic, evolving element of life whose process and outcomes are unpredictable. Its blossoming is rooted in patience, and without it much is lost. Fully accepting that what will be will be and letting go of expectations or attachments to the fruits of our actions requires patience. Patience cultivates peace and is not passive. "Beyond a wholesome discipline, be gentle with yourself. ... Go placidly amid the noise and haste," wrote Max Ehrmann in his 1927 prose poem *Desiderata.*

Again and again, life reminds us to practice patience. *Be gentle with yourself. You're growing.* We treat vulnerable living things such as plants and infants with gentleness. Timing is an important element of our learning and growth, and we need to go at our own pace without rushing. To cultivate patience, we need to be present. If we're distracted or hurrying, we're not in the moment. And more often than not, haste makes waste.

It's often difficult to sense what our natural pace is. Although the Hebrew commentaries known as the Talmud tell us that every blade of grass has an angel over it whispering "Grow! Grow!" those angels are not prodding life to *hurry up.* Too often in our digital age, truth seems like a victim. Information escalates as critical thinking and respect for quality declines. The technological use of information is moving faster than social norms, laws, and human cognition can keep pace. For many reasons, facts are rarely enough to sway campaign rhetoric. With increasing speed hardwired into our culture, deadlines in understaffed workplaces and consumption of stimulants increase.

Patience has been described as an inner expression of great freedom and strength. Freedom takes action as integral service. Consider the pace of life in A.D. 900 when the Japanese poet Ki no Tomonori savored the fleeting beauty of cherry blossoms: "The light filling the air / is so mild this spring day / only the cherry blossoms / keep falling in haste— / why is that so?" Remaining awake throughout our life's journey is supported by the freedom and strength of patience and benefits every stage, including the final process of letting go of life. Patience supports us as we learn to walk and read and as we gradually release the hooks of old conditioning.

In the midst of our busy lives, sustaining the motivation to offer our integral service is often challenging. Distractions abound, and although speed is often exhilarating, it's rarely sustainable. The cultivation of a particular quality or behavior starts with recognition of its value and then clarifying our intention to incorporate it into our lives. When the value of serenity is appreciated, we explore the path of patience on a daily basis. Self-effort draws grace, which in turn supports our goodness to go.

It's useful to practice a state of patience and equanimity *no matter what*. A strong vessel is able to hold the energy and emotions that arise as we engage in life. Small change adds up and strength of spirit shields us in subtle ways. On the path of peace, we start with tolerance for small differences or irritations. As we strengthen our patience muscles, we develop unconditional acceptance for all that is.

"There are no shortcuts to any place worth going," said Beverly Sills, the renowned American operatic soprano who advocated for the fine arts. Naturally, on our journey of integral service, we'll encounter challenges and setbacks. Little that is meaningful comes quickly or easily; every transformative social movement has required tremendous time and patience. Abolitionists in the United States worked tirelessly for decades before President Abraham Lincoln's integral service was added to the battle to end slavery.

The Vitalizing Power of Patience

Patience is a multifaceted jewel and is its own reward. With patience, we recognize, understand, develop, and put our gifts into practice. Like any worthwhile endeavor, our integral service is vitalized by the fortitude, mental strength, and emotional courage present in patience. To rise above the adversities that we'll inevitably encounter, it's useful to strengthen the discipline of resilience in the face of obstacles.

Centuries ago, the Persian poet Rumi wrote, "Patience with small details makes perfect a large work, like the universe." As our goodness to go is activated, strong emotions may arise that are difficult to tolerate or self-regulate. E-motions are forms of energy-in-motion that can hijack us at times. Practicing patience is an antidote, allowing the time and space for us to balance mind and heart instead of escalating the drama. Our world does not need more aggression fueling passionate intensity.

Patience nourishes enthusiasm, a state of being filled with the breath of spirit that allows our goodness to shine. Patience and compassion allow us to investigate and befriend emotions without suppressing or acting them out. Hostile anger often breeds violent words and actions. A more skillful path is to get smart, stop, breathe, watch, and wait until we're still enough to listen to the wisdom that arises. This is one of many ways to activate the "reset" button. When we give ourselves time to recognize the wonder of each moment, the inner strength and freedom of patience grow. Greater intelligence emerges during these conscious pauses. Through the power of patience, we honor an inner state of harmony and equanimity regardless of how "busy," or meaningfully engaged, we are.

From roots of patience grow resilient trunks and branches. The graceful aesthetic of calligraphy, a classic art form that exemplifies inspiration and devotion, requires great patience for the integration of skill and spirit to be realized. In a similar way, through trial and error, we practice patience for the confluence of our inspiration and skillful means to manifest. Our goodness to go is vitalized by the courage, discipline, and forgiveness of patience.

Serving the greater good with patience and resilience often requires the surrender of personal agendas, expectations, and attachment to stories of the past. It's a heroic choice to forgive, to consciously seek the understanding, healing, and peace that come with taking life experiences less personally. Tremendous endurance is required to engage in the work of healing, for those injured or abused as well as for their caregivers. Practice gratitude for the blessings and mercies we've been shown is also an element of patience and forgiveness.

The Patience of Perseverance

"The reward of patience is patience," taught St. Augustine. Patience with small details creates works of art, from Michelangelo's marble sculptures to our life's legacy. The practice of medicine reminds me again and again of how vital patience is to a life well-lived. Every person copes with more challenges seen and unseen than anyone else can know. Judgment is folly.

It's humbling to consider the daily struggles of billions of people. For the past eighty years, a ninety-two year old woman in India has spent six hours of every day obtaining non-potable salty water used for cooking. Lack of safe water sickens, and often results in the deaths of, millions of people. Many individuals have been born with disabilities or have suffered traumatic spinal and brain injuries. The lives of veterans returning with post-traumatic stress disorder and severe physical impairments require nearly unimaginable reserves of courage and perseverance. Lifelong rehabilitation is usually necessary.

The stories of people living with chronic pain and mental illness may be less dramatic but also involve tremendous fortitude on a daily basis. Parenting requires deep reserves of patience and is a call to lifelong service, especially when the child is handicapped in some way. Educating classrooms of children; nursing patients with complex, life-threatening conditions; coordinating volunteers; shepherding environmental and anti-trafficking legislation through the political process; and countless other acts of service are sustained with patient perseverance.

When illness strikes, millions of people contribute their service as the primary caregiver of a parent or spouse. Caring for a loved one with dementia calls forth our compassion and patience and gives unexpected opportunities to practice living in the present, moment by moment. It also requires respite and regular self-care. There are many expressions of our integral service that benefit our families, our communities, and our world.

The power of Nelson Mandela's patience and perseverance made possible the long walk to freedom for black people in his homeland. Although Mandela's early years in South Africa were marked by deprivation and the oppression of white Afrikaners, he was able to attend school for several years. Soon, Mandela was deeply involved in mass grassroots movements of noncooperation with the unjust regime of apartheid. As a political advocate demanding full citizenry for blacks, including free and compulsory education for all children, Mandela led the anti-apartheid movement for decades until he was incarcerated in 1963.

For twenty-seven years in harsh prison conditions, Mandela kept the light of his commitment to social justice burning bright. Mandela became a potent symbol of black resistance, and when his jailers offered release if he'd renounce armed struggle, Mandela refused to compromise his integrity. After years of international campaigning for his release and the inauguration of a new South African president, Frederick Willem de Klerk, Mandela was eventually released from prison in 1990.

Amidst demonstrations and armed resistance, Mandela engaged patiently in a complex political process of intense negotiations. In 1993, Mandela and de Klerk shared the Nobel Peace Prize for their work to dismantle apartheid. The following year, at seventy-seven years of age, Mandela was inaugurated as his country's first black president. As a symbol of global peacemaking, Nelson Mandela's birthday, July 18, is designated as an international celebration of his legacy and a day dedicated to promoting global peace.

The Patience of Peace

We live in chaotic times and yearn for deep peace. In Sanskrit, the word *kshama* means both "patience" and "forgiveness." Although both patience and forgiveness include letting go, they're stable in our core. This still center of our being holds us together when everything else is falling apart and, despite William Butler Yeats's famous lines in "The Second Coming," our center *can* hold. When we allow agitation and resentment to dissolve, more space is available for our breath as well as our goodness to move freely. The possibility begins for difficulties to transmute into the nectar of wisdom.

Patience and forgiveness vitalize the power of peace. They allow our yearning for the well-being of our children and our planet to stay fresh and not spiral down into frustration and fatalism. Individuals growing in self-awareness acknowledge that the path of compassion includes patience with the fact that we're human and will make mistakes along the way. Mistakes are not sins. A mistake is a *missed-take* and frequently leads to creative spin-offs, discoveries, and break-throughs. When we've missed the mark, we can choose to welcome another opportunity to learn more skillful behaviors. Parents and presidents make mistakes, and many teachers are showing their students how to *celebrate* mistakes. The way we respond to mistakes can enhance our compassion and strengthen patience, even bring opposites into harmony.

Our ongoing commitment to both internal and external peacemaking is powered by patience. Perseverance and humility allow us to bear trials and provocations. Access to tranquil states helps to avoid burnout as we care for ourselves and the world. Volunteers don't always show up as promised. The rally or fundraiser that we spent months organizing is rained out. Our commitments are scorned. Fatigue and despair drain our enthusiasm. Thoughts seduce us with the temporary comforts of mindless entertainment: "Just quit your do-gooding. It's time for TV and a warm bowl of popcorn."

Although temptations and impatience abound, it's possible to abide in deep peace that in turn radiates into the world. *Let there be peace and let it begin with me.* The innovative public interest lawyer and social entrepreneur Charles Halpern first experienced moments of deep peace as a teenager. He later wrote that it was in this peaceful state that he experienced "an intuitive intimation that all life on earth is interconnected and interdependent." As we reach out in friendship with trust in our interconnectedness, peace grows. An ancient name for this interpersonal connection is *armicitia*, which is derived from the Latin "to bind by friendship."

The National Peace Foundation proposed the grand notion of a National Peace Academy in the 1980s. Since then, Peace Partnership International and other organizations have joined forces to convene summit gatherings of peacemakers from all sectors of society, including education, business, government, religion, and philanthropy. One vision for the National Peace Academy is to create a decentralized global network that could serve as a resource and training center as well as an academic institute.

Centers for social justice are being created by faith groups such as the Unitarian Universalists as well as by academic institutions around the globe. Another initiative is the development of a congressional bill for a cabinet-level Department of Peace. Many grassroots communities committed to new paradigms of harmonious living are doing a world of good. Deep peace begins in the heart of patience. Cultivating the patience of peace allows us to draw from the wellspring of goodness as we offer our integral service.

Pause, Reflect, and Record

• What facet(s) of patience—courage, equanimity, discipline, gratitude, fortitude, or forgiveness—would you like to deepen at this point in your life? Why?

• In what circumstances do you tend to forget or abandon the practice of patience? How might you approach these situations more mindfully?

• Consciously explore the path of patience. Whenever you're rushing and feel there's not enough time, remember to pause and take a deep breath. Drink water slowly. Before proceeding, give yourself time to be relaxed, centered, and grounded. Draw from the full support of your own being. At the end of each day for at least a week, describe your experience.

• Compassion includes patience for human mistakes. Describe a mistake you've made and the reactions it generated. How might you respond to mistakes of yours and others with greater patience and compassion?

20

The Resource of
Integral Health

We seek to become carriers of new genesis
as the world is getting ready to move
from chaos to renaissance ... a rebirth ...
when the human spirit becomes able to offer
new ways of being and doing.

—Jean Houston, Ph.D.

To leave this world a kinder, healthier, and more interconnected place, personal and community vitality is key. Self care and well being are essential resources to be able to give to the world in positive ways. Without physical, psychological, emotional, and creative energy, our goodness to go cannot be sustained. *Health, whole,* and *healing* share the same Latin root. Regenerative well-being manifests on many levels—global, national, societal, community, familial, and personal.

In addition to sunlight, life on earth depends on uncontaminated water, soil, and air. Water is essential to life, yet over a billion people do not have access to clean drinking water. Many species of fish are important protein sources for millions of people but over-fishing and polluted oceans are decimating their numbers. The integral health of our planet is vital for life to thrive and is a key resource in every environment in which our lives play out. Just as there are toxic buildings, there are psychologically toxic work environments. The mental illness of one family member affects the dynamics of interconnected family systems, often for generations. The wisdom of our actions today will affect the health and wellness of generations to come.

On the level of community health, societies have set aside public places such as libraries and parks to gather for the pleasures of good company, learning, and lively conversation. Ray Oldenburg, author of *The Great Good Places*, describes these common grounds as "the heart of a community's social vitality and the grassroots of a democracy." The health and safety of our common grounds needs our ongoing attention. Troubled individuals of all ages, terrorists, and drug cartels slaughter thousands of innocent people. Ignoring the reality of poisoned environments and impoverished neighborhoods is not sustainable, regardless of the private schools, clubs, jets, and gated communities that money can buy.

The Ecology of Integral Service

Within the great circle of personal health and wholeness, there are many facets. Throughout *Goodness To Go*, we've been exploring four key themes that are integral to weaving the tapestry of our life's service: intention, mindfulness, compassion, and loving connection. Implicit to each is the understanding the environments in which we live, including our physical body and spiritual self, the world of ideas, nature, close relationships, financial circumstances, and our networks of community contacts. Moment by moment we live in, relate to, and are affected by many inner, outer, and even virtual ecologies that can be understood holistically.

The integration of our intention, mindfulness, compassion, and loving connection emerges from a conscious relationship with our heart and mind as one whole. Two distinguished educators, Arthur Costa and Bena Kallick, have articulated sixteen intelligent behaviors they call "habits of mind." Persistence and thinking flexibly are two of these key habits of mind. "If we want a future that is much more thoughtful, vastly more cooperative, greatly more compassionate, and a whole lot more loving, then we have to invent it," the authors write. With empathy and flexibility, we contribute what is ours to give and co-create the future that is living today in our hearts and minds as well as our homes and classrooms.

The habits of mind are tools to invent our desired vision of the future. Other habits of mind are taking responsible risks, responding with wonderment, listening respectfully, remaining open to continuous learning, and thinking interdependently. The Institute for Habits of Mind offers resources about the sixteen thinking dispositions designed to help people develop their critical and creative thinking skills.

Utilizing healthy habits of mind nurtures the clarity of our intentions and the quality of our compassion and relationships. This element of mindful self-care contributes to the flexibility, stability, and resilience essential to sustainable service. Although cultivating personal vitality and harmony of body, mind, and spirit is a wonderful goal, the gift of health is not an end in itself. This vital energy is a resource to share with others, as goodness ripples out with waves of well-being. We give from our abundance.

Personal Well-Being

There is an Arabic saying that when we have health, we have hope. There are consequences that arise from the degree of care that we offer our miraculous bodies and minds. When stress in unrelenting, the depletion of endorphins and neurotransmitters such as serotonin and dopamine lead to increased irritability and insomnia. Enthusiasm for life wanes and resentful rumination increases as our cognition is restructured in a downward spiral. Often, we try to double down and work harder to regain a sense of control and relieve our guilt. Anxiety and apathy often make it more difficult to ask for help.

The emotional exhaustion of burnout is not conducive to mobilizing our goodness to go. Studies have revealed that a third of physicians are burned out. Fortunately, a benefit of our brain's neuroplasticity is that neural pathways can be reconfigured by the ongoing practice of positive thoughts and behaviors. Since we can't give what we don't have, it's important to develop, refine, or rejuvenate a personal plan for wellness. This plan includes managing the key resources of time and energy. Although many books have been written about time management, energy management is especially vital to radiant well-being.

If possible, take a few minutes now to contemplate your action plan to enhance your personal well-being. Before clarifying your intentions for your self-care plan, it's helpful to feel grounded and relaxed in your body. Feel the gentle strength of the earth's support. Breathe slowly and deeply. Let your whole body relax, experiencing gentleness in your own being. Let your mind become serene and your heart expand. From your center of balance, alignment, and firm foundation, clarify simple, specific action steps of your self-care plan. Do you need to drink eight glasses of water and get eight hours of sleep every day? Would a skillful life coach be useful as you navigate a life transition? To thrive, we need both strong roots *and* wings.

When we clearly articulate our intentions and commitments to self-care, we're less likely to succumb to reactive resistance and excuses. The seductions of "stinkin'-thinkin'" are legendary. Many people write their intentions as computer reminders, in day-timers, or on cards they'll see throughout their day. Being mindful of our commitments reduces the seductive power of temptations. The companionship and encouragement of supportive friends and mentors attracts other resources. We notice synchronicities, or meaningful coincidences, along the way. Our "net wealth" is much more than our financial assets, and so many fortuitous, even providential, synchronicities occur in our lives that they might seem to be forms of soulful guidance. A vast mystery surrounds us and we have more allies than we know.

The Mountain Pose described below is a daily practice that increases attunement and alignment with our body. Consider standing in the Mountain Pose for a few attentive moments throughout your day. You can apply its principles to your sitting posture, as well. Gently lifting your heart and upright spine allows relaxing, vibrant energy to flow. The awareness you bring to this seemingly simple standing pose can lead to a greater connection between your mind and heart and enhance your alignment with the energy of life.

Mountain Pose

1. Prepare your foundation: In a place where you can move freely, warm up your body with a few easeful, simple stretches. With feet hip-width apart and parallel to each other, gaze softly just above the level of the horizon in front of you as you relax your jaw and face muscles. Gently smile. Spread your toes wide and feel grounded as you press your feet into the floor. Shift your weight forward and back and from right to left, then come back to center. Slowly firm your thigh muscles, spiraling them up and inward. Gently hold this lifting firmness of your thighs.

2. Lengthen: Aware of the natural curve in your lower back, allow your tailbone to release down toward the earth as the crown of your head gently rises upward. Relax and lift your neck muscles as your tongue rests on the floor of your mouth. Feel the movement of energy along your spine flowing simultaneously up and down as you stand still and steady for a few moments.

> **3. Focus on your heart:** Place your attention on the flow of your breath into your heart. Notice your breath naturally deepen and flow more freely. Aware of the fullness, and power of your heart, be present and mindful of this spaciousness as you move into the next moment of your day.

Offering our goodness to go is sharing the best of who we are. Inattentive to our own well-being, busyness can lead to *dis-ease*. It's wise to don our own oxygen mask before helping another, and it's essential to attend to our lives with the inhalation of self-care. In this way, ongoing exhalations of integral service are possible as we open to cycles of giving and receiving. What goes around comes around. Our generous reception of others' gifts to us includes our gratitude and respect, which in turn enrich our lives with meaning.

Our "bucket" needs to have something life-promoting in it before we can give to others, and the inner goodness that we cultivate uplifts the world in exponentially life-affirming ways. As you breathe beauty, health, and strength into the cracks of someone's life, you breathe them into your own. St. Francis reminded us that it is in giving that we receive. Grounding in your wholeness, you open to the heart of healing that dwells in each moment. This kind of radical self-care empowers you to offer a world of good.

Not Too Tight, Not Too Loose

Musicians know that when tuning their stringed instruments, the strings vibrate best when they're not too tight and not too loose. There's a middle way, a place of balance where creative tension is optimal to create harmony and beauty. People have been aware of states of harmonious balance for millennia. The Greeks referred to this path between excessive indulgence and extreme deprivation as the Golden Mean. The middle way is not a joyless compromise; it is the golden path of enthusiasm and integral harmony. Not too tight. Not too loose.

Fear tightens heartstrings and can make our minds constrict, even freeze in dysfunction. Our energy feels brittle, edgy, and agitated. Sometimes, if fear or stress is intense or prolonged, we collapse or explode emotionally or psychologically. The term "nervous breakdown" is still used. Whether we come upon a tormenter, a new lover, or even think about a change, our hearts pound in our chest if stress hormones flood into our bloodstream. As we engage in social action, many emotions will arise. Some of us fear "getting swept away" by strong feelings, even positive ones

Awakened hearts and minds fine-tune and strengthen their ability to stay open to whatever is happening—suffering as well as happiness. We learn to be poised in the midst of the promise of the present moment and open to possibilities of renewal. The past does not strangle or the future threaten. Gradually, our mind is more calm and clear; useful skills of discernment, self-regulation, and empathic listening become more optimally tuned. By not allowing sensory input and agitated thoughts to convince us that we're overwhelmed, we calmly take one step at a time, one moment at a time. We keep calm and carry on. Peace grows as we manifest our goodness.

Challenges faced and handled with a degree of skillfulness strengthen our confidence and sense of self-efficacy. Throughout our lives, we may need to reinvent ourselves numerous times. Like a butterfly breaking out of its cocoon, stress and struggle may be necessary for a while to make us strong enough to thrive. A butterfly can soar only after it has put forth the effort to free itself from its cocoon, dried its wings, and strengthened in the process.

There is a creative tension between playing it safe and taking a risk. If we overvalue comfort and security, we often lose both the illusions of safety and the possibilities of freedom. Risk can be our most powerful teacher and offers tremendous opportunities for growth. It can also terrify us. We fear that if we open to either great light or deep suffering, to joy or anguish, we'll somehow disintegrate. It's our choice whether to drown in fearful sorrow or remember ways to relax tension, regulate our emotions, and honor our interconnectedness.

Humor is a universal, time-honored way to dissolve tensions and relax sinews that are strung too tightly. Comedy includes social commentary rich in folk wisdom. Comedian Lily Tomlin suggests, "For fast-acting relief, try slowing down." Walk in nature. The pace of industrialized society is not at the speed of life. Cortisol levels are cranked up and many people are wound too tightly, overbooked, overstressed, and exhausted. Movements to "unplug" from technology and set aside days for sacred rest are growing. How do you integrate time for renewal and the gift of humor in your life?

We need time and space for relaxation, recreation, and for the flow of creativity and compassion to arise that nurtures cultures of wellness.

In societies where city lights burn all night and cell phones are rarely turned off, mental illness, autism, and attention deficit disorders are on the rise. Despite increasing technological interconnectivity, loneliness and thought disorders are also increasing; many disenfranchised people are self-radicalizing and harming others terribly. It's tempting to escape with mood-altering substances or hide away in gated communities. Time for self-reflection is necessary so that our needs and options are more clearly understood. As we reestablish healthy boundaries, we preserve our well-being, including our psychological, spiritual, cognitive, emotional, and physical energy. How do you promote wellness in your life, your work place and your community?

Life needs healthy boundaries and space in which to grow. On the microscopic level, cell walls are semi-permeable to allow for the exchange of life nutrients. In his seminal book on interpersonal relationships entitled *I and Thou*, philosopher Martin Buber speaks about the importance of maintaining porous, not rigid, boundaries as human beings. Somewhat paradoxically, as we loosen defensive boundaries of our individual self, fear decreases. Free of dualistic perceptions and rigid boundaries, we unite in friendship; the river becomes the ocean.

Discernment is needed to determine which energies to allow into ourselves in any particular moment. These inputs can come from our minds, external environments and relationships, or the news media. There are days when it serves no one, especially ourselves, to learn more horrific details of an ongoing genocide. Sometimes what we have to offer is prayers and blessings, and at other times we're able to ride into the battle that must be fought.

Honor the flames of discernment and the living torch of intuition that guide you from within. Conservation of life energy is an act of respect. Recognize the people who truly support you and those who seem to drain you. Discover the ways in which you leak your life energy. As you explore your path of service, be awake and aware. Enjoying life is energizing. Learn to pay attention to the wisdom of your inner self and trust your intuition. The power of the living torch of intuition is mighty; its source of inner truth is love. For whom are you keeping your heart healthy?

Orenda—The Power to Promote Well-Being

The natural cycles of giving and receiving are powered by benevolent, beneficial energies. These positive energies of health and healing are resources available to each one of us. In Iroquois tribal traditions, this power that promotes well-being is known as *orenda*. As our generosity and compassion grow, our inner transformation becomes a great service to the world. Multi-dimentional cultures of wellness are created.

The healing that is required by our ravaged earth as well as the transformation of reckless resource extraction, greed, and injustice are beginning. These processes require empowerment and equity to be evident at every system level, from individual to global. The UN Declaration of Human Rights, written in 1948 after the Second World War, is an example of the power to promote our mutual well-being. Another is the Cochabamba Declaration, which was written after local Bolivian people retook their water supply. This Bolivian declaration called for a global agreement to protect the world's water resources, to secure every human's right to water, and to oppose its privatization. Philanthropic organizations such as Water for People put the agreement into action, engaging in participatory development of sewer and water resources in communities around the world.

An Iroquois understanding about social harmony is that its foundation is the strength and wholesomeness of engaged individuals. An element of these societies is their healthfulness, or *reason*—the soundness of mind, body, and spirit. Another is the quality of righteous power that is dispersed throughout society, not concentrated within hierarchies, a power that respects equality. For the Iroquois, righteousness, or *good news*, is "a wholesome doctrine that is good to be heard." Their vision of peaceful, equitable societies is possible when strong hearts and minds use power with sound reason, mobilizing compassion to promote well-being for all. Public health policies are prioritized.

At the heart of *orenda*, the power to promote well-being and the common good, is the perspective of *right relationship*. Right relationship preserves the integrity, stability, and wellness of the individuals and communities involved. A living ecology is sustained by the mutual interdependence of right relationships. Since economic systems often determine access to the means of life, both ecology and economics are domains of right relationship. Awareness of life united in "one law, one heart, one mind, one body" is the clearest understanding of our inter-relatedness within our essential oneness. Universal access to healthcare would reflect this awareness.

One of history's most notable humanitarian achievements occurred when a plant pathologist from Iowa, Norman Borlaug, Ph.D., used his power to promote well-being. The lineage of his goodness to go is described in Chapter 3, which focuses on the theme of our interconnectedness. Borlaug's integral service included the development of more resilient grain seeds that prevented the starvation death of over a billion people throughout the 1960s. With his crossbred wheat strain resistant to disease and capable of producing ten times more grain, Dr. Borlaug launched the scientific agricultural revolution. Countries with millions of hungry people, such as Mexico, Pakistan, China, and India, came to have not only the resource of more robust physical health but also the assurance of agricultural surpluses and food security.

Dr. Borlaug recognized that this increase in food production was a temporary measure allowing humanity time to address its logarithmic population growth on our finite planet. Because famine and starvation are intertwined with injustice, violence, and war, Dr. Borlaug was awarded the Nobel Peace Prize in 1970. He died in September of 2009, and although the agricultural industry is now rife with monopolies, subsidies, political ties, and numerous controversies, Dr. Borlaug bought us time to effectively address pivotal issues of integral health such as the population explosion, food and water security, human rights abuses, and resource disparities.

The economics of resource competition are related to inequities and structural violence that in turn are connected to environmental degradation, oppression, and violent conflict. Survival is a start but it's not enough; people want to thrive as they manifest their full potential. The work of both environmentalists and economists is most beneficial when it's based on a moral vision of the common good. Fortunately, we have the power to choose right relationship in service of everyone's well-being, forge effective new policies, and produce positive changes that benefit our planet and her inhabitants. Ultimately, the rising tide of wellness springs from the commitment of millions of individuals.

As you offer your goodness to go, every bit helps. Positive social connections and collaborations with others support our integral health and service. The vagal tone of our parasympathetic nervous system is increased during social interactions in which positive emotions are shared, however briefly. Health is enhanced and resilience amplified. Find ways that are enjoyable and meaningful for you to connect with others and give back in mutually empowering ways.

Creating Your Personal Plan for Well-Being

For each of the following areas of life related to your holistic well-being and management of life energy, record details about how you are doing currently. Be free of judgment. Then use the A*B*C*D Self-Inquiry process outlined at the beginning of Goodness To Go to clarify your current intentions, commitments, and goals. The three S's of goal-setting are useful as you develop action points that are *small, specific,* and *scheduled.*

1. Diet and Nutrition
2. Exercise and Fitness
3. Health and Self-Care
4. Emotions/Attitudes/Resilience
5. Life Purpose and Service
6. Relationships and Family
7. Spirituality
8. Stress Management

Balance as Integral Harmony

"Life is like riding a bicycle—in order to keep your balance, you must keep moving," observed Albert Einstein. Our natural state is dynamic homeostasis, that exquisitely intricate balancing process within our body as well as the earth's ecosystems. This living state is never static. Think of a mobile moving in space. Rather than a fixed state of balance, its beauty is a result of processes of balancing, harmonizing, and flow.

Some people fully engaged with life may have an irate response to the theoretical notion of "life balance." Although their busy lives may not look balanced, all of its elements have meaning for them and they're not ready or able to let go of some of their commitments. Life balance is not a linear, one-dimensional teeter-totter. The theologian Matthew Fox wrote, "We see that harmony does not mean a *balance-at-rest* but a vibrant, bi-polar energy force that urges on all other energy." Rather than some daily measure of equal weight, time, and space given to all aspects of life, our balancing acts may look different moment by moment. Sometimes we're dancing as fast as we can; at others we're juggling, cooking, cleaning, meditating, and financing creatively. This intricate dance is not about trying to achieve static balance, pinning down and lining up all the ducks in our lives.

Global activist Lynne Twist succinctly states: "I don't even seek that kind of balance. I'm about wholeness and integrity." Twist is passionately involved in numerous social profit projects around the world and is an evolutionary member of the emerging global community of "social prophets" who are manifesting new visions for creating a just, healthy, sustainable world. Social prophets and artists help to manifest the rebirth of our collective vision and a renaissance of spirit. For many members of this emerging community, integration is the new balance.

The quest for a harmonious, meaningful life is mythic and age old. Included are the seemingly mundane as well as the spiritual aspects of life, both of which emerge from one source. As we learn to experience this source and share the goodness within ourselves, we bring about harmony and balance. Happiness arises naturally when our everyday lives are integrated with our core values. Mahatma Gandhi wrote, "Happiness is when what you think, what you say, and what you do are in harmony."

This integrated harmony requires personal effort and courage. Thucydides was an ancient Greek historian whose realism continues to impact our perceptions of international relationships. He wrote, "The secret of happiness is freedom. And the secret of freedom is courage." Freedom empowers responaible action. Gradually, Athenians' courage waned to the point where they wanted freedom *from* responsibility. Wanting the government to keep them comfortable and safe, they soon ceased to be free and their dynamic, creative culture crumbled.

Many wisdom traditions have contributed to our understanding of dynamic life balance and reveal that the cultivation of courage and contentment is paramount. Courage is releasing and manifesting our goodness, and contentment is the deep sense of living in supreme wisdom and peace. Other aspects of contentment are freedom from craving as well as the discipline to contain desires so that we feel a sense of sufficiency.

Insatiable hunger for more undermines individual and planetary health. Excess food damages the natural digestive homeostasis of our bodies. The obesity of overnourishment leads to as much illness as undernourishment. In many cases, excess can be gauche, grotesquely destructive, and numbing. The Japanese term *wagamama* means "it's all about me." Does a family of three need a 15,000-square-foot *wagamama* McMansion? Fortunately, lifestyle patterns of unrestrained consumption of resources, overbuilding, and supersizing can be redefined. The deep contentment of sufficiency—that our needs are met, that we have enough, that we *are* enough—cannot be purchased, grabbed, or hoarded by materialistic mindsets or lifestyles. Sufficiency is a recognition that comes from within.

Finding, creating, and sustaining a health lifestyle may seem so elusive that frustration or cynicism takes over. If life is a river of change, not a static photograph frozen in time, why bother to strive for the seemingly impossible? A response may involve changing our perceptions and definitions of success, meaningfulness, and life balance. In this marvelously complex world, a bird's-eye view reveals a meta-balance inherent in creation. Johann Wolfgang von Goethe wrote, "So divinely is the world organized that every one of us, in our place and time, is in balance with everything else."

In their book *Living in Balance—A Dynamic Approach for Creating Harmony & Wholeness in a Chaotic World*, Joel and Michelle Levy write, "If you can learn to dance with the innumerable paradoxes of your life while staying anchored in an extraordinary suppleness and flexibility, you will create the stability necessary to actually find balance in your life." Each of us is unique, born with our own temperament, constitution, and one-of-a-kind genetic code. Our evolution within changing environments is also unique, providing opportunities to uncover what allows us to dance gracefully with the challenges and paradoxes of life and offer our gifts to the world.

The state of integral health is dynamic and adaptive to changes in our internal and external environments. According to Morihei Ueshiba, the great teacher of the Japanese martial art of aikido, eight forces sustaining the universe affect us: motion and stillness, strength and adaptation, contraction and expansion, and division and unification. Aikido means "the art or way of peace," and harmonizing these energies is key to integral health. We're fortunate to have a mind-body that can be trained, a spirit that can evolve, and a way to move forward. Practice the art of peace in everything you do.

Experience a new kind of life balance. Unite your mind with your breath, inhaling the subtle energy vitalizing life. Rest in the peace of the pause before the exhalation begins. From the still center within, experience and express your inherent goodness. There are numerous teachings, practices, and skills that support an inner state that harmonizes paradoxes, reconciles opposites, and helps us break free from contracting states of mind. What are some practices that you've found helpful in your personal life or that are woven into the cultural fabric of the society in which you live? How do you sustain your motivation to make healthy choices day after day?

Many of us aren't interested in what may be regarded as a spiritual practice or path. The renowned mythologist Joseph Campbell wrote that a spiritual life is the flowering and fulfillment of a human life, not a supernatural virtue imposed upon it. Traditions such as theosophy regard our interconnectedness as sacred. We may recognize the inherent interdependence of all things but choose not to refer to it as a *spiritual* interdependence.

As you develop the capacity to be nurtured by a life of dynamic balance and moderation, return to the still point within and rest deeply in its rejuvenating silence and wisdom. Your goodness will naturally spread its roots and wings, and you come to trust yourself ever more. Rejoice as the positive ripples, shoots, and currents of your actions resonate through the web of life.

Pause, Reflect and Record

- How might you actively work on your relationship with risk and change it in a way that's *not too tight, not too loose*?

- As you engage with inquiries throughout Goodness To Go, how is your understanding of "life balance," or harmonious integration of the many elements of your life, evolving?

- What do courage, patience, sufficiency, and the promotion of well-being have to do with integral service?

- Practice the Mountain Pose described earlier in the Personal Well-Being section of this chapter. As you engage in this practice, notice if you experience a sense of interconnectedness. If so, does this expansive awareness encourage responsibility for the whole?

21

Resilience—The Power
to Adapt and Endure

I am delighted to live in such a splendidly disturbing time.

—Helen Keller

Both life and its goodness to go are sustained by the power to adapt and endure. Since change is constant, and shocks can rarely be avoided, the resilience of our shock absorbers helps us to bounce back and try again as we creatively adjust, adapt, and evolve. Resilience comes from a Latin word meaning "to leap or bounce." Although stamina and fresh effort are involved, resilience is not blindly bouncing back with repetition of old behavior patterns. Innovators and change-agents recognize mistakes as great learning opportunities, and they don't let fear of failure stop them. Rarely do we accomplish a meaningful skill or goal with the first attempt; athletes, artists, and activists around the world remind us that disciplined resilience is required for any worthwhile endeavor.

Several years ago, scientists landed rovers on Mars, designing ways for their advanced technology to survive the impact of landing. The rovers were encased in material that allowed them to bounce repeatedly until coming to rest, and then open like petals, revealing their hardy, high-tech contents. *Spirit and Opportunity* continued their mission on Mars long past their expected lifespan. If we're to sustain enthusiasm for our integral service, we need to be able to bounce back after crash landings, pick ourselves up, dust ourselves off, and strengthen our resiliency.

When my daughter was eight years old, she reminded me, "Don't give up. Keep going. And don't be hard on yourself." A year later, we went for a hike on a glorious summer morning in the foothills of the Rocky Mountains. Starting life as a premature, abandoned orphan from Calcutta, Grace had already demonstrated her resilience in many ways. At times, however, her sensitive reactivity increased her vulnerability to emotional collapse, draining her power in the face of difficulties.

At one point on our long hike, after she'd fallen and scraped her knee, Grace was hot, tired, hungry, and in pain. Her resolve to keep walking the path with a positive attitude was waning. Suddenly, from a meadow of long grass flapped the small wings of a baby bird. It was having difficulty gaining altitude and flew directly at Grace, wing-tip feathers gently brushing my daughter's left ear. Sensing that her vitality had increased, I asked Grace what message the bird had whispered in her ear. After a few more steps along the trail, Grace answered with tender strength, "*Go on.*" This phrase has become my daughter's personal mantra of resilience.

Keep on keeping on. If at first you don't succeed, try, try again. How often have you marveled at the resilience of people? If at first we don't succeed, we're in good company. And we try again. There is a reservoir of energy within us that enables us to stand back up, lift our head, and walk forward. Thankfully, that living ember is never completely extinguished. We have endless opportunities to strengthen our resilience muscles, let go of the shore, and swim with consciousness through Consciousness.

Resiliency is a multifaceted attribute that illumines self-respect as well as confidence, creativity, and courage. Mark Twain observed that courage is not the absence of fear but resilience in the face of fear. Courage is the next best step we take after the one we just took. Vincent van Gogh was a largely self-taught artist who recognized that breakthroughs and creative progress were possible when he skillfully applied what he'd learned from mistakes. Van Gogh's resilient enthusiasm allowed him to unfold his unique gifts, honor the dignity of working people and the vitality of life through his paintings, and become one of the world's most iconic artists.

Self-doubt weakens our resiliency and can prevent us from taking the first step. Practice makes progress, and we strengthen our resilience muscles. As with most training programs, it's recommended to start with simple or small challenges. Experiment with five-pound weights to build capacity. Seek and find the good company of resilience and courage— they're contagious. When we take a stand to serve something larger than ourselves, energized resilience flows in to serve us.

Mindful Resilience

Resilience can lie dormant or thrive. The quality of our attention supports the nourishment and activation of our compassion and resiliency. When we use our attention consciously, instead of being swept into its fleeting, unfocused whirlpools, we connect to the living ground of the present moment. Instead of ruminating on old thoughts and feelings or being mesmerized by dramas and digital input, we're awake and present with the powerful energy of awareness. Trusting our resilience and creativity in the present moment, we have the confidence to rise again.

The *Harvard Business Review* placed resilience on top of a short list of qualities essential to success in life, regardless of how success is defined. Countless challenges, from family and health stresses to geopolitical crises and natural disasters, impact daily life. Our ability to adapt to adversity and start anew determines the quality of our relationships, satisfaction at work, and our ability to respond with wisdom and strength to what threatens to wear us down.

Radical changes of life circumstances as well as physical and mental health challenges are powerful teachers of tenacity and resilience. The ongoing rehabilitation of severely injured people requires tremendous resilience. Millions of people struggle daily with reduced mental and physical capacities. Some have been traumatized by violence, suffered disfiguring burns, or battled cancer and endured the consequences of treatment side effects. It's remarkable how many have been struck by natural disasters, betrayals, or the horrors of abuse and violence have been able to rebuild their lives.

Research on resiliency has described the impact of childhood circumstances, such as violence, poverty, neglect, and parental mental health, on a person's resilience as an adult. Their impacts can be long lasting because these circumstances often shape children's belief systems, which remain relatively stable throughout life without significant intervention. At the same time, having even one kind adult in their lives can be the saving grace that supports the development of children's resilience. *I'm in your court. I've got your back.* Although early environmental factors and traumas cannot be changed, it's possible to change our beliefs and increase our tolerance of genetic and environment challenges.

The positive impact of one supportive adult in a child's life can be psychologically subtle or physically dramatic. Years ago, an orphan in North Africa was wasting away despite sufficient caloric intake. Fortunately, a volunteer health worker recognized that the toddler's malnutrition was due to intestinal worms. Through the treatment process, the volunteer's bond with the child strengthened, and she eventually became the girl's adoptive mother.

It's possible to stand up again and again in the face of adversities and failures. Serving people with chronic disability is a potent reminder of the resilience and dignity of the human spirit. The remarkable Helen Keller, who was brilliant, blind, and deaf, actually *delighted* to live in challenging, disturbing times. Her National Center for Deaf-Blind Youths and Adults empowers the tenacity of people who look beyond disability to possibility.

Imagine the forbearance of an impoverished, uneducated girl crippled from polio living in war-torn eastern Congo whose story was included in Stacey Edgar's book *Global Girlfriends*. Argentine was the eldest of six children. Her mother, desperate to protect the children from armed invaders, would carry Argentine on her back into the bush, where her young daughter hid in a hole covered with brush for days or weeks, singing to herself and praying. After caring for her other children during the day, the mother returned at night to sleep with Argentine, bringing bits of food. Like her mother, Argentine developed a deep trust in providence and continues to marvel at her mother's resilience and love. Today, Argentine's income from a women's artisan cooperative in Goma, Congo pays the school fees for her younger siblings and helps to support her mother. The power of resilient optimism changes destinies.

Seven Abilities of Resilience

Resilience can be cultivated and enhanced. Regardless of the stories and circumstances that inspire service, resiliency is the attribute shared by those whose offerings are ongoing, even lifelong. The songwriter Odetta sings, "Any old way you can make it, baby, keep it movin' on." Other blues songs remind us not to focus on what we've lost but on what we've got left. Recognition of the abundant wisdom available to us inspires our thinking while succumbing to "poverty mentality" depletes us.

During tough times, resilient people don't get stuck in despair about the present or obsess about the past. They continue to engage in self-care that nourishes their well-being and helps them to think and act in resourceful ways. Instead of cracking the whip and trying to go faster or work harder, resilient people may slow down and attend to becoming more patient, kind, creative, and playful. Resilience is giving ourselves permission to make mistakes, mining them for lessons learned, and knowing what to keep and what to let go. We learn to forgive and even appreciate mistakes and respond with more skill.

There are many ways to understand and enhance resiliency. In their book, *7 Essential Skills for Overcoming Life's Inevitable Obstacles*, University of Pennsylvania researchers Karen Reivich and Andrew Shatte describe seven abilities that make up their "resilience quotient." Each of these measurable abilities can be taught and enhanced. In addition, they enrich all aspects of life, including integral service, and enhance communication and conflict skills needed to work effectively with challenges on all levels.

1 and 2: Emotion Regulation and Impulse Control

Self-regulation of our emotions and impulse control allow us to stay calm and cool in the face of unexpected conflicts or under prolonged pressure. Although some temperaments are naturally more skillful with emotions, attention, and behaviors, all of us can learn to apply self-regulation techniques that strengthen our equanimity, such as relaxation breathing, cognitive restructuring, and visualization. The ability to pause and redirect our attention is invaluable.

Children with immature brains and those with neuropsychiatric disorders such as autism are known to erupt with behavioral tantrums. However, most adults have also been hooked or hijacked by a surge of anger and "flipped their lid." This neologism has a degree of neurologic accuracy. Our neocortex, or "upstairs brain," developed around the older "downstairs brain" centers, including the limbic region and amygdala. This area is involved in the swift processing and expressing of emotions, especially fear and anger. When strong emotions activate our limbic system, it's as if our brain is on fire and we flip the regulatory lid of the balancing, decision-making part of our brain. The neuropsychiatrist Daniel Siegel has described this phenomenon in *Mindsight*.

3: Causal Analysis—Our Explanatory Style

Our minds restlessly search for a cause to our problems. "Who's to blame?" asks the grandfather in the film *Whale Rider* as soon as things don't go the way he expects. Our brains tend to react rather than respond, and we jump to blame rather than choose careful analysis. Recall the tendency of most of the jury members in Reginald Rose's play *Twelve Angry Men* to jump to an ill-considered conclusion about the guilt of the accused. It's a complex challenge to calmly and accurately identify the contribution that various elements make to a situation. For many, Monday mornings may be *associated* with excess stress, but this day of the week did not *cause* the stress; association is not causation.

Martin Seligman, Ph.D., the pioneering psychologist who wrote *Authentic Happiness*, has identified various thinking styles that contribute to our causal analysis of a problem. Optimists develop an explanatory style that accurately identifies their personal contribution to a problem, the likely time frame (few problems are permanent and forever), and how pervasive this problem is in their lives. In other words, they acknowledge their contribution to the problem and don't blow it out of proportion. Optimists trust that in all things goodness is at work. This explanatory style is empowering. When we don't feel helpless and hopeless, our ability to act positively and effectively in the world is enhanced.

4 and 5: Empathy and Reaching Out

Our nonverbal clues communicate much more about what we're thinking and feeling than our words. Sensitivity and adeptness with detecting and accurately interpreting nonverbal cues increase our empathy. Mirror neurons may contribute to our empathic ability to imagine what it would be like to be in another person's shoes and to experience compassion. When we're less brittle and judgmental, we're more flexible emotionally and behaviorally. It's easy to assume that other people think like us. Empathic skills free us from narcissistic, "it's all about me" tendencies and reduce the projection of our mistaken assumptions.

When our attention is fully present in the moment, we're more likely to challenge judgments as they arise and free ourselves from being controlled by anger or fear. It's helpful to have the council of wise teachings and a strong open mind and heart. The support of family and community members who understand the importance of being empowered to create one's path in life is invaluable. Doors unlock and windows open. Our example inspires others and thereby increases courage and resiliency in our communities. Many believe that invisible strings connect us and that every time one of us practices being resilient, it strengthens everyone else.

6 and 7: Realistic Optimism and Self-Efficacy

Resiliency is an essential element of our psychological immune system. Optimism, trust, and confidence are positive states that strengthen our hope for the future. People with realistic optimism are skillful at recognizing and then disputing pessimistic thoughts, such as *there are just too many problems in the world for one person to make any difference.* Resilient optimists are grateful for the opportunity to assist one starfish or child rather than bemoaning the impossibility of saving them all. They choose to see the proverbial cup as half full. Resiliency and trust in our ability to make a difference grow as we experience our self-efficacy.

Resilient Optimism

Like gratitude, optimism is an element of emotional intelligence and resiliency. Both are a kind of medicine that protects us from the distortions that conventional thinking often propagates. In 2009, medical researchers analyzing data from the Women's Health Initiative reported that optimism was associated with better health outcomes and increased longevity. Pessimistic, cynical, anxious, or hostile worldviews weaken our immune systems and increase stress hormones that contribute to hypertension and the chronic inflammation underlying many diseases such as coronary disease and dementia.

Optimism and gratitude fuel our flexibility, endurance, and ability to recover from being knocked down or off balance, compressed, overstretched, or traumatized. Resilience includes the enduring self-confidence that grows as we weather the storms in our lives, trust our ability to care for our needs, strengthen the courage to abide by our convictions, and manifest our dreams. Positive actions such as pursuing creative interests, taking classes, participating in bridge or book clubs, engaging in a revitalized exercise program, or serving others renew our sense of agency and control of life. When we're engaged in meaningful behaviors, our brain's fear-rage pathways can't fire at the same time.

Our minds and bodies bear the burden of trauma. Neurologist Robert Scaer's book *The Trauma Spectrum: Hidden Wounds and Human Resiliency* offers hope to those wanting to understand and transform trauma. If we're feeling stuck, there are many approaches to recover from trauma or to get free of the rut of resistance. Humor and laughter nourish optimism and refresh our resilience, even if it's to gently shake up our earnestness. In "laughing yoga," participants smile and exhale *Ha-Ha-*

Goodness To Go

Ho-Ho as they pantomime funny behaviors in exaggerated ways. When grief over the loss of a loved one seems consuming, recall a lighthearted time shared with them. Accentuating the positive and smiling with life's sweet ironies are universal ways to rejuvenate.

Breathe deeply and rest in the pause between exhalations and inhalations. Ask for help from your inner as well as outer guides. Contemplate words of wisdom and incorporate one teaching into your life each month. Create and regularly review a list of your accomplishments, the track record of successes that you've created. Keep a daily gratitude journal. Invaluable teachings about the power of persistence are contained in *When Things Fall Apart* by the American Buddhist nun Pema Chodron.

It's also helpful to stay connected with the goodness of family members and social networks. Setting aside ritual time to grieve losses or honor periods of adversity may release us from feeling pain twenty-four hours a day. Research has shown that just as our mind affects our body, the actions of our physical body also influence our mind. Walking in nature, sitting for daily meditation, visualizing beneficent images, and other mindfulness practices change the brain in ways that are detectable on neural imaging studies. Practicing resilient behaviors, even if you feel despair or grief, can strengthen you. Making the effort to imagine, pretend, or "force" a smile—*faking it till you make it*—has benefits on our neuropsychology.

With a greater sense of resilient well-being, most people feel less burdened and more able to engage with life fully. Many survivors of natural disasters and abuse, parents who've lost their children to illness or violence, and others who've suffered devastating traumas have found that sharing their stories and wisdom, as well as giving of themselves in other ways, is an important part of the process of coming back into their lives. Gradually, the light of the heart beams through seemingly impenetrable darkness. The process of recovering enthusiasm for life requires wellsprings of energy, generosity, discipline, and supportive community members.

Participating in life's ongoing cycles of giving and receiving, including integral service, takes committed resilience. The power and discipline of resiliency sustains loyalty to our convictions, which are not forsaken when they're inconvenient. Those with strong spiritual practices often see their commitment to integral service as a manifestation of living life as worship.

Resilience—The Power to Adapt and Endure

Practical optimists trust their ability to handle difficulties because they've experienced firsthand meeting challenges with flexibility and a degree of equanimity. Their self-esteem is based on real experiences of self-efficacy that are sustained by self-care. Resilience is not a steely resolve forcing us to ignore exhaustion. Resilient optimists experience a deep knowing that no expression of goodness goes to waste. They experience the meaningfulness of offering their time, energy, finances, and skills; they don't fixate on expectations of success, and they're aware of the pitfalls of attachment to praise or blame.

As your resilience muscles grow in strength, let go of the shore and enjoy swimming through and with consciousness moment by moment. Release rumination on old thoughts, feelings, and paradigms. Wake up and be here now, fully present with the powerful energy of awareness.

Goodness to go is sustained by the awareness that there is a greater purpose in everything that happens. Regular self-care rejuvenates us so that we have the energy and resilience to keep on keeping on. Enjoy the entire process of conserving, strengthening, and utilizing resilience. You can dare. Risk. Dream. Help a child. Create a new world. Yes you can.

Pause, Reflect, and Record

- Describe an experience you've had of each of the seven skills that contribute to resiliency: emotion regulation, impulse control, explanatory style, empathy, reaching out, realistic optimism, and self-efficacy.

- How do you maintain equilibrium as life's rogue waves crash over you? In what ways do you or could you strengthen your resilience?

- Revisit a service goal that you're resisting in some way. How could you strengthen your confidence and resilience and change habits of procrastination?

22

Taking a Stand

Give me a place to stand, and I'll move the world.

—Archimedes

We want our lives to be enjoyable and meaningful. When we take a stand to mobilize our goodness in benevolent, skillful ways, we create the life of our dreams. As we commit to global equity and sustainability, we need a place to stand and ways for our voices to be heard. Our souls call to take a stand for something bigger than ourselves. Eleanor Roosevelt lived her conviction that the great task of our time is making international human rights matter. She recognized that there are harmful errors of omission as well as commission. "What you don't do," she once said, "can be a destructive force."

When we take a strong stance for integral service, we're able to hold our ground when the going gets rough; we're rooted in resiliency, not rigid in righteousness. Taking a stand with integrity requires ongoing self-care, self-inquiry, and suppleness in response to changing needs.

In *Yes* magazine, the veteran global activist Lynne Twist wrote:

> Taking a stand is a particular distinction—a way of living, a way of being—that enables a human being to discover a place within themselves that is the very heart of who they are. ... The stand you have taken expresses who you are and enables you to speak and act with authenticity, power, and clarity. ... When you take a stand, you have the capacity to move the world. ... The power of taking a stand can shape people's lives and actions in a way that they have access to profound truths that can empower the emergence of new paradigms and shift the course of history.

Goodness To Go

Our commitment to the stand we've taken makes us who we are. It's an act of radical goodness to take a stand for principles such as global human equity. Thomas Jefferson wrote, "In matters of principle, stand like a rock." This pivotal time in human history calls us to embrace our power. Noble, everyday stories around the world about people who've taken ethical stances inspire us to move into integral service. If not now, when? As we take a stand for what we care about, we move into action with wisdom and compassion.

Dr. Oliver Wendell Holmes was a renowned physician living in the 1800s. Although he understood "taking a stand" as a principled conviction, Holmes was primarily interested in the *conduct* that those principles inspired. Dr. Holmes wrote, "I find the great thing in this world is not so much where we stand, as in what direction we are moving. ... We must sail, and not drift, nor lie at anchor." Dr. Holmes observed that once our minds are stretched by new ideas, they never regain their original dimensions.

Many notable visionaries, including Nelson Mandela, Mother Teresa, Mahatma Gandhi, Jane Goodall, and Jimmy Carter, have taken a stand, stretched our minds, moved the world, and empowered our lives. Of course, there are countless unsung. Abolitionists were hung by fellow citizens. For decades, suffragettes withstood tremendous social ridicule and imprisonment so that women could vote. Recall someone in your life whose courageous integrity inspires you and whose impact has been uplifting.

As we mature and evolve, mindfully engaging in self-care and letting go of attachment to the fruits of our actions, goodness manifests through all of our actions. When we know our own worthiness, our gifts ripple out to help others. Positive change happens from the inside out. The Dalai Lama reminds us, "A positive future can never emerge from the mind of anger and despair." In what ways do you want to be an uplifting presence in the world?

A mind that experiences stillness and equanimity is invaluable. You may have heard maxims such as "Love peace, don't hate war" and "Work for love rather than rage against evil." In 1997, a physicist-philosopher named Will Keepin, Ph.D., spoke at Schumacher College in Totnes, England, at a conference exploring how to take a stand to work for love and peace. Dr. Keepin consistently has taken a stand for gender reconciliation and for the peace that emerges from integrity. His integral service empowers the mutual respect that informs all healthy relationships, whether they're between women and men or humans and the earth.

At the conference, Dr. Keepin summarized participants' dialogues about the application of spiritual teachings to social change. The importance of balancing mind and heart and of grounding actions in both intelligence and compassion was emphasized. The integrity of one's intention and motivation informed the first principle of spiritual leadership. Like many before them, these social change artists recognized the primacy of acting from compassion and doing whatever inner work was required to implement this intention.

Kindness can release life energy that is congealed in negative states, freeing it to become our ally. Inner self-inquiry and maturation goes hand-in-hand with the outer work of social, political, and environmental transformation. One informs the other. Gradually, personal and global metamorphosis occurs.

"Life shrinks or expands according to one's courage," wrote Anais Nin. What we stand for now will determine what future we create for our planet, future generations, and ourselves. If we plant seeds of perennial wisdom and intelligent design, our vision of equitable, healthy communities for our children's children can be harvested. We'll need to imagine and walk into that which we do not yet see. In our busy, noisy world, it requires commitment, patience, and courage to listen to the wisdom of our own heart, awaken our minds, take a stand to live in alignment with our principles, and expand life's possibilities for everyone.

Cultivate the goodness is an inspiring phrase invoked by Hawaiians. In the 1970s, a young graduate student cultivated the goodness when she decided to trust her inner voice and follow her own drummer. In Chapter 17, we looked at the stand that Frances Moore Lappé took as she listened to the promptings of her curiosity and questions. The result of her research was *Diet for a Small Planet*, an internationally acclaimed book that woke us to the political factors underlying and perpetuating world hunger.

After decades of involvement in various social justice initiatives, Lappé wrote *You Have the Power—Choosing Courage in a Culture of Fear*. In it, she speaks about our intense need for connection that can cause us to violate our values and even common sense. Lappé observes, "This is understandable in part when we remember that humans evolved in cultures where being cast out could literally bring death." However, we now have increased opportunities to chart our own life course. "We can be truer to ourselves, consciously choosing those who see us for who we are and encourage us to live our lives fully," she reminds us.

We live is a wired, and even wireless, world. Some media sites refer to communities of like-minded people as tribes. More people in many countries are increasingly able to find or create a tribe that nurtures who they are and what they value. As people e-mail, telephone, Skype, text message, tweet, or share Facebook updates, new connections are forged in real-world and virtual communities. Work, school, sports, artistic, and service communities exist, however, only when people actively build and maintain relationships.

With so many opportunities to interact within a supportive community in our information age, it's easier to find our voice, access our inner courage, and take a stand for our commitments without the fear of being shunned or ostracized. *World Pulse*, for example, is a global media and communication network devoted to bringing women a global voice. Vocal empowerment is on the rise, including in our personal lives. As we see consumerism becoming bloated and full of arrogance, we adjust our behavior and speak out. If we insist that children's agendas be protected, we vote for politicians who've demonstrated their support and get involved with social profit agencies that support children. My daughter's middle school class researched the extent of involuntary servitude on sites like *Slave Tracker*. Many students were dismayed to know that their family's lifestyle depended on slave labor and committed to learning more about the ethics of the companies selling the products that they purchase.

Zainab Salbi, the inspirational founder of Women for Women International, wrote, "This time, like no other time, is a day and a time in history where we need to reassess what is truly important to us as individuals, as a society, as members of a country, as citizens of the world." The plight of our world calls for us, at times, to misbehave with integrity.

Although prolonged emphasis on left-brained logic has produced technologic marvels, we're dangerously out of balance. "Look where reason has got us," pointed out playwright George Bernard Shaw nearly a century ago. We need the natural creativity of our true, wild nature and the integration of both left and right brain hemispheres to devise new paradigms and develop sustainable systems to manage complex issues in just, life-affirming ways.

Beyond Compliance with the Status Quo

Throughout history, the transformative insights and behaviors of artists, visionaries, scientists, iconoclasts, and morally committed individuals have been criticized as being unreasonable. They *acted up* and made history. Nearly everyone who has accomplished positive social transformation has been a nonconformist who has kept the spirit of resistance alive. Rosa Parks kept her seat on the bus and sparked the civil rights movement. Suffragettes marched and acted up on behalf of women's right to vote.

The effectiveness of social and environment activists' noncompliance is based on their discernment that some traditions and customs are not aligned with personal or constitutional core values. Social artists often refuse to conform to unjust prevailing beliefs of their day, and their commitment supports their willingness to be ridiculed or abused and in some cases to give their lives.

Many people across the globe have pledged their lives to ending prejudice, slavery, environmental ignorance, religious oppression, genocide, colonial rule, and gender inequality. Their courage and commitment give us much for which to be grateful. In 1837, President Andrew Jackson reminded us, "Eternal vigilance by the people is the price of liberty, and you must pay the price if you wish to secure the blessing." We share the privilege and responsibility to remain informed and vigilant so that everyone's human rights are protected.

Soon after I began writing *Goodness To Go*, thoughts about noncompliance with the status quo arose as I drove to work one morning. The pithy, aphoristic instruction to "misbehave—with integrity" that Dr. Clarissa Pinkola Estes had inscribed in my copy of her book, *Women Who Run with the Wolves*, came to mind. At one point, my attention shifted to an unusual phrase printed across a gray truck in front of me: DISRUPTIVE THINKER TRANSPORT: In short order, my puzzlement gave way to laughter. *Disruptive thinker transport?*

Initially, the medical part of my brain visualized disabled citizens with delusional mental illness. Was this a division of our local Special Transit? But the van looked so … institutional. Was it part of the penal system? As I passed the truck, I glimpsed the words *creative justice*. Not until later did I learn that this van belonged to an internationally respected marketing firm known for its innovative ideas.

Goodness To Go

Creative thinking is certainly capable of disrupting the status quo. Innovative thinking that includes resilience in the face of resistance is essential to implementing positive changes. Consider the revolutions in computer design and information technology that Steve Jobs accomplished, achieving his aspiration "to put a ding in the universe."

The punishment of disruptive thinkers throughout history may underlie our fears about getting out of line. *Who do you think you are?* The Inquisition killed midwives and healers and many political dissidents are imprisoned, tortured, and murdered. Understandably, we want to avoid the dire consequences or ostracism that could befall us if we're not "well behaved" or dare to question blind obedience to the status quo. We may regress into feelings of being a "bad" boy or girl waiting to be punished.

Life requires courage, which is especially important in the conscious creation of a reverent and just world. What might be provoked by the demeaning taunt implied in *who do you think you are*? Who will you be if you're no longer the eternally compliant, reasonable good girl or boy? Will you be ostracized? Banished? Now is the time to address and grow beyond those fears as we reassess what is truly important as citizens of the world.

The pioneering African American attorney Thurgood Marshall who died in 1993 was named Thoroughgood at birth. He served as the chief council for the National Association for the Advancement of Colored People (NAACP) and as solicitor general of the United States. Marshall wrote, "Listen to others but do not become a blind follower. ... Where you see wrong or inequality or injustice speak out. This is your democracy— make it—protect it—pass it on."

Early in the nineteenth century, the Scottish philosopher Thomas Carlyle declared, "Conviction is worthless unless it is converted into conduct." Actions aligned with our integrity create a more wholesome future. The poet Emily Dickinson wrote, "Sow an act, and you reap a habit. Sow a habit and you reap a character. Sow a character and you reap a destiny."

The paradigm of *We* involves "servant" or service-based leadership. Many people have served as living examples of the leadership that encourages everyone to live as an example to others. Personal responsibility is liberty. We always have this responsibility to our own life and to the entire world. We are all leaders, and whether we're a single mother or the leader of a gang or a country, we can take a stand that moves our communities toward social equality and justice.

230

The Relationship Between Intentions and Goals

Poets and visionary leaders in every culture have noted that dreams are necessary to living life fully. To take a stand and pursue our dreams requires imagination, strong intention, resilience, confidence, discipline, and other resources. Learning to live intentionally with trust includes the development of skillful means, experiences of personal efficacy, and clarifying our inner and outer priorities. Author Phillip Moffitt and others describe outer priorities as external actions or goals we'd like to achieve and inner priorities as our resolve about the way we intend to be as we act.

The inspiration to take a stand and share our gifts naturally springs from our gratitude and compassion. The active expression of gratitude is applied appreciation for all that we've received. Skillful means allow us to translate our deepest values into practical assistance that empowers everyone involved and uplifts the situation. For example, it's more effective, respectful, and skillful to first ask people what they need rather than deliver donations that are unsustainable, of little use, or that disempower the recipients with dependency.

Intentions are based on our motivations and *how* we'll be as we act. Both surgeons and assailants may have the goal of slicing open someone's chest but their intentions are very different. The surgeon moves her scalpel with the intent to assist the process of healing while the intentions of knife-wielding assailants are less wholesome. Right intention, taught the Buddha, is to treat yourself and others with loving kindness and compassion.

The practice of setting our clear intent includes awareness of our state of mind in each moment. Our ability to act from our clear intent blossoms as our understanding of our inner values grows. Clarifying, refreshing, and applying our intentions is a practice that requires daily renewal that includes being mindful and ethical. We may have a goal to ace next week's test; whether our intention is to cheat or to relish the opportunity to prepare with diligence determines how we'll manifest that goal.

Goals focus on *what* we'll do to create an envisioned future. This future orientation is useful in deciding how to allocate our resources. Intention and commitment are interrelated. Although to err is human, and our alignment slips out of place at times, our sustained commitment to personal integrity allows us to reset our course. Honorable intentions are not codified moral laws where noncompliance spurs guilt for errors of commission or omission. Judgment and guilt drain life energy that could be directed to what matters. We need all of the strength and courage available to us to work for peace, listen to all sides, transform dysfunctional systems, and empower people.

Living our intentions is *being* our values in this present moment. When we're grounded in the meaning and larger context of our true intentions, we're more resilient. As we meet obstacles or setbacks, we keep the big picture in mind as we evaluate our inner state, our skillful actions, and our approach to manifesting our goals.

Cultivating Clear Goals and Intentions

As we take a stand and initiate offerings of integral service, it's useful to contemplate and articulate our inner and outer priorities on a regular basis. Our intentions, motivations, and goals evolve. When our intentions are aligned with our values, we have an increased sense of authenticity and more clarity about our external goals.

At times, our priorities may be unclear or in conflict. Uncertainties and challenges often arise that can be seen as unexpected opportunities for growth or as obstacles that stop us in our tracks. Many factors affect how we interpret and respond to our thoughts and feelings about life's uncertain reference points and difficulties. Do we collapse in disappointment, quit in frustration, or remember the value we place on serving humanity? Active self-care involves the process of self-inquiry and identifying what may be sabotaging our best intentions.

Ask yourself, "How might I be getting in my own way?" or "What are the effects of my attachment to this outcome?" Answering with deep honesty frees us from self-imposed limitations and decreases fixation on achieving a particular goal. Although it's liberating to redefine what is within our field of possibility, it is counterproductive to cling to a goal or whip ourselves with harsh criticism. Many things are simply out of our control. Clarifying inner priorities about our values and the inner state with which we intend to act enhances our resilience and flexible balance when external events don't go the way we planned.

Like setting intentions, goal-making is a valuable skill. Goals focus on the future and on *what* we want to accomplish. Commitment to a future outcome provides direction to our actions and helps to organize our time and energy. Remembering to be free of attachment to the fruits of our labor is very helpful. We do our best and let it go. Often this is much easier said than done. It's challenging to both engage in the achievement of a cherished goal and witness the unfolding of events with equanimity. How do you let go and not give up?

Periodic reappraisal of both our inner and outer priorities within the context of what is going on in our lives is valuable. It's also helpful to break down goals into small, specific, scheduled steps. Before scheduling those steps—the *what* you intend to do—reflect on the *whys* and *hows*. Begin by focusing your self-inquiry on these key questions:

1. *Why am I drawn to this course of action?*
2. *How does this goal align with my personal integrity?*
3. *Do I have, or can I attract, sufficient resources?*
4. *How will I track the results?*

Goals are more easily reached if they express core values, are beneficial to yourself and others, and energize you. Integral service goals are nourished by altruistic motivation. How clean are your intentions? Will you free up the time and summon the courage required to manifest your goal? How important is it to track progress? Are you willing to let go of attachment or aversion to success or failure, to the outcomes and fruits of your labor?

Phillip Moffitt, the founder of the Life Balance Institute, explores the clarity of our intentions and the goals that spring from them. In *Emotional Chaos to Clarity: How to Live More Skillfully, Make Better Decisions, and Find Purpose in Life*, Moffitt suggests that we have two responsibilities if we want to manifest our intentions: one responsibility is self-inquiry and the other is self-effort.

An aspect of self-inquiry is checking in with ourselves regularly throughout each day, remembering our deepest intentions for our lives, and asking ourselves if we're being true to them. If we're not, our responsibility is to put forth the effort to immediately start doing so to the best of our ability. Pause. Remember. Inquire. Realign. It wastes precious life energy to criticize ourselves for forgetting. We can hold the intention that when we remember to realign with our values, we'll celebrate with a moment of self-acknowledgment.

Like any muscle or habit, the resolve to live according to our values develops strength and consistency by daily practice. With gentleness, we nurture and cultivate something we care about. Experience the benevolence of gentleness in your own being. Remember to be patient when you forget or get lost in emotional reactivity. With loving kindness, come home to yourself. It is an intention to live intentionally, not a goal to be grasped.

Pay attention all along the way. It can take years of mindful practice to make steadfast the commitment to living intentionally day by day. Being less controlled by fear is one of the many benefits experienced as our resolve deepens. The muscle of resolution creates a joy and satisfaction that removes or transcends fears fed by ego-mind. There is freedom in knowing that our allegiance is with things more important than fear.

Thousands of years ago, wise beings articulated their intentions and took a stand for the unification of our hearts and minds. In the sacred Hindu text known as the Rig Veda, a prayer says, "Let us be united. Let us speak in harmony. Unified be our hearts and perfect be our unity." Positive intentions usually lead to positive results, even if those results are mostly about who we become as a result of our commitment to manifesting meaningful goals. By remembering our heart and mind's clarified intent, we share the gifts of self-respect and peace of mind, whether or not we achieve the desired outcome. Do what you can with what you've got where you are.

Strengthening Resolutions and Goals

- Clarify a service goal that you want to achieve. Why do you want this to happen? What is the strength of your commitment to its manifestation? Be enthusiastic and specific. With clear, simple language and strong resolution, articulate your dream, vision, or goal.

- With this positive frame of mind and gentle smile, imagine yourself achieving your goal with the best possible outcome for all involved. Fuel your visualizations and resolutions with empowering images, energy, and emotions, articulating them in the present tense.

- Remember and repeat your resolution throughout each day. Consider connecting this practice with a daily activity, such as when you drink a glass of water, sit down at your computer, or step over the threshold of your home.

- While honoring your present responsibilities, take s stand and focus the eye of your heart on your resolution. Create action steps related to the service project that interests you. Expand your horizons and dare to have big dreams so there's room to grow into them. List your intentions and goals, and schedule specific steps of your action plan. Find or create communities that support you and your commitment to manifesting your dream.

Pause, Reflect, and Record

- What are your core values and priorities at this point in your life? How might you cultivate and sustain a strong intention for a specific service goal that is grounded in your core values?

- What is one thing for which you are willingly to take a stand? Describe in detail.

- What is your deepest intention for your life?

- For at least a week, practice mindfulness. Notice gaps between thoughts and breaths. In those brief gaps, extend the pause and consciously choose whether to nurture a specific thought or to abide in silence. Describe your experience.

- Record questions, insights, inquiries, and action steps from Section Two with which you'd like to engage further.

Section Three

Mobilize Integral Service

23

Moving from
Concern to Action

My actions are my only true belongings.
I cannot escape the consequences of my actions.
My actions are the ground on which I stand.

—Thich Nhat Hanh

In the first two sections of *Goodness To Go*, we've summoned our awakened heart and empowered our mind. We've experienced how the in-breath of self-care sustains our resilience with daily practices of compassion and mindfulness. We've looked at freeing ourselves from fear and changing the way we think to create the world we want. And we recalled that for millennia, wise beings have taught that the intention to benefit all beings is the best of all thoughts and a key to being wholly alive.

In this section of *Goodness To Go,* compassion moves into action. Although integral service is rooted in compassion and conviction, it takes flight as benevolent action. Edward Everett Hale, a brilliant historian and Unitarian clergyman who supported the anti-slavery movement, wrote, "I am only one, but still I am one. I cannot do everything, but still I can do something. And because I cannot do everything I will not refuse to do the something that I can do."

Our world needs our concern and conviction to move into conduct. Whether we're passionate about the just, the sublime, or both, it's time to become warriors of the human spirit. As we pause now in the potency of potential, it's important to recognize that the breath of inspiration grounds in sustainable action. Otherwise, it tends to fade away with the next breeze, global threat, or negative thought that comes along.

This is a place of transition and threshold on our journey of discovering and manifesting our goodness to go. Resourced with the inspiration of well-being, we're ready for the out-breath of integral service. From whom much is given, much is required. Personal freedoms and resources such as time, energy, skills, and education are privileges that are accompanied by the responsibility to use them well. Financial resources beyond those necessary to meet genuine needs flow most meaningfully when others benefit as well.

On the transpersonal level, it's a time when new paradigms of thought and social action are emerging even as consequences of old mindsets based on fear and abuse of power run rampant on the physical plane. Nearly every social contract, including trust in our religious and banking institutions, has been broken. Scandals injure individuals as well as societies. Despair may be understandable but staying stuck in it wastes our creativity, compassion, and energy. Life asks us to care for life.

Imagine and explore paths of integral service. Beware of analysis paralysis. Some creative forms of goodness to go include teaching impoverished children to express themselves through art, photography, and poetry. Social artistry calls others to engage in challenging political and environmental arenas. For millions of people, Earth Day is every day. The generous patience, humility, and fecundity of the Earth feed us and offer ground that we call home. For our violence and poisonings of her beauty, we ask forgiveness, wrote the Irish poet and philosopher-priest John O'Donohue.

A grassroots affiliation based on activist spirituality is called Reclaiming. This organization is founded on earth-based spirituality, which claims that nature and the physical world are sacred and one with spirit. One of its founders understands the resistance people may feel as they consider becoming socially or politically active. In her book *Pagan Visions for a Sustainable Future*, Starhawk writes:

> No sane person with a life really wants to be a political activist. ... Activism tends to put one into contact with extremely unpleasant people, whether they are media interviewers, riot cops, or at times, your fellow activists. ... Nonetheless, at this moment in history, we are called to act as if we truly believe that the earth is a living, conscious being that we're part of, that human beings are interconnected and precious, and that liberty and justice for all is a desirable thing. ... Reclaiming folks have been out there—taking part in marches and demonstrations and protests ... and doing proactive work beyond the protest—helping to organize our communities, providing

healing, food, nurturance for children, music, art, and ritual—all the things that embody the world we want to live in.

As we begin to contemplate the forms of goodness to go and embody the world we want to live in, maxims of our parents may echo through our minds: "A winner never quits, and a quitter never wins;" "Be up, be doing. Busy hands are happy hands." We've probably heard the phrase "Just do it" several times in our lives, or "There's no trying, there's only doing." Think of a time when you've worked toward a goal despite the real possibility that obstacles, mistakes, and other setbacks could prevent its achievement. What helped you to *go for it* and possibly *get it done*? Reflect on internal and external factors that support your transition from motivation and concern to skillful, beneficial action.

Allow Compassion to Be Your Guide

A life well lived leaves a legacy of benevolence, of beauty and healing, or the enhancement of others' opportunities. How do we begin to embrace our integral service? A good place to start is waking up to the present moment. The nineteenth-century English poet Percy Bysshe Shelley implored us "to remove the scales from our eyes." Like many, Shelley observed how we get caught in habits of ignoring the environment and people around us. Stuck on automatic pilot, many of us tweet and text and miss the sunrise glory shining through the window.

In 1836, inspired by Eastern spiritual texts, Ralph Waldo Emerson set out the values of the American Transcendentalist movement in his book entitled *Nature*. Emerson wrote, "To the attentive eye, each moment of the year has its own beauty, and in the same field, it beholds, every hour, a picture which was never seen before, and which shall never be seen again." Many forms of goodness to go are inspired by deep awe and respect for the gift of life. The love of nature and animals draws many people to environmental or wildlife protection. Abolishing all forms of slavery that continue around the world compels others to act.

Spiritual and religious communities in every culture have service or mission work that calls forth their members' goodness to go. We may be inspired, invited, or drafted into offering our skills and resources. Of course, even if we're drafted for service, it's usually our choice whether we agree to participate. Many conscientious objectors choose jail, exile, or community service over military service.

Goodness To Go

Even when we've chosen to heed a calling to integral service, there are many ways to dodge or qualify our commitment to its less desirable aspects. Although it's easy to enjoy the adorable moments of parenting, pulling ourselves out of bed again to attend to a screaming child requires fortitude. Every night, pagers and cell phones wake firefighters, physicians, and other professionals who provide 24/7 on-call service. It often takes time to accept wholeheartedly the service that calls us on any particular day, and if we're unwell or exhausted, it's especially important to allow compassion to be our guide. Initially, we might agree halfheartedly, submit, succumb, or surrender to our commitment. For our service to be sustainable, eventually we need to embrace it fully.

Individuals have unique histories, constitutions, and personalities, and there are countless paths of service. Each of us has our own journey of readiness to express our goodness to go. People genetically predisposed to anxiety benefit from working gently and diligently to calm their nervous systems, strengthen their resiliency muscles, and maintain a degree of mental health. Others have experienced emotional or physical traumas that impact their current ability to commit to sustained service. There are many effective somatic and psychoanalytic therapies available to support the healing process. Often, the compassion that deepens through these experiences is a gift that wounded healers share in their integral service with others.

Only you know the thickness of your skin, the facets of your temperament, your current state of resilience, and the vitality of your health and energy. At different times in your life, you may have more or less space, time, and energy, physically or psychically, around the focus of your concerns. Sometimes you're able to send a check to support a peace initiative. In other chapters of your life, you might create a philanthropic foundation, volunteer in a classroom, write a letter to a political representative or media source, join the global abolitionist or reproductive justice movements, or organize a local rally to end gender-based violence and inequity.

Go at your own pace and forgo judgment of yourself and others. Time contains our moments of life, and how we allot our time determines the quality of our lives. Although time management is useful, skillfully managing our life's energy is especially valuable. As we learn more about ourselves, we'll discover activities and ways of being that energize us. We'll identify habits that leak or squander our life's energy. Start to notice and map your personal rhythms, involvements, and patterns of energy.

Below are five variations on the theme of *Yes! I will show up in service*. Your experience may be a combination of any number of these categories—or something entirely unique. In a sense, all of these ways of engagement in integral service are a response to a calling. Which are most congruent with your personal style?

Five Styles of Showing Up

1. Diving in

Some folks are divers whose courage to leap into the deep end of activism seems apparent from an early age. They know there's no lifeguard on duty but trust that they'll build fins or wings along their way. Divers also know how to flow around or over obstacles and how to circumvent them when necessary. Like most people whose goodness is on the go, divers often have had powerful mentors and role models whose example, inspiration, and teachings inform their lives of service.

Frequently, activism arises from viewing or experiencing injustice. Think of some of the countless unsung heroes who've given their lives to creating a just society. In 2001, four mothers in Colorado were concerned that the rights of children would be overshadowed in the aftermath of the terrorist attacks on the World Trade Center in New York. They dove in with their pro-child agenda and created Mothers Acting Up (MAU). For ten years, MAU inspired and mobilized advocacy on behalf of the world's children.

One of MAU's co-founders, Joellen Raderstorf, has a long history of diving into situations where injustice is present. Raderstorf is the fifth of six children whose father worked for the railroad. Her next older brother was born with Down's syndrome, and she experienced firsthand many prejudiced reactions to his differences. Raderstorf's love for her brother led her to value differences, honor the uniqueness of individuals, and to "love the underdog." These values motivated her to mobilize courage to speak up for positive change.

As the mother of three sons raised to be global citizens, Raderstorf is a go-giver. Her years of speaking truth to power began as a lobbyist for pro-justice and anti-poverty policies with a citizen activist group called Results. In several of her high-powered industrial engineering positions, Raderstorf was the only woman on her work teams. She started an organic food cooperative, and after barely escaping the 2004 tsunami in Thailand was stranded with her family on a hilltop with people from all

over the world. As she grows more grounded in an awareness of impermanence, the knowledge that anything can change at any time, Raderstorf's advice is "keep stepping through each moment and give the best
you can."

2. Direct connection

Some sort of direct connection with an issue may be the most common
source of inspiration for starting on the path of service. Very likely it
plays a part in all of the styles of showing up with heart in hand. Kari
Grady Grossman, author of the award-winning book *Bones That Float: A
Story of Adopting Cambodia*, founded a school in Cambodia after adopting her son from a nearby orphanage. Following years of international
philanthropy associated with their Cambodian school, Kari and her husband, George, expanded their vision to form Sustainable Schools International.

Being an adoptee can also inspire the heart of service. Ana, an infant
girl in Peru, was adopted by a couple who provided her with a privileged
life in the United States. As early as her adoptive mother could remember, Ana Dodson longed to see her birthplace where her biological mother
had died. When Ana was eleven, her parents took her to Cuzco, Peru,
where they came across a struggling orphanage for girls. Ana knew she
could have ended up there had she not been adopted.

With passion ignited to assist the Hogar Mercedes de Jesus Molina orphanage, Ana founded Peruvian Hearts when she returned to the United
States. Donor funding has created lunch programs and library projects,
purchased chickens, financed installation of a hot-water system for the
orphanage, created greenhouses and education funds, established partnerships with medical missions, and purchased a candle-making stove
for the girls to make candles to sell. Ana has received numerous commen-
dations including the Kids with Heart Award, and is one of the young
leaders of today who is changing the world one heart at a time.

3. Concerned sensibility

People are sensitized to humanitarian and heed calls to direct action in
many ways. Initially, we might offer compassionate words or make philanthropic donations. Tom Hayden has been an outspoken advocate for
civil rights, social justice, peace, and environmental protection for over
fifty years. It was Dr. Martin Luther King, Jr., who first encouraged the
young writer to cross the line from observation to direct action.

Gratitude for our blessings and good fortune often fuels a desire to offer thanksgiving in the form of direct service. Many people understand service as the rent we pay for the space and resources we use on this magnificent planet. Good deeds are a way to begin to repay our debt. Although it may be that we can never pay off our debts completely, we can "pay it forward." We support the next person in need who we meet, the next species, landscape, or endangered natural resource, as well as the next generation. For nearly forty years, the abolitionist William Lloyd Garrison resolutely moved against the tide of opposition, laid the moral groundwork for the abolition of slavery, and bent the arc of history. When one door was closed for a while, he'd find a window that would open and collaborators to join the cause.

One mother shared a thread of her journey toward global service. When her daughter was eighteen months old, the child was diagnosed with leukemia. Although the little girl is well now, her mother continued to contemplate her gratitude for living in a country with so many financial and medical resources. "I just couldn't imagine being a mother with a sick child and not having any way to help my child," Julie White said, and went on to found One Mother, a not-for-profit organization that empowers women with HIV/AIDS to generate sustainable incomes and create compassionate communities in which their children can thrive. One Mother partners with other nonprofits to teach women the skills needed to create handmade quilts and other items made from old fabrics, bringing financial independence to the women involved.

"Travel is fatal to prejudice, bigotry, and narrow-mindedness," wrote Mark Twain. International travel often educates our minds and opens our eyes and hearts to the urgent needs of others. John Wood's *Leaving Microsoft to Change the World* is a captivating story of the transformation he experienced from high-powered software industry executive to global philanthropic entrepreneur. While on vacation in Nepal trekking in the Himalayas, Wood struck up a conversation with a friendly Nepali man whose work was to find educational resources for seventeen poor rural schools that typically went only to the fifth grade.

The Nepali man's great efforts and concerns about his country's 70 percent illiteracy rate inspired Wood to visit a school with 450 children. An avid reader since childhood, Wood was stunned by the absence of books. He went on to found Room to Read, a nonprofit organization that has established over 5,000 libraries and 400 schools, has awarded long-term scholarships to more than 3,000 girls, and has given more than a million children the lifelong gift of education. Increasing numbers of relatively small grassroots philanthropic efforts working in direct partnership to address local problems are blossoming globally.

4. Invited

Sometimes we receive a direct invitation to extend our heart of service. Bay Roberts is an environmentalist who explored the rural countryside near her home when she was a child. When the tanker *Exxon Valdez* spilled oil off the coast of Alaska near Roberts's study sight, she joined the cleanup efforts. Later, after working as a schoolteacher, Roberts and her husband decided to adopt an infant girl from China.

Like many new parents, Roberts began to experience a growing sense of connectedness with children in need everywhere, especially those abandoned or orphaned. With the opening of the heart that caring for her daughter inspired, Roberts said, "My heart was so tender, it wanted to help all children. I felt that *any* child could be my child."

One fateful day, Roberts received an e-mail from a friend who had moved to Africa to help with the AIDS crisis. The e-mail was an invitation seeking sponsorship for a young girl named Juliet recently orphaned by AIDS. Before Juliet's single mother had died, she'd been able to make plans only for the care of her two older children. As Roberts gazed at the powerful photograph of Juliet, her heart called out to adopt this girl. Quickly, Roberts learned that Uganda had restrictive regulations, including living in the country for three years before being allowed to begin adoption proceedings. It took years to finalize legal guardianship and obtain a passport for Juliet.

While she waited to welcome Juliet to her new home in America, ideas about other ways to help arose in Roberts's heart. Through e-mails, she learned which school Juliet would attend and decided to support it. Roberts inspired another mother and together they founded One School at a Time. Only two months after first seeing Juliet's portrait, the women had gathered enough resources, determination, and family support to travel to Africa. One School at a Time built a safe, sustainable building and water storage system for Juliet's school, and its funding systematically expanded to assist other schools. Never underestimate the power of an invitation whose offer enters open minds, fertile hearts, and is shaped by willing hands.

5. Drafted

Another launching point for integral service is being drafted unexpectedly. As a renowned philosopher and expert on esoteric spiritual texts of India, Paul Muller-Ortega, Ph.D., has explored ways that we ascertain our integral service. Dr. Muller-Ortega observed, "Some of us volunteer for our next service and some of us are drafted!"

When Carolyn and Paul Zeiger were growing up in the 1950s, neither thought much about movement disorders. Carolyn became a respected psychologist who wrote *Doing It All Isn't Everything*, and Paul worked as an innovative electrical engineer, computer science consultant, and respected university professor. They married, raised their daughter, and offered tremendous amounts of service to various organizations.

In 2005, Paul began to move more slowly and tentatively, and eventually was diagnosed with Parkinson's disease. Carolyn, who had her own health issues, had retired from her psychotherapy practice and was open to learning about her life's next contribution. She trusted that she'd recognize it when it appeared.

Medical conditions lead us to re-examine our current values, goals, and needs as expectations and attachments to the status quo are shaken up. After some initial resistance, Carolyn recognized that embracing Parkinson's as her husband's care-partner and serving as an advocate for others affected by this disease were elements of her next life work.

The Zeigers began to fly around the United States, speaking about Parkinson's disease, leading care-giver support groups, teaching university classes, and offering hatha yoga as well as various complementary therapies to clients living with this movement disorder. Both laugh as they describe how they were "drafted," using their philosopher friend's term, into their new roles as advocates for people with Parkinson's disease.

The five styles described above—diving in, direct connection, concerned sensibility, invited, and drafted—are ways of accepting a calling and showing up on the path of service. Undoubtedly, there are other modalities, motivations, strategies, and paradigms. Many kinds of giving, including socially responsible investing, are pragmatic, and some embrace spiritual inspiration.

To succeed at just about anything, from the creation of our personal life to changing the world with new paradigms, our inspired resilience has to be greater than our fear of failure. We are our future not yet unfolded and realize that the best way to foretell the future is to create and navigate it consciously. Our intentions and goals are not flimsy wishes. Strong with mindfulness and compassionate self-care, we gently exhale our compassion in action as we create our future.

Pause, Reflect, and Record

- What style or hybrid of styles best outlined in this chapter best describes the way that you commit to something larger than yourself?

- When have you experienced the inspiration to move from concern to direct action? Describe.

- How strong is your current interest in fully embodying your values and living an integrated life where you walk your talk?

- Challenges can bring forth transformative growth, and hardships contain lessons that can strengthen resilience and refine character. Describe some examples of this from your life.

24

Principles of a
New Activism

Service is a relationship between equals.
The wholeness in us serves the wholeness in others
and the wholeness and mystery in life.
We serve life because it is holy.

—Rachel Naomi Remen, M.D.

Woven throughout *Goodness To Go* are principles of a new paradigm of activism. Its vision is based on the recognition of our interconnectedness and that the wholeness in us serves the wholeness in others. Our actions are relevant and they matter. Citizens of planet earth don't have to succumb to learned helplessness. When the world is on fire, positive transformations and the creation of new stories in our hands.

The power of large social movements, including the efforts of abolitionists, suffragettes, civil rights workers, and others unafraid to confront oppressors and exploiters, has fueled progressive reform. When apartheid or bloated monarchies dominated their societies, reform was insufficient and unjust systems had to end so that new paradigms could emerge. Vibrant citizenship has an obligation to the promise and power of democracy, says Liz Coleman, a pioneering innovator in education. Complacent tolerance, denial, and avoidance are maladaptive reactions. We're interdependent and what affects one affects us all.

Early in the twentieth century, the Irish poet William Butler Yeats expressed his concern about laissez-faire living when he wrote, "The best lack all conviction while the worst are full of passionate intensity." In times fraught with fundamentalism, terrorism, and self-radicalization, "benign neglect" is a delusion. There are no innocent bystanders and when urgent need exists, what we don't do can be as damaging as actions made with harmful intent. Recently in the United States, a coalition of civil liberties groups, labor unions, and environmental organizations united to form the Democracy Initiative aimed at removing political roadblocks to progressive legislation. In other parts of the world, many of the millions of protestors raising their voices for freedom have given their lives for liberty.

Seven principles of activism for the twenty-first century have been described by members of the Global Renaissance Alliance. Now called the Peace Alliance, the foundation empowers civic engagement toward a culture of peace. Several principles focus on the in-breath of feeling, being, and self-care. Others emphasize the out-breath of thinking, doing, and integral service. Which, if any, of the following acts of peace and power especially resonate for you?

1. **Stillness as an act of power:** Cultivation of a quiet mind is the most effective antidote to chaos. We begin to experience harmony as an operative principle in the world as we sit simply in silence.

2. **Envisioning as an act of power:** In the twenty-first century, power will be determined by one's wealth of imagination and consciousness, not merely by material or financial resources.

3. **Interpersonal healing as an act of power:** The source of war and peace lies in each of us; as we rid our hearts of the sparks of violence, we are fostering peace in the world.

4. **Depth of insight as an act of power:** The depth of a commitment or a conversation is more important than how many people are involved in it.

5. **Radical goodwill as an act of power:** Forgiveness, compassion, and loving kindness are our most powerful transformational tools.

6. **Creating sacred space as an act of power:** The power of ritual gatherings harnesses energy for the purpose of spiritual healing.

7. **Spiritually centered action as an act of power:** By making a stand for a new possibility, rather than fighting what is, we attain the power to create what could be.

A great change is upon us. What is broken can be made whole; there is still time. We have many opportunities to repair and heal our damaged home planet and her inhabitants. Biomimicry is growing in many design and engineering applications. From the natural world, we're learning about coevolution, cooperation, and social harmony. The change that is needed asks that our goodness be offered in the co-creation of new global cultures. A wise leader in Ursula Le Guin's novel *The Other Wind* says, "We must join together to learn what that change is, its causes, its course, and how we may hope to turn it from conflict and ruin to harmony and peace."

A new activism aligned with life-affirming values will be based on enduring principles of sustainability. It won't be the application of unsustainable band-aids or neocolonialism dressed in wolf's clothing. Colonialism and top-down development are an enforced presence, regardless of how benevolent the stated intent. Commitment to deep democracy is central, where every voice is valued, brought forth, respected, and included. Participatory development is its natural expression. Community members know what their needs are and want to be actively involved in all stages of healthy development.

Global citizenship is on the rise. Andrew Harvey's book *The Hope: A Guide to Sacred Activism* describes the growing revolution of social activism and supports our longing to give back. Emma Seppala is one of many who has expressed her appreciation for the opportunity to know herself, be herself, and give herself away: "If my tears roll, let them be of gratitude. If I'm shaken to the core of my being, let it be by the intensity of wonder. And if I am filled with impassioned longing, let it be to give more, know more, love more, connect, and uplift."

This new revolution of activism includes laughter, song, and dance. Music is a universal language that moves, uplifts, refreshes, and strengthens us. Integral service supported by enjoyment and self-care is infused with meaning and happiness, despite the painful and exhausting experiences that it may include. It gives voice to the joy of being alive. Self-care is essential to prevent compassion fatigue and burnout. As we care for ourselves and each other, we clarify our motivations and develop increasingly skillful means. Our goodness is leveraged with more potency.

Citizens in consumer countries are learning more about the people who are providing the products that they purchase. In the United States alone, coffee is a $40 billion industry. The impoverished women and children who pick coffee beans earn very little money; brokers, roasters, and corporations make tremendous profits. Women executives in the coffee industry are facilitating change through empowerment of the growers as well as socially responsible purchasing. By mentoring the women working in rural Africa and Central America to learn entrepreneurial skills, direct sales from coffee growers to buyers lead to more income for their families and to more resourced local communities.

Social networks like Facebook, LinkedIn, Twitter, and MySpace foster social change on an enormous scale (witness the online success of Barack Obama's presidential campaigns) and make social activism profitable. Two young social entrepreneurs founded Virgance, which uses the power of the Internet to channel the good intentions of millions of individuals into specific causes. Virgance supports One Block Off the Grid, brokering deals for neighbors to get inexpensive solar setups; Carrotmob, to reward businesses for making socially responsive changes; and a green news online site.

From Global Awareness to Action

"Knowing is not enough; we must apply. Willing is not enough; we must do," wrote Johann Wolfgang von Goethe. Around the globe, we're awakening to the possibility and imperative of social justice and environmental sustainability. James Hansen, Ph.D., is a NASA climate scientist who has stated repeatedly that halting global warming requires urgent, unprecedented international cooperation. The protective ozone layer is nearly 20 percent depleted by mounting carbon emissions, and cancer rates related to increased exposure to solar radiation are rising

At the Copenhagen Summit in 2009, the crucial issues of decreasing carbon emissions and deforestation were discussed. One effective strategy that emerged was to invest in equatorial countries in ways that conserve their invaluable reserves of biological diversity. With sustainable economies, the slashing and burning of irreplaceable forests could be prevented. The entire planet needs the lungs of the rainforests, not the carbon pollution of their smoke. Industrialized nations emit disproportionately large amounts of carbon into the earth's biosphere. With only eight percent of the global population, the United States consumes 30 percent of its resources and emits 25 percent of the greenhouse gases polluting our atmosphere. If other countries seek to emulate the United States' path through industrialism to the information age, the earth could become uninhabitable for humans.

In the journal *Science,* a Canadian biologist, Boris Worm, Ph.D., published his team's research on the sustainability of marine life. The loss of whole species puts entire ecosystems at risk. Declining biodiversity is hampering the ocean's ability to filter pollutants, resist diseases, produce seafood, and rebound from such stresses as overfishing and climate change. If current trends continue, biologists predict the collapse of virtually all fish stocks worldwide by 2048.

In the Gulf of Mexico, the 2010 explosion of British Petroleum's offshore oil drilling operation hemorrhaged millions of barrels of oil over many weeks. This preventable disaster killed untold life, devastated ecosystems, destroyed many families' fishing legacies and livelihoods, and further polluted our oceans. Years later, the cleanup and recovery efforts continue. Many gushing oil "spills" of similar magnitudes occur on a regular basis off the coasts of African nations, although they receive virtually no media coverage.

The powerful earthquake and tsunami that hit Japan in 2011 spewed toxic radioactive materials into the ocean and caused tremendous loss of life and property. Hydraulic fracturing, known as fracking, releases toxic air emissions and pollutes underground water supplies as it extracts natural gas. Wells stretching horizontally under the earth's surface for about a mile are fracked in dozens of sections, requiring millions of gallons of water. Academic and other research institutions receive large sums of money from the oil and gas industry, and faculty members are losing their jobs if they speak out against fracking. Obviously, there is an urgent need for environmentally safe energy sources and for wise care of the world's water and air on which life depends. Business as usual will simply not suffice,

Although many disregard the mounting scientific evidence of current climate changes, glaciers and ice caps are melting at unprecedented rates, and polar bears are drowning as they hunt for food because ice flows are thinner and further apart. Some "climate cynics" teach their children that any information about global warming is merely propaganda. More people are accepting the reality of climate change but continue to deny that human activities contribute in any substantial way. Social commentators have noted that we may be entitled to our own opinions but not to our own facts. Ill-informed opinions deny and multiply while factual evidence grows. If we close our minds to what we're doing to our only home, we're not serving ourselves or our children.

In her first book, *Diet for a Small Planet*, Frances Moore Lappé explored global food systems, including the cultural, social, political, and ecological economics associated with the production and distribution of food. Over the decades since the book's publication, many people have learned about the global role that livestock plays in environmental degradation and food scarcity. Cattle eat grain that could feed hungry populations of human beings. On an equal weight basis, beef produces ten to twenty times more greenhouse gases than chicken or salmon. Climate change has brought drought to many regions that grow corn, which is a major food source for cattle. Food insecurity increases as governments subsidize farmers and food prices escalate.

Political and ecological economics affect the production and distribution of food that the earth is able to provide. Too often, people starve while available food surpluses rot. The ingredients used to make a single container of fruit yogurt can have traveled over 5,000 miles. If a household chooses not to eat red meat or consume dairy products for a year, it saves the same amount of carbon emissions as if they'd cut about 8,000 miles out of their driving. The production of food and our attachment to eating *what we want when we want it* promote harshly polarizing reactions.

Our decisions about what we eat, the number of children we create, and our willingness to mobilize our compassion affect the network of life. Many pressing global issues, including hunger and malnutrition, disease epidemics, extreme social inequality, and the population explosion, abound. In 2007, an emergency medicine professor at the University of Toronto took a leave of absence to volunteer near Darfur, Sudan. In his book *Six Months in Sudan: A Young Doctor in a War-Torn Village*, James Maskalyk, M.D., explores altruism and its motivations. "Rather than finding the answer to the question of how I can fit this kind of work into my life, I realize the real question has become: *How can I fit a life into this kind of work?*" Many individuals around the world are contemplating how their life can care for life.

How can you fit your life into your integral service? The response to this question is a unique, evolving tapestry for those willing to mobilize their goodness. Committing to service as a defining priority in one's life is radical compassion at work. Dr. Maskalyk continues: "Once you experience doing such work, you can see it goes beyond all rational explanation, and that it's just what you're compelled to do. ... We're just part of that greater thing that is life, and all life wants is to go on. Life wants to explore this ecological niche on Earth; it wants us to take care of each other; it wants us to make sure life goes on. This is life caring for itself, and that's why we do it."

Life cares for itself, flows, changes, and evolves. There are no short-cuts to the communal vision, effective strategy, and sustained effort required to co-create our vision of positive transformation. Like the earth creating clear, strong, beautiful diamonds, the development of our resilient courage and creative intelligence requires the grace of ongoing pressure and sustained effort.

The social activist and artist Kazauki Tanahashi articulated some commonplace truths and principles of engagement to create positive change. This understanding begins with a deep trust that no situation is impossible to change and makes it clear that everyone is responsible to help make a difference. Decades ago, a wise woman walked alone across the United States sharing her understanding of the relationship between inner peace and integral service. "To change your life, change your motive to service. Know and do your part in the Life Pattern. Do all the good you can each day. No one finds inner peace who avoids doing his or her share in the solving of collective problems," the Peace Pilgrim wrote.

Social artists of all kinds strengthen their self-confidence and nourish trust in their ability to make positive contributions to the world. The human potential pioneer Jean Houston, Ph.D., has lived a mythic life that inspires us to remember the power of our natural goodness. She writes: "These are the times when we stand humbly and boldly in the presence of our own great promise. These are the days when through our decisions and actions, we determine our legacy for those to come. ... Let's do what we came here to do." Contributing in meaningful ways to the world beyond our personal needs has been described as paying rent for our space on earth, as humanitarian service, as forms of social or spiritual love, and as sacred activism. Yours may be a changing kaleidoscope of intentions and actions. Our world needs everyone who has the capacity and willingness to offer time and skills, heart, head, hands, and other resources to the creation of a healthy, harmonious global community.

Pause, Reflect, and Record

• How can *you fit your life* into a life of integral service?

• What is an example of *radical goodwill* that you've experienced or been inspired by?

• How might action intended to increase social justice become *sacred activism*?

• Maya Angelou, a Nobel laureate in literature, shares insights gleaned from life's challenges. She wrote: "Try to be the best human being you can be. ... Do it because it is right to do." How might you be the best that you can be in your home, workplace, community, or place of worship?

25

What Did You Do
Once You Knew?

*This is the true joy in life, the being used for a purpose
recognized by yourself as a mighty one... Life ... is a sort of
splendid torch ... and I want to make it burn
as brightly as possible
before handing it on to future generations.*

—George Bernard Shaw

We are living the history of our future. Our purpose can be mighty and our actions beneficial. It's possible to free our children from suffering the consequences of current abuses of the earth and one other. With keen appreciation for the maturation of our moral sense, we'll care about the lives of generations to come. As we learn from our mistakes and offer our goodness to go, we're more resourced to co-create a positive, equitable future, refusing to continue with business as usual.

Humanitarians want to be awake, aware, and informed in as many aspects of life as possible. The truth can set us free. It's important to learn about political and financial arenas of human society, as power plays in these sectors have led to legal and human rights violations for centuries. Every day, we learn more about environmental devastation, human trafficking, carbon footprints, child labor in sweatshops, collapsing economies, and stock markets dominated by fear and greed. We've seen that as economic dominos begin to fall, the process can develop the intensity of a runaway train that hurts the most vulnerable.

Our children and grandchildren may ask us how we responded to the momentous challenges of this time: *What did you do once you knew?* What are you doing now at this critical time for life on earth? What do you want your answer to be as you prepare to let go of your human life?

Goodness To Go

It's been said that *whatever any human is capable of, I am capable of.* Everyone makes mistakes or missed-takes. A Greek word for sin is *amartia*, to miss the mark, and it's not a moral sin to make a mistake. We can forget, resist, or deny our capacity to express our inherent goodness and thereby miss our mark. Both nature and nurture affect this capacity: there are biochemical and social factors as well as genetic, educational, and parenting influences.

We've been conditioned by our cultures. Our confidence and compassion are affected by numerous influences from within our bodies, families, and communities. Although we're not able to know enough about someone to judge, we can assess the value or harm of their behaviors. Understanding the intention that motivates a behavior is relevant to this determination, as well.

Recent stampedes to sacrifice the future for short-term profit contradict healthy conservatism. Cultures based on conspicuous consumption and overdrawing assets have degraded global ecosystems and concentrated power into a financial elite, resulting in a tremendously inequitable distribution of wealth. Psychologists might describe the elements leading to the 2008 recession as a perfect storm of passion, aggression, and ignorance. By ignoring our highest principles, we allowed passionate ideology and aggressive greed to damage the integrity of our conscience and investments as well as the global economy.

Although capitalism has many flaws, no other economic structure of the 20th century provided as many opportunities for citizens. A dominant economic ideology has been Milton Friedman's free market movement. In Naomi Klein's book *The Shock Doctrine: The Rise of Disaster Capitalism*, the curtain of deception that has been fueled by free market myths was pulled back. Tremendous human misery and repeated violence advocated by political and corporatist machinations have resulted from forcing this doctrine on resisting countries, including Chile in 1973 and Iraq more recently. Klein's book reveals a disturbing narrative of hubris and malfeasance on the part of many with resources and power.

The dynamics causing the 2008 global economic meltdown were in operation for many years before major banking institutions began to fall. Human behavior is often driven by incentives and assessment of risk. If a behavior reaps large profits and is perceived to have little risk, it's difficult to resist. Laws that promised loan guarantees absolved bankers from any risk if they lent money to people who didn't qualify for home mortgages. Behavior changed predictably when financial workers knew that the government would bail them out if they made loans to people who couldn't pay them back, or when they over borrowed, or over leveraged.

Mortgage lending standards that stood the test of time determined that borrowers had to save about a third of the price of the home they wanted to buy and banks assumed 100 percent of the risk of their own lending. During the Reagan administration, deregulation of the financial sector began in earnest. By 2009, subprime mortgages, ongoing tax cuts, political players cutting oversight regulations, and uncivilized greed created a toxic bubble. Bankers, CEOs, and mortgage lenders paid themselves billions in bonuses or severance packages while millions of jobs and homes were lost. Unemployment was rampant and retirement savings disappeared. In the foreclosure crisis, growing distress escalated domestic violence and suicide rates.

In many ways, the economic collapse was like a Greek tragedy of epic proportions. When the meltdown began, some financiers anxiously asked for regulations that would control their behavior, acknowledging that "the temptation was just too great." However, when they saw no negative consequences coming their way, requests for oversight stopped. We tend to assume that most people, especially professionals, will act ethically. "Creative" financing does not equate with unethical behavior. Bankers who broke the rules and destroyed trust went on to receive bailouts; they were too big to fail and apparently too big to jail.

Most old paradigms die hard. Greed frequently uses deception and manipulation to grab as much as it can from old systems before their final dissolution, regardless of the harmful consequences to others. A Hong Kong–based investment commentator, Marc Faber, forecasts a "collapse of our capitalistic system as we know it today." For individuals, crippling debt often leads to forms of servitude and "financial imprisonment." Yet many bankers and financial corporations whose actions and poor performance put millions into huge debt continue to strategize ways to profit from an economic collapse that devastates the world.

In the United States, tax rates are not applied fully to corporate elites and those with private fortunes. Over 25 percent of U.S. corporations pay no income tax at all. Many, including the oil industry, are government subsidized while acting as separate sovereign entities globally. Lobbyists spin loopholes for their interest groups to avoid taxation.

The U.S. debt, which has been increasing by $1 trillion annually, is expected to exceed $17 trillion by the end of 2013. Following the "Summer of Debt Discontent" in 2011, protestors occupied Wall Street and quickly the Occupy movement spread around the world. People of all ages whose futures had been compromised by debt or loss of pensions raised their voices together in recognition of the need for fair tax codes and effective, transparent oversight of financial institutions.

The healthy flow of currency in the form of taxes supports institutions and services for the common good. We all benefit from transportation systems, energy and scientific research, national parks, safe streets, elder care, emergency services, public education for citizens, and democratically controlled public institutions. Taxes are the price we pay for these collective goods and services; it's not useful to frame them as a burden. The legendary Supreme Court justice Oliver Wendell Holmes, Jr., wrote early in the twentieth century, "Taxes are the price we pay for civilization." Collection of taxes by government agencies assists citizens and communities devastated by increasing numbers of disasters such as wildfires, hurricanes, tsunamis, and floods. Taxes pay for security forces that perform surveillance and special operations to decrease our exposure to violence.

There are many lessons from this recent global recession that are too important to forget, ignore, or gloss over. Systemic over-leveraging of borrowed money and government loan guarantees need to be reevaluated. Financial institutions need oversight and fraud needs to be regulated. We need to fully understand the riskiness of our financial behaviors and investment strategies. Citizens and institutions that lend or borrow money need to do so responsibly and ethically. Will we learn from the past and remind ourselves to apply those hard-won insights? In doing so, we'll serve as midwives to new paradigms that catalyze positive transformation for everyone in our interconnected global village. With compassion for mistakes made, let's survey some of the factors that nearly resulted in a global financial meltdown.

The Recession's Shadow

When light falls on the material world, shadows form. And wherever there's a crack, light comes through. Human shadows are usually the result of a lack of understanding or ignorance. Ignorance may be due to insufficient information or serve as a way to deny or cope with difficulties. Frequently, we forget that we're a spark of divine light and that both light and darkness are informative. As cracks in the economic bubble destroyed its temporary illusion, they allowed in the light of understanding and the possibility for wiser, more ethical and humane courses of action.

Balancing the regulation of business practices is an ongoing dynamic. Over-regulation of some industries leads to monopolies, fewer choices, reduced quality, and higher costs to citizens. However, we know now that with few government regulations and little oversight, financial systems become legally corrupt. Economic tactics of institutionalized injustice where the rich get richer and the poor get poorer are somewhat akin to apartheid where wealthy, pale-skinned Afrikaners prevented disenfranchised South Africans from gaining access to privilege and power.

Arrogance and greed are not marks of a character that is noble and strong. Financial traders covered their tracks in many ways, including setting up off-shore accounts in housekeepers' names. Reports about the epidemic of insider trading and securities fraud continue to appear. A disturbing trend that has been increasing over the past twenty years is the number of members of Congress who've become extremely wealthy from trading on their insider information. New rules have been suggested that would stop a great deal of the corrupt cronyism that takes place in Washington: the investments of members of congress are put into a blind trust while they're in office; their pensions are paid from their salaries as public servants; and they cannot have direct family members involved in special interest lobbying.

Unbridled capitalism does not benefit everyone involved. The head of Goldman Sachs made $485 million in 2010 and some hedge fund directors make more than a billion dollars a year. The acquisition of money can become addictive, fueling insatiable greed. In the first century, a Roman philosopher named Seneca observed that greed's worst point is its ingratitude. Another is its frequent disregard for the suffering it causes. Political observers have noted that representatives of financial institutions who were given bailout money rarely expressed any gratitude. Wall Street workers have displayed an entitled arrogance—*of course we had to be bailed out*. Despite unethical practices, their businesses were saved by those they harmed.

When More Is Less

Our commitment to upholding our values and integrity needs to be rejuvenated on a regular basis, in much the same way as we refresh our intent to exercise daily. Every day, we're exposed to marketing campaigns that stimulate desires we didn't even know we had. Turbo-capitalism fuels obsessive materialism. Catchy advertising phrases tell us: "Less is a bore. Consume more." Often, we demand instant gratification and complain of boredom in the midst of beauty and plenty. Many suffer from the dis-ease of *more*—demanding more calories, more addictive substances, more entertainment, more consumer goods, more status. Although animals in their natural environment do not take more than they need, ego's greed wants *more, more, more*. Native Americans and other indigenous cultures have considered it a form of mental illness to accumulate more than one needs.

Consumption is not a virtue. Insatiable is not sustainable. Credit bubbles precipitate economic crises. Global currency markets are unbalanced and turbulent. The alliance of the Eurozone is in crisis. Enormous federal debt tempts governments to inflate their way out by printing more money. It is untenable to shift blame for budget shortfalls onto elders' health care when most corporations pay no taxes due to clever loopholes. It is not true that our only choice is to either care for elders who created our societies or invest in young people who will create the future. With sufficient ethical and political will, we can redesign social systems so that everyone thrives.

The earth's abundance is able to provide for our needs but not our greed. A medical condition may underlie addictive behavior, and in other circumstances moral and ethical codes succumb to temptation. In the years leading up to the 2008 economic collapse, incentives and compensation practices fueled unethical behavior. Mortgage brokers received bonuses if they sold financial products at a higher interest rate than the borrowers would otherwise have qualified for. Sixty percent of subprime mortgage borrowers were actually eligible for regular, lower-rate loans but their lenders steered them away in order to increase their own compensation.

The banking industry has a social contract to help stabilize economies and assist entrepreneurs to finance businesses that create jobs, provide necessary commodities, and develop innovations. It is usually the dynamic private sector that creates innovation and employment opportunities, and it is the private sector—not the privileged sector—that deserves tax break incentives, freeing capital to invest in growing businesses. People need to work, and tax codes benefitting the private sector (including small businesses and the middle class) make sense for the common good.

Five years after Wall Street collapsed, most of its banks were bigger than ever but reluctant to provide loans. Every profession should first do no harm. Many people believe that systems lacking integrity need more than simplistic reform, they need to be regulated and redesigned with respect for universal values in mind.

Economic Fantasia

At the heart of the economic crisis is a moral crisis. *As we are, such are the times.* With varying degrees of clarity, financial analysts described credit swaps, upticks, naked shorts, backwards incentives, distressed debts, toxic assets, and collateralized debt obligation. Many in the banking sector succumbed to technically legal tricks and traps that lined their pockets with millions of dollars. Caught up in a financial joyride, many didn't bother to comprehend the risks of what was going on.

Members of federal financial oversight committees acknowledged that they did not understand credit default swaps and other novel financial vehicles, including derivatives. When we don't take the time to understand something, our minds tend to ignore, fear, or worship it. Derivatives are essentially insurance policies, bets, or swaps between banks that give a paper guarantee shifting risk to the future. For a time, they seem to inject liquidity into a market that gives some investors a way to hedge their bets. In this financial shell game, derivative markets accumulated close to $600 trillion.

Pipe dreams promising easy profits seduced many people. In the stampede, human values were swept away. Warnings about over-leveraged derivatives markets occurred in the late 1990s, truth-tellers spoke up, and Enron imploded in 2001. For over a decade, we ignored cracks in financial markets that eventually ruptured in 2008, devastating the global economy. During the aftermath of this recession, free-market enthusiasts and others have realized that without oversight and regulation, the "invisible hand" of an unregulated economic system will rob the till. The call for "conscious capitalism" is sounding around the world.

Intelligence alone does not equate with ethical decision-making. Fraud, manipulation, bogus deals, and blatant scams prevailed among brilliant, deregulated financiers. During the derivative and mortgage mania, cynical Enron executives were taped as they snickered about "granny losing her retirement fund." Their comments lacking empathy for "gullible suckers" who had lost everything reflected attitudes of corruption. When actions have harmed others, a healthy conscience usually experiences remorse. Ways are sought to make amends, if possible, and to change behaviors for good.

Goodness To Go

Some analysts contend that obedience to the economic philosophy of Alan Greenspan and compliance with the advice of Ivy League economic advisors fueled unethical decision-making and deception within the financial sector. Throughout his career, including eighteen years as chairman of the Federal Reserve, Greenspan bet his money on the unregulated, libertarian separation of state and economy popularized by the writer Ayn Rand.

Laissez-faire and libertarian financial ideologies have been on the loose for decades. This economic philosophy and its tide of deregulation was made to order for the Reagan era, after which the U.S. debt doubled in eight years. The doctrine of libertarianism upholds absolute, unrestricted "freedom" to extract financial resources in any way that an individual sees fit. This unregulated incentive to profit financially has created monopolies, privatized water supplies, sold arms to terrorists, and used child labor in sweatshops.

Greenspan was awarded congressional medals and was called a rock star by President George W. Bush. Some called him "The Wizard," awed by the intelligence of this free market acolyte who seemed to pull financial strings inside a black box. During heady days of booming markets, critical thinking was replaced by slogans such as "In Fed We Trust" as well as simplistic, antigovernment rhetoric. Atlas shrugged. The Greenspan credo insisted that "markets get it right," financial risks were adequately distributed, and fraud did not require regulation. Predictably, incentives drove behavior. The chance to pocket vast sums of money was so tempting that fraud expanded into spectacular scams described as "bankster" behavior.

Canada shares thousands of miles of border with the United States. However, none of its banks fell during the economic recession whose epicenter was Wall Street. The Canadian government had in place sufficient oversight regulations of financial institutions so that none of the tempting tricks used by colleagues to the south could be utilized.

When something sounds too profitable to be true, it usually is. The bubble economy was a snare and a delusion. Real capital invested in real products generates real economies that create useful goods and services. Bubbles and dreams can seem harmless and enticing. However, when nightmares manifest, terrible harm can be done. Whether global financial eminence shifts north, south, east, or west, responsible governance is needed to protect our welfare, our communities, and our home planet. Clearly, long-term, win-win integrative systems solutions are needed.

Many people ask whether financial institutions that are too big to fail are too big to exist, yet the banks remaining since the beginning of the global economic collapse are bigger than ever. They've learned that their industry will not only be highly subsidized but also bailed out. Citizens question why there has been so little investigation and litigation of the economic engineers. Those injured want to understand why perpetrators of so much harm are not being brought to justice after running rampant with predatory lending that "lost" billions of dollars belonging to philanthropies and individuals.

In the years following the economic collapse, even modest attempts to put protective financial regulations in place were immediately attacked by those who preferred to operate without regulations or transparency. Some 30,000 lobbyists—five for each member of Congress—spend billions to gut laws that protect citizens. Many citizens regard it as a travesty that financial systems continue to lobby against regulations that are clearly essential for the ethical protection of all people involved in financial markets.

The Fallacy of "Free" Markets

For decades, economists and political journalists published warnings about the damage that unregulated "free" markets would bring. One commentator was Henry Fairlie who had coined the term "the Establishment" years ago. Global corporations often misuse free market systems and trade policies in ways that hurt people with impunity. International trade prices do not take into account the negative impact of harm to the environment, human rights abuses that afflict countless workers, and other externalities.

Ethical freedom is not license, which interferes with the freedom of others. Corporate managers are "free" to buy cheaper materials from sources using slavery that keeps retail prices down and social costs exorbitant. Across the globe, approximately 27 million victims of human trafficking are working in slave conditions. Although the American Civil War was more than 150 years ago, involuntary servitude fueled by undemocratic systemic forces continues to be rampant in the United States and in over one hundred other countries.

When the playing field is not level and unethical businesses are subsidized, free markets compensate abusive practices. A level playing field makes an equitable, competitive market more possible and factors in the social and environmental costs of making products fast and cheap. Although a "living wage" varies from country to country, many businesses don't offer benefits or a minimum wage in line with the communities' economy. They undercut business owners committed to offering health benefits as well as protecting employee safety and the natural environment. Cheaper resources and manufacturing costs translate into cheaper prices, but cheaper at what cost?

Democracy for Sale?

Long ago, the brilliant philosopher Johann Wolfgang von Goethe warned, "None are more hopelessly enslaved than those who falsely believe they are free." Plutocracy is governance by a rich, controlling class. Democracy is a grand experiment of government by and for the people, not by wealthy ruling aristocrats. We cherish the principles of democracy and the recognition that all people are created equal.

A 2010 U.S. Supreme Court decision supported plutocracy rather than democracy when unlimited corporate spending on political campaigns and issues was allowed. In effect, corporations were granted "personhood" by the votes of a few individuals. Although citizens need full disclosure about who is financing the campaigns of their elected representatives, the *Citizens United* provision allows wealthy individuals and corporations to remain anonymous as their fortunes manipulate political agendas.

An invisible, capitalistic structure underlying many democracies has been described as a financial pyramid scheme. At the narrow top of this pyramid is one percent of the population, the privileged "haves." Rather than being a "meritocracy," this one percent controls 40 percent of the total national wealth. A thriving, informed middle class sustains democratic values and is the foundation of a stable economy.

In the 1890s, income inequity led to massive unemployment, uprisings in several countries, and the first industrial depression. The most recent time that income inequality and the number of bank failures approached current levels was 1928, just before the Great Depression. Banking oversight regulations were put in place soon thereafter and bank failures dropped to nearly zero. When the Reagan and Carter eras initiated the decrease of financial oversight regulation, both income inequality and bank failures increased. Economists have noted that curves representing bank failures over the past century match graphs of income gaps between the rich and poor.

Income inequality in the United States is worse than in India. Nearly 25 percent of the money generated in the United States each year is controlled by the richest one percent. Although the middle class is the engine of the U.S. economy, its net worth decreased by 20 percent in the past few decades. The financial health of African Americans and Hispanics has been losing ground disproportionately since the economic recession began in 2008.

There also has been a stagnation of wages. A median worker in 2011 makes less than a similar worker in 1969. Excessive income inequality is destabilizing and is associated with decreases in savings, health, and trust as well as increases in crime. Low social status is associated with increased health and social problems that are more prevalent in unequal societies. The rising strength of Brazilian, Indian, and Chinese economies is based on increasing the education and opportunities of their middle classes.

Is one of the first duties of government to protect the powerless against the powerful? Enforceable oversight regulations make it possible for free people to combat tyrannies in economic and other realms. Is it a democracy when "those who have the gold make the rules?" Lobbyists control much of the congressional process, and U.S. politicians claim that they're held hostage by Wall Street. When the U.S. government prints money to borrow money, buying Treasury bonds from Goldman-Sachs, and then buys back these bonds of debt, Goldman Sachs keeps a significant profit. Meanwhile, the tremendous economic danger of devalued currency increases exponentially.

We allowed ourselves to be intimidated, bamboozled, and seduced by easy profits and the apparent brilliance of the deregulators. Why didn't engaged citizens thoughtfully consider warnings about the reassurances of financial wizards before laissez-faire economics failed? A culture of greed and conspicuous consumption hijacked financial responsibility and discipline. While governments deregulated financial systems, millions of consumers were asleep at the wheel. Repeatedly, citizens of democracies have been reminded that the cost of freedom is constant vigilance.

Our task is to be consciously aligned with our core values so that self-absorption doesn't take over. Fortunately, we have access to resources on many levels that enable us to do this. Our inherent goodness, life energy, financial resources, social networks, and other forms of personal power support our confidence, resilience, creativity, vision, and the courage to take risks. At the end of the day, net worth has little to do with the size of our bank accounts. Crises hold both danger and opportunity. We can rekindle our respect, appreciation, and commitment to the principles of democracy. Opportunities abound.

Strengthening Our Moral Compass

We no longer live in the twentieth century and are moving beyond its old paradigm of "wealth now; philanthropy later." Economic values are moving from simple accumulation of capital to nurturing it systemically and holistically. Socially responsible business build around principles of sustainability, care of the commons, humane treatment of all workers, and environmental stewardship. There is such a thing as money that is too fast, companies that are too big, and finance that is too complex.

Real worth is our simple goodness and our measure of giving, not our accumulated financial wealth. Former president Gerald R. Ford wrote, "Always demanding the best of oneself, living with honor, devoting one's talents and gifts to the benefits of others—these are the measures of success that endure when material things have passed away."

Instead of "wasting a crisis," we can reflect on the moral issues at the heart of it and learn what beneficial changes are needed, inside and out. We can learn to harness power of all kinds without letting it harness us. Power, including economic power, is not the problem just as money is not the problem. Wisdom traditions remind us that the root of the problem is our *attachment* to money and power. Power systems that develop elites by excluding or hurting others need to be redesigned from the inside out.

If we're not part of the solution, we're part of the problem. Prevention of another economic collapse due to lack of financial regulation is possible, and oversight is part of that solution. Overseers need to be completely independent and should not be paid by those requiring the supervision. Experience has shown that accounting firms hired or paid by the company they're overseeing miss or overlook many more accounting discrepancies.

Academic assessments lose credibility when the authors have financial ties with the corporations whose behaviors they're assessing for public safety. Physicians uncovering medical problems related to water systems polluted by chemicals used in natural gas fracking operations shouldn't be "gagged" from sharing this important safety information with the public.

Although it may be an appropriate role of government to support and protect markets so that they can function, the consumer-credit market relationship needs to be redefined. What have we learned about running and regulating financial institutions and the global economy? The energy of money is not the issue so much as our relationship to it. Wealthy politicians could use their financial independence to be free of lobbyists' agendas. Ethical politicians would not use insider trading information or focus on preserving the power and exclusive privilege of the financial elite.

Freedom comes with the responsibilities of citizenship. Citizens in democracies have not only have the privileges and rights of personal initiative but also responsibility for vulnerable citizens, including children, elders, and those suffering from serious disabilities. It is the responsibility of immigrants to contribute financially and participate politically in their host country, and those of reproductive age need to be responsible about the number of children they bring onto an environmentally stressed planet.

As we strengthen our moral compass, we continue to learn from opportunities provided by the 2008-and-beyond recession to reassess our relationship with the energy and resource of money. The historic Dodd-Frank financial-reform bill was passed about two years into the recession, creating a new agency to regulate the credit industry. An umbrella group of progressive organizations called the Americans for Financial Reform worked to pass this consumer protection legislation. To revitalize democracy, we must maintain vigilance about the spin and influence of the "lobbocracy," the massively funded financial sector lobbyists on Capitol Hill. We'll need to find allies within and without to help us engage in this ongoing battle for financial and political integrity.

A New Economics

Global optimists are calling for a new story of economics that reflects our interconnectedness, our goodness, and the energy of innovation that creates more equitable institutions and healthier environments. The arc of evolution is doing more with less. Charles Eisenstein writes about the themes of civilization, consciousness, money, and human cultural evolution. His book entitled *Sacred Economics: Money, Gift and Society in the Age of Transition* explores the roots of present financial crises and the convergence of the worlds of spirituality and activism.

The collapse of the deregulated economy presents opportunities for communities to create more sustainable and humane ways of doing business. Some corporations have demonstrated their commitment to social as well as financial profit. Healthy businesses thrive in environments where progressive approaches to private-public partnerships are fostered. Success in business is being redefined by the B ("Be the change we seek) Corporation movement. Through rigorous standards of social and environmental performance, accountability and transparency certified B Corporations define success as creating the best *for* the world rather than being the best *in* the world.

There are encouraging signs and points of light. Social investing is on the rise, and the Slow Money movement is an example of the alliances that are accelerating the transition to economies based on preservation and restoration rather than extraction and consumption. Slow Money investors share new ways of thinking about relationships between food, money, and soil health, and want to *bring money down to earth*. By investing in local food enterprises, food security, safety and access in enhanced, nutrition and health can be improved, and cultural, ecological, and economic diversity is promoted.

Many consumers are insisting on "fair trade" business practices. In 2009, a $4.5 million corporate donation sponsored a program in India called All for Children. Families who work in cotton fields were given financial assistance to allow their children to go to school instead of working in the fields. Recently, Domini Social Investments helped to convince the steel company Nucor that it could reduce human misery, including slavery, through discernment about its sources of raw materials. Small change counts. Millions of small acts add up to transformation. History rises from the hearts and minds of millions of people dedicated to democratic, humanitarian principles.

Our actions affect the future of our children and our planet. A great nation is a compassionate nation. Poets and prophets have reminded us for millennia that whatever we love, we are. If we want money more than anything, we'll be bought and sold. It's also useful to recall that one of the first signs of a society's decline is a shift away from cooperation and caring about others' well-being to self-centeredness. Self-absorption is often characterized by greed as well as lack of empathy and responsibility. The practice of self-inquiry is useful to free ourselves from the clutches of self-absorption.

Generosity begets generosity. Since the recession began, DonorsChoose. org has seen a substantial rise in the number of donors. Characterized by a spirit of abundance, generous people are more fulfilled as they give their time, friendship, expertise, and other resources. According to a study conducted at Case Western Reserve University, generous, compassionate individuals also live longer, happier, healthier lives.

Even our banknotes feature "the gracious and the good". Human beings are capable of great clarity and extreme confusion, of so much good and so much evil. If we acknowledge the distorted as well as glorious facets of life, if we accept our shadow as well as our light, we can evolve. Recognition of the value of compassion and generosity is expanding and we're learning that agitated minds can be trained to rest within a tranquil heart.

The grand convergence of mind, heart, and hands is the true, sustainable wealth. As warriors of the twenty-first century, our confidence arises from our allegiance to compassion and truthfulness, including transparent disclosure of interactions and agreements. Let's support and encourage humanitarians and entrepreneurs serving more people using fewer non-renewable resources. Innovative microsolutions as well as international cooperative projects around the planet manifest human creativity and goodwill.

Take a moment to be awake and aware of the potential and peril of this historic time. With our collective awareness and action, these challenges will provide opportunities to fuel environmental restoration and social reform as we work together for the common good.

Pause, Reflect, and Record

- Many citizens believe that *every* donation to political campaigns should be public information. If money did not control politics and "clean" election campaigns were funded by the public rather than wealthy individuals, labor unions, and corporations, how might the democratic process be affected?

- What is one step you could take to learn more about or change systemic injustice?

- In what ways is massive national debt one of the biggest threats to a nation's security?

- How is society destabilized when the middle class diminishes?

- How could humanity develop principled, equitable, global structures based on universal values?

26

Making a Life with Meaning

We make a living by what we get.
We make a life by what we give.

—Sir Winston Churchill

Human beings seek meaning and our brains are wired to find patterns in our complex perceptual fields. Life in all its forms, including giraffes, trees, and bacteria, live, reproduce, and die but human consciousness seems to know there's more to life. We feel there's a purpose or significance to our lives that's not obvious or directly expressed. *Who am I? Why am I here?* Clarifying, developing, and sharing our unique contributions to the world is an important element of making a life with meaning.

In a Nazi concentration camp, the psychiatrist Viktor Frankl experienced the profound importance of having meaning in one's life, of having something positive to strive for. Amidst the horrors, Dr. Frankl strove to self-determine his own response to his experiences and not be crushed by terror and degradation. With tremendous resilience, he chose compassion and courage over despair and fear.

"Being a great human being ... depends on caring about the well-being of all our fellow sentient beings," wrote Wu Yin, the abbess of Taiwan's Luminary Temple. Many people find it meaningful to perceive every moment as sacred and to socially engage their spiritual practices. Others strive to finish high school, find fulfilling work, save for a home, educate their children, or endow a philanthropic foundation. Some aspire to enhance at least one person's happiness every morning and decrease someone's suffering every afternoon. Toward what purpose, goals, or dreams do you strive? Your response determines the investment of your time, energy, and money as well as what dividends you may reap.

It's up to each one of us to make good use of the limited time we have on earth. Most people don't want to have lived their lives but missed the meaning. Goodness to go integrates our compassionate hearts and clear minds with physical action. What our hands offer is informed by our values, principles, and knowledge and is sustained by self-care. Joan Halifax is a respected teacher of Zen Buddhism. She wrote, "Recognize your limits with compassion; share your joy, stability, strength, openness, and humor; help to create a strong, supportive community; and above all, don't neglect the practice of self-care. If you really want to take care of the whole world, start by taking care of your life."

Self-care sustains integral service, including social justice activism. The Scottish philosopher-economist Adam Smith noted that injustice "will utterly destroy" society. Starting in childhood, we hear our deeply ingrained insistence on this globally shared ethic as young voices cry out, *"But that's not fair! It's not fair!"* At the heart of our sense of fairness is the recognition that all people are free and equal and should be treated equitably. It's not fair that our gender or skin color locks doors of opportunity or "justifies" abuse. If injustice is experienced throughout a lifetime or for generations, it can sour hearts and enrage minds. When we value generosity, honor the interests of others as well as our own, and continually add value to others' lives, justice will naturally be honored.

How do we create meaningful lives? One key element is our integral service. "Give and you shall receive," says an ancient proverb. Elements of our consumer culture that foster materialism, competition, and greed tell us to get out there and be go-getters. In the inspiring tale called *The Go-Giver*, the protagonist learns that his true worth and degree of influence are determined by how much more he gives in value than takes in payment, how many people he serves well, and how abundantly he places others' interests first.

Norman Lear, the writer-creator of many socially relevant television series, including *All in the Family, Maude*, and *The Jeffersons*, is a go-giver. Lear is an esteemed elder whose servant leadership takes the form of political and social activism as well as philanthropy. He funds youth programs from the proceeds of his new music endeavors and says, "I want to wake up every morning and do something that matters. That brings me great pleasure." Who do you especially admire in the growing global community of go-givers?

Some part of us knows that when we give with respect, we always receive. Giving to others in meaningful ways expands the quality of our lives and can increase our life spans. The most valuable gift we can offer is ourselves. Although we respect authenticity, justice, generosity, and purposeful benevolence, we're not sure at times how those values translate into ongoing action in our lives. Many people have experienced that committing to the path of integral service brings them the transformation they seek. At the same time, they don't duck personal responsibilities such as financial security, health and exercise, career development, relationships, and spiritual growth.

Ducks are moving targets. Is it ever possible to line up all the changing aspects of our lives in a prescribed way? Will our lives really be in mythical balance if all our ducks are somehow in a row? When we believe that our personal ducks come first, our goodness to go can get stuck. A useful question is not *How do I fit in community service or global citizen initiatives into my life?* but rather *How do I design my life around my commitment to integral service?* With this question as our compass, we'll take a stand to mobilize our goodness to go. Then we clarify what issue calls us most strongly. We may volunteer to an hour a month at a local Head Start program or articulate a larger-than-one-lifetime vision, such as universal education for all children.

The Song Within

With clear commitment to contribute beneficial service, other facets of life come into perspective. Social artists and activists let go of fixations that all personal ducks must be lined up before being able to create meaningful lives. The Bengali Nobel Prize–winning poet Rabindranath Tagore wrote about the lament of many: "I have spent my days stringing and unstringing my instrument / while the song I came to sing remains unsung." Each of us has a heart song yearning to be sung. The *song within* inspired the film *Music Within* based on the true story of a Vietnam veteran deafened in the line of duty. Eventually, his voice joined many other engaged citizens committed to civil justice for disabled individuals. Richard Pimentel joined the ranks of disability rights activists whose efforts led to the Americans with Disabilities Act of 1990 and the legal end of work, housing, and educational discrimination against disabled people of all ages.

From justice for the disabled and disenfranchised to global hunger, environmental degradation, and terrorism, the sheer magnitude of world suffering can be overwhelming. Violent attacks by mentally deranged individuals are increasing. Destabilized governments often lead to social chaos and violent criminality. Global temperatures and natural disasters are on the rise. Hopelessness and helplessness can creep in. However, if our intent is to create a meaningful life and manifest our purpose, then it's our responsibility to engage in sufficient self-care to enable us to do what we can.

Most of us will experience some trepidation as we step outside our comfort zone, and avoidance seems like an attractive alternative at times. We think we'll wait for the perfect moment in some fantasy future when we've attained eternal fearlessness and our proverbial ducks are in a row. Other tactics are workaholism, distraction, cynicism, self-sabotage, playing small, making excuses, withdrawing in guilt, hiding in apathy, or insisting on self-imposed limitations such as *I can't afford it or I don't have time.*

A familiar yet deceptive belief is that we don't have enough. How sensible and convincing ego sounds when it tells us that once we have enough, we'll listen to and act upon our deep life forces, yearnings, and callings. "Good things come to those who wait. Someday your ship will come in and then you'll have enough to start on those dreams. Take care of number one." This broken record keeps spinning in the illusory groove of current lack, promising future milk and honey when there will be enough of the right combination of time, money, emotional intelligence, energy, education, experience, psychological and spiritual maturity, good karma, auspicious astrological omens, and grace. Beware of poverty mentality and fantasies of some future perfect present.

Sing your song now. Mahatma Gandhi taught, "Live as if you were to die tomorrow. Learn as if you were to live forever." In Section Two, we explored ways to free our empowered minds from control by fear. Many spiritual traditions emphasize meditation, prayer, contemplation, and service as ways to disentangle ourselves from thoughts that fuel fear. Centuries ago, we were encouraged us to rise above fear and flow in widening rings of Being by the Persian poet-saint Rumi.

Others with a pragmatic psychological approach recognize that fear is going to be an element of our brief, vulnerable lives. Life is tough; fortunately, there are many ways to deal with its challenges with wisdom and compassion. We're encouraged to redirect our attention, rise above difficult situations to gain perspective, *or get over it.* Note the fear, and do it anyway. Trust yourself. Get on with living and doing what you came here to do.

Courage in Uncertain Times

In her book Insecure at Last, award-winning writer and international activist Eve Ensler challenges our obsession with security and safety. With powerful stories and insights, she reminds us that inherent in the quest for security is its undoing. Fearful clinging to illusory guarantees of safety makes us hypervigilant to who or what may threaten our fantasy of security. Fear reinforces dualistic thinking. Always seeing others as potential threats, we separate the world into "us" and "them," a duality that undermines our humanity. Love and compassion erode dualisms.

How do we become more comfortable with insecurity and uncertainty? The American Buddhist nun Pema Chodron has written extensively on ways to develop four limitless qualities that support freedom from fear: love, compassion, joy, and equanimity. Chodron writes: "Openness doesn't come from resisting our fears but from getting to know them well. We can't cultivate fearlessness without compassionate inquiry into the workings of ego." The wisdom practices described in Chodron's books support an ongoing evolution of opening our hearts and minds as we act in the world. This opening includes letting go. As we release old habits of clinging to hopes and fears, we become free of pairs of opposites, such as gain and loss or praise and blame. As we release attachment and aversion, we see that trying to find certainty in absolute rights or wrongs is just one more illusion of our insistence on security. "Am I going to practice peace," Chodron asks, "or am I going to war?"

Our cerebral cortex is regarded as the control center of the essence of our humanity. Its frontal lobes are the seat of empathy, understanding, humor, decision-making and problem solving. Cognition is able to override biological drives and ego reactivity. The frontal cortex overlays a more primitive region related to instincts and feelings that are potentially useful for survival, such as fear and anger. The evolved anatomy of human brains offers opportunities to develop and integrate the abilities of our "upstairs" and "downstairs" brains as well as the skills of both hemispheres of our brain. A fiber bundle connects the language and logic of the left hemisphere with the spatial creativity, sensation-informed, usually less verbal right hemisphere.

Courage and the integration of our brain's abilities are required to free ourselves from the dualistic, fear-based thinking that is a prison, or "optical delusion," of consciousness. Einstein reminded us that problems cannot be solved at the level of thinking that created them. It's difficult to optimize our life's potential if we're trapped in limited thoughts and behaviors. "Why do you stay in prison when the door is so wide open?," Rumi asks us to ponder deeply. Dualism is based on fear that fuels more fear. From everyday lapses of kindness to global atrocities, this fear-based thinking is the true threat to humanity.

Political power games and fanatical obstructionism waste precious time and energy. In destructive games of extreme polarization, players disrespect, distort, and even demonize worthy opponents. At this pivotal time in human history, we're called to mature, evolve, and engage our frontal cortex in mutually creative and productive problem solving. The future of our children and life on earth depends on how we navigate this potent time of peril and promise.

Woven through this book are reflections on the nature and sources of fear as well as the ways to manage fear. When others need our help, anxious feelings of overwhelm may hinder our goodness to go. Note the fear and take the first step. "Once compassionate vision is awakened, then your strength, longing, and inspiration increase in unexpected ways," writes Cynthia Kneen, a business consultant who explored personal courage in *Awake Mind, Open Heart.*

Open hearts and awake minds naturally care about the well-being of fellow beings and manifest compassion in action. Recall the many ways that courage and generosity shone in Haiti after the catastrophic earthquake in 2010. A woman trapped under rubble for over a week was pulled out singing. Orphans were adopted as emergency rations and medical support poured in. About ten days after Port au Prince collapsed, killing over 200,000 people, performers around the world gathered for a "Hope for Haiti Now" fundraiser, which was televised internationally. In spite of Haiti's cholera epidemics and electoral irregularities, the resilient Haitian spirit—with the goodness to go of many individuals—will gradually rebuild a more sustainable nation.

It Feels Good to Do Good

It feels good to celebrate our lives as we engage in self-care and the care of others. "The reward of a thing well done is to have done it," wrote Ralph Waldo Emerson. Self-acceptance and trust arise naturally when we experience our inner goodness, and the phrase *it feels good to do good* can be understood in several ways. One is that we enjoy and appreciate our commitment to benevolent action, and another is that we respect excellence: it feels good to perform well.

When we put forth the effort to perform with excellence, it feels good. We've offered our personal best and "been all that we can be." *Good job!* we say as we congratulate one another with two thumbs up. There's a healthy pride in doing one's best. The competence of a job well done is empowering and energizing, and that, in itself, feels good. Personal alignment and authenticity, the quality of our engagement in the process as well as beneficial results of our integral service are all sources of positive feelings.

Integral service is often an experience in which our goodness and our competence intersect in a grand convergence. Offering beneficial action makes us feel good. We feel more alive when we share our resources and abilities, when our lives have purpose and meaning. Imagine what it would feel like if no one was interested in you or the gifts you have to share.

Good feelings that are intrinsic to integral service can be experienced on individual, institutional, and community levels. When financial resources are invested in responsible ways to maximize social benefit as well as profit margins, investors feel good and do well financially. Growing numbers of corporations are committed to inclusive, sustainable growth and to doing well by *doing good.*

Endless accumulation and hoarding of excess don't sustain good feelings. Despite our assumptions, mounting evidence indicates that having more money than required to meet basic life needs does not make us happier. Money can't buy love, and the state of happiness cannot be purchased. Aligning our actions with universal principles and heeding our call to integral service nourish and sustain positive states of being.

The inestimable Helen Keller was very clear about this. She said, "Many persons have a wrong idea of what constitutes true happiness. It is not attained through self-gratification but through fidelity to a worthy purpose." In my daughter's home country of India, this is described as aligning yourself with your *dharma*, or sacred duty. An Indian business ethos is, "We can only do well when we do good, and we can only do good when we do well." Compassionate capitalism recognizes the triple bottom line of people, profits, and planetary health, and its corporations orient their business strategies to address social problems. Their definition of success is doing what's best for the world.

Our lives are more than self-improvement projects. Health and maturity are not ends in themselves. Thoughts like "When my self-esteem is better, then I might think about volunteering" or "Someday all my ducks will be in a row" are attempts to justify procrastination. This kind of thinking was explored at the beginning of Section Two: *When I've fixed enough pieces of myself and my life, when I've had enough therapy and saved enough money, when my ducks are lined up, I'll be ready to serve.* It's time to move outside the box of "personal wealth first, philanthropy later" thinking.

It's possible to spend our entire life in a never-ending process of consumer upgrades and self-improvement. This is not to say that daily practices that purify our heart and minds and sustain our connection to spirit are not valuable. The eco-philosopher Joanna Macy, Ph.D. and many others recognize the value of contemplative practices to reclaim personal power and nurture our inner resources of attention and compassion to increase freedom. Self-care empowers social action, "freeing us to respond in simplicity and immediacy to our fellow beings," Macy writes.

A familiar maxim exhorts us to *get our good going!* Spending available time *planning* to mobilize our intent to serve without moving into action wastes a lifetime. At some point, magnetizing available support internally and externally is much more fruitful than making more lists and attending more workshops. One small positive action helps to ground feelings of inertia or overwhelm. Actions usually speak louder than words and nurture the experience of self-efficacy above and beyond the delightful helper's high.

Competence and contentment are distinct from inflated self-esteem, the elusive element that was thought to be an essential prerequisite for positive behavior. Self-efficacy is not the same as self-esteem. Actions that emerge from our integrated wholeness offer the best of ourselves. When life is caring for life, it naturally feels good. The deep satisfaction and contentment that arise from our generosity and wisdom lead to a happiness more subtle than elation or pleasure.

Hundreds of research projects have shown that an experience of one's usefulness and competence is key to self-efficacy. Genuine self-esteem does not come from praise. Telling children how "special" they are often translates into feelings of entitlement, not genuine esteem or efficacy. Repeating "*Good job!*" ad nauseum and pressuring teachers to artificially inflate grades aren't meaningful and don't promote integrity.

Rather than nourishing self-esteem, praise often inflates a sense of superiority. Loyal patriots don't need to feel superior or demonize other countries. Hierarchical judgments inherent in some kinds of praise, such as insisting that our team, idea, or country is *the best*, lead to feelings of separateness and can fuel violence. Comparison creates conflict. Alienation has led to distorted thinking, self-radicalization, and senseless violence. For most us, resilient self-worth doesn't come from external, inflated praise or even from mere participation in an activity. What is key is the quality of authentic presence and effort as we participate.

Self-esteem and self-respect most often develop as a result of consistent effort toward a meaningful goal. In turn, doing well is about self-efficacy and the discipline needed to become proficient at anything. Earning good grades, making friends, learning to play an instrument, and living with integrity all take practice and nurture self-confidence. Nothing great comes easily.

Learners around the world participate in various programs and classes, training groups, and rehearsals. Many have experienced that the brief spark of inspiration after a weekend seminar is difficult to maintain unless their learning is consistently applied. Activities that are the most fun and sustainable and that make the most positive difference are those where participants work together over time toward shared goals. Community doesn't just happen; we have to build it. Meaningful employment, life goals, and service projects motivate people. In so many ways, it feels good to do good.

Our World Needs Us Alive

"You are closer to glory leaping an abyss than upholstering a rut," wrote the poet James Broughton. Our communities, nations, and planet need us to be awake, engaged, and well informed. Throughout *Goodness To Go*, we've looked at processes that build authentic self-regard, efficacy, and resilience. Recall some of the experiences, skill-building activities, or spiritual practices that have enriched your life. For many, faith in a higher power and regular meditation, contemplation, and centering prayer strengthen their resilience.

As we create meaningful lives that uplift others, genuine social, political, and religious freedoms are invaluable. If we've experienced freedom, we have an ongoing debt of gratitude to the innumerable heroic individuals whose integral service has contributed to freedom. We stand on strong shoulders. For those living in authoritarian regimes, simply knowing that freedom is alive on this planet and that global humanitarians are committed to social justice can be sustenance in dark times. The constant vigilance required to protect freedom and advance justice is deeply meaningful. Reigniting on a daily basis our reverence for life and profound gratitude for freedom is a torch lighting our path of service.

Life cares for life in infinite ways. The skills of resiliency noted in Section Two—emotion regulation, impulse control, causal analysis, empathy, reaching out, optimism, and self-efficacy, among others—are useful to the creation of a meaningful life. If they're consciously applied, we're less overwhelmed in the face of all there is to do to manage our lives and offer our gifts to the world. We learn to be present in the moment, do one thing at a time, cultivate confidence, and embrace change with suppleness, curiosity, and joy.

When you feel rushed or suffocated by limiting thoughts and feelings, remember that the door to freedom is wide open. Take whatever steps are necessary—deep breaths, writing to the newspaper, volunteering at a safehouse—to cross that threshold to inner freedom. The world needs us resourced, resilient, empowered, and alive. Patience withstands both good and ill. Fear, worry, greed, and cynicism constrict our lives and imprison our hearts and minds with bars of anger, judgment, and guilt. We serve no one by making ourselves trapped, small, or weak. It's empowering to focus our attention on the freedom to be fully alive in each moment.

Fear not. When we forget and are tempted to hunker down in the illusory safety and comfort of the status quo, the glorious game of life demands that we grow and evolve. George Leonard, a respected participant in the human potential movement, challenges us to embrace the play of life in which we act out various roles. Classroom volunteer, social rights activist, grandmother, or political representative may be some of many roles that we include in our life's changing cast of characters.

If the first few steps of your vision for integral service seem a little daunting, inhale self-care and then exhale your goodness to go. The magic of *mojo*, or self-assuredness, moves energy and makes space for the next step. *Get it done.* Get that first step made and out of your way. George Leonard writes: "Life is designed to keep us at the point of maximum tension between certainty and uncertainty, order and chaos. Every important call is a close one. We survive and evolve by the skin of our teeth. We really wouldn't want it any other way." Some days our response is *Wow!* and at other times *Whoa!*

Although we may be able to adjust its speed or mitigate its intensity for a while, life is an ongoing process of rebalancing, harmonizing, and letting go. Homeostasis is the natural state of exquisitely intricate balancing processes within our body and the earth's ecosystems. This dynamic living state is never static. For human beings to maintain their vitality, it's helpful to discern which elements of life need to be integrated and what needs to be released.

Part of the whole is missing when we're not available to show up and offer our gifts as well as ourselves. At times, we keep ourselves in the isolating doghouse of self-criticism, guilt, or other self-generated punishments to avoid full engagement in life. When we're present and give ourselves permission to shine, it's possible for our creativity and goodness to get going. Listening to our heart, integrating its wisdom with our mind, and moving our compassion into action makes us whole. From that wholeness, we offer our best to the world.

A lifespan is brief; love and wisdom live on. During our brief sojourn on planet earth, let's find creative ways to activate and express our unique gifts, profound generosity, and courageous goodness. Although death is a natural, inevitable stage of life, it's tempting to deny that it will happen to us. As curious or understandable as it may seem, most people prefer not to think about, accept, or embrace the death that many traditions describe as a mirror in which the true meaning of life is reflected.

Social movements are growing that encourage people of all ages to gather in small groups and engage in dialogue and exploration of issues related to death and the dying process. Numerous reports of near-death experiences describe luminous interconnectivity, awareness of the continuation of consciousness, and an absence of fear about death.

From the flaming edge of his short life, the young rebel James Dean modified Gandhi's reminder, saying, "Dream as if you'll live forever. Live as if you'll die today." As we contemplate our death, we realize that we must look into our lives right now. Obviously, if we wait until we're on our deathbed to wake up, it's far too late. We are free to live fully engaged with each moment and to die with confidence and the contentment of having created a meaningful life.

Pause, Reflect, and Record

- What is the song you came to sing? If you're not singing it now, what are you waiting for?

- In what thoughts and forms does avoidance of discovering and living your life purpose show up in your life? How might you counteract these habits and strengthen new, supportive strategies that expand life's possibilities?

- Describe a time when you *felt good by doing good or did well by doing good.*

- Recall a person or an experience that set off a metamorphosis that made you feel more fully alive. In what ways did this experience strengthen your sense of self-efficacy or self-confidence?

27

You're Already Enough

Do the thing you believe in.
Do the best you can in the place
where you are and be kind.

—Scott Nearing

You are already enough and are sufficiently resourced to offer your goodness to go. Life is a mystery, death is certain, our path is unpredictable and change is inevitable. Change is inherent to physical growth and cell renewal, yet there are no genetically determined processes on the emotional, cognitive, and spiritual levels of human development. We get older and our bodies reach adult proportions, but there's no guarantee that we'll mature psychologically.

What leads to emotional, psychological, and spiritual maturation? Without reflection and integration of our experiences, we tend to make the same old mistakes. Thoughts and feelings change constantly, yet it takes discernment and commitment to "grow up." If we stay stuck in a habit of blame, who and what we blame may change but we don't evolve psychologically. Learning to forgive can be difficult inner work, but the pain of spinning in old mental ruts prods us to try something new. Evolution is possible on many planes other than the physical.

With sufficient clarity about your goodness to go, everything else tends to take care of itself. "Sufficiency is the exquisite state of being where you are enough, you have enough and you envision a world where this is true for all," writes Kay Sandberg, the founding director of the Global Force for Healing. Wherever we are on our path, we're "good enough" just as we are right now. Earlier, we looked at the delusion about lining up our ducks before extending to others. It's not that we need to evolve first and then find the perfect time to offer service. The process is more akin to an interweaving double helix than a simple linear equation as our personal growth spirals with our interpersonal generosity. *We have enough and are enough* already to offer our integral service, and as we serve, we'll simultaneously engage the process of personal evolution.

An inspiring vision or meaningful direction for your personal contribution may be clear for you at this point. The Women Roofers are volunteers in North Carolina whose mission is to fix roofs for people who cannot afford the repairs. This group of mothers, grandmothers, and widows started as a church project. Years later, with donated materials from the Rutherford Housing Partnership, the women continue to enjoy their goodness to go. They've experienced that loving service makes life worth living.

We're explorers and inventors of our own life's journey. For positive transformation to occur on a personal or global level, thinking or even visioning differently is a good beginning. Then, we need to practice *being* different—awake, compassionate, and resilient—and *doing* differently. If we try to visualize world peace without addressing the violence in our lives and communities, the wish becomes a vapid mush of "whirled peas." *Let there be peace and let it begin with me.*

It's up to us to make good use of the time we've been given and manage our energy on physical, emotional, cognitive, psychological, and spiritual levels. A creative service endeavor may spark enthusiasm for a day or a week but, without careful tending, the demands of everyday life dampen the fire. While the embers of creativity never burn out completely, there are many habits that clutter our world or drain our energy and time. The support of positive habits and commitments is helpful when temptations to succumb to unhealthy choices creep into our day. Muscles, including our resilience and courage muscles, get tired. Nourishment and rest are needed to recover vitality and strength.

Few people want to waste their lifetime or leave undeveloped the gifts, talents, resources, and creative intelligence with which they've been blessed. Goodness to go doesn't require great amounts of time and energy. Even brief, positive social interactions are investments in each other's well-being. When we laugh together, stress hormones are reduced and our brain's activity synchronizes with the other person's. Although we measure time with clocks and say that time is money, the priceless gift of time is regarded as sacred by many people.

The energy of time wants to be uplifted by our actions. A few of the ways that we drain the profound gifts of time and energy are rushing, procrastination, mindless escapes, addictions, obsessively collecting information, and workaholism. Desperate to avoid judgments about being *not good enough*, perfectionism whips us or tempts us to not start or finish anything. On the otherhand, with gratitude and mindfulness, we live as if every moment is a miracle.

Co-Creating Our Vision

Imagine all of us serving the common good in a fellowship of humankind. "Human kindness is overflowing, and I think it's going to rain today," sang Randy Newman decades ago. To co-create the world of our dreams, our kindness will cultivate the courage to act together with a shared vision. Realistic optimism is implied. "Optimism is a political act," wrote Alex Steffen, one of the world's leading voices on social innovations, sustainability, and planetary futurism. "Those who benefit from the status quo are perfectly happy for us to think nothing is going to get any better. In fact, these days, cynicism is obedience."

Passive acquiescence to a status quo of *business as usual* is harmful at this point; fortunately, processes of co-creation are emerging around the globe. Charting our own course, being a follower, or assuming leadership roles are familiar choices. Yet, we're all creators with infinite things we can make: we can make trouble, make excuses, or *make good*. Will we make peace or make war? The evolution of our new We paradigm requires that we create together as respected equal partners sharing benevolent intent. Of course, this is enhanced by inner work that increases self-understanding so that we bring clarity and compassion to our relationships.

In order to co-create a mutually beneficial future, we need accurate information and intelligent predictions, not opinions or rumors. Warren Washington, Ph.D., an internationally esteemed climate researcher, has garnered numerous awards and inspired other African Americans to serve as scientists. In 2010, Washington was awarded the National Medal of Science for his valuable contributions to humanity's understanding of the effects of climate change. He explains how increased environmental carbon dioxide acidifies the oceans and kills marine life. Global temperatures are rising, which increases the frequency of tropical rainstorms and the ferocity of cyclones. As glaciers melt and sea levels rise, millions of climate refugees will lead to humanitarian and national security concerns. Clearly, our collaborative creative intelligence is needed to address these complex issues.

Buddha taught that the wise shape their lives as carefully as a carpenter shapes wood. A clear vision of what we want to create and how we want to be on this good earth is invaluable. Helen Keller, with tremendous courage supported by the creative resilience of her teacher Anne Sullivan, transcended blindness and deafness to create her life's vision. Having experienced that happiness is attained through fidelity to a worthy cause, she wrote, "The most pathetic person in the world is someone who has sight but no vision." As a social activist, Keller committed her lifetime to doing a world of good, and longed to acquire more normal speech cadences because of "how much more good" she could have brought about.

Helen Keller's empathy for the human condition ran deep, and it's unlikely that she thought we're pathetic if we lack the guiding light of a clear life vision at times. However, the suppression or crippling of our willingness to discover and manifest our life's purpose is tragic. Why allow any part of our short lifetime on earth to die prematurely? Fearful or hostile avoidance of our integral service is a waste of precious time and energy and denies others the benefit of our contributions.

Discomfort is part of life, and is distinct from the suffering that is related to our reaction to pain. The temporary psychological pain experienced as ego breaks through a limitation and we wake up is ultimately beneficial. Often, as we see through false assumptions, our path becomes smoother, we suffer less, and our potency is leveraged in ways that we couldn't foresee. Staying tightly bound is usually much more painful than blossoming. Like flowers, our *choiceless choice* is to open, blossom, and give of ourselves. Staying stuck in self-suffocating habits is a cause of suffering; nearly every birth involves some pain. It serves no one when we refuse to blossom fully or try to hide our light and stay small.

Wisdom traditions teach that even as we feel pain, we can release suffering that may accompany the pain. The release of suffering is a surrender, a relinquishing of our resistance to pain, and when we change our relationship with pain, suffering is often released. Many people with severe chronic pain come to accept its daily presence and are able to move on with their lives quite cheerfully. Despite ongoing pain or disability, they've developed the resilience and ability to free themselves from suffering. Roger Ebert was a passionate film critic who refused to feel sorry for himself and kept working after cancer surgery removed his larynx and disfigured his face. For decades, despite a debilitating neurological disease, the theoretical physicist Stephen Hawking has directed research institutes and contributed to humanity's understanding of cosmology.

As we strengthen our mind and cultivate the qualities of an awakened heart and mind, including courage and patience, we develop wise and beneficial ways to respond to personal and planetary challenges. As discussed in Chapter 4, one self-care technique that benefits others is the practice of *tonglen*, utilizing the breath of compassion. Making art or music about an issue that concerns you, fundraising, offering vocal empowerment workshops, writing to politicians, planting extra vegetables in your garden to alleviate others' hunger, or mentoring a child are forms of the out-breath of compassion in action.

What Is Readiness?

Consider that you are already enough and have sufficient personal resources to step into your integral service. Moment by moment, you're as ready as you'll ever be. What are ways that you've cultivated a state of readiness with which to meet a new endeavor or a familiar fear? "The readiness is all," wrote William Shakespeare. What is readiness and how do we cultivate it? Before we can answer the question "Ready for what?" we sense the value in making our state of readiness and response-ability more conscious and skillful.

A Zen teaching states that wisdom is a ready mind. We're not talking about the kind of readiness suggested in the comment "Ready or not, here I come!" Research scientists note that engaged, inquiring minds are prepared to recognize the importance of emerging patterns of data, anomalies, and new insights. Being present, informed, and attentive are basic elements of a ready mind that respects accurate facts, shaping them into knowledge and wisdom.

Volumes have been written about a person's readiness to make a change. Motivation is a very complex subject. Although language tends to be linear, and the notion of stages, steps, and levels seems to imply a lockstep progression, our emotional, psychological, and spiritual processes don't follow linear sequences. At different points in our lives, we may have more or less energy to devote to civic engagement. However, if we're committed to taking a stand, we'll find a way to serve in some capacity. Usually, all we have to do is ask what is needed.

Simply being aware of an issue is a start. Are we willing to shine the light of consciousness, integrity, and knowledge on a social injustice or environmental ill? The philosopher Alan Watts commented, "Normally, we do not so much look at things as overlook them." Can we slow down and really see beyond the surface? The potential to cultivate an open mind that dwells in the deep silence at the heart of things is available to us. In that silent stillness, it's possible to acknowledge and appreciate the infinite, changing levels and facets of reality.

A strong, supple mind is able to rest in paradox and hold the validity of opposing ideas. This can be especially challenging in our age of staccato signals of constant information and misinformation. Paul Simon sings about loose affiliations of millionaires and billionaires, and observes that often we see what we want to see and disregard the rest. It's difficult to discern the integrity of our news sources and the quality of our thinking. Yet, a wise and ready intellect seeks to be informed not deluded, and puts forth earnest effort to be as unbiased and discerning as possible.

The readiness of a prepared mind that has done its "own work" as well as homework perceives patterns, relationships, and synchronicities. Think of the preparedness of Isaac Newton's mind whose insight about gravity was triggered by the falling of an apple. Such a mind is relatively free from conditioning about the limits of what is judged to be true or possible. An awake and ready mind understands and integrates new experience with a mature capacity for wisdom and keen discernment. Its freedom allows us to offer our best while remaining unattached to outcomes.

"If there is to be any peace," observed the twentieth-century writer Henry Miller, "it will come through being not having." This includes claiming or "having" the fruits of our actions. As we regularly refresh our readiness to engage our goodness to go, it's valuable to be free from attachment to its outcomes. If we want something, the poet Rumi suggested, release the wish and let it light on its desire, completely free of the personal. We do our best and let it go. This is what some call "selfless" or unconditional service.

A prepared mind may not have every piece of information that is stored in its memory's warehouse or in global storehouses of knowledge, but its intellect does have the capacity to choose sound ends and appropriate means. For many people, the integrity of the means employed to realize their dreams is as important as the integrity of their goals. Through experience, they've learned that unscrupulous means do not justify seemingly positive ends.

The wisdom of a ready mind is an element of character. When our daughter was eight years old, we were reading a bedtime story in which a reference to a person's character was made. I asked Grace if she knew what character meant. "Yes," she replied. "It is a mindful, heartful, kind person who always speaks the truth.

That just about sums it up. If we want to develop the kindness, awareness, and depth of character that supports our life's service, it invariably means that we'll choose to participate in uncomfortable, even difficult circumstances. Our willingness to strengthen endurance and deepen our tenderness contributes to the development of a ready mind.

Vision in Action

Yasuhiko Kimura is an integral philosopher ordained as a Zen Buddhist priest who founded Vision-In-Action, a public benefit corporation whose mission is to promote original thinking as a creative approach to restore wholeness to our troubled world. Among his many writings is a collection of essays entitled *Think Kosmically, Act Globally* in which he shares his passions about human evolution and the integration of spiritual philosophy and physical science.

Kimura and many others articulate key elements of integral service and express the importance of inner work leading to self-knowledge. "As authentic self-knowledge begins to unfold, our principles, thoughts, commitments, and actions rise up to be in accord with who we truly are," wrote Kimura. "Then we are able to sustain our commitment ... because it is now an authentic expression of our Authentic Self and is based on authentic Self-knowledge. ... We can sustain only the kind of commitment that is in accord with who and what we are and with our principles and values."

How do you sustain valued, long-term commitments in your life? To what or whom, including yourself, your values, your community or your planet, are you committed? What roles do loyalty, long-term friendships, deep bonds of love, and steadfast commitments play in your life? Reflect on what realigns and refreshes your aspirations. How do you ready your mind to be sufficiently present, open, and courageous to make the first step on a new path?

Einstein noted that he never made mistakes; rather, he always learned from experience. Having a problem can inspire an intention and commitment to move forward on our path of human evolution. We may try to blow off engagement with challenges to the status quo by glibly saying, "*What-ever.*" The callous indifference often inherent in this comment doesn't foster deep understanding of systemic forces underlying current problems. Creative problem solvers care about turning data and ideas into humane solutions and intelligent designs.

Many social commentators remind us that challenges are creative evolutionary tensions and essential elements of our life's journey. New approaches to solving today's problems with curiosity and wonder are emerging. Some problems may not be delightful but serve as obstacles in our path that we must overcome in order to move forward. We learn from the experience and the light of our awareness creates solutions that will uplift tomorrow. In the exquisite words of poet Elizabeth Barrett Browning, "Light tomorrow with today."

Gathering Your Resources

It takes awareness, intention, and commitment to continually weave threads of inspiration into our daily lives. William Stafford celebrated the way of the thread that's often difficult for others to see in the poem "Last Words: The Way It Is." In this poem, Stafford wrote about the thread that we follow through life's changes and don't let go of, even when others don't understand our path. Calvin Coolidge, the U.S. president during the 1920s a decade of dynamic social change, reminded us that persistence is far more important than talent, genius, or education to the manifestation of our vision.

In *The Rhythm of Compassion*, Gail Straub outlines four phases that you may experience as you prepare consciously and conscientiously to offer yourself and your gifts in service:

1. **Preparing the ground.** When you're awake to the rhythm of compassion pulsing between your in-breath of self-care and your out-breath of caring for the world, you'll choose when to serve and what kind of service is right for you.

2. **Uncovering your social shadow.** As you bring light to the dark burdens of ignorance, guilt, shame, shoulds, selfishness, and egotistical arrogance, personal suffering dissolves and energy is released that can benefit others.

3. **Developing mature compassion.** Unconditional presence, a calm mind, and open heart allow your wisdom, mercy, and right action to uproot pain and suffering. You're free to act from your heart's pure intentions.

4. **Practicing socially engaged spirituality.** Suffering is transformed as shadowed places, states, and situations are illumined with compassion and integrity. As your willingness to open to suffering expands, beneficial action naturally emerges.

We have unique capacities and there are many ways that diverse personalities and constitutions make life changes. Some of us dive in. Others circumvent obstacles by flowing around boulders on their path. Devotion to a higher calling can transform lives and many choose to methodically research, organize, and prepare for an intended change. Our readiness needs to be continuously refreshed and flexible since life's changes are often unintended, surprising, and tend to blindside us at times.

Be playful and have fun along the way. "A little nonsense now and then is relished by the wisest men," said British fighter pilot and writer Roald Dahl. Both pleasure and purpose are part of a fulfilled life. The discomfort of resistance to change is reflected in humorous comments—*change is good; you go first.* Blur the lines between service, work, and play. Remember compassionate self-care, which includes enjoying your life.

Consider this: if you're alive, there's a reason you're here. And if you're here, you're needed. You are the world and you're invited and encouraged to contribute who and what you are. The ocean refuses no river, songwriter Sheila Chandra reminds us. From every direction, in whatever state they may be, the ocean welcomes all rivers flowing into its depths. We're good enough and ready enough, just as we are, to offer the river of our life's service.

Pause, Reflect, and Record

- What has been your usual response to challenges to your status quo? For example, how have you approached the decision to raise a child, change careers, commit to daily meditation practice, or expand your circle of giving?

- How could you enhance your skillfulness in managing your life resources of space, time, money, and energy?

- What values are compelling life forces that guide, inform, and inspire your life? (Consider taking the Signature Strengths Survey developed by psychologist Martin Seligman, Ph.D. at www.authentichappiness.org.) How could you apply these to your goodness to go?

- Are you willing to incorporate integral service in your life and ready enough to design your life around it? What changes do you need to make to address that calling?

28

How Do I Start?

The … deeper spirit of altruism … that is visible is minor compared to what people carry in their hearts unreleased or scarcely released. Mankind is waiting and longing for those who can accomplish the task of untying what is knotted.

—Albert Schweitzer

In the previous chapter, we claimed our readiness to enter the river of integral service. Many people have come to the understanding that only a life lived for others is worth living. Choosing not to dally in the shallows, they reflect deeply on causes of injustice and inequity as well as on the mobilization of goodness. Repeatedly, Martin Luther King, Jr. asked himself, "What is the moral assignment?" After understanding a situation to the best of his ability, he'd determine a wise course of action, start moving, and keep going.

Make a plan, put it into action, and follow-though. "Action is the foundational key to all success," observed the renowned artist Pablo Picasso. A proverb reminds us that the good we do is not lost, though we forget. The hopeful impulses that inspire our compassion in action are part of our legacy. At this point in your engagement with *Goodness To Go*, is there anything that seems to be preventing the initiation of your integral service? What do you need to take the first step of your action plan? What would you like to contribute to the world that would support your experience of a life well lived?

Our legacy as wise and compassionate ancestors will benefit generations to come. As we imbibe that responsibility, each of us can do small things with great love, spreading our love everywhere we go. With mindfulness, we get our game back and focus on working with what we have. Extending beyond our psychological comfort zone expands our creative courage and frees up energy to take our next step. "It is the mind that makes the body," said nineteenth-century abolitionist and African American social reformer Sojourner Truth.

As you increase the capacity to be mindful of your intent to offer integral service, a new relationship with your life develops. President Theodore Roosevelt encouraged us to dare greatly, spending ourselves on a worthy cause. His distant cousin, President Franklin D. Roosevelt, later said, "Do what you feel in your heart to be right—for you'll be criticized anyway." Turn within, listen to your inner wisdom, summon the power of your heart, and live an intentional life.

Even with the resilience to withstand misunderstanding, false accusations, and criticism, it's helpful to explore how we approach the decision-making process. One style is to avoid making decisions and succumb to a lazy laissez-faire mode. Slide by as a drifter. Even dead fish can go with the flow. Whatever will be will be. Don't make waves. Another style tries to leave our interests and dreams out of the equation and go for the impersonal and practical. Internal tug-of-wars characterize other approaches to decision-making as various factors, risks, benefits, and values are considered.

Does your heart and soul call out to be an artist or change agent while your mind clings to job security? Sometimes we're stuck in passivity or let our upbringing, cultural conditioning, or engrained habits choose for us. At other times we clarify courses of action that are guided by unconditioned wisdom and are more likely to be beneficial. "No matter how far you have gone on the wrong road," a Turkish proverb reminds us, "turn back."

Making Decisions Mindfully

Mindful decisions are informed by kindness and intelligent use of accurate information. Let's look at an approach to decision-making that we can choose with more or less consciousness. A coin might be a metaphor: tails—we run and hide away; heads—we take a responsible approach that integrates mind and heart. Even an avoidant laissez-faire mode—*whatever; we don't need oversight; let it be; go with the flow*—is a choice. However, if our goal is to lead our lives intentionally from a place of generative wisdom and efficacy, passive avoidance of our decision-making responsibilities is unhelpful.

When we're tempted to avoid making an active decision, our reaction may be to rock back and forth between possible, even seemingly opposite ideas. "Yes, I'll exercise today. No, maybe I'll start when I might feel more motivated." When we're infants, we're rocked in a cradle. It's comforting on many levels and appropriate at that age and stage of our development. We're innocent and understandably ignorant of critical issues facing our fellow human beings.

When we're older, swaying in a hammock soothes our nervous system and offers comforting rest and relaxation. Then, it's time to raise the sails and set forth again. Although it may seem wonderful for a while to avoid the decisions of daily life, we're abdicating responsibility for our lives if we let others make decisions for us. If we allow naïve innocence, ignorance, and avoidance to take over, we can get stuck in a reactive rocking stage—*should I do this or that?*—and end up going nowhere in a geriatric rocking chair.

A more mindful approach to making decisions is to engage in personal introspection, articulate our goals, and develop action steps. Different personality types have stronger predilections for this kind of active decision making. It takes more than a great idea or vision of your path to manifest your integral service or creative expression. A Japanese proverb reminds us, "Vision without action is a daydream. Action without vision is a nightmare."

Self-inquiry, reflection, and contemplation are elements of engaged approaches to decision making. Why do I want to extend my service beyond my immediate family? What are my strengths and interests? What social issue consistently attracts my attention and concern? What do I value? What do I want my legacy to be? Introspection and contemplation include the wisdom of the heart as well as the mind; for many people, the integration of heart and mind is one seamless awareness.

As you begin to envision and articulate the types of service that are aligned with your values and interests, it's important to keep your heart in mind. Be attuned to images that arise from dreams or intuitions. An unexpected synchronicity might fire your imagination. Ideas about what constitutes an ideal model or approach to solving a problem meet the reality of facts on the ground. Having a long-term notion about how to reduce the population explosion needs financial and medical data as well as compassionate understanding of the short-term needs of impoverished people. Otherwise, the worthy attempt will invariably end up on the dust pile of great ideas from talking heads.

Sometimes our stated goals are sabotaged by less conscious conflicting goals or beliefs. For example, we may say we'll delegate responsibilities to other volunteers but have a hidden goal or agenda that we want to be seen as indispensable and in full control. We wish we could be slim and healthy but have no intention of disciplining our nightly cookies and ice cream habit. Conflicting goals stand in the way of stated goals. An adult education professor at Harvard University, Robert Kegan, Ph.D., consults with organizations and individuals about useful ways to achieve positive change. He suggests five steps that help to identify goals that conflict with our stated goal:

1. **Sabotaging behaviors.** List things you do (and don't do) that inhibit progress toward your stated goal. One example is when you've realized that early morning is an optimal time to exercise but you continue to go to bed too late to support that intention.

2. **Underlying fears.** For each inhibiting behavior, ask yourself, "When I imagine myself doing something different, or even the opposite, what fears arise?" You might fear you'll lose personal time to relax in the evening. Or you may resent losing the autonomy to eat whatever you want whenever you want, or fear being hungry or unable to sleep if bedtime snacks are reduced.

3. **Conflicting goals.** Rewrite fears in ways that express your attachment or commitment to hidden or conflicting goals. For example, "I insist on eating *what* I want *when* I want it."

4. **Challenging assumptions.** Look at each of your fears again. Describe your assumptions, mistaken ideas, and irrational fears about the worst consequences that could happen if you let go of your conflicting goals. For example, "If I follow other people's health advice, I'll no longer be the boss of me." Challenge this conflicting belief by asking, "Is that true? How do I really know that is true? Could the opposite be true?" Simplistic reactions aren't expressions of true freedom. Uncover your core values. Instead of resisting the helpful suggestions of others, embrace healthy eating when that is your free choice after careful consideration.

5. **Consequences of pursuing a stated goal.** List possible negative and positive consequences of committing fully to your goal relatively free of internal resistance. For example, "I'd have to reduce the number of tasty bedtime calories and perhaps spend

money getting smaller-sized clothing. On the other hand, internally motivated and sustained discipline would enhance my self-respect as well as my state of wellness. I'd be healthy enough to enjoy my grandchildren and continue the work that I love."

Although it's efficacious for some people to make several significant behavior changes at the same time, small changes are more sustainable for many others. Our hidden, conflicting goals are often based in beliefs that shape our sense of who we are or were. When new intentions and stated goals challenge these old beliefs, our minds frequently react and resist strongly. For example, if we haven't updated an early belief about the invincibility of our health, we may react defiantly when reminded that to be optimally healthy, we can no longer smoke, eat whatever we desire, sit most of the day, and refuse to exercise.

Dr. Kegan reminds us that it's fairly common for ego to set us up for failure to prove that it was right in the first place; this is a form of self-sabotage. It's helpful not to attach any importance to negative thoughts or feelings of unworthiness. They're not who we are and they come and go like clouds in the vast blue sky. As we look for the sun in their midst and concentrate on our good qualities, our minds become stronger and more peaceful.

Sweeping proclamations without a long-term plan rarely achieve the success of specific, scheduled steps made with clear intent and commitment. The familiar New Year's resolution to "exercise more" quickly falls to the wayside whereas the mindful intention to walk for fifteen minutes after lunch five days a week is more likely to result in cardiovascular fitness. Consider inviting a motivated colleague to walk with you. It's also useful to discuss goals and change behavior with those who will be affected by those changes. Their understanding of our intent and reasons for new behavior increases the likelihood of their support.

As we've discussed, both tempered reason and an open heart are required to articulate and manifest our ideas and visions. The ability to give voice to our thoughts and feelings through the right of free speech is empowering and deeply valued. Global vocal uprisings are connecting through digital media but technological advances that can speed up the change that builds a better world continue to be double-edged swords. The interconnectedness of our world made possible by the Internet allows individuals to spread mutually beneficial ideas or caustic virulence that feeds flames of fear, hatred, and violence.

Former president Bill Clinton has noted that we live in a contentious and partisan time. "We are more connected than ever before, more able to spread our ideas and beliefs, our anger and fears. As we exercise the right to advocate our views, and as we animate our supporters, we must all assume responsibility for our words and actions before they enter a vast echo chamber and reach those both serious and delirious, connected and unhinged."

The loose cannon of manipulative rhetoric has led to assassinations, genocide, senseless violence, and increased global terrorism. Internet bullying has been a contributing factor in the suicide of young people. The Anti-Defamation League's Scott Levin said, "The reckless and irresponsible spread of such vitriol only heightens the divisions in our communities at a time when we should be finding ways to diminish, not increase, hateful rhetoric in public debate." Some people argue against any kind of "speech control," regardless of how untruthful, hateful, or incendiary it may be. Nevertheless, with great freedom of speech comes great responsibility.

Moving Intention into Action

"If a man would move the world, he must first move himself," Socrates and others have observed. We know that a journey of a thousand miles begins with a single step. Begin within. Identify aspirations and choices that you have and a worthy cause that draws your commitment. Get started. Write down your vision of integral service and develop an action plan. Find ways to make the process as gentle, enjoyable, and easeful as possible.

Try a practice run. Take one small step in the direction you'd like to go, and then another. Movement shakes up the anxious thoughts and cobwebs of inaction that create the illusion of being stuck. Your intention for positive change and contribution will attract the most amazing synchronicities: a global philanthropist lives in your neighborhood, another guest at a party knows a valuable resource for you, or your intuition leads you to a useful book or event.

More than 2,000 years ago, the Roman philosopher and statesman Cicero reminded us that the beginnings of all things are small. The courage to risk change and take responsible action arises from alignment with personal values and clearly articulated goals. Beware of getting trapped in analysis paralysis. Make a move and get unstuck. The nature of energy and our human bodies is to move. If we are, as Einstein said, more energy than matter, then move we must.

There are many ways to move, of course. We can contract or expand, flow or resist. We can move aggressively or gracefully. It's most meaningful to move toward our stated goal, aware that it will continue to evolve. From a wheelchair, a lawyer fought until her last breath for the rights of the disabled. A photographer went to Calcutta and eventually created the award-winning documentary *Born into Brothels*. Her organization has funded the freedom and educational opportunities for many children who otherwise may never have been able to escape sex-trade slavery.

We're called to integral service in our own unique way. Chapter 23 looked at some of the ways people move from concern into action: diving in, direct connection, concerned sensibility, and being drafted or invited onto a path of service. As we begin to mobilize our goodness to go, it's helpful to find or create a community of people who have similar commitments. We may not be able to sustain our motivation or accomplish our goal on our own, but we can do it together. The importance of creating community will be discussed further in Section Four of *Goodness To Go*.

The poet Mary Oliver has described her own moment of mobilized concern as the day she finally knew what she had to do in spite of the warnings, sneers, and skepticism of voices inside and out. "Do not be too timid. ... All life is an experiment. The more experiments you make, the better," wrote Ralph Waldo Emerson. People of all ages, including children, scientists, artists, and inventors, make countless mistakes from which they learn along the way.

Whether with trepidation or joy, it's time to get going. If fear creeps in, ask, "If I take just this one step, what else might I be able to do in my life? What goodness and joy might I bring to myself and others? If I'm willing to take some heat and pressure, if I'm willing to tolerate the discomfort of trying something new, how might I be transformed? What diamonds might be created?" Clarify your values and goals, listen to your heart, and take the first steps on your path of integral service.

Pause, Reflect, and Record

- What are you deeply concerned about? What fills you with wonder and enthusiasm? In what ways are you willing to conserve, protect, or expand what you value? Articulate your intentions related to this concern and one step that you could take this week.

- Make a list of personal energy leaks, ways that you drain or waste time and energy. How could you conserve your resources that could be redirected toward service?

- Have you resisted a call to compassionate action, such as insisting that you *can't be bothered* about immigration or reproductive justice?

- If you sometimes just go with the flow or opt out with a laissez-faire attitude, could there be an underlying fear or conflict that keeps you from inaction? If so, use Dr. Robert Kegan's five steps described in this chapter to explore the resistance or resentment of a conflicting goal that sabotages your stated goal.

29

Rippling Through the Web

Service rests on the basic premise ...
that life is a holy mystery ...
Only service heals.
From the perspective of service,
we are all connected.

—Rachel Naomi Remen, M.D.

We are interconnected and our actions ripple through the web of life. When we've untied knots that block our goodness to go, our compassion is free to move through our lives and around the world. Visionary artists and mystics throughout the ages have sought to express a net of interbeing that connects us all. In daily lives that are frequently ego bound, it's easy to overlook our subtle interconnectivity and oneness. We may long for a deeper communion, said the poet T.S. Eliot, but our attention is repeatedly distracted by the demands of daily living. It requires steadfast commitment to sustain focus on the light of our highest intentions for our lives.

What goes around comes around. Again and again, as we bring our attention and imagination back to the goodness rippling through the web of being, we free ourselves from narrow self-centeredness. Instead of grasping at life's goodies, we offer our goodness. The faculties of mindful awareness and creative imagination allow us to envision the goodness that is ours to give as our love for life is expressed kindness, appreciation for the unique beauty of each moment, and devotion to one another. Our integral service is infused with a delight that is uniquely ours.

Understandably, the image of a web was used to describe worldwide computer interconnectivity that continues to expand exponentially. In addition to providing information, connecting social networks, sharing innovations, and promoting commerce, websites and community networks are promoting reciprocal trade or cash-free bartering transactions that include swapping products and services. Social media—using online and mobile tools to communicate user-generated content—is a powerful tool. Although they provide easy ways to spread opinions and unfounded rumors, the diffusion of innovative ideas as well as interdisciplinary collaboration and networking has increased significantly as well. In relationships, communications, and actions, the integrity of our intent and discernment is paramount.

Our global community needs us to release any knots confining our spirit of altruism. Possibility and opportunity abound. Our goodness to go may be at a crossroads where shadowy fears meet the light of courage some are ready and eager to integrate integral service into their daily lives. Numerous related issues great and small affect life on earth today. It's empowering to know that our actions springing from positive intent ripple out and affect untold nodes of this interconnected web.

As we offer our goodness to go, we "connect the dots" of understanding, aspiration, and compassion through the net of inter-being. Issues and actions are linked together in a global web of networks that include nodal points of individuals, nonprofit organizations, social enterprises, philanthropic foundations, and government agencies. Networks of motivated people are more creative and adaptable than hierarchies.

In hierarchical structures, various levels tend not to share information and ideas freely or encourage innovation beyond the status quo. This systemic weakness of hierarchies was evident in the fall of Kodak, a corporation that made film for millions of cameras used around the world. Kodak was an industry giant that failed to connect the dots and imagine the demise of the need for their product. Networks of creative individuals in other companies developed effective ways to adapt to the new digital technologies that made the use of film obsolete for most people.

Top-down hierarchical models that have been dominant for centuries in many countries exclude most people from opportunities to fully develop their potential. As new opportunities for online education, microfinance, promotion of social movements, and other forms of global interconnectivity develop, the time for trickle-down paradigms is ending. We can do better than slowly drip a few beneficial changes and resources down to those on lower tiers of an economic pyramid. Evolution toward greater equity and justice, mutual respect, and reverence is emerging in many parts of the world. World Pulse is an action media network powered by women from 190 countries who tell their stories, reform laws, and co-create a better world.

Civil and human rights movements are spreading their wings to include immigration and reproductive justice issues. As we embrace paradigms such as networks and webs that are more inclusive, it's counterproductive to be naïve or gullible. As we've explored, the powerful tool of the Internet spreads ideas and information that can be used to uplift people or exploit and attack them. Sadly, predatory humans continue to prey upon those who are most vulnerable. At this point in our evolution, not every node in the network is a light-reflecting gem. Recall that a primary goal of the terrorist Osama bin Laden was to create "a thousand bin Ladens" with interconnected webs of darkness.

In *Mountains Beyond Mountains,* Pulitzer Prize–winning author Tracy Kidder chronicled the inspiring work of Paul Farmer, M.D., founder of the acclaimed international philanthropy Partners in Health. Kidder writes: "Many people find it easy to imagine unseen webs of malevolent conspiracy in the world and they are not always wrong. But there is an innocence that conspires to hold humanity together and it is made up of people who can never fully know the good they have done."

This is the kind of innocence that is inherent to our goodness to go. The ice cream company Ben & Jerry's is known for its good works as well as its frozen confections. One of the co-founders, Ben Cohen, reveals the awareness of webs of interconnectedness when he says, "As we help others, we cannot help but help ourselves." On the other hand, contamination is literally spread through our interconnectedness. In January of 2013, China's increasing numbers of coal burning plants resulted in thick, caustic air pollution that limited visibility to a hundred yards, endangered citizens' health, and canceled flights to and from Beijing. Dark days in China affect us all. Smog compromises people's ability to breathe, raises carbon dioxide levels around the planet, and acidifies the oceans we share. Will we choose to use our creative intelligence in global collaboration for the common good?

Small Change Adds Up

Discernment about the beneficence of one's intent is essential, as is clarity about helpful ways that it can be mobilized. Marian Wright Edelman is the founder of the Children's Defense Fund and recipient of the Albert Schweitzer Prize for Humanitarianism. She reminds us, "It is a time not just for compassionate words, but compassionate action. ... We must not, in trying to think about how we can make a big difference, ignore the small daily difference we can make which, over time, adds up to big differences that we often cannot foresee."

Throughout *Goodness To Go*, we've explored positive ways of perceiving the world and appreciating the rare opportunity to be alive on planet earth. It is empowering to know that our "bucket"—our worldview of conscious perceptions—is flowing over with energy from an inexhaustible source. Empowering worldviews are based on abundance, not on a poverty mentality that insists that there's not enough. Living in the miracle of the present moment with accurate perception and skillful means brings great joy. When we manifest the awareness that we give from our sufficiency, we can move the world.

An innovative thinker whose inventions moved the world and increased opportunities for humanity was Robert Noyce, Ph.D. As an integrative engineer, Noyce pioneered silicon microchips, co-founded Fairchild Semiconductor in 1957 and Intel Corporation in 1968, mentored entrepreneurs such as Apple's Steve Jobs, and created the egalitarian culture of creativity in California's Silicon Valley. As the son and grandson of ministers, Noyce skillfully held the creative tension between ethics grounded in integrity, respect, and kindness and the unchartered frontier of the emerging high-tech industry.

The new paradigm of business teamwork valued openness over hierarchy, risk over certainty, and innovation over the status quo. It has allowed creative intelligence to flow through networks of resourced, empowered individuals, making possible such technological advances as space flight, personal medical devices and computers, and the World Wide Web of global interconnectivity.

Small changes add up on many levels. As we consciously live with an awareness of gratitude and sufficiency, even our vulnerability is empowered. Our tenderness is called forth to meet the needs of each moment. Sensitivity is a key element of our personal power and not a liability with which we retire from robust participation in life. The subtle vulnerability of our senses, faculties, and intuitions helps us to understand what is happening on multiple levels and summons the courage that seeks to be made greater by what it meets. We are the leaders needed at this time, and in spite of some trepidation, we can push the edges of convention, create new solutions in the face of "random catastrophic failure," and contribute in positive ways to our global community.

If you have the opportunity, time, life energy, and ability to read this sentence right now, you are greatly privileged. If you have clean water to drink, food in a refrigerator, clothes in a closet, a bed to sleep in, and a roof over your head, you are more privileged than the vast majority of human beings. With this privilege of having a little extra, follow your natural inclination to give back. Every little bit helps. Small changes inspired by kindness weave a tapestry of goodness. Be willing to be ignited by your gratitude for life and your calling to serve. Allow that flame of inspiration to reveal your golden heart in all its goodness.

Social Media and Social Responsibility

We're responsible for who we are and what we'll be as we weave together vast numbers of influences in the tapestry of our lives. Who is in charge of telling the stories that shape us and our cultural belief systems? Although direct experience of the world has been our primary teacher for millennia, messages mediated by our families, storytellers, churches, schools, and media sources play increasing large roles. It's important that these secondary, mediated versions and voices of reality be as accurate and numerous as possible. Interpretations and representations of the world are not direct experience with reality. A waterfall on a computer screen cannot be the real thing; the glorious reality that we experience on multiple sensory and cognitive levels is infinitely more than digital input.

Nevertheless, after decades of consolidations, only six corporations control virtually everything that Americans see, hear, and read. Media monopolies focused on profit margins own dozens of other media entities and storytelling formats. Investigative journalism plummets. As independent newspapers fail, billionaires acquire them to frame and spread their political messages. For responsible citizens to be educated with critical thinking skills and for democracy to flourish, strong, independent news media committed to serving the public are essential.

Today, the Internet and television determine which stories are most widely disseminated and thereby are most influential within society. Although it's our responsibility, it's very difficult to ascertain their accuracy. In addition to being a primary news source, the Internet connects billions of global citizens using it for business and personal reasons. Social media has increased meaningful engagement and global connections as well as awareness of social justice and environmental protection issues for many people As Facebook, Twitter, LinkedIn, and other online social media multiply, it's useful to remember that increased connectivity does not necessarily lead to increased communication or commitment to social activism.

Andy Carvin, known as "the man who tweets revolutions," has served as an online community organizer since 1994. Through collaboration with the public, he's become a leading player in the breaking news business. Carvin, the senior strategist for National Public Radio's social media desk, revolutionized journalism during his coverage of the "Arab Spring" uprisings. As a one-man social media hub, his online "mobcasting" harnessed first-person citizen reporting to gain new insights into current social issues and events.

Like any tool, social media can be used for good or ill. Crowdsourcing is a process that outsources a task to an undefined public that is often online. It may be used to gather opinions about a current issue or to raise funds for a documentary film. Although social media can make it easier for some people who are relatively powerless to collaborate and give voice to their concerns, it also allows misinformed or malevolent minds to spread their contagion globally. Authoritarian regimes use social media to track down participants in nonviolent protests in order to imprison, torture, and even murder them.

Social media networks are usually built around weak ties that may be effective at increasing participation in some causes by decreasing the level of motivation and commitment that participation requires. It's fairly easy to donate a few cents to Darfur or sign a petition online; it's another thing to engage in higher-risk activism and the real sacrifices that it may incur. Although both are useful, many social artists do not regard digital protest as strategic activism. There are many positive features of the nonhierarchical, consensus-driven structures of networks. However, the discipline and strategy required to articulate a unified philosophical direction or make difficult tactical decisions are rarely strengths of sprawling networks.

Malcolm Gladwell, a Canadian writer best known as the author of *The Tipping Point*, has commented on what he regards as the outsized enthusiasm of digital evangelists. In a 2010 *New Yorker* article, Gladwell questioned their belief that organized establishments and the powers that be can be taken on by so-called Twitter revolutions. Garnering votes for an election is not equivalent to the sustained commitment required to effect real change. "Activism that challenges the status quo—that attacks deeply rooted problems—is not for the faint of heart," Gladwell wrote.

Of course, not all acts of integral service require the deep motivation required by high-risk activism.

Civil rights activist Dr. Martin Luther King, Jr. believed a person's character is revealed in times of challenge and controversy, and that "no one really knows why they are alive until they know what they'd die for." Both the strategic organization and profound commitment that supported the high-risk activism of the civil rights movement were crucial to its success. Other essential factors were the strong ties, personal connections, and critical friendships within the movement that provided ongoing support and motivation. This *strong-tie phenomenon* that is a key factor in the resilience and success of social change initiatives was described by the Stanford sociologist Doug McAdam. Unless individuals develop their own strong intrinsic motivation and personal support systems, social media just makes the existing social order more efficient. Those who benefit from the status quo, even an unjust one, are usually less motivated to change it.

Social media communities reach out to the world. Protestors in Egypt yearning for the implementation of democratic principles have been using social media for several years. In January of 2013, citizens again summoned their hearts of courage and defied curfews to protest the policies of Egypt's Islamist president, Mohammed Morsi. Citizens in many countries continue to sacrifice their lives in the fight for freedom against regimes that monopolize power and ignore multiple social problems.

Ways to use social media for social change are growing exponentially. Social media communities can both alert people about floods and tornadoes, and promote violence; they can uplift communities with news of social justice victories or spread hateful rumors. Assistance for many beneficial causes has been enlisted through social media communities. Individuals, organizations, and governments choose whether or not to utilize this communication tool for good. Those who choose anarchy and terrorism send hate messages and instructions for basement bomb production. Others fund documentaries to educate people about global warming or the importance of educating girls.

Many governments' policies punish freedom of speech. Despite the firewall of Internet censorship in China and other countries, citizens on planet earth are finding ways to connect and empower each other in remarkable ways. True freedom is not simply access to designer labels and consumer goods. Social media are platforms to celebrate the freedoms that are possible in a genuine democracy and they can enhance opportunities for individuals to survive. One potent, inspirational social media campaign saved the lives of two young Indian men who both needed to find a rare bone marrow match and transplant to combat acute leukemia.

Those who operate with integrity and relevance in the World Wide Web can attract very large, well-intended audiences. Open access to accurate facts, not merely avalanches of opinions, is essential. Beliefs we thought we'd die or kill for often change. The importance to the democratic process of a free press that reports all sides of a story as accurately as possible cannot be overestimated.

Every person on earth has unique life circumstances and experiences that color the particular lens or bias through which the world is seen. Although bias is not equivalent to malicious prejudice, legislative changes and diversity trainings do not necessarily lead to truly inclusive cultures. Can citizens set a beneficial course to the future and create a righteous peace without accurate, relatively unbiased information?

We're at a threshold of a new frontier where we can look inward and find the compassion and skillfulness to create healthy, just, and sustainable civilizations. In the early 1960s, President John F. Kennedy set the course for another kind of frontier when he said, "We choose to go to the moon ... because that goal will serve to organize and measure the best of our energies and skills, because that challenge is one that we are willing to accept, one we are unwilling to postpone." The ever-changing, multifaceted complexities involved in returning astronauts safely from a moon landing required networks of creative thinkers from many disciplines working brilliantly together.

It is a privilege to face the challenges of our time and to have within us the ability to respond to these challenges. The Children's Defense Fund's Edelman, reminds us, "If you don't like the way the world is, you change it. You have an obligation to change it. You just do it one step at a time."

As we continue on our path of personal evolution and summon the power of heart and mind, let's move into action. We're empowered when we move from "I can't" to "How can I?" The journey of a lifetime is often in the movement from "no" to "yes." Yes is a world. Even if our courage seems a little shaky at time, we keep moving forward. Our actions ripple through the web of being and are also the ground on which we stand. We can't escape their consequences. In many ways, every action contributes to an energetic field of interconnectedness in which we all live.

A social artist mentioned earlier in this book, Frances Moore Lappé, celebrates the awareness that "each of us is a 'node' whose actions can ripple through all the links. ... There are only entry points into the network of life. If we think of our actions as entry points, each affecting a node in the pattern, then we see we are in fact shifting the whole pattern when we act with clear intention. The ripples through the network are potentially infinite. What a sense of power!"

A Buddhist teaching says, "There are only two mistakes on the path to truth: one is not starting and the other is not going all the way." Let's refuse to allow fear and dysfunctional beliefs to stifle our goodness to go. Let's stop fighting for old paradigms and ways of being that bolster an inequitable status quo carring on with business as usual. When we release these limiting habits, creative energy is freed up to discover new realities, rich new possibilities, and unexpected opportunities to uplift our communities and our world.

Pause, Reflect, and Record

- List three or more networks of people to which you belong. How do they affect your life and the world?

- Evolutionaries engage in personal evolution as they contribute to global evolution. Describe an experience in your life in which the personal began to ripple through the collective?

- How many hours a day do you spend in front of a screen? How reliable are your news sources? Consider ways to increase your direct experience with the world and the accuracy of the stories that you hear about it.

- Reflect on your personal bias and worldview. What is a lens or paradigm though which you perceive your part in the grand story of life?

- What contributed to the development of the lens through which you perceive your world, including parents, teachers, and media? Describe a facet of this lens that you'd like to change in some way. Why?

30

Social Profit and the
Flow of Money

Money is like water. It can be a conduit for commitment,
a currency of love. Money moving in the direction of our
highest commitments nourishes our world and ourselves. ...
Let your soul inform your money and
your money express your soul.

—Lynne Twist

Nearly every enterprise in which we invest our energies, including humanitarian service, requires reliable sources of financial support. The manifestation of our goodness profits society, and *social prophets* bring social profit on many levels, including the field of finance. Although money doesn't make the world go round, it has proven to be a useful form of energy exchange that moves in the direction of our commitments. The flow of money in our lives can express our soul's vision, and an income is usually necessary to support us as we mobilize our goodness to go.

If we think we have access to a golden goose, it's tempting to run after it and get attached. Recall the folktale image of a long line of people stuck together after trying to steal a golden feather from a reportedly magical bird. King Midas's golden touch destroyed the life of all he loved. Many people have wasted much of their lives shackled by the "golden handcuffs" of a substantial paycheck for work that has lost its meaning. Our mistaken faith in the orthodoxy of the gold standard and a laissez-faire approach to the financial sector led to global economic calamities at the beginning of the twenty-first century.

It's important to understand the ways that money moves through our lives. If you follow the money trails of financial gain and profiteering, you'll have a clearer understanding of most social and environmental issues. For example, in cities around the world, including New York City, hundreds of sweatshops exploit vulnerable youth for corporate financial gain. The mining of diamonds frequently devastates environments and spills the blood of endangered workers paid slave wages.

Thousands of children are trafficked into and within the United States each year, and millions more are trafficked internationally for various types of businesses, including the sex trade. In the first half of the twentieth century, the poet-physician William Carlos Williams trusted that if people worked together, their empathy, imagination, and commitment could move that century a few inches forward. The lives of twenty-first-century visionaries, volunteers, entrepreneurs, CEOs, servant leaders, and social activists are deeply committed to moving this century many miles forward and abolishing slavery of all forms forever.

Throughout history, very few people have accumulated massive profits in ways that were not tainted by exploitation. In the 1600s, impoverished children on the streets of England were shipped to new colonies across the Atlantic Ocean. As European settlers invaded territories inhabited by Native Americans, they used the children as indentured servants. The wealth of plantation owners was built on the backs of slaves. Apartheid institutionalized white privilege in South Africa.

During the Industrial Revolution, many American children were forced to work such long hours that they had no time to attend school. In 1903, children in Philadelphia went on strike to protest the suppression of their educational opportunities. Signs of protest read "We Want to Go to School!" Many citizens summoned the power of their hearts, minds, and spirits to decrease the industrial servitude of children.

New ways of thinking, human rights legislation, and reformed social systems are gradually improving conditions for children and other exploited classes in many parts of the world. The dynamic expansion of global commerce has brought about greater prosperity in many nations, increasing the diversity and resilience of world economies. With sufficient commitment, current economic restructuring could create more equitable global access to financial opportunities.

Sufficiency and Abundance

A Hindi word *sant* comes from a Sanskrit verb meaning "to be good" and "to be real." Human beings can choose to bring real goodness to every living thing. When we recognize that we are one in spirit, our compassion in action naturally empowers those living in extreme poverty to live more humanely. Meanwhile, fear and global crises trap our life's energy in knots and shadows. On a psychological level, our shadow contains elements that are unknown, unwanted, unwelcome, or unloved. "Every man is a moon, and has a dark side which he doesn't show anybody," Mark Twain observed.

When we acknowledge our dark sides and demons, we're able to discover the needs behind their confusion, to care for their woundedness, and to nurture their transformation. The light of our goodness illumines dark corners as we approach the unknown with compassion and curiosity. Accepting and embracing all aspect of ourselves with gentleness allows us to live in abundant kindness and sufficiency. Kindness begins with the sown seed. What seeds of kindness do you want to plant?

How do we restore our experience of inner abundance with radically kind self-care? Years ago, I met a wonderful elder who used a bucket as a symbol for our container of life energy, and spoke about the psycho-spiritual metaphor of the empty bucket. Exhausted emptiness is a feared consequence of frantic overworking, draining our life's force, and burning us out. We're familiar with the sinking spirits that accompany the old refrain: "But I'm *just* one person; anything I offer is *just* a drop in the bucket."

An ocean is made drop by drop. It's disheartening and inaccurate to believe that all of our concern and effort is *just* a drop in the bucket. This belief also assumes that every bucket has leaks through which goodness inevitably drains away. We can see things differently and live in the understanding and creative goodwill for all that ancient Greeks called *agape*. This spontaneous, overflowing love seeks nothing in return, as its unconditional presence redeems and transforms the soul of the receiver as well as the giver.

Many of us have been conditioned by old stories and definitions of what a *good person* is. When we're trying as hard as we can and feel out of touch with our abundant source, our energy can seem depleted. Old paradigms resorted to using the metaphor of an *empty bucket* to describe good people: instead of filling their own buckets, good people gave everything away, keeping nothing for themselves. However, an empty bucket is a hollow container, not a vibrant, resourced human being. We've judged thoughts focused on our own well-being as selfish and defined truly good people as "generous to a fault," tirelessly giving away all of their time, resources, and energy. Only when we penetrate deeply into our habit of judgment will we live in peace and true prosperity. It's time for new stories and a new paradigm of human goodness and generosity.

Goodness To Go

Many people are reimagining the empty bucket as a soup pot whose overflowing abundance nourishes those who are hungry in some way. We give from our strength and abundance, not our lack. The first time our young daughter decided to make soup for dinner, she was delighted to nourish everyone. "It has water, vegetables, protein, and flavor," Grace exclaimed. "What else does anyone need?" We want the abundant soup of our lives to be created in ways that are delicious, nutritious and sustainable.

We don't want to get scorched on the bottom and burn out. When fresh water, healthy ingredients, and self-care are added continuously, our resources are abundantly sufficient. It's also useful to discern the soundness of our vessel so that we don't leak our goodness and life force. Although the source of life may be bottomless, our physical energy is not. If we're sick or exhausted, we need to rest and heal. With a strong container, we feed ourselves and others with our soulful, seasoned abundance.

In new paradigms, needs for self-care are harmonized with our aspirations to give back to our world. Self-care is not selfish; selfishness is greedy attachment to getting more than we need at the expense of others and taking credit for everything. As we engage in practices that refresh and rejuvenate our souls, we give from our inner abundance and generosity. This kind of abundance has nothing to do with accumulation and hoarding. It's about the generous allocation of our resources, including money, integrity, compassion, and life energy.

Cycles of giving and receiving are the flowing forth of our natural goodness and are evident throughout the natural world. Self-care takes us deeper into the world, and caring for the world takes us deeper into our true self. We season the rich and hearty soup of our lives, nourish ourselves fully, with plenty to share. Rather than seeing our life's bucket as a limited container of finite time, energy, and caring that eventually empties out, we experience being in touch with an ever-renewing source that fills us to overflowing.

Our giving is our flowing over. This shift in perception and energy leads to other shifts in perspective. We experience that there is no hole in the bucket that can't be mended. No caring effort ever disappears or goes to waste. Goodness on the go is always significant. Quantum physics confirms that every thought and action reverberates throughout the cosmos, so let's make that resonance beautiful and meaningful. The image of the old wooden bucket has evolved into intricate worldwide webs and networks of expanding consciousness.

Social Profit and the Flow of Money

The Energy of Money

Money is a form of energy that is a medium of exchange and is most beneficial when its currents are flowing freely. The quality of our relationship with money affects us: we can grow in generosity and discernment or allow greed, attachment, and lack of financial discipline to determine our attitudes and choices. We choose whether to swirl down a drain of fearful despair or wake up to the opportunities that new paradigms offer.

The flow of currency, like water, is healthiest when it is treated respectfully. For several decades, charitable giving has been somewhat recession resistant. Despite recent precarious financial situations, about two percent of our average disposable income continues to flow in philanthropic directions. At the same time, several governments have increased their outsourcing of social services onto patchworks of private corporations and nonprofits that rely on the steadfast generosity of individuals.

Social democracies in Scandinavia collect about 40 percent of their gross national product (GNP) in taxes for their countries' infrastructure and for public sector services such as health care and education. In contrast, the United States collects only 25 percent of its GNP, and only three percent of this is allotted for civilian spending, including energy, education, scientific research, highways, and all levels of the country's infrastructure. As world economic crises intensify, fear stifles financial markets and decreases investments in new industries and job creation. Although financial discipline and strategic discernment are sensible, anxious hoarding stagnates currency.

Several paradigm shifts in the nonprofit sector are occurring. Some reformers no longer use the words *nonprofit* or *charity*. Charity has come to be associated with a top-down model: the *haves* give handouts to the *have-nots* in ways that can be somewhat demeaning for the recipients. Indigenous peoples in various parts of the world have clearly stated: "If you're coming to *help* us, no thank you. If you're coming because you know that your liberation is bound up with ours, let's work together." Current philanthropic models emphasize investment and partnering in mutually respectful relationships where the resources of all are recognized and honored.

After being awakened to a new paradigm of sufficiency by Buckminster Fuller in the 1970s and serving many global initiatives for decades, Lynne Twist wrote *The Soul of Money*. She replaced the term *nonprofit* with *social profit* as a more uplifting and accurate description of the benefit provided by the millions of humanitarian organizations around the world.

Twist refers to social profit workers as "social prophets." She invites us to have compassion for the fear generated by myths of scarcity, and radiates the mature awareness that it is a great gift to release yourself to a life committed to something larger than "your life starring you." It's time to move from destructive greed to wise stewardship of our financial and environmental resources. The daily practice of gratitude supports appreciation for the life we have and the integral service that it enables us to contribute to the world.

Ignited by Twist's book, a website called the Global Sufficiency Network was launched to explore how to live in sufficiency, free of a fearful sense of scarcity regardless of our circumstances. Some multimillionaires fear they don't have enough money as they shuffle between gated communities and private jets. Impoverished parents *know* that several of their children will die from malnutrition or disease, leading to more children being born and dying in their attempts to be provided for in their old age.

When we fear that we'll have insufficient energy supplies, we resort to oil and natural gas extraction practices such as hydraulic fracturing, or fracking, that contaminate groundwater and release toxins into the air. If we insist on burning even a fifth of the oil and gas reserves remaining on this planet, scientists predict that the poisoned environment will be incompatible with human life. Renewable energy enterprises and other elements of the growing green economy create environmentally sustainable jobs as well as social and financial profits. The possibility of generating tremendous amounts of clean energy through solar power is increasing rapidly. More jobs are being created as newer thin-film technologies become more efficient and manufacturing costs decrease.

Networks of global conversations about sufficiency are catalyzing actions that address fear of scarcity as a fundamental root cause of global crises. Consider how this fear underlies the population explosion crisis, the environmental crisis, the social justice crisis, the spiritual crisis, and the economic crisis. Does a fear of scarcity affect your life in any way?

Trusting life's abundance, we feel the delightful power of being alive, awake, aware, and it's natural to express our gratitude and appreciation in creative, concrete ways. In his book *Enough Already*, Alan Cohen discusses the power of radical contentment. Practicing contentment and the awareness of sufficiency amplifies our generosity. Giving is the new getting. Be ignited. Rather than just getting rich, *be* rich.

Socially Responsible Investing

Integral service is a calling to invest our resources in our interconnected world. The word *integrity* emerged from roots that mean "unified wholeness, a state of being complete and incorruptible." Too often we feel fragmented. The power of integration guides fragmentation toward unity, and hatha yoga is one practice that supports multi-dimensional alignment and flexibility. When our values, perceptions, thoughts, words, and actions are flowing in alignment, we experience the essential empowerment of being in integrity. *We walk our talk and put our money where our mouths are.*

We're interconnected across time and place and authentic integrity takes a stand for sustainability. In 1987, the United Nations defined *sustainability* as the ability of current generations to meet their needs without compromising the ability of future generations to meet theirs. This includes future generations of other species, despite the tragic fact of rapid species extinction. All of life has a right to be here. The interconnected wholeness of life is an external manifestation of our internal integrity.

One element of our commitment to full integrity is the way we spend and invest money. Economic systems, including capitalism, can be informed by humanitarian principles. What are the policies and ethics of companies from which we purchase products and services or that are in our stock portfolio? It's instructive to scan our checkbooks and credit card statements to see where we direct our financial energy. More people are aligning their environmental, social, and ethical values with their investment strategies, choosing social investment organizations to help them decide which stocks and mutual funds support their highest commitments.

The founder of the Institute for Global Ethics in Maine, Rushmore Kidder, wrote *Shared Values for a Troubled World.* According to Kidder's research, some of the underlying values and social virtues that people from widely differing world cultures share are respect for life, responsibility, truthfulness, and fairness. Justice—fair, respectful treatment of all beings—is particularly important.

There can be no lasting peace without justice. Around the world, the possibility of equity for all children is held in billions of human hearts.

319

Yet a child dies of preventable causes every three seconds. Of the more than 25,000 children who die every day, at least half of those deaths are due to malnutrition. It doesn't have to be this way.

Since 1999, innovative, nutritional protein spreads that don't require clean water, refrigeration, or heating have been available. One distributor of these spreads is the Child In Need Institute's Nutrimix Social Business, located on the outskirts of Calcutta, India. Jobs are created for community members who make the low-cost protein packets from locally grown grain. In another endeavor to combat malnutrition, UNICEF has invested in Ethiopia's first factory that makes a high-protein peanut-based paste used to treat severely malnourished children and AIDS patients. This low-cost therapy, which can result in a 90 to 95 percent recovery rate, is one of several effective approaches available today. With sufficient moral and political will, no one needs to suffer from hunger and malnutrition.

We have a responsibility to the generations who will come. At least half of the world's children live in poverty. Two-thirds of all war casualties are children. The impact of our political, economic, and environmental choices on this generation is appalling. Imagine having lived your entire life in any of the impoverished or war-torn regions of the world? How many more generations locally and globally are to suffer from this legacy? The health of children born to mothers who are obese or addicted to drugs is at grave risk, with significant social costs and consequences.

Wherever we're going, we're going together. The executive director of Global Action for Children, Jen Delaney, recognizes that it is in everyone's best interest "to help prepare impoverished children to become healthy, educated citizens contributing to the global economy and political stability, not detract from it." She calls for children's ambassadors to prioritize and coordinate critical children's programs in foreign aid budgets. How might you take a stand for children?

Networks of Goodness

Networks are patterns of connections. A physicist at Notre Dame, Albert Laszlo Barabasi, describes the networks that are the key to understanding our world. In *Linked*, he wrote that small change affecting only a few of the nodes or links can open up hidden doors, allowing new possibilities to emerge. The Estonian Bank of Happiness is an example of these emerging possibilities. People with skills or services they'd like to share

are linked with those who could benefit. No bank notes are exchanged, only thank-you notes.

Microcredit loans are filling people's "buckets" all over the planet. The growing trend of microloans primarily involves women in developing nations who are starting small businesses. Studies reveal that women entrepreneurs invest more of their profits to enrich their communities than men. These resourceful women virtually always repay Microcredit start-up loans, and a financial leg up allows them to care for and uplift their families and communities. The power and combined leverage of microcredit networks and personal resourcefulness enables people living in poverty to help themselves in sustainable ways.

In the past thirty years, microcredit has spread to every continent and has benefited over 100 million families. The pioneer of this innovative banking program and founder of Grameen Bank is Muhammad Yunus, Ph.D., a Bangladeshi economics professor who was awarded the 2006 Nobel Peace Prize. Social business is his next step in creating a world without poverty through more humane forms of capitalism.

Dr. Yunus describes two models of social businesses. One provides a social benefit, such as poverty reduction, social justice, and health care for the poor, rather than focusing on maximizing profit. The other model consists of profit-maximizing businesses owned by the disadvantaged whose equity growth goes to benefit the poor. Microfinance isn't banking; it's humanitarian investment in building the financial capacity of impoverished people.

Although microfinance has philanthropic roots, any good idea can be tainted by greed and lack of transparency. In his book *Confessions of a Microfinance Heretic*, Englishman Hugh Sinclair reveals how shifts toward microloans for consumption, rather than to start businesses, become primarily profit driven. Unscrupulous lenders intimidate borrowers. This type of microfinance results in downward spirals of poor people taking out more loans with very high interest rates to pay back old loans.

Microfinance consumption loans to pay for food or medical care usually don't include income-generating plans for repayment, and borrowers often default on their loans. "Sometimes, children are forced into labor and women into prostitution," writes Sinclair. "In India, several dozen women have even committed suicide because they were pressured to repay their loans." International laws governing microfinance are needed to protect both the borrowers and investors, as well as to return it to its humanitarian roots.

Many reputable organizations invest in the financial empowerment of people. Through one called Kiva, potential investors can make microcredit loans online. The Kiva website allows micro-lenders to make loans starting at $25 to small businesses in need, choosing which country and type of budding entrepreneur they'd like to support and follow online. This is one way that the interconnected web of the Internet helps generosity to flow. "When we give and receive, giver and receiver are on equal ground," writes Buddhist teacher Judith Lief. "Generosity is an exchange, not a one-way street. Generosity connects us with each other, whether we are the giver or the receiver, and enriches us both."

It may be true that we can't manage what we can't measure. However, not everything that can be counted matters, as Albert Einstein observed, and not everything that matters can be measured. We choose whether we'll align our energies with what matters most to us. Will we trust the flow of sufficiency or remain stuck in fears of scarcity? When we've reflected on and articulated our deepest values, we want our words, thoughts, deeds, and investments to be aligned. Integral service and integral investment matter. Our choices determine the actions that are our entry points into the network of life.

Pause, Reflect, and Record

- Who is a "social prophet" whose integral service you admire? Describe.

- What is the nature of your current relationship with money? Are there any ways in which you'd like that relationship to change?

- How full is your "bucket" of resourcefulness? Are there ways in which you leak, squander, or drain your life energy? Describe.

- Are there areas of your life where you feel that you don't have enough? How might you begin to feel a greater sense of sufficiency and abundance?

- In what social enterprises are you interest in investing your resources, such as time, creative energy, and money?

31

Transitions—
The In-Between Times

Have patience with everything unresolved in your heart. ...
The point is, to live everything. Live the questions now.

—Rainer Maria Rilke

If you're in a transition period or your path of integral service is not yet clear, be patient. Life is constant change, and the ongoing process of integrating service into our lives naturally includes many seasons of transition. As health and finances wax and wane, we may need time to rest and rejuvenate. Immersed in the care of young children or starting a new business, we may have less time and energy for other forms of service.

Although we often fear it, change is what makes hope possible. Dreams for the future that our imagination envisions come true because time flows and things change. At every crossroad in life, we're presented with opportunities for wonder, doors opening to new beginnings, and fresh opportunities to share our gifts with the world.

The rhythmic phases embedded in our daily lives as well as the transition times between them can be acknowledged and honored. Sunrise, midday, and sunset have their own energies. Childhood, adolescence, early adulthood, midlife, and our elder years have within them cycling times of planting seeds, incubation, flowering, and fruition. Some describe our Mother Earth as having a yearlong cycle of breath, with the Summer Solstice as a finale of her expansive, six-month exhalation, and Winter Solstice as the deepest in-drawing of her inspiration. Traditionally, the darker winter season is a time of inward reflection and contemplative transition to a new phase of our lives.

Goodness to go is sustained by the in-breath of self-care giving way to the out-breath of integral service. Between the phases of our breaths and heartbeats, there are natural pauses of transition. We're reminded to mind the gap. The space between the in-breath and the out-breath, between the past and the future, is not just a passing moment. That space is beyond time, and it's an ongoing process to be here now in the timelessness of the present moment. The potent moment beyond the confines of linear time is a special, even sacred, kind of transition. Many feel that it is a gateway to an eternal, divine Self.

On the physical plane, there are many other kinds of transitions, including graduations, divorces, and job changes. After serious illnesses, we need to rest and recuperate before jumping back into hectic schedules. Our minds and bodies require sufficient sleep, nurturance, and revitalization on a regular basis. We need times of stillness, contemplation, and darkness; it's neither wise nor sustainable to burn the candle at both ends or keep the lights burning bright 24/7.

Surfing Change with Wisdom

Since constant change is inherent to life, there are countless transitions that we'll navigate. Many of us enjoy days and even years of relatively clear sailing. It's full steam ahead on paths of schoolwork or professional training, running a household or a global corporation. Much of the time we feel secure, in control, and in charge. With a fair degree of resilience, our coping mechanisms are grounded in our competency. We have, or can find, the answers to most of the problems that arise in our day-to-day life. Then night follows day.

In the wake of economic and environmental upheavals, the birth of a child, graduation, retirement, or illness, transitions, thresholds, and crossroads inevitably present themselves. We can feel that we have less control and are more vulnerable. Fear, dismay, despair, or anger often arise. On the other hand, we may find our way to a state of curious, open-hearted presence in the face of change and the unknown.

During the in-between times, it's important to be gentle with yourself and others. Nurture your inner strength and freedom as you practice patience; the clarity of peace is achieved by patient understanding and cannot be forced. Contemplate the peace that is the greatest good. Trust that the seeds of the next phase of your life will take the time they need to incubate. Don't try to push the river. Just as there are times to get moving, there are times to turn within, be still, let go, and listen. Any veils that are temporarily blocking your vision of what is next are necessary for now.

Charles Halpern, a social entrepreneur, pioneer in the public interest law movement, and long-time meditator, places the development of wisdom and compassion at the center of his life. Halpern has created several exceptionally effective institutions dedicated to human betterment. In *Making Waves and Riding the Currents—Activism and the Practice of Wisdom*, Halpern writes, "The practice of wisdom doesn't give answers, much less assure that we will arrive at a state of wisdom. But it can give resilience, balance, and depth ... and create a space for the emergence of wisdom."

It's a profound gift of conscious awareness that we can choose to redirect our attention. As we practice bringing attention to the spaces between breaths or to the bodily sensations of feelings, we tap into the energy of awareness itself. When our nervous system is more regulated, with fewer surges of agitating emotions and more skillful at working with them, we can access the resonant stillness of unity awareness.

Poets, mystics, spiritual teachers, and artists throughout the ages have emphasized the quality of our awareness and attention. Aldous Huxley's novel called *Island* emphasizes the importance of paying attention. *Attention. Attention.* The word resounds through its pages and remains a wake-up call to *be here now*. Practicing mindful awareness in the eternal present is refreshing and rejuvenating to our hearts, minds, bodies, and spirits.

Many wisdom traditions emphasize the importance of experiencing the unconditional presence in the space within and beyond the world of forms and actions. Even in the midst of rendering integral service, it's possible to place our attention in the potent pauses between thoughts and breaths, in the spacious presence of serenity and timelessness. The power of peace is in the pause.

As we rest in this clear, calm energy, it's possible to imbibe the ever-present peace that is always available to us. For a moment, there's nowhere else to go and nothing more to do. Instead of constant preoccupation with our roles and responsibilities, we identify with our essence, the simple exalted state of *I AM*. Relaxing into that awareness, we witness, accept, and appreciate all of existence and our part in it.

Multi-Environmental Mindfulness

Every day we create and interact with at least three environments: our inner world of thoughts, feelings, beliefs, and values; our local niches of home, neighborhood, and work; and our extended community and global environments. The quality of our awareness at all three levels—internal, local, and global—contributes to our personal well-being and our service to the world.

As we participate in the dramas of life's integral service, internal reactions, including thoughts and feelings, are triggered. Whatever arises contains our greatest lessons. As we march for freedom, are we able to remain calm when hateful words or fists are hurled our way? Where we place our attention is a key determinant of our state and our behavior. If we align with gratitude and equanimity, we find value in all of life's experiences.

As we redirect our attention to the present moment, we acknowledge everything that we're experiencing. We face and work with all of it, which includes the option of releasing thoughts that distract us or states that suffocate us. Mindful awareness frees us to learn, mature, and skillfully share our gifts instead of lashing back in righteous indignation or fury. We're able to access our discerning frontal lobes and self-regulate our autonomic nervous system with self-care tools and practices. Wise, non-violent, even graceful responses include consciously ignoring the provocation, opting for a calculated retreat, seeking legal counsel, or keeping our seat and standing our ground.

Commitment to being fully present is a lifelong practice that supports the expression of our goodness to go. Gradually, we strengthen our ability to redirect our attention when we're temporarily hijacked by experiences of injustice, betrayal, disappointment, and other difficult emotions. Our energy isn't drained by critical judgments about others, including fellow volunteers who renege on responsibilities. When a service project is derailed, defeatism doesn't hook us.

We're mindful that our planet's ecosystem is in a period of transition. Climate change is raising global temperatures rapidly, and environmental devastation is imminent in many regions. It is our choice whether to protect our environment, contain carbon emissions, reduce population growth rates, and respect the rights of all life. Food supplies need to be safe and clean water freely accessible to everyone. Creating a world that we cherish and want our children to inherit is a life worth living.

Many social commentators have suggested that the need for deeper meaning is a central crisis of our time. As trust in our ability to be present with *what is* strengthens, we have the opportunity to redirect our attention in meaningful ways. With this freedom of awareness, we envision more clearly and choose the next most meaningful step in our lives, whether it's embarking on a retreat, contacting political representatives, or volunteering with a social profit enterprise. Doing our part may be to empower children, protect the environment, abolish involuntary servitude, or end violence against women and girls.

Navigating Turbulent Times

Although some transitional moments are literally the pause that refreshes, there are times that rock and even fracture our world. What happens when things fall apart? We may feel empty or exhausted by battles with chronic disabilities or life-threatening illness, and traumatized by the loss of a loved one. Veterans with amputations and traumatic brain injuries try valiantly to return to civilian life.

Millions of people have been forced to leave their homes due to natural disasters, violence, or financial devastation. Graduations come and go but we're not sure what's next. Our management positions disappear in corporate mergers. Our dearly anticipated child is born with severe disabilities. We ache when marriages end, when work no longer feels meaningful, or our soul yearns to take flight.

We're hardwired neurologically to react cautiously to detected movement, unexpected changes, and potential dangers in our environments. Fear can offer a survival advantage, and it's usually beneficial to pause and reflect on the wisdom of a proposed course of action. *Look before you leap*, we're cautioned. *Pause before you speak.* Conscious reflection and discernment are acts of love and wisdom, not reactions ignited by resistance. In these fruitful pauses, insights arise.

When we slow down and relax a little, we may come to understand that we're not trapped by situations; it is fear itself that is suffocating us. It's not the integral service we're considering that's the problem, it's our anxiety about feeling burned out or overwhelmed. Fear often makes us stomp on the brakes and screech to a resistant halt when it catches wind that we're transitioning away from our status quo, contemplating a change, or hearing the first chords of a calling.

People who have developed a degree of skillfulness at navigating turbulent times are more likely to enter the unknown. There seems to be a genetic basis to our propensity to take serious risks, but we all can develop the capacity to extend beyond our comfort zone, whether keeping our seat on a segregated bus or running for political office. Whatever our degree of risk seeking or aversion, we can learn to handle the discomfort of risking new behaviors.

What allows us to surf times of change? One factor of readiness for change is the strength and clarity of our intention to let go of dysfunctional habits and beliefs. Insistence on blaming our woes on the state of the economy, the world, or our partner keeps us stuck in disempowered victimhood and serves no one. Ego-mind regurgitates assumptions and succumbs to toxic myths: *The situation is out of hand, and there's nothing I can do to make a difference; that's just the way it is.* At these times, contemplative practices such as centering prayer or journaling allow the mind to be spacious and still enough for wisdom to arise. We train our mind to relate with emotions rather than being completely identified with or hijacked by them. Insight therapy, meditation, yoga, regular sessions of reflective self-inquiry, and other practices invite wisdom to guide our lives.

There are many behaviors that are useful in the adventure of navigating change and some that are not. Ruminating about colossal obstacles confronting us often reinforces the problems in our neural and collective circuitry. The brain experiences imagined fear as intensely as "real" terror; nightmares and PTSD flashbacks trigger the same stress hormones that flood us when an assailant threatens us. For the most part, however, as we focus creatively on positive outcomes and not the size of the issue, contexts shift, and constructs dissolve. Solutions and resources present themselves as new paradigms emerge. Synchronicities abound. As we embrace change with resilience, flexibility, and creativity, beneficent outcomes are more likely.

Some transition times provide a crucible for anxiety, grief, and a sense of meaninglessness to transform into activism. Many young people around the world die from malnutrition, disease, and violence, devastating their families and communities. In many countries, massacres of people unknown to the assailants and who are gathered in public places are increasing. In 2012, a gunman slaughtered moviegoers in Aurora, Colorado, and another deranged man with a semiautomatic rifle murdered twenty first graders and six educators in Newtown, Connecticut. Sufficient public will was galvanized to sustain a growing movement to control access to assault weapons through legislative reform. Sadly, many political representatives have not been unwilling to vote in support of gun control reforms.

Many adolescents die as a result of gang violence, suicide, and motor vehicle accidents. The grief process of surviving friends and family members can be agonizing and, at times, redemptive. Although it's difficult to predict how long any transition period will last, many people make significant changes in their lives and incorporate integral service into their daily lives. Several years ago, a bereaved mother woke one morning after an extended period of mourning and heard herself say, "I've *got* to do something for someone else." Before long, she found herself in Africa volunteering with orphans as she gradually created her new life's direction and purpose.

Civility in Dangerous Times

Civilization matters. Democratic constitutions are ennobling. Without the social institutions and civil codes of behavior evident in relatively stable cultures, chaos reduces much of life to the lowest common denominator. Witness Somalia's swift decline into anarchy. We're at the crossroads of transition into the promise of the twenty-first century. Although the challenges are tremendous, this is a time to evolve our consciousness as a species. Unchecked greed, inequity, and violence inevitably destroy civilizations and allow barbarism to proliferate. If we choose to discipline ego's greed for *more*—more power, more money, more resources, more speed, more comfort—we can create an earth where its bounty is shared equitably.

Violence must be curtailed whenever possible. Reasonable restrictions on assault weapons are consistent with democratic constitutions and are repeatedly supported in bipartisan polls. Nevertheless, following the Newtown massacre, the National Rifle Association continued to challenge reform of background checks and refused restrictions on access to semiautomatic rifles. When an assailant in China attacked school children with a knife in the same week, none died.

What rational or righteous argument justifies a citizen's right to own assault weapons that can spray hundreds of bullets in minutes? Carnage from the use of automatic rifles in public spaces, including universities, movie theaters, retail malls, and elementary schools, is increasing.

At the same time, it is essential to consider the violence in our midst with compassion, wisdom, and discernment. As our tears join with those of the victims' families, our vision need not be blurred or myopic. The aftermath of tragedies is understandably a time for grief and deep reflection about how to prevent similar occurrences. We've learned that many perpetrators of premeditated homicides and suicides use the Internet as a new form of soapbox or confessional. In-depth community and national conversations about improved health care for those suffering with mental illness as well as effective controls on access to automatic assault weapons are both needed.

It may never be possible to detect or predict when an individual's mental health or thought processes become unbalanced but we can rouse the political will to develop effective gun control legislation and enforcement. Social movements have abolished institutionalized slavery; overcome entrenched resistance to women's right to full participation in society, including the right to vote; and expanded civil rights to all people. Assault weapons are intended for trained members of a well-regulated militia, not for citizens who insist that they have the "right" to own this kind of destructive power. If gun control issues call you, thousands of violent deaths may be prevented by your integral service.

The human experience spans the spectrum from egregious acts of contempt to the sublime beauty of Bach's *Magnificat*. In 2001, on the evening following the terrorist attacks on September 11th, my family gathered with others for a time of silent reflection in the midst of emotional turmoil. Many tears fell. At one point, my one-year-old daughter wriggled out of my arms and crawled to a woman nearby. Gradually, the distraught woman opened her eyes into the glistening darkness of Grace Shanti's eyes, and a smile gently spread across her face. Grace then crawled from one person to another, rekindling the light of faith again and again. Afterward, Grace's godfather said that as he witnessed the effect of her sweet innocence, he thought, "All of a sudden, the good is back."

Every day of our lives—especially during transition times—is rich with opportunities to mature and evolve, to explore our gifts and share them. Create space in your daily life for the emergence of wisdom. Treasure the lessons of both the valleys and the peaks of your life. Listen for the voice of your inner guidance. When the student is ready, the teacher appears in a multitude of forms, from subtle insights and synchronicities to wisdom teachings and the gaze of a child.

Maturing—The Inner Adventure

For everything there is a season. The positive intentions of your aspirations and actions never go to waste. It's not unexpected to feel fear or frustration during plateaus or transition periods in life. You may sense that something new is coming or feel a calling but can't yet see what it is. This is the time of *inventure*, the inner adventure of maturing that prepares you for your next adventure. It's an *innernet* rather than a world wide web of the Internet. Although there are no external maps to navigate times like these, learn to anchor within, take a stand, and then set sail, come what may.

Every stage of life requires that we develop new, ever-changing skills. Throughout his life, the renowned inventor of the telephone, Alexander Graham Bell, utilized his creative intelligence to become a pioneer in communications for the deaf. "To face tomorrow with the methods of yesterday," wrote Bell, "is to envision life at a standstill." Life continues to evolve. If the transitions between childhood, adolescence, and young adulthood are Act One, we may have the good fortune to experience Act Two, the second half of life.

During their middle decades, some people experience a midlife crisis while others celebrate a midlife expansion. We can sink or swim, build a new boat, chart a new course, or crash on rocks in a murky passage. Do we jump ship, drown in anxiety, or take the helm? Any crisis holds both danger and opportunity for growth on multiple levels. Even when we feel overwhelmed by roller coasters of ever-changing thoughts and moods, we can wake up to the present moment and remind ourselves that these times call for all hands on deck. We're needed now.

One of the great inner adventurers who heeded his calling was the Swiss psychiatrist Carl Jung. He perceived that every crisis at its core is a spiritual crisis. When asked if we'll make it, Jung would reply, "If enough individuals do their inner work." Introspection is an element of relating with crises, spiritual and otherwise, that reveals meaning in one's life. It's fruitful to reflect on current global challenges through the lens of spirit as well as pragmatism.

Three key elements of human spirituality that help us through transitions are our core values, our relationships with others (as well as our relationship with ourselves), and a meaningful purpose in life. Values. Relationships. Purpose. The human soul and imagination have a vast richness, and we yearn to find value and meaning in life experiences. Many people who've felt a sense of emptiness in their lives, especially during the in-between times, have experienced the meaningfulness of engaging in beneficial service to others.

In their book *Spiritual Intelligence*, Danah Zohar and Dr. Ian Marshall discuss their experience of the soul's spiritual intelligence as an integrative force. It weaves together the full complexity of our intellectual and emotional intelligences. Spiritual intelligence, the authors contend, facilitates a dialogue between reason and emotion while respectfully incorporating the body's wisdom. As we tap into the transformative and unifying power of our spiritual intelligence, transition periods become especially potent times to dream, envision, and strive to express our creativity and goodness in lives that are meaningful and satisfying.

Many social commentators have suggested that the need for deeper meaning is a central crisis of our time. However, even when the mind constricts with fear, we also have the capacity to notice our state and smile at fear with curiosity and courage. With mindfulness and spiritual intelligence, we ripen and mature. As we identify more strongly with our potential for equanimity and compassion, we're able to sustain our goodness to go in enjoyable, meaningful ways.

During periods of transition, many people have wrestled with the decision to speak truth to power. Workers in nuclear and oil industries, law enforcement, pharmaceutical companies, and many government agencies have blown the whistle to alert victims and potential victims about corruption, theft, and toxic products. Think of the sacrifices of freedom fighters, social justice activists, and spiritual teachers and disciples throughout the ages. Many people risk their lives and others accept the risks of bringing unethical practices of their employee or their government into the light of public awareness. Their power is in their courage and integrity to hold to both their goodness and their ground.

Maturity is required to serve as a responsible truth-teller. One clarion voice throughout the decade before the economic meltdown of 2008 was that of Brooksley Born. As the financial litigator and director of the Commodity Futures Trading Committee, Born was repeatedly attacked as she warned about the dangers of markets whose record keeping and reporting were kept in the dark. Although the chairman of the Federal Reserve, Alan Greenspan, insisted that the financial fraud that Born revealed did not require regulation, the Banker's Trust fraud soon became evident, followed by the Long Term Capital Management derivatives hedge fund fiasco in 1998.

As a public servant, Born repeatedly spoke up with the intent to protect people's homes, jobs, and finances and expressed her grave concerns about regulatory gaps. Regardless of attempts to deny, misrepresent, or ridicule Born's legitimate concerns, toxic "assets" did cause banks to fail and markets to collapse. Eventually, it was painfully evident to the entire world that a corrosive bubble had been constructed with mortgage-based securities that had no real value but could cause enormous damage, nevertheless.

The strength of character demonstrated by truth-tellers such as Brooksley Born is inspiring. In the 1800s, the innovative publisher of the *New York Tribune*, Horace Greeley, wrote, "Fame is a vapor, popularity an accident, riches take wings. Only one thing endures and that is character." The in-between times can be valuable even when what it is needed is to rest deeply, relax fully, and restore energy supplies. Hold your questions gently in your heart. Honor them with patience. Reframe difficult transitions or crises in your life as opportunities for spiritual and personal growth. Actions become habits. Habits become character, which creates our destiny. Character matters.

Transition times provide opportunities to develop new skill sets, strengthen our character, and enhance our readiness to meet what's next. They're times to expand our horizons as we integrate the capacities of our heart, head, and hands. For millennia, when the right season arrives, trees have blossomed and born fruit. Trust that guidance especially designed for you will come when the time is right.

One spark of goodness can inspire, uplift, challenge, and comfort many others. Consider the blazing torch of beneficence that would be kindled if millions of us brought the flames of our goodness together. With this spirit of adventure, patience, and generosity, let's continue our explorations of how to meet the adventure of living our life's calling with equanimity and enthusiasm.

Pause, Reflect, and Record

- *Change how you see. See how you change.* Describe a time when you "changed the prescription of your glasses." How did you change when your perception about a personal situation or social issue changed?

- What are some life transitions that you've navigated? What did you learn from these times of change?

- How have your core values, your relationships, and your life's purpose evolved as a result of a challenging transition?

- As you mature, how do you approach painful or difficult situations differently?

32

Sustain-Ability—
More Good, Less Harm

*If you want to build a ship,
don't herd people together to collect wood
and don't assign them tasks and work but rather,
teach them to long for the endless immensity of the sea.*

—Antoine de Saint-Exupery

The integral service of each irreplaceable, unrepeatable person is unique, and its manifestation depends on one's circumstances, resources, and abilities. Although motivation may spring from visions of endeavors that are immense with meaning, how do we sustain our longing for that endless immensity? We've discussed how mindfulness helps to clarify the wellspring of compassion and enthusiasm that nourishes our asspiration and resilience.

To keep our resiliency resilient and our sustainability sustainable, regular self-care is essential. When we've suffered a trauma or are living with illnesses and other circumstances that drain our energy, it's especially helpful to feed our brain with positive memories, thoughts, and states of mind. If our nervous system is particularly reactive, we dampen its trigger by offering our mind more calming stimuli; we wear earplugs to deepen our sleep, we soak in warm water, listen to gentle music, stretch and rock gently, walk in nature, and meditate. Other ways to support our state of wellness are to eat healthy food, chew slowly, inhale incense or a favorite fragrance, sing, dance, and socialize with friends, find our purpose, breathe fresh air, oil our skin gently, get a massage, and pause to appreciate the unique beauty of this moment. When we modulate, balance, and self-regulate our nervous system, we replenish our energy stores.

Goodness To Go

It's easier to find enjoyable ways to offer goodness to go when we blur the lines between work and play. If we have thin skin psychologically, we might feel like the proverbial canary in a coal mine during times that feel toxic. Although we may not be able to grow thicker skin, we can practice gratitude for all of life's lessons and reframe many vulnerabilities as strengths. Radical sustainability is rooted in the source of our inner self; it flows out in service with the power of our hearts, minds, and hands. When our interconnected life energies and their expression as integral service arise from this internal source, they're naturally sustainable. Although it changes its form of expression throughout our lifetimes, integral service is not an add-on to life's to-do list. Service is inherent to life.

Life continues because it serves and cares for life. The myopic plight of ignoring our interconnectedness is satirized in a familiar cartoon image. In it, a family is riding high in one end of a rowboat while another family desperately scoops water out of their end that is sinking due to a ragged hole in the boat's hull. With smug relief, the temporarily elevated family exclaims, "I'm sure glad the hole isn't in our end of the boat!"

We're travelling together on this good earth and cooperative collaboration of our hearts, minds, and hands is needed. In Barack Obama's January 2013 inaugural address for his second term of service, the president put sustainable energy sources front and center. "We will respond to the threat of climate change," he declared, "knowing that the failure to do so would betray our children and future generations." This is the conservatism that conserves and protects what we cherish.

Although newly found natural gas reserves will change economic dynamics and global energy politics, pressing risks remain—methane from extraction sites leaking into the atmosphere and water supplies becoming contaminated from hydraulic fracturing. Will we choose long-term environmental degradation for short-term financial gain?

Humanity, especially in industrialized nations, spews 90 million tons of carbon emissions each day into our shared atmosphere as if it were an open sewer. This carbon dioxide (CO^2) falls as acid rain into the oceans that cover two-thirds of planet earth. Marine life that is required as a protein source to sustain millions of people is dying off at alarming rates in acidified oceans. Although China now emits close to double the U.S. rate of CO^2, it is investing in sustainable energy sources and utilizing "cap and trade" as well as carbon tax programs more aggressively. Governments set a limit, or *cap*, on the amount of a pollutant that may be emitted, and firms are required to hold emission permits (or carbon credits) equivalent to their emissions. The buying and selling of permits is a *trade*, where, in theory, companies that reduce their emissions most cheaply will sell their permits and reduce pollution at the lowest cost to society.

In 2007, former vice president Al Gore was awarded the Nobel Peace Prize for his role in educating humanity about the reality of man-made climate change and the measures needed to counteract it. Many scientists and citizens regard climate change as a planetary emergency. "CO_2 is the exhaling breath of our civilization, literally," Gore warns. "Changing that pattern requires a scope, a scale, a speed of change that is beyond what we have done in the past."

Our creative imagination can step up to the task of sustaining life on earth. Recall the incredible ingenuity and scientific collaboration that were mobilized to save the Apollo 13 astronauts. Complex problems arose and were solved with out-of-the-box thinking in rapid-fire succession and returned the crippled spacecraft safely to earth. Our imagination also allows us to envision the endless immensity of goodness. We don't ignore current-day realities as we imagine and work toward a world at peace where all people are able to care for their families with dignity and confidence. Practical, sustainable ideas, such as malnourished families rising out of poverty with livestock investments from Heifer International, emerge from our humanitarian vision.

Take a moment to envision a home planet where oceans and forests thrive, the soil is rich, the air and water are clean, and every facet of globalization evolves with ecological intelligence and social justice. Strong commitment to social equity would make it possible for no one to go to bed hungry and all children to be safe and resourced sufficiently to explore and develop their gifts.

These are noble goals. Meanwhile, paradigms of cynicism or greed belittle compassion and inflame fears, warning that "we have enough problems at home." We have the power to speak up and stand our ground in the face of rhetoric that denounces international aid for brutalized civilians as "policing the world". Our shared commitment to global equity is resilient and sustained through challenging times.

Sir Wilfred Grenfell was a medical missionary whose decades of service to immigrants and aboriginals living on the fierce coasts of Labrador and Newfoundland began in 1893. He commented, "The service we render others is the rent we pay for our room on earth." When we have a responsibility and aspire to serve a valued goal, it's useful to refresh our vision and longing for that goal.

The intentional collaboration involved in teaching and mentoring one another may be a uniquely human activity. Although other species demonstrate pro-social behaviors such as tolerance and empathy, we've developed the capacity to encourage one another with enthusiasm, to share and record our discoveries, to enhance our understanding, and to create evolving cultures and civilizations of increasing complexity.

It's time to mentor one another, to consciously align with, manifest, and sustain the power of the possible. The value of sustainability is being invoked in nearly every aspect of life on earth, from natural law to political law. In order to sustain themselves, animal populations adjust according to available resources of food and shelter. President Lincoln and the abolitionists didn't work to stop slavery for a few years; they were abolishing it and making freedom sustainable for all time. Nelson Mandela devoted his entire life, sustaining his vision through decades of harsh prison conditions, to see the end of apartheid in South Africa and the creation of a democratic government.

A paradigm shift known as *slow democracy* is a call for citizens to reinvent government by working on local levels and governing themselves with a balance of freedom and unity. In *Slow Democracy—Rediscovering Community, Bringing Decision Making Back Home*, authors Susan Clark and Woden Teachout propose three key elements of a paradigm shift that is occurring in the democratic decision-making process: inclusion, deliberation, and power. The principle of inclusion ensures diverse community participation. Public deliberation of problems and potential solutions is based on sound information and respectful relationships. Connections between citizen participation and power structures are necessary. Citizens in true democracies are active producers of decisions and the resulting public policies and actions.

Governance based on citizen ownership and the responsibility of decisions made democratically involves advocacy, not fighting one another in polarized power struggles. With cross-community connections, citizens come together to make the best decisions possible for everyone involved, moving beyond the winner-loser paradigm. Although our ancestors might not recognize what passes as democracy today, we need not be passive recipients or consumers of policy. If the noble, ongoing experiment of democracy has been "hacked" by privileged interest groups on the congressional level, we need to wake up and be vigilant in our protection of invaluable freedoms on local, national, and global levels. What systemic changes would support politicians' service of society rather than obsessions about tactics to get re-elected? Through ongoing deliberations, we may re-evaluate the presence of lobbyists and term limits for elected representatives.

Life on earth needs citizens engaged in creating sustainable policies and practices to preserve essential natural resources. Regulations such as carbon taxes and international treaties are not the only answer. Global political will is required to invest in new paradigms and renewable energy economies so that we're not dependent on polluting carbon-based oil and coal technologies. Boom-and-bust cycles are inevitable in the old extract-and-consume paradigm. To pass on an inhabitable world to future generations, we're at a profoundly critical point where human impact on our finite environment needs to be substantially reduced.

Compassion and self-discipline are other types of energy sources that can be cultivated in sustainable ways. While running a marathon, we need to pace ourselves mindfully so that we can sustain our disciplined effort through the finish line. In much the same way, when we choose to explore the path of integral service, we need to be aware of inspirations and practices that sustain us. What has motivated you to keep going when the going gets tough?

In her book *Making a Change for Good*, Cheri Huber emphasizes the happiness that accompanies radical self-acceptance and compassionate presence. She describes self-discipline as allowing the intelligence and generosity of our authentic nature to guide us in every moment. It's important to honor the yearning, intuitive insights, and guidance about our integral service that arise from within. Antoine de Saint-Exupery's quote at the beginning of this chapter reminds us to refresh our yearning for the vision that initially inspired us to serve

We've seen that sustainability doesn't imply a permanent fixture or static condition that is incompatible with the dynamic change inherent to life. Rather than attaching to a fixed structure, sustainable systems expect, and even welcome, the unexpected. Small farms, for example, are dynamic systems that are sustained by recycling manure and compost to fertilize soils, investing in hydro or wind power, saving rainwater, and rotating crops according to nature's changing conditions. True sustainability is flexible; its stability is based on sensitive responsiveness to continually changing needs in ways that don't limit future generations from meeting their needs. Patience, endurance, compassion, and creativity are all part of sustainability.

Voluntary Simplicity

"'Tis the gift to be simple, 'tis the gift to be free," sang the Shakers, a sect committed to voluntary simplicity and equality of the sexes in the eighteenth century. For many cultures, *reduce, reuse, repurpose, and recycle* continues to be a way of life, often due to physical necessity, and voluntary simplicity movements over the centuries have incorporated the value of sustainability. In the nineteenth century, Henry David Thoreau lived simply and deliberately on Walden Pond, and a renowned twentieth-century architect, Ludwig Mies van der Rohe, proclaimed, "Less is more."

What's worth doing is usually not worth overdoing. It's best to take exactly enough physical resources required for our sustenance and no more. Thousands of years ago in Athens, Euripides wrote, "Enough is abundance to the wise." Sufficiency suffices. However, during economic boom times in the last half of the twentieth century, many people embraced the notion that *more is more*. Small families built homes with tens of thousands of square feet. Are supersized McMansions necessary? Mahatma Gandhi lived nonviolent simplicity with profound integrity, requesting that we "live simply so that others may simply live."

In 1977, Duane Elgin was part of a think tank at Stanford Research Institute that studied voluntary simplicity movements. Researchers observed that when an individual chooses to live on a simpler, more human scale, other values such as material simplicity, self-determination, personal growth, and environmental awareness naturally evolve to sustain their commitment.

Desiring less creates more space for things that really matter. In his new edition of *Voluntary Simplicity: Toward a Way of Life That Is Outwardly Simple, Inwardly Rich*, Elgin writes, "Simplicity creates the opportunity for greater fulfillment in work, meaningful connection with others, feelings of kinship with all life and awe of a living universe."

The physicians' Hippocratic Oath emphasizes, "First, do no harm." Zoe Weil, the co-founder and president of the Institute for Humane Education, coined the phrase "most good, least harm". Like Duane Elgin and many others, she's experienced increased mindfulness as she lives more simply. Also, with more time and energy to make thoughtful choices, our negative impact on our environment, including our carbon footprint, decreases. A rich, simpler life often moves at a slower pace with more time for the in-breath of self-care and the out-breath of service to our community, environment, and the planet.

A central theme of *Goodness To Go* is our intersubjectivity. As one Subject, one interconnected whole, it's a fallacy to think we could be a completely objective observer. We live and perceive through the lens of humanness within a vast, interactive, interpersonal field of Being. We are all facets of one whole, one ecology.

Thich Nhat Hanh refers to *inter-being*, the dynamic interpenetration of mutual influences affecting our adaptation and evolution as a species. Our interbeing is our ecology. Each generation builds on the best learning of previous generations, and we all stand on the shoulders of those who came before us. As we educate our children and ourselves in the broadest sense of eco-literacy, we can create the most wholesome ecology possible for ourselves and for future generations.

Getting Unstuck

Have you ever intended to start a meaningful project but seemed stuck in endless stages of planning and procrastination? There are many ways to shake out the cobwebs and get moving beyond the confines of our comfort zone. Late in the nineteenth century, the German philosopher Friedrich Nietzsche wrote, "The secret of the greatest fruitfulness and the greatest enjoyment of existence is: to live dangerously!" The uncomfortable, exhilarating, even paralyzing experience of fear is the clearest indicator that we're at our edge. Generations of spiritual teachers have challenged students to cultivate and sustain the courage that is willing to experience and work with fear skillfully.

When we're mindful of our natural courage, we're less hesitant to engage in the present moment. The more we practice jumping over or through fear, the stronger our courage muscles become. Paradoxical statements that encourage intuitive insight over reason are known as *koans*; one challenges us to *leap—and the net will appear*. The net, not physical or literal, is our inherent courage to be free of deception and capable of spontaneity.

While courage grows as we notice, engage, and even befriend our blind spots, biases, and fears, the habitual reaction to play it safe can be tenacious. Tired clichés like *better safe than sorry* echo through generations.

Goodness To Go

Although instinctive caution is hardwired into human anatomy that has supported our survival for millennia, we don't have to be enslaved by it. If curiosity killed the cat, our ancestors chose to temper curiosity with discernment when survival was at stake. Our brains have 100 billion neurons, each of which has an average of 10,000 connections to other neurons. If our minds didn't filter out most sensory input, if we weren't able to focus our attention on concerns that we judge to be priorities, we'd be driven to distraction by overwhelming oceans of stimuli.

Thankfully, we also have the ability to over-ride prehistoric wiring and reptilian brain conditioning. The calming parasympathetic "rest and digest" nervous system balances the "fight or flight" sympathetic nervous system. Our large frontal cortex allows us to reflect, rethink, and respond rather than react rashly. Despite habits of fearing and doubting, our ethical mind and courageous heart call us to the challenge of righting a wrong or entering the unknown. It's a hero's journey that is ours to undertake. Daniel Ellsberg risked his livelihood and liberty by releasing the Pentagon Papers. Volunteers clear land mines. Musicians sing out against injustice. Millions risk their lives in protest against brutal regimes.

Sustainability itself requires fresh sustenance. The numerous environments in which we live support and reflect who we are and who we want to become. The health of our mind and body, our work, home, spiritual, educational, social, community, technological, and political environments affect us in many ways and are influenced by choices we make.

We can move beyond the dualism that is often implied by the word *environments*, suggesting that we exist separate from them. Dualistic thinking turns environments into objects; one nineteenth-century philosopher used the phrase "the objectional objective world." When we objectify anything or anyone, compassion and awareness of our interconnectivity tend to decrease. Non-dual awareness recognizes the interdependent nature of the ecology in which we live. The science of ecology explores the interchange within relationships between organisms and their environments. Our sustainability depends on the quality of these relationships. It includes the intelligence and compassion of our collective relationship with all life and all ecosystems on our home planet.

In many ways, our lives are a mythic journey through ecologies of the unknown and we're often touched by the "fine hand of synchronicity." Joseph Campbell explored the call to the adventure of life in his seminal book *Hero with a Thousand Faces*. As we leave the known of our familiar habits, environments, and status quo, we cross thresholds into the unknown and enter liminal dimensions between the old life and the new. These transitions are ripe with opportunity and potential, peril and promise. As we summon the courage to follow our calling, untold meaningful, synchronistic coincidences appear. Doors open and our lives are enriched in sustainable, meaningful ways.

Pause, Reflect, and Record

- What resources sustain your well-being on all levels— physical, intellectual, emotional, psychological, political, and spiritual?

- Explore in what ways more is *not* better. What is something that is worth doing but not worth overdoing?

- When you've found yourself procrastinating, what has helped you to get unstuck?

- In what ways have you been willing *to give up greed for freedom*?

33

Generativity—Giving Back

Many an individual has turned from the mean,
personal, acquisitive point of view to one that sees
society as a whole and works for its benefit.
If there has been such a change in one person,
there can be the same change in many.

—Mahatma Gandhi

The essence of goodness to go is giving back. As our generative commitment to society, it is seen in the countless ways we offer our gifts. The expression of our humanitarian principles generates healthy ways for future generations to prosper in equity and peace. By empowering children, growing organic food, making art, transforming toxic habits and beliefs, engaging in social justice and environmental activism, or developing beneficial organizations, we take care of our communities and our planet. Optimism about humanity is inherent in our generativity.

In 1950, the psychologist Erik Erikson noted that generativity also stems from impulses for our creative energy to flow. Dr. Martin Luther King, Jr., devoted his life to generative actions and didn't merely condemn the injustice of prejudice and discrimination. "It is not enough to say we must not wage war. It is necessary to love peace and sacrifice for it," he wrote.

Words are not enough; we need to mobilize our deepest values into beneficial actions. A man who grew up in an urban slum shares the story of his recovery from heroin addiction. Deep gratitude for the people and programs that gave him a second chance inspired his generative commitment to give back. Now he volunteers at a drug rehabilitation program and says, "I've been given so much and feel so blessed. It's my duty to rise above this, and make my world and that around me a better place."

Goodness To Go

The Challenge of Living Our Calling

If we remain overly attached to the predictable, we may miss the calling of our lives. The habit of avoiding the unfamiliar is like any habit: it can exceed its useful boundaries. Discernment can collapse into judgment and evasion. Recall Jonah's predicament before he was swallowed into the proverbial belly of a whale. Jonah didn't fall asleep at the wheel of life; he fell asleep in the dark hold of the ship on which he was trying to escape his calling.

Although Jonah was chosen to preach to the Ninevites, he judged them as unworthy of being saved and fabricated a flimsy excuse about his incompetence as a preacher. While escaping in a sailing ship, Jonah encountered the Lord's stormy appeal for his change of mind but chose denial instead. Attempting to avoid the storm that he had responsibility for creating, Jonah went to sleep in the bottom of the boat.

Regardless of how strong the temptation to deny our calling, there is a generative element within that is awake and whose voice will not be silenced. Awakened by the strong voice of the captain, Jonah acknowledged his responsibility for the ship's danger and offered himself as a sacrifice, thinking it to be the only way to calm the storm. Eventually, under duress, the sailors agreed and threw him overboard. Three days later, the whale that swallowed Jonah spewed him onto the shores of Nineveh. Transformed after his deep contemplation and soul-searching in the dark abyss of the whale's belly, Jonah embraced his calling to serve humanity unconditionally. To this day, some call him the patron saint of refused callings.

Stories and parables have been important teaching vehicles throughout history. Arthur Koestler in *The Act of Creation* writes that the source of Jonah's remorse was that he clung to the trivial, trying to cultivate only his own little garden when he was being called to a larger task. It can be easy to succumb to illusions of safety and comfort, even mediocrity, with which the familiar can seduce us.

Our innate goodness calls us to responsibility even as we cling rather desperately to the comforts of the status quo. The Buddha taught that attachment is the root of dissatisfaction and suffering. We're all connected, and freedom from attachment is subtly distinct from detachment. In the Afghani tongue, the verb *to cling* is the same as *to die*. Fear of death often stems from clinging to life and all that we think we'll lose. It's an act of courage to live with the awareness of our mortality and not hide out in dismay, distress, or denial.

346

Renowned developmental psychologist Abraham Maslow calls truancy from living our authentic life the "Jonah Complex," which he describes as "the evasion of one's own growth, the setting of low levels of aspiration, the fear of doing what one is capable of doing, voluntary self-crippling, pseudo-stupidity, mock humility." Sometimes we insist on denial or evasion, refusing to wake up to our life's calling. In the Navajo tradition, there is a proverb that suggests it's not possible to awaken someone who is pretending to be asleep.

The theme of the sleep of avoidance that precedes awakening is age-old. Although playing small serves no one, the potent forces of denial, resistance, and avoidance spawn refusal to live our authentic life. If we move at a frenzied pace, faster than the speed of a life, we'll collapse eventually and hunker down in exhaustion and avoidance. We convince ourselves that we have "the right not to know" about the calamities, atrocities, and injustices in our world. Somewhat defensively, even defiantly, we say that we're busy enough with our own personal lives.

We've taken birth to share our true selves with the world, not to cling to temporary comfort. If we're walking on thin ice, say the Eskimos, we might as well dance! Our life stories are outer expressions of our soul's intended journey to use the lessons of our pain, as well as our gifts, to make the world a better place. We can find ways to nourish our aspirations and actions; the world needs us resourced and resilient, able to sustain our generative service.

Concern yearns to move into action; our worldview and actions influence each other. William Gibson, the writer who coined the term "cyberspace," observed that we see in order to move and move in order to see. Many people consciously consider what kind of legacy they want to leave for future generations, and others simply dive into their currents of connectedness with the living world. In any case, the world needs our willingness and commitment to transform the multiple dangers that threaten civilization.

For this transformation to occur, we give of ourselves. Yogi Bhajan was an influential entrepreneur and spiritual leader who introduced new forms of Sikhism and hatha yoga to the world in the twentieth century. He taught, "First commit, then live to the commitment and then experience the commitment. There's no other way to be happy." This insight about the path to generativity and happiness is found in nearly every culture.

For the past half-century, nearly 200 individuals have participated in one of the longest-running social science studies of our time. One of the researchers, psychologist Paul Wink, co-authored a book entitled *In the Course of a Lifetime* that presents the findings of what constitutes a happy life. This research also found that an important key to creating a happy life is generativity, our capacity to give to others. The happiest and most vital study participants practiced gratitude, felt joy in giving to others, and reframed life difficulties as opportunities to enhance empathy. They honored the lessons that life's valleys hold as much as those of the sunny peaks.

Beyond the experience of a temporary helper's high, practicing gratitude and making positive contributions to others enhances mental and physical health. Wink and his colleague learned that high school students who scored high on generativity were healthier and happier fifty years later. How affirming it is to know that when the altruism of adolescents is cultivated, their current well-being as well as their future wellness is enhanced as they contribute to the health of the world.

Serving your family and community may help you live longer, too. At the American Geriatrics Society meeting in May of 2009, researchers presented their findings that volunteers had half the death rate of those who didn't volunteer; the findings were adjusted for factors such as chronic illness and socioeconomic status. The study authors suggested that improved self-esteem and expanded social networks might help explain volunteers' lower mortality.

Generativity fosters healthy self-regard, which in turn fuels our goodness to go. Experiences of personal efficacy and optimism support the confidence that we can make a difference in our troubled world. Empathic generativity can grow to the point where the welfare of others is as important, or even more important, than our own. Empathy is expressed in many faith-based organizations, including traditional religions and eclectic spiritual paths. Engaged Buddhism has a rich history of compassion in action, and within the Catholic Church are members who choose a life of poverty, devoting themselves to serving others around the world.

The generative contributions of individuals have protected and enriched millions of lives. Recall the integral service of Irena Sendler, the young social worker who smuggled 2,500 Jewish children out of Warsaw, Poland, during World War II. With the support of courageous citizens, an underground network was woven together around their commitment to saving as many children's lives as possible. Sendler miraculously survived the war years and died in 2008, about the time *The Oprah Winfrey*

Show televised another of its "pay it forward" episodes. The goodness to go of Irena Sendler and others endures far beyond their lifetimes.

Inspired by Oprah's "pay it forward" challenge, a banker in North Dakota cut each of his 460 employees a $1,000 check—with the condition that they had to pay it forward. Projects and foundations helping more than 100 schools and hospitals, 300 families, and 200 nonprofit and community groups in the state were established. "We became more compassionate people," said one employee. Others asked themselves, "What else can I do?" and found it thrilling to give in ways that were meaningful for them.

There are innumerable stories about people from all walks of life who've mobilized their generative ability to serve and contribute their life's assets, financial or otherwise. A college student founded an orphanage in India. A grandmother in her seventies ascends some of the planet's most magnificent mountains to raise contributions to help find cures for various illnesses. To assist a generation of students in a faltering Arkansas town, the Murphy Oil Corporation pledged to pay college tuition for nearly every student in town for twenty years.

In 2007, Peter G. Peterson became an instant billionaire at eighty-one when his company went public. Like many, he had a passion to do good and contemplated which of many worthy causes called him most clearly. He decided to commit $1 billion to his foundation focusing on fiscal sustainability. "Our children are unrepresented," he wrote. "The future is unrepresented. The moment is overdue for us to become moral and worthy ancestors." Like many, Peterson understands that borrowing money from the future to shore up an unsustainable current paradigm is folly, suffocates countries with debt, and harms the lives of our children.

It's deeply fulfilling to breathe new life into situations where it's needed. Fan the embers of your intent to offer your integral service. The impact of your teachers, mentors, and ancestors is honored and celebrated as you mobilize your ability to give back or pay it forward. Integral service leads to a healthier, more beautiful life for you as well as for those who receive your gifts.

Prasad—The Cycle of Giving and Receiving

As we expand our circles of caring, we participate in many overlapping cycles of giving and receiving. One purpose of our lives on earth is to know the love in our hearts, receive guidance and support, and share with love our talents and inspirations. Divinely superfluous beauty surrounds us. In the context of nature's *prasad*, which is a reciprocal interplay of life and death, we each have our allotted time on this earth; we can't live forever or "have it all." The reciprocal balance at play in the natural order is evident as predators and prey maintain sustainable populations within an ecological niche. Plants utilize our exhaled carbon dioxide and we inhale the oxygen they give.

Eventually, what goes around comes around. Nature gives and receives; those who are generous with life experience life as generous. When there is simple, open space inside us, there is room to receive. Like an acoustic guitar, we need inner vibrating space in order to give our music to the world. In this offering, there is great freedom. A philosophy professor at Oregon State University, Madronna Holden, writes: "There is certain justice in the way life works upon and then returns to us what we give to it. We cannot know how the results of our actions will come back to us—or to those who follow us onto the vast canvas of life and time. We only know that natural reciprocity makes such a return inevitable."

Gratefulness for life strengthens us. Appreciation for *what is*, even when it's not all that we want, is a receptive state that has been called perfect allowing. A heart overflowing with gratitude naturally takes form as integral service. In the Sanskrit language, the word *prasad* reflects the beauty of the natural cycles of giving and receiving that are a sweet dance of generosity and connection between equals. Prasad is the flow of blessings experienced by the one who gives as well as the one who receives.

We reap what we sow. A handful of wheat becomes a harvest. An acorn becomes a mighty oak. Our hearts open, receive, and offer life. Giving of ourselves unconditionally is a natural impulse, and what we give is what we receive. We can't give what we don't have, and to let in goodness is to give it. Giving and receiving are acts of love that are harmoniously interdependent.

The literal translation of the word *kabbalah*, the ancient teachings of Jewish mysticism, is "the receiving." Honoring the receiving, holding and imbibing teachings that have been given, allowing the in-breath of self-care and the loving service of others, is at the heart of prasad. It is then natural to want to give in return. In the Chinese culture, reciprocity is emphasized; indeed, repaying one's gratitude is a basic rule of being human. Relationships are maintained with reciprocal exchange.

Receiving is a medicine that heals and strengthens. A West African teacher named Sobonfu Some believes that life is infused with spirit and that we receive energy from the spirit that is alive within relationships. Sobonfu, whose name means "keeper of the ritual," wrote: "Receiving heals us individually, and the gifts of that relationship can then be offered back to the community. ... We receive from an abundant source that can offer whatever we need. There is always enough for everybody. Everything from spirit is free. There is no price in receiving. We don't need to earn what we're given. We just need to turn toward spirit with an attitude of service."

We uplift the world with the power of our respect and kindness. Thousands of years ago, the Taoist philosopher Lao Tzu noted, "Kindness in words creates confidence. Kindness in thinking creates profoundness. Kindness in giving creates love." When we give without expectations, that offering bears its fullest fruit. The light of our goodness brings out the best in others, which is the greatest integral service of all.

The PRASAD Project

The PRASAD (Philanthropic Relief, Altruistic Service, and Development) Project is an international not-for-profit organization committed to improving the quality of life of economically disadvantaged people around the world. During medical school, it was my good fortune to volunteer on PRASAD's mobile hospital in the rural Tansa Valley north of Bombay, as Mumbai was called in the 1980s. For many years, PRASAD's exceptional programs have served as models of compassion and efficacy for other philanthropies.

The intention of the PRASAD Project is to empower people to become self-reliant and live a life of dignity in healthy communities prospering in harmony with the natural environment. For more information about the PRASAD Project's community-wide economic, educational, environmental, health, and agricultural programs and events, visit www.prasad.org.

Goodness To Go

It feels good to do good, and we're wired in such a way that we can't help but experience good feelings when we give. Neuroscientists have learned that neurons that fire together wire together: when nerve connections are repeatedly stimulated and reinforced, the stronger and more efficacious their interconnectedness becomes. In much the same way, people that "fire" or work together for a common purpose "wire" together. Their social cohesion and happiness increase. Our collective human resonance as we work collaboratively for a positive overarching goal magnifies our individual effect. Together we can revitalize life on earth.

Neuroscience research also has documented that levels of "feel good" neurotransmitters like dopamine, which is associated with enthusiasm and motivation, and the hormone oxytocin, which affects emotional bonding, increase with giving. Altruism is not puritanical do-gooding; it benefits the giver as well as the receiver on many levels. This inherent receiving does not make our giving less pure. Genuine giving and receiving occur simultaneously and are reciprocal in nature.

In a popular modern parable called *The Go-Giver*, some laws of "stratospheric success" are described. The fifth law states that *the key to effective giving is to stay open to receiving*. Staying open to receiving includes letting go of what we don't need, including dysfunctional beliefs and habits such as excessive materialism. Receiving also allows and respects the contribution of others.

The glory of receiving from others and giving of ourselves is that the blessings spread like ripples in the ocean, touching other beings and other parts of the earth as well. Booker T. Washington, an African American born into slavery who became a leader of the civil rights movement at the beginning of the twentieth century, expressed the cycle of blessings given and received in a beautifully practical way: "Lay hold of something that will help you, and then use it to help somebody else."

With gratitude for life, we receive what helps us and use it to help others. The courage that releases and expresses the goodness in our hearts and minds is expressed through our generative actions. Rumi, the Sufi mystic wrote, "In generosity and helping others, be like a river." The river of our goodness to go is our generativity. The optimism, generosity, and nobility of our potential for generativity can be cultivated throughout our lives. As we give back to communities that have made our lives possible, we're also paying it forward to enhance the lives of future generations.

Pause, Reflect, and Record

- Recall a time when you received an unexpected, deeply appreciated gift. Remember another time that you truly gave of yourself unconditionally without expectation of reciprocation. Describe how each experience felt. What did you learn?

- How does the awareness of *prasad*, the natural cycle of giving and receiving, impact your life? In what ways have you experienced that everyone involved in the circle of giving is also a recipient?

- Consider a social or environmental issue that is especially concerning to you. What is one action step that you could take today to make the world a better place for future generations?

- Record questions, insights, inquiries, and action steps from Section Three with which you'd like to engage further.

SECTION FOUR

INTEGRATE HEART, HEAD, AND HANDS

34

You're Good to Go

It's time for greatness—not for greed.
It's a time for idealism—not ideology.
It is a time not just for compassionate words,
but compassionate action.

—Marian Wright Edelman

Throughout the first three sections of *Goodness To Go*, we've explored several elements in the sphere of human existence that are interconnected facets of our integral service. We've recognized our hearts, minds, and bodies are one interdependent whole and that after we dream, we act. Our actions ripple through the dynamic web of space, time, and life. As we embark on the spiraling adventure of summoning our heart, empowering the mind, and mobilizing benevolent action, we'll meet tests and trials as well as allies. No clouds are here to stay. We'll have opportunities to evolve beyond dualistic, fear-based thinking and uncover the inner treasure of wisdom that we offer to our community.

Goodness is on the go in our personal lives and around the globe, and there is a growing understanding that philanthropic giving is an auspicious privilege. One entrepreneur shared that he regards the art of philanthropy as a noble path. Although we cannot *make* change happen in situations outside of ourselves, we are responsible for our personal maturation as humanitarians. Our response to life, moment by moment, creates our destiny. If enough of us do our inner work, we'll serve together as a force of goodness and positive planetary metamorphosis. Compassion in action gives strength to the heart and clarity to the intellect; we become kinder and wiser.

An iconic image in Indian philosophy of the infinite interconnectedness of nature and the cosmos is known as Indra's net. Like a multidimensional, bejeweled web, our actions of goodness ripple through its nodal points, which have multiple threads to other points throughout the universe. Some people sense vibrations of this net as a cosmic hum that animates existence. In many ways, the celebration throughout this book of the adventure of integral service is a microcosm of the vast interconnectivity of multifaceted goodness.

Our actions now create our future. Former U.S. president John F. Kennedy reminded us that we can change our human story. He wrote, "In the total of all those acts will be written the history of this generation." His brother Robert F. Kennedy was a humanitarian statesman who celebrated the exponential leveraging of goodness. He said: "Each time a person ... acts to improve the lot of others ... a tiny ripple of hope is sent forth. ... Those ripples, from a million different centers of energy and daring, build a current that can sweep down the mightiest walls of oppression and resistance."

The integration of hearts, heads, and hands grown strong with wisdom and love is required to embrace the paradoxes inherent in our complex world. Our readiness for undertaking integral service emerges when our inspirations, thoughts, willpower, emotions, and skills work together. The pioneering Jewish Expressionist Marc Chagall wrote that when he created only from the head, almost nothing worked. For centuries, poets and visionaries in every culture have wondered what the world would be like if our hearts could do the thinking and our minds began to feel.

Fundamentalist and patriarchal cultural beliefs often separate mind from heart, with dualistic worldviews that reinforce separateness and competition, racial and religious discrimination, subjugation of women, and exploitation of nature. The dualism implicit in these mindsets has devastated environments, extinguished many species of irreplaceable life, and continues to threaten human existence on this uniquely generous, exquisite planet. Important developmental, spiritual, and evolutionary tasks for human beings are to free ourselves to bring heart, head, and actions together as one, integral whole. With this unified power, our goodness is on the go.

Benjamin Franklin, the eighteenth-century Renaissance man and polymath of great and varied learning, was a person of action who created a remarkable legacy of integrated heart, mind, and hands. As the son of a candle maker, he experimented with electricity and invented the lightning rod. As postmaster for the American colonies, he set up the first national communications network. As a printer, statesman, and political philosopher, he defined a new ethos that was opposed to political and religious authoritarianism. It wove together the practical values of education, hard work, thrift, community spirit, and democratic self-governing institutions. Although the torch of integral thinkers continues to illumine each generation in every region around the world, tremendous efforts are required to create and nurture paradigms of equity, justice, and freedom.

The power of our heart and will is as important to the releasing of old ways of being as it is to harnessing energy for new endeavors. With self-effort and unshakeable faith in the values of democracy, President Abraham Lincoln wrestled with his racial prejudice. Eventually, he was able to release and rise above it, evoking the better angels of human nature. The deep respect Lincoln engenders is not because he is superhuman, but fully human. Freedom is paramount in the pursuit of genuine peace and happiness. Lincoln let go of limiting beliefs and joined with the abolitionist movement committed to increasing possibilities of freedom and happiness for all, including opportunities to create self-sufficient lives and healthy, equitable communities.

Abraham Lincoln continues to inspire generations because his aspirations informed his actions as well as his thoughts. He evolved in a way that integrated his heart, head, and hands by growing resilient through repeated failures, respecting the decades of ethical foundation laid by the abolitionists, unifying a severely fractured country, and upholding the truth that all people are created equal. His thoughts, feelings, speeches, and actions were pivotal in abolishing slavery in the United States for all time. As Lincoln lived life in integrity with his core values and with life's creative vision for his destiny, he freed himself and millions of others.

Give More to Live More

The poet Adrienne Rich wrote about casting her lot with the everyday goodness of individuals who, through the ages, "reconstitute the world." While I was writing *Goodness To Go*, a dear friend died after an arduous journey through cancer. Anne was in her forties, with a young son, devoted husband, and a large, loving community of family and friends. As a teacher and outdoor educator, Anne was a social artist who reconstituted the world. With every rising of the sun, she saw her life as just begun. Anne's luminous heart uplifted hundreds of children and families who were empowered by her enthusiastic confidence in their strength of spirit and goodness of heart,

People of all ages were inspired by the joyful way Anne greeted, acknowledged, and celebrated their goodness. She was a beacon of light who saw that same light in everyone, and a "No Judgment" zone radiated from her. During the last birthday that Anne was physically present to celebrate, friends and family gathered to honor her generosity and countless gifts to the world. In the midst of the festivities, Anne said in her straightforward way, "Nothing I do is original. When I see someone doing something that I like, I just do it, too!" Her goodness appreciated the goodness in others and was always on the go.

Although cheerfully engaging a near stranger in an elevator and inviting her to tea may not be an original action, Anne was an original. Her spirit of service was unique, fresh, and alive in each moment. In the same way, each one of us is an original. Our inner journey is uniquely ours, and what we do has our individual signature and unique personal tapestry of influences brought to bear on our actions. Our response to our life's calling can be *Yes!*

We weave, construct, envision, and evoke the path that our life's adventure will take with our responses to big questions: *Who am I? What brings happiness and meaning to life? What legacy am I to leave?* The renowned mythologist Joseph Campbell encouraged us to follow our bliss and to honor what kindles the rapture of being fully alive.

What are some of your responses to the big questions of life? Campbell felt that the grand question is whether or not we're going to say a hearty yes to the adventure of our lifetimes. Individual callings often link with the callings of others for the common purpose or overarching goal of creating a positive, equitable future for all. When goals are shared and we realize that we're all in this together, we shift from individual and resource competition toward cooperation and mutual respect, restoration and rejuvenation.

We may do no great acts, but we can offer small acts with great love, Mother Teresa reminds us. Small acts of kindness make changes that add up. Their living wisdom keeps life whole in a world where nature's central impulse is an irrepressible drive toward wholeness, not a struggle for dominion. Think of how bees live and die to make their hive, their honey, and their entire community better. In addition, their integral service pollinates 90 percent of plant life on earth, and human environmental contamination is bringing them to the brink of extinction.

Small change adds up. Howard Thurman was an African American philosopher, theologian, and educator who inspired leaders from every ethnic background in the struggle for equality and civil rights. He wrote, "Do not think lightly of these little gestures—it is their multiplication from all over the world that creates heaven on earth." It's been said that there's no such thing as an innocent bystander. Even young children can report the bullying of a classmate to their teacher. Consider the positive ripple of consequences through the web of interbeing when we choose to be an upstander in our communities and beyond.

The combined actions of many people contributed to the miraculous survival of Malala Yousafzai, the Pakistani girl who was shot in the head in 2012 by Taliban extremists for being an advocate for girls' education. Two days later was the inaugural International Day of the Girl. Early in 2013, with a reconstructed skull and left ear cochlear implant, Malala released a video statement. With profound courage she vowed, "I want to serve. I want to serve the people. I want every girl, every child, to be educated." Thousands of upstanders join Malala in the global movement for gender equity and empowerment.

Together We Are More

An interconnected whole is much more powerful than the sum of its parts. Consider that each of our brain's ten billion neurons makes 10,000 connections with other neurons, or think of the computational power possible with integrated circuits of microchips. Teams and networks of empowered individuals are significantly more creative than isolated lone rangers or stultified hierarchies. In *The Bond: Connecting Through the Space Between Us*, author Lynne McTaggart describes how brain-wave entrainment between two individuals can resonate between members of larger groups, creating a collective resonant identity.

Over 2,000 years ago, the eminent Jewish scholar Rabbi Hillel wrote, "If I'm only for myself, what am I? If not now, when?" He understood that if the wealth of our experience and knowledge is not shared, it becomes a burden. Life is good. We are defined by our essential connectedness, not the illusion of our separateness, and there are many ways that we express this awareness.

The twentieth-century analytic philosopher Bertrand Russell was a prominent anti-war activist for over five decades who wrote *Introduction to Mathematical Philosophy* while in prison for his pacifism during World War I. In addition to campaigning for women's suffrage and against nuclear weapons, Russell was awarded the Nobel Prize in Literature in recognition of his varied and significant writings in which he championed humanitarian ideals and freedom of thought. This renowned logician experienced that the integration of mind, instinct, and spirit is essential to a full life. The life that is to be sought, Russell wrote, develops all three in coordination, "intimately blended in a single harmonious whole." We offer our harmonious integral service in collaboration with others who share a common goal or activity, no matter how different we may seem to be.

When we experience our connections with nature and one another, we know how to nurture those physical and emotional ecologies. The Buddhist teacher Chogyam Trungpa Rinpoche wrote, "Human beings destroy their ecology at the same time that they destroy one another. From that perspective, healing our society goes hand in hand with healing our personal, elemental connection with the phenomenal world."

The sacredness of all life is served as we serve the earth and our fellow beings. When we open our hearts and welcome fresh insights needed for our world, we naturally acknowledge and celebrate our interconnectedness. Saying *Yes* to our integral service, we discover how to use fresh enthusiasm to create meaningful transformation in the world. Simultaneously, we behold our own happiness. The Bengali poet Rabindranath Tagore, who won the Nobel Prize in Literature in 1913, wrote, "I slept and dreamed that life was joy. I awoke and saw that life was service. I acted and behold, service was joy."

Countless individuals have recognized that our service is our life's joy. Our shadowed ego often seems to be an adversary of goodness, hiding out in curses and excuses. "For me to get what I want, someone else has to lose," ego argues. Regardless of ego's pessimistic worldview, one candle lighting another is not a zero-sum game: the source of the flame is not diminished by igniting others. It's better to light a candle than to curse the darkness, a proverb tells us. Light increases and darkness recedes. It's the win-win paradigm of *Yes, We Can.*

For millennia, we've been inspired by metaphors that evoke light's beauty as the transporter of radiant goodness and awareness. Edith Wharton, a major American figure in literary history who was honored by France for her philanthropic work during World War I, reminded us, "There are two ways of spreading the light: to be the candle or the mirror that reflects it." In every community around the world, humanitarians are serving as both the candles that illumine the world and the mirrors that reflect the light of everyone they meet.

Love and unconditional happiness cannot be purchased. Rather than hiding your light under a proverbial bushel, allow its illumination to spread in service of the welfare of the world. Former president Woodrow

Wilson, a minister's son, was committed to representing the citizens' interests. Early in the twentieth century, he developed a program of progressive reform and asserted international leadership in building a new world order. Wilson understood the importance of community networks of support and wrote, "Provision for others is a fundamental responsibility of human life."

Social scientists have known for decades that strong support systems contribute to a longer life. In *The Longevity Project*, psychologists Howard Friedman and Leslie Martin describe the findings of an eighty-year Stanford study about factors that contribute to lengthy life spans. A key predictor of longevity is not what you have or get in the course of your life but what you do for friends and family.

Embracing a Multi-Truth Reality

We have the marvelous task of evolving and integrating the diverse elements of who we are. There are many facets and levels of integrity, perspective, and truth within a single human being. Just as each blind man experienced only a small part of the elephant, we perceive the world through the lens of our unique point of view and it's far too vast and complex for a single perspective to be wholly accurate. Rigid *black or white* thinking is rarely useful. Although resorting to simplistic dualism may be tempting, which my daughter called "either-or-itis" when she was twelve, there are far more than two sides to any true story.

Integral service is a manifestation of goodness. With mindfulness in the present moment, wrote the Buddhist lineage holder Sakyong Mipham, we manifest our courage by wholeheartedly relating "to the manifest quality of goodness." What does it mean to relate to the manifest quality of goodness? During times of deceit, terror, or betrayal, how do we maintain allegiance to the manifestation of our basic goodness? Within us is the great treasure of a mind that can open and see clearly, free of filters and prejudices, and has the profound ability to choose. This endless sky flows naturally with compassion and it is our great good fortune to be able to focus our awareness on the sun in a sky much vaster than any obscuration. The heart breaks in.

Relating to the goodness in ourselves and others is very challenging at times, especially when stress hormones, fear, and anger create internal infernos and external explosions. When we're in conflict with someone who acts like an enemy with antagonistic, even hostile values and goals, how do we cultivate on-the-spot courage? How do we remain steadfast in acknowledging, appreciating, and manifesting mutual respect with skillful means?

As we've discussed throughout *Goodness To Go*, there are many ways to resource our resilience. Inner calm is enhanced by remembering to pause, grounding our perceptions in what is present in the moment, recalling our heart's intent, and deepening our balanced breath. Healing emotional wounds of the past allows us to be more present now and for our actions to be more effective and beneficial in the future. First do no harm. With more access to inner peace and wisdom, listen for guidance about the most beneficial response for all involved.

Unattached to our actions, we dedicate any merit of our actions for the welfare of all. Developing the confidence and skillful means to trust that we can maintain our equanimity and genuine regard for the other in the face of conflict and aggression takes time and committed practice. This is as true for parents and politicians as it is for warriors, and the example of many wise beings assures us that it can be done. It's a noble, ongoing discipline to free ourselves from the prison of small-minded ego and embrace a multi-truth reality.

There are multiple voices in a multi-truth reality. In *The New Media Monopoly*, journalist Ben Bagdikian outlined the dangers of corporate consolidation and control of media sources to democracy and the marketplace of ideas. The root process of democratic change is respecting the right of every voice to be heard and developing beneficial courses of action committed to justice, respect, and responsibility. Frequently, what aggrieved or disenfranchised people express shakes up a status quo that resists embracing multiple perspectives. The more ways we have of looking at the world, the better will be our ideas for pragmatic, positive transformation.

To fully embrace life, it's valuable to include all of its dynamic play of diversity, constant change, and purposeful thrust toward evolution and optimization. When we're stuck in sorrows and regrets about the past, or caught in anxiety about the future, we're not fully present and we're not free. It's possible to let go of old patterns of thoughts and behaviors and be free of ruminating about problems and grievances. We can forgive ourselves and others for mistakes made and move on.

Philosopher-fisherman David James Duncan wrote an acclaimed novel called *The River Why*. Twenty years after his epic was published, Duncan reflected on his love of fishing and his concern for our planet's health. He wrote: "Knowing justice is inescapable, and not in human hands, I want to ask, finally, Why judge? Why hate or rage? Why not just serve, wherever and however and for as long and as gratefully as we can, step by step, heart to heart, move by intricate move?" We may have insights, evaluations, and discernments, but reflexive, harsh judgment is rarely helpful. No one has nearly enough information about any one or any action to judge. Instead, we can choose to look deeply into the nature of judgment and gradually release all notions of superiority, inferiority, and ultimately, even the *judgment* of equality.

We are meaning-seeking creatures and Duncan's questions are meaningful to contemplate. Why judge? Why not just serve for as long and as gratefully as we can? Life is multifaceted, multidimensional, organic, and, at times, messy with competing needs, rights, and truths. Even in times of chaos and aggression, we can put aside limiting beliefs and allow ourselves to see through the lenses of others' perspectives. We can extend our intelligence, imagination, and compassion to include all of life.

New Millennial Warriors

Social artists, activists, and other twenty-first-century warriors of compassion integrate the wisdom of their hearts, heads, and hands. Buckminster Fuller was the design innovator who championed doing more with less, and he passionately lived his understanding that integrity is the essence of everything successful. "We have to think with *feelings* in our muscles," recommended Albert Einstein. Courage and mindful attention are needed to manifest our gifts for the world. Generations of humanitarians, including singers, teachers, writers, artists, and volunteers, have offered the gift of their creativity to inspire movements for social and environmental justice.

As we heed our wake-up call to integral service, it can be challenging to put evolving insights and transformations into the world, or simply into words. In *Callings*, Gregg Levoy discussed the temptation to evade life's challenges that many of experience at some point in our lives. Each of us is called to the hero's journey, as mythologist Joseph Campbell called it, to venture into uncharted territory, grow stronger from the challenges that we inevitably encounter, and return to share our wisdom with our communities. Goethe wrote that as soon as we trust ourselves, we will know how to live the adventure of our lives. And although we may not always see it, we're encouraged to trust that everything plays to our greater good.

Goodness To Go

Our courage and generosity as everyday heroes and teachers enriches our world and the human story. Ulysses, whose odyssey was largely ego driven, exemplifies an old-paradigm hero or warrior. Our millennial age needs new kinds of warriors—warriors of compassion who are awake to their inherent goodness, act with integrity, are share the wealth of their experience and knowledge. In this paradigm, warriors in training develop the willingness to approach and embrace their inner fears, act with compassion rather than aggression, and speak truthfully. The bravery required to look our fears in the face is power grounded in integrity and responsibility.

Following his imprisonment in a Nazi concentration camp, Viktor Frankl, M.D., wrote *Man's Search for Meaning*. In it, Dr. Frankl asserted that individual freedom from oppression has little meaning unless it's linked to responsibility for our actions. We're only truly free if we accept responsibility for that freedom. Frankl suggested that a Statue of Responsibility be built to complement the Statue of Liberty, a gift that was given in international friendship. Funding has begun to sculpt two hands holding each another. One hand symbolizes responsibility for our personal needs, and the other represents those for whom we feel responsible—children, ecosystems, the sick and poor, our planet, and all species as a whole.

The willingness to relate with difficult or darker aspects of human nature, as Dr. Frankl did, is an important aspect of manifesting goodness to go. We've looked at how the fear of being stretched or even overwhelmed can prevent the integration of service into our lives if we succumb to it. On the other hand, as we develop skillfulness in relating with emotions, including fear and anger, we increase access to our inherent generosity, wisdom and confidence.

Discomfort can be a clue that we're close to something important for our soul's authentic growth. Ralph Waldo Emerson, a leader of the Transcendentalist movement in the mid-nineteenth century, wrote, "Bad times have a scientific value. These are occasions a good learner would not miss." Sometimes fear means *GO*. Within and beyond fear lies the joy and strength of our tender hearts and trained minds. As we develop the wisdom that resides within, trust in ourselves overcomes fear. This kind of confidence allows us to respond to our calling to serve and to smile gently in the face of fear.

As new millennial warriors, we're campaigning for and creating systems of integrity and transparency. When our interactions with one another are based on those values, the world changes; deals made in the shadows of crony capitalism come into the light of day. As we embrace the responsibilities of freedom with deep gratitude to those who've made freedom possible, we won't allow democracy to be sold out from under us. We'll be vigilant in protection of the freedoms that define democratic nations and institutions.

People in every nation are protecting the rights of all life on earth to sustain their lives in healthy environments. Increasing numbers of species are disappearing, mostly because human populations and pollution encroach on their habitats. Park rangers in Africa risk their lives to save elephants from armed poachers. More than 200 "dead zones" in the world's oceans are acidifying, and 90 percent of all large fish are gone. Deforestation has destroyed 75 percent of forests and 30 percent of the earth's invaluable topsoil has eroded in the past forty years.

We are co-inhabitants on planet earth, and we've discussed how sustaining its health contributes directly to the quality of our lives. Developed countries consume excessive amounts of energy whose source is mostly carbon based. Many other nations, in their haste to match those lifestyles, are relying on coal to fuel their growth. China's contribution to global air pollution has been exponential. Flights to and from Beijing have been cancelled due to thick, caustic pollution reducing visibility to less than a hundred yards. Toxic waterways flow into oceans made acidic by increasing carbon dioxide levels.

International treaties have done little to contain global contamination. It may be necessary to create international councils with the authority to impose carbon taxes and other sanctions designed to protect natural resources such as air, soil, and water. The urgent need for great change often requires that we make hard choices. If humans are to continue to live on this blue jewel of a planet, what difficult choices need to be made to address these issues?

The acceptance of a calling is an attunement with something larger than our individual ego-mind. This surrender requires courage and serves as an initiation and evolutionary unfoldment of our life's purpose. Carl Jung followed his calling as he pioneered an understanding of archetypes in the human psyche. "For Jung, individuation and realization of the meaning of life are identical," wrote his student Maria von Franz, "since individuation means to find one's meaning, which is nothing other than one's connection with the universal Meaning."

Goodness To Go

"My heart is set on living," declared the poet Edna St. Vincent Millay. Attributes such as courage, compassion, gratitude, patience, generosity, and wisdom are our great treasures and make life worth living. Self-care is pragmatic: it preserves the gift of life energy and prevents burnout. Thornton Wilder was the three-time Pulitzer Prize winner who wrote, "The only time we're truly alive is when our hearts are conscious of their treasures." As warriors of kindness, we'll tend to our needs while widening our sphere of benevolent engagement in the world. With delight, courage, and vision, let's get our good going. Together, we can light tomorrow with today.

Pause, Reflect, and Record

- What are your deepest, most valued principles? What is your current degree of integration of these principles?

- In what ways could you uplift the human spirit with integrity, happiness, and meaning?

- If you could be a part of the effective, equitable solution to one local or global issue, what would it be?

- What is the meaning and purpose of your life?

35

From Motivation to Mobilization

We frail humans are at one time capable of the greatest
good and, at the same time, capable of the greatest evil.
Change will only come about when each of us
takes up the daily struggle ourselves
to be more forgiving, compassionate, loving,
and above all joyful in the knowledge that,
by some miracle of grace, we can change
as those around us can change too.

—Mairead Corrigan Maguire

The process of moving from concern about a social or environmental issue to active engagement is unique for each individual. In all cases, however, imagination, courage, compassion, and perseverance are required.
In Chapter 23 of *Goodness To Go*, we looked at some of the ways that
people start on their path of service. Some dive in and others gradually
dissolve familiar boundaries of the status quo in their personal lives,
communities, and the world. Since goodness to go is compassion in action
and not dabbling in dreams, it's useful to revisit the often challenging,
ongoing process of mobilizing and sustaining our integral service.

Each of us has key commitments that inform our lives, including the
callings of our inner self, the affection for our loved ones, and the meaningfulness of our work and service. By engaging in courageous conversations about them, we're living that which holds everything together.
Often these conversations, whether internal or external, lead to a moment when we are inspired to move from concern to action. Commitment
transforms potentials and promises into reality.

Human beings are capable of the greatest good and the greatest evil.
In the midst of genocides, humanitarians have risked their lives to save
as many victims as possible. Firefighters run into collapsing infernos to
rescue fellow citizens. The greed to power over others and grab land and

resources has been prevalent throughout history. Rhetoric promising benevolent assimilation has belied the savage behavior of conquerors. The good news is that we can wake up to the learning available in all of life's experiences and evolve with integrity.

Long ago, St. Francis pointed out that it's easy to sense the divine in the beautiful; much more challenging is to see the divine in all that is. While the valleys of life hold as many lessons as the sunny grandeur of life's peaks, it's often difficult to feel gratitude for *everything*. Although this book's intent is to clarify and mobilize our goodness, it's unwise to ignore or avoid the shadow side of human nature.

Carl Jung originated the psychological concept of shadow—the banished, disavowed, or suppressed aspects of the self that we condemn, deny, reject, and project. "One does not become enlightened by imagining figures of light," Jung observed, "but by making the darkness conscious." We bring illumination to dark corners. What we resist not only persists, its force can increase. When we integrate the lessons of our shadow, we regain lost energy and functionality. Our character matures and our actions more clearly reflect our basic goodness.

Although we may be sparks of the holiness that is life, temptations abound and our behavior is often flawed. Money and the power associated with it can be very seductive. We mistakenly think we'll be happier or safer with more of it. The arcane language of money seems to hide secrets behind a curtain of obscure mystery, somewhat like the *Wizard of Oz*. However, most people are capable of understanding key concepts of any subject when provided with pertinent information and transparent, full disclosure.

Our creative intelligence and inherent goodness are resilient, inexorable forces with which to meet life's challenges. Sticking our heads in the sand is a waste of time, and we can't afford to repeat our mistakes. Plato's warning echoes across millennia: "The price of apathy is to be ruled by evil men." Nearly everyone has contended with aspects of the ego such as apathy, arrogance, and greed, and many people deal with significant psychological imbalances. It's important to recognize, too, that incentives and disincentives drive most human behaviors. If financial institutions are deregulated and incentives exist for bankers to sell riskier mortgages, they'll be aggressively sold to citizens who cannot afford them. If fraudulent, profitable behavior has few consequences, it increases.

As we mobilize our integral service, discernment and vigilance are required. Addictions of all sorts abound in every profession, including sports, entertainment, banking, law, politics, and medicine. The mental health of many heads of state has been deranged, and some rulers meet the diagnostic criteria of psychopaths. Adolph Hitler declared: "Make the lie big. Make it simple. Keep saying it and eventually they will believe it." However, if something is a lie, if the emperor truly has no clothes, we need the conviction and resilience to speak up and act up again and again.

The Responsibilities of Freedom

The price of apathy is to be ruled by evil men. Empathy transforms apathy; as our hearts and minds relate to suffering, our goodness to go becomes part of the solution. Throughout history, we've been reminded that freedom has little meaning unless it's linked to responsibility, as Dr. Frankl wrote after living through the monstrous tyranny of Nazi death camps. The current politics of representation and participation needs revitalization. The very nature of bureaucracies and organizations, wrote German sociologist Robert Michels more than a century ago, leads to dominion of the elected over the electors. Michels determined that even democratic political parties inevitably become impenetrable and elitist. In patriarchies, citizens become subordinates. More egalitarian social movements such as the Pirate Party use the Internet to inform members and gather their opinions.

Ours is a time of political crises and global democratic movements, including in the United States. *We the people* have the right and responsibility to continuously co-create an equitable society. Engaged citizens continue to challenge the 2010 U.S. Supreme Court ruling that established "corporate personhood," making it legal for corporations to not disclose contributions to political campaigns. Citizens have united across ideologies in initiatives calling for a constitutional amendment to ban corporate personhood and to make all political funding transparent.

While the First Amendment protects the right of free speech, including political speech for "associations of citizens," the intent of the constitutional rights was to protect individual citizens within the entities. The entities themselves are not human beings and do not have personhood. However, the expenditure of money by any person or entity, including labor unions and corporations, to influence elections without full transparency is not to be equated with constitutionally protected free speech.

Money is not speech. An individual casts a single vote. A corporation in not an individual and can't be granted citizenship. Some citizens

371

recommend that elections be publicly funded, believing that it's undemocratic to allow wealthy sectors, including private citizens, labor unions, and corporations, to spend millions of dollars to preserve privilege and power. Many believe that no political campaign advertisement should be blind and that every donation should be public information. The goodness to go of many committed citizens is required to effect equitable systemic change and have their informed values reflected in their laws. Indefatigable support of democratic ideals is important since well-funded, dedicated minority opinions continue to distort politics. Do you sense a calling to this kind of integral service? If so, what might be your part to play?

Engaged citizens are key to the ongoing integrity of democratic processes. Tom Atlee is a "wise democracy" political pioneer and co-director of the Co-Intelligence Institute in Eugene, Oregon. His book, *Empowering Public Wisdom: A Practical Vision of Citizen-Led Politics*, describes citizen councils that offer a platform for "collective intelligence" to inform public policy. Atlee emphasizes that it is our calling to create the capacity for public wisdom to manifest in the twenty-first century.

Informed deliberation about issues is described by Atlee as "thorough, thoughtful consideration of how to best address an issue or situation, covering a wide range of information, perspectives and potential consequences of diverse approaches." As policy evolves, citizens engaged in ongoing public conversations integrate differences and generate consensus. More than a half-hearted ritual of casting a vote every few years, true citizenship is "getting well-informed about an issue, thinking and talking with others, and working things out together about what the community should do," Atlee writes.

If we insist and persist, governments can develop strategies that benefit all life on earth, instead of resorting to neocolonialism or tributary-system thinking where money is lent to less stable countries merely to obtain their resources. Many countries, including the United States, and several in Europe, Asia, and Africa, have brutal histories of inflicting imperialism and colonialism on others. Some nations have experienced being the prey as well as the predator.

Functional economies need production, not just consumption. They need clean, safe, renewable energy sources, not only extraction of resources. When multinational corporations flood vulnerable countries with their cheap products and food, indigenous businesses often fail. A classic example of this occurred in 1994 when Haiti was re-entering democracy after years of military corruption. Poverty, joblessness, and systemic dependency increased when local businesses were undercut, robbing the people of hope. In 2005, a report on the costs of importing liberalization and free trade was published. The international development charity Christian Aid estimated that Malawi, for instance, would have had a gross domestic product eight percent higher if it hadn't opened itself to cheap imports. As economies globalize, let's first do no harm.

Recently, many movements for democratic reform have developed in countries with authoritarian regimes. Will such uprisings have the necessary support and resources to lead to meaningful change? To replace systems of suppression and domination with participatory democracy, allies are essential. Interim governments and interventions are frequently needed, such as France's reinforcements in Mali early in 2013 that were intended to halt the spread of invading extremists. Citizens and nations of the world, global media, international foundations and corporations, and diplomatic envoys have the ability to support the emergence of the voice of the people.

Be Mindful of *Unreason*

As we participate in engaged citizenship and humanitarian service, it's useful to recognize that there are built-in kinks in human recall and reasoning. Neuroscientists have discovered how mutable memory is. Also, our brains are wired to search for patterns and often insist on quickly assigning a cause to an effect. Even though a respiratory viral infection has a natural history of seven to ten days, we believe that the reason for our recovery was the antibiotic that was unnecessarily prescribed. What we "know" to be true is simply our knowledge, although it may not be accurate.

Our minds have at least two styles of mental operations and use all sorts of irrelevant criteria in decision making. One style is fast, superficial, and easily misled. Although we acknowledge that it's irrational to ignore truly relevant information, we do it all the time. We tend to filter information based on our previous experiences, and often ignore facts that don't fit with our existing worldview. We also pay more attention to information that comes from people who seem to be like us; we trust familiar lenses through which the world is seen. Thankfully, we can choose to think more deeply.

Research conducted by psychologist Daniel Kahneman, Ph.D., who was the 2002 Nobel Prize winner in economics, has explored human unreason and errors of logic. Our attention is easily distracted and our minds are usually so attached to stereotypes and seduced by vivid descriptions that we seize upon them to make quick decisions, even if they defy logic. Knowing that human thinking can be predictably unpredictable allows us to consciously shift to a slower, deeper kind of thinking so that we can evaluate a decision more thoroughly.

When we take time to consider data and decisions carefully, seeking informed outer council and listening for inner guidance, our actions are more deeply aligned with our core values. It's invaluable to remind ourselves and each other to *think about our thinking* since we're often unaware of our blind spots and prejudices. Then we'll be less likely to be falsely reassured by patronizing comments or misled by partial truths.

Participants in citizen councils are more effective in arriving at useful, innovative solutions when they listen compassionately and support each other in clearing away mental cobwebs with more deliberate, critical thinking. To understand an issue, we need factual information from all sides. The tactics of "dirty" politics that dismiss "fact checks" and impose false information and unfounded opinions are disrespectful of engaged citizens committed to informed deliberations regarding their civic duties.

If we value freedom, then our active participation is required to protect everyone's democratic rights. Citizens in democracies grant for themselves and others the right to live freely in accord with their deepest values in ways that respect the rights of others. Citizen engagement and constant vigilance is required to safeguard free, just, and equitable governance.

Those who recognize the importance to a democracy of well-educated citizens will fund unbiased, investigative news reporting from high-quality organizations committed to integrity and transparency. Citizen journalism is on the rise, and Internet communities and connections can facilitate the exchange of useful information. Rather than assessing the wisdom of a few people in a demonstration, investigative reporters use social media to leverage "crowd wisdom." Of course, discernment is always necessary.

Human rights abuses and political uprisings are recorded on cell phones and "go viral" over the Internet. Public broadcasting corporations around the world that operate free of market constraints empower citizens and strengthen the democratic process. Vigilant citizens and democratic governments will recognize, value, and fund unbiased, independent sources of accurate information free of political agendas.

The Freedom of Attention

By enhancing our awareness of where we choose to place the light of our attention, we increase access to the vibrant power of life. When used consciously, attention is a bridge that connects an individual's awareness with the powerful freedom and potential of the heart.

With practice, it's possible to free ourselves from contracted states of mind and learn to see with the wise and fearless eye of the heart. There are many approaches to letting go of unhelpful thoughts, releasing the suffering caused by attachment to limiting ideas, and allowing empowering thoughts and new habits to open our lives to uplifting possibilities. For decades, Byron Katie has shared her insights about a transformative process of self-inquiry that she calls The Work. In *Loving What Is*, we're invited to challenge thoughts by asking ourselves four questions: Is that thought true? Can I absolutely know that it's true? How do I react, what happens, when I believe that thought? Who would I be without the thought? Slower, deeper thinking facilitates the emergence of wisdom.

A later step in The Work's process of freeing ourselves from attachment to limiting thoughts and beliefs is to turn around the statement embedded in the thought. For example, a "can't" is turned around to become "can." "He doesn't" becomes "I don't." We then find at least three specific, genuine examples of how each turnaround is as true or even more true for us. If judgments or contracting, fear-based thoughts arise about integrating service in our lives, we apply this self-inquiry process with openness, curiosity, and compassion. We summon our strength, let go of the shore, and swim in and with consciousness, using attention consciously. Choices that we make now will reverberate through time.

Envision yourself offering uplifting service with joyful energy rather than from a place of lack, guilt, or judgment. Then make one small step as you begin to manifest that vision. If times look bleak, it's helpful to shine your inner light on the power of possibility. When you feel empty, pause, resource your resilience, and fill your bucket. As you tend your flame of inspiration and act from your source of creativity, generosity, and trust, you share the gift of yourself. How can you be the change you wish to see for the world?

The Ongoing Resurrection

In 2001, elders of the Hopi tribe gathered to compose a message of inspiration for our time. "There is a river flowing now very fast," they wrote. "Know that the river has its destination. ... The elders say that we must let go of the shore ... see who is there with you and celebrate! The time of the lone wolf is over. ... Gather yourselves. Banish the word *struggle* from your attitude and vocabulary. All that we do now must be done in a sacred manner and in celebration. We are the ones we've been waiting for."

It's often necessary to let go of old ways to allow new forms and ways of being to emerge. Several years ago, I had a vivid dream that ended with an unusual question, "What is the ongoing resurrection?" Startled awake, this enigmatic inquiry resounded through me. There are probably many ways to contemplate this question and perhaps as many responses as there are people interested in reflecting upon it. When I mentioned this dream to my daughter recently, her immediate reply was that people are born in every age and every culture who continue to carry the torch of goodness.

It has been noted that the call to be "reborn" is an ongoing human theme. After yet another fall, resilience rises once again. What is the source of continual renewal and revitalization? When I shared this question with a friend, her initial response revolved around the willingness to summon the power of one's heart again and again. As she spoke, I sensed that there are living embers within everyone. No matter how difficult or discouraging our circumstances may be, those embers never go out completely. Our breath, our trust, our resilience, and our awareness can fan the resurrection of other flames of goodness.

Discover ways that work for you to summon and manifest the power of your heart. Paying attention to where you place your attention is a valuable discipline. Many contemplative practices, such as centering prayer and meditation, help to strengthen this ability to choose how we'll use the profound gift of consciousness. Consider finding or refreshing a practice of mindfulness or self-inquiry to which you'll commit on a daily basis. Apply it to your inquiries and action plans for mobilizing your integral service.

At the same time, be free from attachment to making the world a better place. "There is only one corner of the universe you can be certain of improving," wrote Aldous Huxley, "and that's your own self." In this process of inner transmutation, small shifts can have big consequences as they ripple through the web of life. Along the way, celebrate mistakes as portals of discovery. Einstein remarked that he didn't make mistakes, he learned from experience. Regardless of what others may think, have the courage of your convictions while remaining open to new insights, people, and points of view. Change is an inside job, so begin within. Your inner work serves in the regeneration of others; remind yourself that practice makes progress.

A well-known sentiment by Mark Twain reminds us to live life fully: "Twenty years from now you will be more disappointed by the things you didn't do than by the ones you did do. So throw off the bowlines. Sail away from the safe harbor. Catch the trade winds in your sails. Explore. Dream. Discover." Each one of us has a role in co-creating the future of our world, in making difficult choices, and in developing new, life-sustaining paradigms. Let's come together, within and without. This is the time to wake up to our inner courage and consciously contribute our goodness to the gathering current of transformation. Potent with the power of the possible, we flow with the river of change and create our future.

Pause, Reflect, and Record

- What resources sustain your well-being on all levels— physical, intellectual, emotional, psychological, political, and spiritual?

- Reflect on a time in your life when you moved from concern to action, when you created more good and less harm.

- How might you enhance your ability to sustain service as an integral part of your life?

- How can you maintain and express your appreciation for the goodness within and surrounding you?

36

Yes is a World

Lift up the banner of your heart boldly
and commit your very next step
to what you love most dearly.

—John Fox

Offering integral service is saying *yes* to life with our heart, head, and hands. An unfettered yes is a vast, magnificent world of affirmation and commitment. If an automatic no of resistance is a naysayer, the voice of yes is a celebratory tribute to that which creates transformative break-throughs, uplifts the human spirit, and makes the world a better place in which all life can thrive.

Sometimes, the journey of a lifetime begins with the single step from "no" to "yes." Years ago, my heart was clenched by resistant fear. As a busy physician with insomnia trying to multitask my way through my midforties, I was tired. For several years, I'd been riding the emotional roller coaster of trying to conceive a pregnancy and finally had accepted that adoption was an option. Even though I'd let go of my cherished goal of giving birth to a child, lingering fears surfaced about adding the huge responsibilities of parenting to an intense schedule.

As months rolled by, I rocked back and forth between hope for fecundity and fear of loss. Wretched sadness and anger shredded equanimity at times. A particularly mighty battle raged within me one morning. The voice of yes was on the side of hope and trust in life. On the other side, the naysayer of fear lashed me with thoughts like *how can you add the responsibility of caring for a child to your exhausted, busy life? With your energy and time limitations, do you really think you could care for a child in a way you'd feel good about?* I felt sad and suffocated, threatened and defensive.

It was tempting to avoid further struggle as my heart seemed to wither and lose courage in the face of this aggressive onslaught. Although I was drained and emotionally vulnerable, I chose to meet with some kind friends for lunch. One woman shared an instruction that our teacher had given in a recent talk and, unexpectedly, my state was transformed by her words: "If you want to do something to express your gratitude for life's blessings, do something for children."

The undeniable light of *YES!* was my heart's spontaneous reply. A door opened into an expansive world of affirmation where fear transformed into peace. It was crystal clear that I would do something for children by joyfully welcoming a child from the other side of the world into my life. Literally, I could feel constrictive bands around my heart bursting as fresh courage pulsed with the healing energy of yes. All of the effort to make the decision to adopt Grace, to choose life and love rather than succumbing to fear, became effortless.

As fate would have it, a small photo of a newborn girl sent by the adoption agency arrived soon after this metamorphosis. Later, I learned that she'd been born on Mandela Day, an international celebration devoted to inspiring peacemaking and to building a global movement for good. In many ways, the seeds for *Goodness To Go* were sown that day. The power of yes opened the door to adopting Grace Shanti, and the ongoing yes of love deepens between us and uplifts our lives.

At a conference several years ago, an elderly nun who'd served as a social activist for most of her life shared her experience of the power of *yes*. Instead of saying "Amen" at the end of her prayers and blessings, she said *Yes!* with love and enthusiasm. Love is our greatest wealth, and through it we are connected throughout time. Learning to reduce anxiety and to make choices unburdened by fear reduces what psychologists call "behavior despair."

Perhaps you're experiencing even the whisper of a yes that could mobilize your goodness to go. Recall Eleanor Roosevelt's trust that "the future belongs to those who believe in the beauty of their dreams." The beauty and goodness of our dreams inspire our hearty yes to take action. In his second inaugural address, President Barack Obama envisioned our yes to the future as our response to the threat of climate change, "knowing that failure to do so would betray our children and future generations."

Many people around the world are honoring and affirming life by applying their creative intelligence to solving today's problems with tomorrow's ideas. Innovative solutions to generating clean electricity are emerging and solar panels are rapidly becoming more efficient and cost-effective. Materials engineers and chemists are developing artificial photosynthesis and bioplastics. Small Bloom Boxes are powering entire high-rises. Car and tire manufactures are using plant-based oils to reduce plastic and rubber waste. Instead of corn, biomass from waste wood, crop residues, and grasses is being converted into ethanol, which reduces gasoline emissions.

Growing numbers of high-combustion industrial plants burn garbage, using technology that does not pollute and adds power to electric grids. Fuel cell cars are becoming more efficient, and the by-product of combusted chicken feathers develops nanopores that absorb hydrogen for the fuel cells. Let's celebrate the yes inherent in the ongoing expression of our creative inventions and goodness to go. Consider a local or global issue to which you'd like to offer your *Yes!*

Walking Our Talk

For a dream to mobilize into a sustained vision and possible eventuality, we get moving and walk our talk. We formulate small, realistic goals and do something. It takes a degree of trust and courage to find our integral service and walk our soul's intended journey. Often, we're asked to let go of a life that we thought we wanted in order to participate in the one that is calling us. We are not alone, and as we step into the new unknown, allies (both internal and external), synchronicities, and wise support present themselves.

Life's quests lead us deeper into our hearts as well as to the edges—more the frontiers than the fringes—of what we think we know. While acknowledging that parts of our brain are wired toward defending against perceived survival threats, we can regain and sustain openness and receptivity to more resilient, empathic ways of being. As we strengthen access and utilization of our brain's frontal lobe and increase interconnectivity between its two hemispheres, we can also cultivate lightness and humor. "Laughter may be the shortest distance between two brains," wrote Daniel Goleman, the author of Emotional Intelligence. Laughing at ourselves and with each other enhances both our resiliency and interconnectivity.

In his "Callings" workshops, Gregg Levoy suggests steps to encourage the voice of yes. One is to list allies and resources, such as supportive friends, mentors, health, wisdom teachings, money, personal experience, and ritual. Some have found it invaluable to create a personal board of advisors or to read the stories of those who have followed a similar path. Other ways to resource our resilience are relaxation breathing, being in nature, meditation, warm baths, retreats, and connecting with loving friends through enjoyable activities and meaningful conversations.

Every person defines and redefines what the good life is and what it means to live well. Socrates taught, "Living well and beautifully and justly are all one thing." In about A.D. 200, there lived a great mystic and Greek pagan named Plotinus. In his treatise *On Beauty*, Plotinus discussed how the good reveals itself as beauty to lovers of the good: "For the good is the cause of life, of thought, of being. Seeing, with what love and desire for union one is seized—what wondering delight!" When goodness is on the go, there is the beauty and consciousness of our interconnected oneness.

"What's good for me is also good for you" is a phrase that recognizes the interconnectivity of the flow of goodness. Now is the time to help those we're with, and a tale by Leo Tolstoy illustrates several related themes about how to live a good life. The story's seeker is a king who consulted many wise and learned teachers about what he felt were three essential questions: when was the right time to begin, who were the right people to be with, and what was the most important thing to do? Despite the teachings inherent in the story's dramatic turn of events, the king needed them to be mirrored back and spelled out because he didn't take time to reflect on his life's lessons.

In Tolstoy's story, an old hermit patiently explained to the king that there is only one time that is important—now. It is the most important time because it is the only time in which we have power to discern, choose, and act. The necessary person is the one we're with now because no one knows when death will come. The most important thing to do is to do good for the person we're with because for that purpose alone humans were sent into this life. Whether we're farmers working a small plot of land or employees of an international corporation, we all have social responsibility.

To respond with clarity and creativity during pivotal times in our lives, it's helpful to know what our most cherished priorities are. The mystic Persian poet Rumi wrote, "This is a subtle truth; whatever you love, you are." When we remember our primary allegiances, it supports the release of habits of fear and resentment that weigh us down. Angels can fly, we've heard, because they take themselves lightly. Embarking on our path of integral service doesn't mean we have every step mapped out precisely. When you're packing for you journey, remember that you usually need only enough for liftoff.

Good to Go Includes Letting Go

Learning to live and learning to die is learning to let go. Letting go is not tuning out. An influential inventor of the twentieth century, Lin Yutang, used discernment in his relationship with action and inaction. He wrote, "Besides the noble art of getting things done, there is a nobler art of leaving things undone." The world of yes includes our willingness to let go of attitudes, beliefs, identifications, and involvements that drain our vitality. A belief is just a thought to which we've been attached over time. Not every item on our crowded to-do lists needs to be done today, if ever.

More space and energy is available when we let go of things we don't need. In this jet age of information, piles and files of information clutter our lives. There's simply more exponentially expanding information than a human brain can memorize for instant recall. Discernment is paramount since irrelevant facts can elbow out useful ones.

Consider asking, "Is this truly *worth* storing in memory?" Although there's nothing wrong with appreciating knowledge, addiction to accumulating information suffocates inspiration. Repeatedly ask, "Do I truly need this? Can I give myself permission to let go of this? What is enough? Am I willing to trust that this moment is enough, and has enough, just as it is?" The compulsive gathering of information doesn't make us wiser; it drains our energy and distracts us from seeing the bigger picture. Other hindrances to our creative intelligence are reactive habits of mind and dysfunctional beliefs. A tiresome habit of ego is to generate judgmental thoughts nearly constantly; committed practice can lead to freedom from attachment to them.

Computer technologies have expanded possibilities in many ways. On the other hand, prolonged interaction with content on screens alters our attention spans and consumes our time; unconsciously, we can bypass important developmental tasks and limit the full expression of our humanity. Sending a quick mobile phone text reading "sorry" doesn't build the relational capacity that expressing our remorse in person does. Social media and video game overuse often takes on compulsive tendencies that have addiction potential as our brain's reward centers are repetitively stimulated. Saying yes to living as a full human being is hindered if we avoid creating connections with real people in the real world. Also, without a personal relationship with the natural world, it's more difficult to care about environmental stewardship. A movement to regularly *unplug* from technology is growing.

Goodness To Go

To be awake in the present also includes releasing attachments to the past or future and resisting the burden of chronic anxiety. "Worry does not empty tomorrow of its sorrow, it empties today of its strength," wrote Cornelia "Corrie" ten Boom, a Dutch Christian woman who helped many Jews escape the Nazi Holocaust. Through an ongoing dialogue with our heart's wisdom, frantic fears and wearisome worries can be released into its resonant stillness. What are some habits—mental, psychological, or physical—that would be useful to release as you commit to acting in service of others?

There's a tale about master sculptor Michelangelo in which he says he adds nothing to the block of marble because perfection is already present within it. All he must do is remove the unnecessary stone obscuring that perfection. An ancient Taoist text attributed to Lao Tzu teaches that to obtain wisdom, reduce and reduce again until all action is reduced to non-action. "Then nothing is done yet nothing is left undone." Releasing that which obscures the clarity and beauty of our integral service often takes persistence as well as confidence and skillfulness. Surrender pettiness and serve the goodness of life.

Gratitude Is a Living *Yes*

Wise beings throughout the ages have affirmed that love is gratitude and gratitude is an expression of love. The daily practice of gratitude is a living yes. In our community, a cheerful woman living with incurable cancer is deeply devoted to the experience of ongoing gratitude. In daily prayers, she thanks her Maker for her loving family, for each morning's sunrise, and for physicians who diagnosed her disease as quickly as possible. Others afflicted with life-threatening diseases seek this wise woman's lightness of spirit and compassionate council. As she receives rounds of intravenous chemotherapy, she gives thanks to those who've gone before her and helped to optimize dosing regimens. Loving gratitude is the great wealth that she freely shares.

The expression of gratitude creates our lives. Although we make a living by what we get, observed Winston Churchill, we make a life by what we give. Mother Teresa reminded us that it's not how much we give, but how much love we put into giving. This gift may be as simple as a genuine smile or as subtle as continuing to listen deeply while not reacting defensively to a false accusation. It is possible to extend the practice of gratitude to include everything and everyone.

Cultivate forgiveness and gratitude. Offer a simple act or perhaps a not-so-simple act of kindness. Goodness does not go to waste. Let go of expectations of reward. Attitude and intention are key. We're still learning and growing, so remember to be gentle with yourself. All humans forget and make mistakes.

Traditional wisdom tells us that if we love something, let it be free to create its own destiny. Part of us wants to hang onto the things we think make us happy. We don't want good times to end and it's not always easy to go with the flow. Happiness, courage, and kindness, it's been said, are reflections of wisdom. Releasing our grip and surrendering ego's desires and attachments is supported by the trust that the source of our contentment and gratitude lies within.

Many of us are initially uncomfortable when we hear the word *surrender*. An echo of Winston Churchill's command to never give up or give in is emblazoned on many psyches. Taking these societal messages too literally, we may assume that they're urging, even whipping, us to soldier on no matter what. It's easy to misunderstand the practice of sweet surrender, thinking it means to be weak and inconstant. Fickle. To lose heart and faith. Yet from another perspective, surrender is an element of sacrifice, of making sacred.

Surrendering small-minded agendas, fears, and attachments is the essence of an awakened life. It is also a living yes. Releasing old habits of defensiveness or judgment frees us to expand our understanding and recognition of our oneness. Letting go allows space for our goodness to blossom. The multicultural writer Anais Nin recognized that "we don't see things as they are, we see them as we are." When we allow ourselves to open into the world of yes, we blossom. We have come here to surrender every more deeply, wrote the poet Hafiz, to freedom and joy.

Collaborating with Chaos

For our goodness to blossom and give birth to our integral service, it's helpful to develop tolerance for the paradoxical aesthetic appeal of chaos. Clearly, great waves of change are pouring through our lives. Humanity is now facing a crucial threshold where we're called to create the conditions that can welcome a wholesome future for all life. Times of great change contain both chaos and crisis where danger and opportunity dance together.

Goodness To Go

What does it mean to collaborate with chaos? Theoretical physicists are exploring new theories of chaos. In their book *Seven Life Lessons of Chaos*, F. David Peat and John Briggs define chaos as an "underlying interconnectedness that exists in apparently random events: ... We're all a part of the whole. By staying open to a constant, even turbulent flow-through of energy, ideas, and materials, systems survive by creatively self-reorganizing."

The brilliant nineteenth-century philosopher Friedrich Nietzsche wrote, "One must still have chaos within oneself to give birth to a dancing star." Human creativity has a high tolerance for ambiguity, ambivalence, and the ability to hold the tension of paradox and apparent dichotomies. Through our creative, integral service, we acknowledge not only our uniquely individual gifts but also our indivisible connection to the whole.

As we let go of old, consensual structures, ideas, and paradigms, we're more able to tolerate doubt and uncertainty. Then it's possible to co-create adaptable, resilient, equitable solutions, paradigms, and organizations that serve us now and in the future. We embrace the paradox of beneficial structures emerging from creative chaos. Like crisis, chaos includes opportunity, and is not synonymous with dangers that we need to escape, avoid, or deny.

A classic environmental crisis of opportunity happened on earth millions of years ago. The oxygen from vegetation and trees reached nearly unsustainable levels until the emergence of animals that needed to breathe oxygen. These new animal life forms created a dynamic biosphere where animals and plants were in respiratory equilibrium. However, we've acted against nature for so long, ignoring our essential interconnectedness, that ecological and climate changes crises urgently require our attention.

In numerous kinds of crises, the inadequacy of old ways of thinking, perceiving, and being is painfully apparent. Currently, we're in crisis nearly continuously—terrorist crises, food crises, water crises, debt and banking crises, and many others. Dr. Martin Luther King, Jr. spoke about "the fierce urgency of now." An egocentric, materialistic mode of consciousness that has dominated our thinking for centuries has led us to a perilous point in the human story and our creative problem-solving is needed now.

It's time for a new ways of thinking and being. Consumerism, addiction to fossil fuels, profit-driven globalization, and environmental devastation are capable of destroying our ability to live on this jewel of a planet. We see that accumulating more things and defenses will not bring us the happiness, security, ease, and peace we want. Peace means more than the absence of war. Peace is the ability to provide for our families in dignified ways, to banish fear, to give up old misunderstandings and hatreds, and to embrace one another despite differences. It's the power to open our hearts into the light of yes.

The poet Elizabeth Alexander read verses of life praising life before President Obama's first inaugural address. Her words honored the courage and the love that empower our willingness to walk forward into the light of each new day. We cannot know the full impact of every ripple of our goodness as it radiates into the world. There are countless ways to use our gifts to make our world a better place, and it's a great adventure to track the signs and messages that reveal our path. This journey of discovery and meaning and goodness to go begins with our heart-opening YES!

Pause, Reflect, and Record

- When have you said yes wholeheartedly to a calling and weren't stopped by the voice of fear?

- List the people, places, things, and beliefs that are supportive resources for the fruition of your goals and dreams.

- Is there a naysayer anywhere in your life, inside or out, that you'd like to challenge with respect and confidence? Describe.

- What could be removed from your to-do list that would simplify your life and free up space, time, and energy for the revelation and manifestation of what's truly important to you?

37

Creating Community

The community stagnates without
the impulse of the individual.
The impulse dies away without
the sympathy of the community.

—William James

Throughout *Goodness To Go*, we've looked at different ways that people embark on the journey of moving from empathic concern to humanitarian action. For some, there's a pivotal moment that dissolves hesitation; others experience a more gradual awakening to service. The mobilization of our inherent goodness is often inspired by deep recognition of our oneness. Recently, my twelve-year-old daughter exclaimed, "Oh, I get it! We're not just all connected. Everyone *is* everyone!"

Inherent to compassion in action is the flow of goodness through interrelated networks of communities. As we embark on our path of integral service, we're influenced by a unique symphony of genetic and environmental factors. A grandmother in Somalia and a graduate student in London will have different opportunities calling forth their goodness. Although we move forward with individualized motivations and create distinct paths and legacies, collaboration with others is essential along the way. No human is an island and every person needs the support of others throughout life.

The essence of community is mutual support. When survival is threatened, when we face times of great challenge, more commitment, endurance, and courage may be required than we're able to muster on our own. Relationships serve as crucibles for personal and collective transformation, and healthy reciprocity is the flow of goodness to go. When we've nurtured relationships with family, friends, and other communities of fellowship, we're tended in return when our spirit or energy wanes. Embers of resilience are gently rekindled and our compassion returns to action. "Call it a clan, call it a network, call it a tribe, call it a family. Whatever you call it, whoever you are, you need one," wrote the English novelist Jane Howard.

Modern physics and global wisdom traditions remind us of the interrelatedness of our cosmos. For centuries, the unity of the great web of life has been a fundamental belief among traditional Native American and other indigenous peoples. "All things are connected like the blood that unites us all," said Chief Seattle in the mid-1800s. Indian philosophers and yogis describe a nondual state of consciousness that perceives the unity of subject and object. With the recognition of our interbeing, it's clear that what's genuinely good for one is good for all. Since empathy is wired into our neurological nature, the communities that human beings create have ethical orientations. Life cares for life.

Our interconnectedness has also been referred to as collective resonance, the Bond, and Indra's Net. The Islamic movement of Ahmadiyya, which originated in India, teaches the oneness of the human species, and in the Baha'i faith, a core belief is the "Oneness of Humanity." The French Jesuit priest and philosopher Pierre Teilhard de Chardin observed that we're not merely a collection of separate objects. We're joined in invisible ways that make the world a communion of subjects who are "collaborators in creation of the Universe."

Acting for the Greater Good

The writer George Bernard Shaw valued moral integrity and community. He wrote, "I am of the opinion that my life belongs to the whole community, and as long as I live it is my privilege to do for it whatever I can." Humans have taken into account the interests of others long before Socrates asked, "What is justice?" Over the ages, many ways have been developed to support the common good and protect vulnerable community members, such as children, the sick, and the elderly.

"You are here to enrich the world," wrote former U.S. president Woodrow Wilson. Many people living in both cosmopolitan and rural communities are becoming global citizens who approach conflicts of cultural values with mutual respect. Individuals' different capabilities contribute to communities characterized by social equity and justice. Although capacities or resources aren't equal, each person has equal dignity and requires conditions that support that dignity. Clearly, abject poverty and all forms of slavery and degradation shred human dignity and are profoundly unjust.

390

In 1961, humanitarian lawyers founded an international community of human rights activists called Amnesty International. When they learned that two young Portuguese men had been jailed for raising a toast to freedom, a network of goodness was mobilized to support prisoners of conscience. Since then, hundreds of people around the world who've spoken truth to power have been imprisoned and tortured. The living flame of a candle wrapped in barbed wire became Amnesty International's logo. Human rights abuses anywhere are the concern of people everywhere. An international community of concerned supporters continues to write thousands of letters to assist in the release of people imprisoned for nonviolent protest of injustice.

Increasingly, humans are creating networks of communities within cities, and the global urban population is swelling by a million residents every week. By 2050, demographers predict that at least two-thirds of our planet's nine billion residents will live in cities. Although cities draw together major environmental problems such as population growth, pollution, resource degradation, and waste generation, vibrant urbanization also drives social progress and innovation. With shared knowledge sparking new ideas, advanced public transportation, energy efficiency, and lower birth rates, some urban communities are beginning to create smaller ecological footprints.

Communities grow stronger when residents, human services, congregations, local associations, and businesses work together in partnerships to address important problems and actualize sustainable solutions. Asset-Based Community Development, or ABCD, is a powerful approach focused on discovering and mobilizing productive resources that are already present in a community. Relationship building and collective commitment among all stakeholders is key to supporting the common good for all citizens. Communities don't just happen; they're consciously created.

People, rather than programs, are the solution. Civic engagement is especially effective when it's recognized that every citizen has a gift, institutions are servants to people, and citizen-centered organizations are the key to community partnerships. Everyone is needed and nothing, including freedom, can be taken for granted.

There are inspiring stories from every corner of the world about people regenerating communities and environments. In 2001, Majora Carter, a young woman who'd lived in urban devastation, founded Sustainable South Bronx in her former neighborhood. Carter brought together the assets within her community to transform a dump into a waterfront park and plant urban gardens and green roofs. Carter is an urban revitalization strategist who continues to create green job infrastructures and advocate for environmental justice. No demographic or socioeconomic group should be dumped with the garbage and toxic environmental burdens of the entire community.

Creating Cultures of Health

It's been said that wellness is the fuel for prosperity in the 21st century, and healthy communities contribute to the health and generativity of their citizens. During both World Wars, "victory gardens" grew fresh produce in public parks and in the small lawns of private residences. These gardens provided about 40 percent of the food production in the 1940s and they're needed today more than ever. Social movements of food justice and food sovereignty recognize that healthy food is foundational for our health. In many communities, it's far easier to find and afford unhealthy food. Most businesses, including the food industry, operate in accord with demand for their goods and their ability to supply those goods. As more people grow accustomed to high fat, high fructose diets, demand for fresh produce decreases.

Obesity has reached epidemic proportions in many communities, threatening the physical health of individuals and their children as well as the fiscal health of their countries. Obese individuals who've consumed excessive unhealthy calories tend to be blamed for their condition. Although demand for fresh vegetables has declined for many reasons, communities could come together to create a culture of health rather than blaming individuals. When the wellness "value equation" changes, we value a healthier life more than a quick fix of nutrient-poor food that contributes to the diabetes epidemic. A focus on wellness rather than disease and its prevention would increase the demand for healthy food. Local vegetable gardens could supply relatively inexpensive fresh produce to meet the demand.

In addition to education, values clarification, and a focus on wellness, creating a culture of health includes making it easy for people to make healthy choices. A safe, clean neighborhood makes it easier for people to walk and play outdoors. Exercise integrated into the work day of sedentary employees is an efficient way to increase their health and productivity. Easy access to affordable produce is also important. The growing movement of urban agriculture is especially valuable in impoverished "food deserts" where residents have virtually no access to grocery stores. Community gardens in these areas make it possible for farmers' markets to provide healthy alternatives to convenience store items containing saturated fats and high fructose corn syrup. Another benefit of gardening is that it increases connectivity and relationship with the earth.

In our global village of interconnected societies, our responsibilities extend beyond friends and family members to the world community. Human life flourishes to the extent that we acknowledge this interconnectedness and share our goodness. As we come to recognize the ways that our communities as well as our individual lives interpenetrate, we enhance our capacity to give and receive. Drawing on the collective energy that is our substratum refreshes our innovation. We'll create healthier cultures of sustainable wellness supported by good choices and not focus solely on disease prevention by trying to stop unhealthy behaviors and their negative consequences. Knowing that the earth's resources are finite, we'll contain the population explosion and stop irrational, accelerating exploitation of natural environments.

What moral obligation do we have to do something helpful, and not merely *do no harm*? The eye of the heart recognizes our interdependency, and life-threatening natural disasters and diseases bring this into clear focus. Each one of us needs the support of community members at every stage in our life cycles. This is true not only for orphans, the developmentally disabled, and the physically or mentally ill. An accident, a serious illness, or a loss of financial resources can affect any one of us. Personal vulnerability or disability is a political issue if it leads to social repression and isolation, or decreases options that support dignity.

How do we reduce suffering for ourselves and others? Awareness of our mutual interdependence as a condition of life is fully baked in the marrow of those who've experienced war zones and medical crises. Throughout history, the inborn social ethic of mutual aid has manifested in numerous ways, from direct medical care and trauma therapy to delivering meals, sheltering refugees, reading sacred texts to the dying, rebuilding communities devastated by earthquakes, floods, and hurricanes, and offering child care to mothers who need to work to support their families. At times, the serene, unconditional presence of someone we trust is the greatest gift of all. Recognition of life's interdependence leads to natural responses to utilize whatever power and resources we have for the benefit of all.

Goodness To Go

Collaborating in Difficult Times

The remarkable power of team spirit has been extolled from football fields to corporate boardrooms. Successful athletic teams create small, collaborative communities. Sometimes, their stories are epic tales of the triumph of resilience, forgiveness, and reconciliation. During the violent 1994 Rwandan Hutu-Tutsi conflict that had been generated decades earlier during Belgium colonialism, a seven-year-old boy obediently ran from the killing fields that took the lives of six of his brothers. Adrien Niyonshuti's astonishing journey from genocide survivor to mountain biking Olympian is documented in the film *Rising from Ashes*.

Several years, an American cycling coach brought together promising young Rwandan cyclists from both sides of the genocide. Gradually, a small team of survivors with tremendous physical and psychological endurance began racing internationally, bringing their weary country together around a communal vision of competitive excellence. Adrien's remarkable equanimity and forbearance made him the natural choice for team captain and he served as his nation's flag bearer at the 2012 Summer Olympics in London. His small community of traumatized, formerly polarized young men has been a positive inspiration globally, and bicycling teams are being formed in neighboring African countries devastated by civil war.

Long before their contact with Europeans, indigenous communities were aware of life's mutual interdependence. Warring tribes of Native Americans came together to create the Iroquois confederation whose first and most important principle was that the people of the different nations were one people. They believed that a harmonious society is a collaboration created and maintained through the cultivation of reason and righteous power. A political philosopher and spiritual leader known as the Peacemaker inspired the Iroquois confederation to create "The Great Law of Peace" or the "Big Harmony." This government's purpose was not only to put an end to war but to eliminate the causes of conflict through the establishment of universal justice.

For the Iroquois, justice was the process of healing relationships so that each element in the cosmic order of creation could live its natural power and fulfill its responsibility. These native people wrote: "We were instructed to carry a love for one another, and to show a great respect for all the beings of this Earth. ... In our ways, spiritual consciousness is the highest form of politics."

The word *politics* comes from a Greek word meaning "for or relating to citizens." The acquisition and application of power is a great responsibility for all citizens, especially those in leadership roles, and shared struggle for the common good makes our sacrifice a sacred offering. Those entrusted to serve as trustees of the community need to reconcile political power with the spirit of service, and in turn trust that informed citizens can create effective solutions to their collective problems.

One example of a wise community trustee and social activist is Grace Lee Boggs whose autobiography is entitled *Living for Change*. For more than fifty years, she has committed her service to redefining, respiriting, and rebuilding the urban disintegration of Detroit, Michigan. Engaging unemployed young people in neighborhood revitalization, Boggs has shown that the collapse of Detroit as an industrial giant has become an opportunity for different cultures and communities to emerge. *To turn an obstacle to one's advantage is a great step towards victory*, states a French proverb.

It is with humility and respect that we honor the profound resilience of the human spirit, which prevails even in the midst of horrors. Outside Prague, in a remote Nazi work camp called Terezin, imprisoned Jews in 1943 chose to re-create their choir as choral members were continually sent to death camps. Czech pianist Rafael Schachter conducted this awe-inspiring artistic uprising. The hungry, exhausted community of Jewish prisoners rehearsed a Catholic funeral mass in Latin by night and gave sixteen performances of *Requiem* by Giuseppe Verdi, regarded as one of the world's most difficult choral compositions, within Terezin's walls of captivity.

The choir's final audience of German army officers and gullible Red Cross officials did not decipher the singers' defiant demand for justice and liberation. In a documentary film entitled *Defiant Requiem*, an elderly survivor of this remarkable community recalled how the beauty of heavenly music nourished her soul. To give voice to their integrity, their dignity, and their longing for liberation, they sang as one. "In the world that we created, there was goodness and meaning and healing," she said. "The Nazis could not take our spirit even as they shot our body."

Tragically, in much of central and eastern Europe, the horrors of Nazism were followed by the terrors of Communism. Soviet officers, secret police, and local communist recruits not only suppressed the freedom and artistic expression of subjugated communities, they tortured and murdered many dissidents in attempts to crush resistance to their brutal regime. Most of these criminals have not been brought to justice and museums documenting that dark period are scattered throughout Europe. The profound state of freedom cannot be taken for granted and the integral service of many before us have made it possible for us to be alive in this moment so rich with possibility.

The Great Turning

Both the natural world and human societies are webs of relationships. Joanna Macy, Ph.D. is a deep ecologist and social activist who suggests that all living systems—whether organic like the human body or supra-organic like a society or an ecosystem—are *holons*. Being a holon means that we're both whole as ourselves and, simultaneously integral parts within larger wholes. Macy believes that this epochal time in which we're living may come to be called the Great Turning.

Although we're encountering crises on personal and global levels, we have this moment. Within it exists the opportunity to be present and still, to sense our connectedness and choose to face the rising sun. We are not alone, and can cherish and celebrate all of life together. One facet of the Great Turning is the growing interest in reducing our carbon footprint, the amount of carbon dioxide produced by behaviors that pollute ecosystems. Automobile congestion emits more carbon dioxide than efficient public transportation systems. Burning fuel to fly food from thousands of miles away leaves a large, polluting carbon footprint on planet earth. Eating locally grown foods is an aspect of this ethic of community responsibility.

Deceptive marketing by businesses large and small that tries to usurp the "go green, feel good" quality of genuine green economies is called *greenwashing*. "Localvores" aren't fooled and consistently choose healthy seasonal food that is not flown or driven thousands of miles. However, it's too expensive for many urban people to purchase locally grown, organic food, especially those living in food deserts without grocery stores in their neighborhoods. Creating vegetable gardens in small plots of land, even in pots or raised beds on balconies and rooftops, is one of many ideas discussed earlier as we address economic and ecologic issues of food justice and security.

Thomas Jefferson was one of the founding fathers of the democratic model of governance who believed that every generation needs a new revolution. In the Great Turning, we're shifting from runaway, industrial growth dependent on accelerating consumption of resources to innovative, life-sustaining societies. Out-dated philosophical frameworks of competitive individualism, in which people are set against nature and each other, fade as clear recognition of life's interconnected cooperation and partnerships emerges. Many regard the creation of a global society free of abject poverty and human rights abuses as the new revolution of this generation.

A few years ago at a TED Global conference in Oxford, England, then–prime minister Gordon Brown called for global ethics in a connected world living in a digital age. The prime minister encouraged listeners to act "when we see wrongs that need righting or problems that need to be rectified. ... What we see unlocks the invisible ties and bonds of sympathy. ... We do feel the pain of others and we believe in something larger than ourselves."

The Internet gives us opportunities to see what is happening across the world. Images sent from mobile phones in 2011 prevented some election fraud in Uganda, and in 2001 the "Coup de Text" in the Philippines involved more than a million people texting about the repression of their dictator. Satellite surveillance can provide real-time footage of human rights atrocities and environmental devastation.

A free web-based software application called Ushahidi encourages citizen participation and democratizes information channels by providing ways for people's voices to be heard through an interactive mapping tool. *Ushahidi* means "testimony" in Swahili; the software has helped humanitarian workers operate efficiently during Haiti's earthquake, track floods in Venezuela, and map incidents of violence and peace efforts during Kenya's bloody postelection fallout in 2008.

Monks in Burma involved in the 2007 Saffron Revolution blogged about the atrocities of their country's military junta. This repressive regime refused the world's relief efforts in 2008 that were intended to help the Burmese people devastated by Cyclone Nargis. Although Burma, also known as Myanmar, now has a reform-minded government, media reports of serious human rights abuses continue.

Over a billion people are connected through Facebook's social media community. Increasing digital connectivity spreads images, opinions, and information that can mobilize action for good or ill or any place in between. Social media connectivity is lucrative for many businesses and fuels consumerism; in some countries, thousands of dollars are spent on stylized photos of high school seniors, in addition to prom gowns, catered dinners, and limousines. Both inspiring video clips and pornography can "go viral."

With knowledge comes responsibility. Cell phone videos have shown the world civil rights abuses during elections but have also been used by malevolent forces to identify peaceful protestors who are then captured, tortured, and killed. This is a shadow side of the enhanced access to information and shared innovation that technology provides. It is the intent that we bring to the use of this remarkable tool that is paramount. In this digital information age, the power of our moral sense can be linked to the power of modern communication systems to create global communities committed to social justice.

Nobody Gets There Unless Everybody Gets There

Marcus Aurelius, a Roman emperor and philosopher, believed that participation in society is an essential element of being human. Testaments to our impulse to care for one another are the millions of philanthropic individuals and organizations around the world. A prominent global citizen and physician, Dr. Paul Farmer, is the celebrated founder of Partners in Health. From his decades of service in Haiti and internationally, Dr. Farmer is exceptionally aware of the power of community to heal lives broken by poverty.

Addressing root causes of hunger and poverty makes peace possible. Since 1944, Heifer International has brought help, healing, and hope to communities worldwide. The hunger and poverty of more than ten million families has been reduced through livestock and agricultural programs that reinvigorate the lives and communities of the recipients who in turn pass on the gift. Several presidents and numerous humanitarian awards have honored the effectiveness of Heifer International's programs to eradicate hunger in ways that are sustainable and empowering.

The respected journalist-anchorman Walter Cronkite, who supported Heifer International during his life, wrote: "If there is one thing I could give to the struggling people of the world, it would be self-reliance. Everyone deserves the dignity of providing for themselves and their families." Dignity and self-respect can lead to the creation of sustainable lives in an equitable world.

It's been said that it's our choices, not our abilities that show us who we are. Communities don't just happen; genuine community is consciously created and maintained. What kinds of communities do we want to create? Do we choose to be engaged citizens, to sing out and rise up when necessary? How do we choose to use resources and spend money? Nearly everyone has something to give, regardless of age, health, or socioeconomic level.

The power of community is at the heart of all positive social change. Democracy is a collective project requiring collective action; its birthing process often demands tremendous sacrifice and its vitality requires vigilance. The collaborative efforts of Nelson Mandela and millions of courageous individuals ended apartheid in South Africa. Vaclav Havel, philosopher and former president of the Czech Republic, wrote, "Genuine politics … is serving the community and serving those who will come after us. Its deepest roots are moral because it is a responsibility expressed through action, to and for the whole."

Thousands of protestors around the world are motivated by the power of love that yearns for freedom, justice, and peace. Yoani Sanchez is an influential dissident blogger who was blocked twenty times from leaving Cuba before its communist government allowed her to visit Brazil in 2013. She's committed to speaking up for the reforms dreamed of by fellow citizens: the freedom of association and expression within safe, thriving communities.

The power of love and peace can be fierce as well as tender. "The art of Peace is not easy," wrote the founder of Aikido martial arts, Morihei Ueshiba. "On occasion the voice of peace resounds like thunder, jolting human beings out of their stupor." The transformative, nonviolent example of Mahatma Gandhi jolted the British Empire awake, freed India from colonial domination, and reminds us to this day to be the change we wish to see in the world. The numerous global challenges we face require the global ethics of a global community working together to create sustainable, just solutions.

Health, Care, and Wellness

Wellness is a dynamic experience of vitality and purpose. It is an alignment between the values and goals of our external social self and our internal essential self. Although wellness may include optimal health, it is not limited to physical well-being. The degree of wellness of individuals, businesses, communities, and countries energizes their ability to prosper on all levels. Communities intent on creating cultures of health and wellness recognize that access to affordable, quality health care is a basic necessity.

Goodness To Go

What is our vision of individual and societal prosperity in the twenty-first century? In what ways does wellness fuel prosperity? In countries without universal healthcare, income inequity becomes a social justice issue. Wealthy citizens purchase the best medical care that money can buy while millions of citizens living below the poverty line suffer unnecessarily, die prematurely, or hope that an emergency room won't turn them away in a medical crisis. In many countries around the world, most people have virtually no access to medical care.

Although the United States is the only industrialized nation to spend more that 12 percent of its total economy on health care, it does worse than most countries on almost every measure of health outcomes. Like other nations with patchworks of private insurers, millions of citizens in the United States aren't able to afford health insurance and end up in emergency rooms with pre-existing conditions. The Affordable Care Act, commonly called Obamacare, is an attempt to increase access to integrated healthcare and contain skyrocketing medical, societal, and personal costs.

If we value universal access to decent health care with good results at an affordable price, then a free-market model cannot work. For health care needs, markets don't work well, wrote Nobel Prize–winning economist Kenneth Arrow, because people don't know when they'll need these services. Cancer, heart failure, and other diseases usually strike unexpectedly and treatment costs are prohibitive, bankrupting many families. People afflicted with serious illnesses often are unable to work, and insult is added to injury as they lose health care coverage when their job is terminated. This is unjust to victims of unexpected illness. Also, the link between employment and health care is excessively bureaucratic and inefficient: changes of employment or insurance carriers usually mandate different forms, policies, restrictions on pre-existing conditions, and finding another physician who is contracted with the new insurance plan. Lack of coordination and gaps in care, refusal of coverage for needed services, and wasteful retesting are a few of the significant issues of free-market health insurance companies whose CEO salaries are in the millions.

Many people are questioning the link between employment and health insurance for different reasons. Global businesses seek a level global playing field, yet U.S. firms pay tens of billions of dollars to provide health care for their employees and former employees. Business counterparts in Britain, Germany, Canada, and Japan pay a fraction of related costs because their countries' insurance models provide access to universal health care. Although social realities are often messy and complex, every industrialized nation that provides universal health care, including free-market havens like Switzerland and Taiwan, has needed an insurance or government-sponsored model. National health care is an excellent example of collective action for the greater good.

Microsoft billionaire-philanthropist Bill Gates has an innovative take on wealth, compassionate capitalism, and corporate responsibility. Gates writes that there are two great forces motivating human behavior: self-interest and caring for others. His goodness to go responds to world poverty in multi-faceted ways, including sharing technology, providing small-business loans, and eradicating preventable diseases in developing nations.

Sustainable Economies and Communities

Throughout *Goodness To Go* we've been reminded that the in-breath of self-care honors our individual lives and the out-breath of service honors our communities. It's in our self-interest to care for others and to remove systemic injustice hindering their ability to create thriving, equitable communities and a wholesome life for their families. Millions of human beings simply request that we remove the roadblocks from their path.

Ours is also a time for a new ethics of capitalism. Economic ethics in the twenty-first century is not about abolishing the rich or leveling everyone to some lowest common financial denominator. The values-driven goal of a new economics is to abolish poverty, starting with extreme poverty in which people live on less than $2 a day. One of the many social issues that impoverished individuals face is lack of access to justice systems; legal council is expensive, interpretation of the law is confusing, transportation and time off work may not be available, and identity papers are often missing. The vulnerability of the poor to the violation of their rights continues to be addressed by the International Justice Resource Center and other organizations.

In many parts of the globe, the rich are getting much richer and the poor much poorer Global economic interest in income inequality is increasing. Poverty is being recognized as an extension of capitalism, not a failure that is separate from it. Motivated to combat the Great Depression, the influential economist John Maynard Keynes began articulating new understandings about the socioeconomic roots of poverty in the early 1930s. The importance of full employment was emphasized and his theories were later used to analyze the rise in income inequality that began in postwar America.

Keynes believed that in times of economic depression, it was essential to stimulate capitalist economies and maintain supply-demand dynamics; increased government spending promoted full employment and productivity which maintained citizens' purchasing power and demand for goods. In our post-Keynesian world shaken by another global recession, both unemployment and income inequality have become prevailing social issues.

Financial necessity is inventing new economic systems. When community members share their personal resources, from gardening and child-care skills to financial expertise, social trust grows and daily life is less stressful. Time banking, where volunteer hours can be "cashed in" for needed help, is one of many ways that communities can support their members. Directories of community time banks serving neighborhoods, churches, schools, or agencies are available online. Sustainable communities interested in the vital well-being of their members create nurturing containers that support life caring for life in innumerable ways.

Local and global communities are also creating "gifting economies" where goods are swapped, traded, or borrowed. An example is the Freecycle Network, whose members in thousands of local groups give away their household items to others who need them. One peer-learning community is the global collaborative of YES! in which facilitators from twelve nations work for social transformation on five continents. Issues they address include indigenous rights, innovative education, community media, environmental protection, and social justice. Yes to the awareness that *everyone* is *everyone*.

At the heart of community is communion, the fellowship of sharing in common, and offering pragmatic altruism is natural within communities. A seminal book about economic sociology is *The Gift Relationship: From Human Blood to Social Policy* by Richard Titmuss. When community members regard their blood donations as gifts rather than marketable commodities, the energetic difference of the donors' motivations affects entire systems. Titmuss compares the United Kingdom, where blood supplies are sufficient and no paid labor is used in its collection, with the United States, where large amounts of money are spent collecting blood, often from impoverished, diseased donors, with tremendous wastage and frequent shortages.

The gift relationship is at the heart of many acts of integral service. A genuine gift is motivated by affection and respect, without expectation of reciprocation. In other circumstances, people mobilize their goodness to go and collaborate to achieve a common purpose. The Transitions Town Network is an example of a grassroots community-building movement where everyone involved shares information and power democratically. Rather than relying on institutions and governments to solve local problems, these communities are determining what is required to create equitable, thriving local economies as well as finding ways to reduce both dependence on fossil fuels and carbon emissions. These intentional communities are examples of "slow democracy" principles coming fully alive.

Transition towns reflect the understanding that renewable energy contributes to sustainable peace and that resiliency to environmental and economic stressors is strengthened by enhanced community connections. Rob Hopkins started this movement while he was teaching a practical sustainability course in Ireland. His book, *The Transition Handbook: From Oil Dependency to Local Resilience*, has inspired numerous towns and cities worldwide to change the way they live.

Wholesome communities prosper on many levels, and investment in each other's well-being enhances the health of individuals, families, and communities. Even brief positive social interactions increase our cardiac vagal tone and the ability to self-regulate our emotions and behaviors. The peace that begins with us ripples through our world as our goodness to go is leveraged and amplified. "Never doubt that a small group of thoughtful committed individuals can change the world," observed the cultural anthropologist Margaret Mead. "Indeed it's the only thing that ever has."

Pause, Reflect, and Record

- What communities or groups do you participate in, including family networks, sports teams, alumni groups, professional organizations, social media groups, and others? In what ways does inclusion in each of these groups enrich and support you?

- Is there another group, community, or tribe that is drawing your attention at this point in your life? Describe.

- In what ways does wellness—the dynamic alignment of vitality and purpose - fuel prosperity in your life and in that of your community?

- Do you regard access to basic healthcare a human right? Why or why not?

38

Social Artistry and Entrepreneurship

There was a star danced, and under that was I born.

—William Shakespeare

The social artistry of integral service contributes to a world where everyone can thrive. It is our great privilege to help bring about a *possible* society in which we actively love peace and equity not merely hate war and injustice. Increasing numbers of social artists are stepping forward and taking a stand to create a mutually uplifting future for life on earth.

The International Institute for Social Artistry was founded by Jean Houston, Ph.D., a pioneer in bringing new ways of thinking and doing to global challenges. Dr. Houston has lived a mythic life and speaks boldly of a regenesis of human society. With a passion for the possible, she's served as a leader in the human potential movement for decades. Dr. Houston is the author of dozens of evocative books, teaches online courses for social artists, and has worked with the United Nations Development Program to train global leaders for the twenty-first century.

Another social artist and entrepreneur is the renowned philanthropic fundraiser Lynne Twist who created the Pachamama Alliance after writing *The Soul of Money*. In addition to working with indigenous people in South America, the Pachamama Alliance sponsors "Awakening the Dreamer" symposia. These inspiring programs explore three interrelated facets of our interconnected world: environmental sustainability, social justice, and spiritual fulfillment.

Social artists and entrepreneurs are forming international networks that manifest creative solutions for community and global problems, and they're developing profitable, environmentally sustainable companies committed to social justice. These aspirations can invigorate every type of business. Entrepreneurial principles are used by many ventures to organize, create, and manage initiatives that are creating social change for the highest good of humanity. One example is a low-cost, highly effective water filter that was developed by a young woman in China.

The Unreasonable Institute based in Boulder, Colorado, offers dynamic support of social entrepreneurs from every walk of life around the globe. In January of 2013, the institute launched a pioneering program called Unreasonable at Sea. Through a rigorous application process, the institute identified ten young entrepreneurs from around the world whose technological ideas could provide tremendous social benefit. Together with mentors and social investors, these young people sailed the globe, collaborating together and visiting government officials in many countries whose citizens would benefit from their innovations.

When entrepreneurial businesses address social or environmental problems, ideas need to be scaled up to affect enough people to build a financially sustainable base. One definition of "scalable" includes the condition that solutions impact at least a million people. Rather than measuring their success in terms of financial and geographic profitability alone, social entrepreneurs measure their effectiveness in terms of resolving, one by one, global issues threatening the planet and humanity.

Financial profit is important to keep energy and currency flowing in sustainable ways. However, clarity of vision and strength of commitment to the social venture's humanitarian mission is even more important. "Copy cats" may try to mimic true authenticity, but deception is soon detectable. The socially minded TOMS shoe company clarified their mission to donate a pair of shoes for every pair purchased. The connectivity and reach of social media helped its business thrive, but when Skechers tried to mimic the "donate a pair" shoe campaign, it failed because consumers quickly smelled the lack of authenticity.

The integration of profit and purpose requires keen integrity. In addition to authentic vision and commitment, skillful means must be developed to manifest a mission for social transformation. The bombastic Venezuelan president Hugo Chavez, who died in March of 2013, wanted to lead a socialist revolution to assist those living in poverty but did not develop a management team and effective strategies to sustain structural change. Despite Venezuela's large oil reserves, the country's infrastructure is crumbling, its middle classes are decimated, and the lives of the poor have not changed substantially.

Social Artistry and Entrepreneurship

In contrast, Paul Polak, a former psychiatrist who is also committed to uplifting the lives of billions of poor people, is remarkably effective in achieving his mission. Dr. Polak grew up in Canada, learned to listen "with all his soul" to the impoverished, mentally ill people he served in Colorado, and went on to found several companies that design affordable, simple solutions to problems of poverty such as irrigation of crops and safe drinking water. Dr. Polak thinks outside the box, develops skillful teams of creative problem solvers, mentors young entrepreneurs through the Unreasonable Institute, and manifests sustainable solutions that help millions of lives.

The founder and CEO of the Global Fund for Women identifies herself as a social venture capitalist. For over twenty years, Kavita N. Ramdas, with the support of the J.P. Morgan Chase financial institution, has invested over $70 million in thousands of women's initiatives in sixty-seven countries. Through her international experience, Ramdas has recognized how essential it is to invest in women as key players in social change. The Global Fund for Women and many other philanthropic organizations catalyze a ripple effect that strengthens and stabilizes economies as well as individual lives.

Old paradigms where charity is viewed through a handout mentality are ending. Women are a widely underutilized resource in world economies, and every stable, profitable country needs their contributions as educated, independent citizens. Women are creative at preventing war, developing inclusive communities, and at reframing situations and changing their terms of reference. If governments and businesses refuse or neglect to include over half of the world's population, their budgets need to build in the cost of this failure. It's time for a new bottom line.

Too often we've focused on either developing a profitable, "efficient" business model or on giving money away in an attempt to repair social inequities. Entrepreneurs operating from the worldview of "we're all in this together" aren't caught in this either-or dichotomy. They realize that by investing in equity, every business and country will get more efficient outcomes.

One example of corporate social responsibility is Green Mountain Coffee Roasters. This Vermont-based company is one of the world's largest coffee wholesalers and makes ethical and sustainable practices a key part of its business. Green Mountain's vision and business model are about making positive change in the world. Employees are inspired, the energy within the organization increases, and the marketplace embraces

407

the company's product and its vision. This is the win-win effect of creating business cultures of multi-level wellness.

Green Mountain's research staff continues to assess the social and environmental health of communities throughout their supply chain as sales of their fair trade coffee increase. Recognizing that the new social venture model is investing in people rather than giving handouts, Green Mountain invests five percent of pretax profits in grants to social and environmental organizations in coffee-growing communities, including a microcredit agency called Root Capital. Whereas "throwing money" at a problem wastes valuable resources, social investments are profitable on many levels. Caring for people and the planet as well as financial profits is the new bottom line.

Extreme Poverty Is the Absence of Human Rights

Although there are numerous definitions of poverty, it is described by social justice professor David Gordon as the absence of two or more of the following basic human needs and rights: sufficient food, safe water, shelter, sanitation facilities, health care, legal and financial services, and access to information. The eighth basic right is the educational opportunity to become literate.

Poverty is a denial of choices, opportunities, access to services, and a violation of human dignity. Sixty percent of the global population lives on only six percent of the world's income, and half of the world lives on $2 a day. Over one billion people live on less than a dollar a day, and the frustration, despair, and hostility generated by this injustice are threats to peace everywhere on the planet.

One reason that millions of people living in poverty are excluded from legal market systems is that they do not have access to documents verifying their legal identity and property rights. In addition, camps for most of the world's millions of refugees from political violence or environmental devastation are often dangerous and are located in underdeveloped nations. It's extremely unlikely that vulnerable refugees will find employment in their struggling host country, and in some cases, refugees are met with violent resentment.

A young Mexican father was desperate to earn money for his son who required a kidney transplant. With hope and courage, he left for the U.S. border and died attempting to cross into the land of opportunity. Children of undocumented immigrants are not always granted citizenship in the country of their birth. The unjust exclusion of millions of extra-legal entrepreneurs and their families results in unstable political and economic environments that are potentially dangerous for everyone. In Peru, for example, 98 percent of businesses are extra-legal, using non-cash systems that try to operate outside of the state's top-heavy, bureaucratic structures. Most of the people living in extreme poverty—less than a dollar a day—have no legal documents.

For his service as a microcredit pioneer and his efforts to alleviate global poverty, Muhammad Yunus, Ph.D., founding director of the Grameen Bank, was awarded the Nobel Peace Prize in 2006. In his book *Creating a World Without Poverty*, "banker to the poor" Dr. Yunus describes how social entrepreneurialism has been an integral part of human history. Dr. Yunus supports free markets and outlines ways that social business entrepreneurs can be a solution to many of our world's economic and social justice problems.

Dr. Yunus's book highlights the pivotal point at which a philanthropic organization operates beyond its cost-recovery point into the zone of profit, thereby overcoming the gravitational force of financial dependence. He sees this as a critical moment of institutional transformation, when a business that does good for others also makes money. When more currency flows, more people rise out of poverty. Dr. Yunus proposes the creation of a social stock market attractive to investors who are not only oriented to personal gain but also to achieving social goals. Strong, equitable economies are good for everyone.

If we create the right environment, writes Dr. Yunus, social business entrepreneurs can make the market an exciting place for fighting social battles in increasingly innovative and effective ways. Many have asserted that short-term financial gain is blinding us to the importance of long-term good. We have thousands of years of history to learn from and perhaps thousands of future generations will be affected by our choices today.

Investing in Long-Term Good

Social entrepreneurs invest in long-term good. Monique Alvarez, founder of Nourish the Children, says, "Business for monetary gain alone only allows me to have more of what I already have, but business for the sake of helping others allows me to live with clear purpose and passion." Investing in the upliftment of life and the human spirit has inestimable long-term gains.

Goodness To Go

Several countries are introducing a new era of governance whose intent is to restructure, not repeat, the abuses of power rampant in oligarchies. Designs for simple and elegant financial reporting with continuous, radical transparency are being implemented. The number of ethical financial institutions, such as Triodos Bank in the Netherlands, is increasing, as are microfinance organizations critical to developing economies. The ability to access microloans from ethical lenders gives budding entrepreneurs the security and confidence needed to set up their own small businesses. The opportunity to provide for one's family with dignity is priceless.

South Africa has a Social Investment Exchange, and other social stock exchanges have been launched in Europe as well as North and South America. Social stock exchanges connect donors and investors with nonprofits and businesses that have a social mission. Other efforts for social-purpose businesses and like-minded investors are under way in India, New Zealand, Portugal, and Thailand.

An ethical era is being ushered in by the current generation of graduating business administrators. Harvard's MBA oath acknowledges that the goal of a business manager is to serve the greater good. The public vow attests that business managers will act responsibly, ethically, and refrain from advancing their "own narrow ambitions" at the expense of others. The Leeds School of Business at the University of Colorado, Boulder, has a progressive social enterprise department. At Columbia Business School, all students must pledge to an honor code that states in part: "I will not lie, cheat, steal or tolerate those who do."

Some students protest that having to commit to a code of ethics is paternalistic. Others are ethical relativists, believing that ethics are always embedded in context. This backlash may serve to fuel meaningful dialogue and contemplative inquiry about personal and professional codes of behavior. In the new generation of activists, many promise to consider a corporation's effect on its workers, the community, and the environment, not only on its earnings. Their commitments contribute to sustainable business models that integrate heart, head, and hands.

Schools offering programs in social business entrepreneurship are increasing and bank branches may soon specialize in financing social business ventures. Working at the high school level in Africa, the organization Educate! is developing social entrepreneurial leaders. An example of a Danish and Dutch college-level program is KaosPilots, an educational program in new business design and social innovation. KaosPilots students share the passion to make the world a better place by bringing about the change the world needs now.

Our times call for a conscious capitalism of sufficiency, where satisfactory rather than maximum profit is enough, and the contribution to social welfare or social justice is central. There are many ways to organize for comprehensive, effective change that decentralizes the financial system. One web-based activist network is the *structural reform thinking group* called A New Way Forward that is dedicated to structural change in the political economy. Another group, Americans for Financial Reform, is a broad coalition of more than 250 organizations representing consumers, labor, seniors, small businesses, and low-income citizens who have joined together to fight for banking and financial system reform.

Growing numbers of philanthropic organizations are dedicated to social entrepreneurship, such as the Skoll Foundation in California and the organization for Pan African Entrepreneurship in Education. Each year, *Entrepreneur* magazine recognizes the brilliance of 100 leading entrepreneurial companies. Social artistry includes principles of leadership such as whole brain thinking and collaboration that are needed in the twenty-first century. In the development of an individual's leadership potential, there are often transformative moments of testing, from burying a child to losing an election, from which opportunities arise to emerge with integrity and power. Forbearance is a process that can clarify vision. With compassion, persistence, support, and patience, we need not be decimated by hardship but can rise wiser and stronger from its grip.

In their book *Leading for a Lifetime: How Defining Moments Shape Leaders of Today and Tomorrow*, Warren Bennis and Robert Thomas describe these potentially pivotal moments as "crucibles" that force us to decide who we are. In fires of transformation or in the belly of a whale, we hone our commitment and resilience to manifesting the furthest reaches of our capabilities. Creative solutions to any level of problem require active imagination and as we imagine, envision, and dream, we design, plan, and create.

Social artistry takes many forms. During their Run for One Planet in 2008, a young Canadian couple ran 11,000 miles and raised about $100,000 to inspire action for a healthier environment. These runs are ongoing endeavors to support environmental activism one step at a time. The grand hope that we can begin to heal our world with justice and peaceful harmony is not a pipe dream. In nature's preservation and the mobilization of our social artistry is hope for the world.

Pause, Reflect, and Record

- Has there been a "crucible" moment in your life that has forced you to define who you are?

- In what ways are you a social artist or entrepreneur? What needs do you see in the world that inspire you to take action and use your gifts?

- How closely do your financial expenditures align with your deepest values and goals? What changes could you take to bring them into closer alignment?

- What traits do you think characterize an effective, twenty-first-century leader?

39

Blessed Unrest—
The Interdependence Revolution

In order to change an existing paradigm
you do not struggle to try and change
the problematic model.
You create a new model and
make the old one obsolete.

—Buckminster Fuller

It is a state of blessed unrest that often initiates our goodness to go. Around the world, awareness of our interdependence is growing and shaking up complacency with a status quo that puts us to sleep. As consciousness wakens and unitive visions inspire us, global shifts are beginning.

Paul Hawken, a social activist and best-selling author of several seminal books and articles, published *Blessed Unrest* in 2007. In it, Hawken described the explosive involvement of a global humanitarian movement arising from the grassroots of communities. By his estimate, there may be two million groups worldwide intermingling their concerns for social justice and ecological rejuvenation that constitute a kind of invisible, developing superpower. This galvanized humanitarian movement is supporting governments to generate economic dynamism that evolves in healthy, sustainable ways. As a result, stronger economies and new job sectors are being created.

This is a time of metamorphoses and we're living in a grand moment of opportunity which holds radical opportunity: ignorance, fear, and apathy transform into empathy that moves into positive action. Blessed unrest is a yearning that implores us to remain open to possibility and aware of the urges that motivate us. Contributing to the design of a healthier, more equitable world is the creative work of many kinds of social artists.

Goodness To Go

An innovative modern dancer and choreographer described the blessed unrest of artists as a "divine dissatisfaction." Martha Graham felt that this creative unrest makes artists more alive, and wrote, "There is vitality, a life force, a quickening that is translated through you into action, and because there is only one of you in all time, this expression is unique. If you block it, it will never exist through any other medium and be lost. The world will not have it. It is not your business to determine how good it is; nor how valuable it is; nor how it compares with other expressions. It is your business to keep it yours clearly and directly, to keep the channel open."

A maturing, compassionate global consciousness may ensure the survival of the human species. For millennia, the idea of an all-extensive world soul has existed and a French sociologist Emile Durkheim coined the term "collective consciousness." The renowned Swiss psychiatrist Carl Jung extended this concept a century ago. He believed we inherit a second, universal psychic system that consists of pre-existent symbolic forms, which he called archetypes. Mayans and other indigenous peoples have predicted that ours is a time not only of chaos but also of potent opportunities to expand our awareness of our collective consciousness.

In the 1930s, Soviet geochemist Vladimir Vernadsky and French philosopher Teilhard de Chardin suggested that the increasing planetary convergence of humans could create a "noosphere," or energetic sphere of human thought. In this theory, the noosphere is the third in a succession of phases of development of the earth, after the geosphere (inanimate matter) and the biosphere (biological life). The concept that human cognition is able to transform the biosphere is being researched as part of the Princeton Global Consciousness Project. Wisdom traditions have predicted that breakthroughs in human consciousness are possible at this time in history and that expanding human potential will change conditions for life from the inside out.

Many believe that thoughts and feelings in the energetic sphere affect life on earth through energetic frequencies emitted and behaviors prompted. The awakened mind of prayer and meditation resonates at slower alpha frequencies that are said to be more conducive to insight than the brain's usual beta frequencies. Basic forces motivating human behaviors are the energies of fear and love. As we become free of fear, we're able to act more effectively from the wisdom of the heart. The more we give, the more we're inspired to give, and the receiving happens naturally. "Evolution and all hopes for a better world rest in the fearlessness and open-hearted vision of people who embrace life," wrote renowned social artist and musician John Lennon. Attending with open hearts and minds to our needs for self-care and our feelings of blessed unrest allows our creative potential to flourish.

An empowering dynamism is flowing from ongoing innovation, adaptation, and change. Economist Joseph Schumpeter described capitalism as an evolutionary process where resources used in new ways improve standards of living over time. Even monarchs didn't have flush toilets or dentistry a few centuries ago. He labeled the inevitable changes to old industries and obsolete jobs as "creative destruction" as we learn to do more with less. Many social artists of the interdependence revolution encourage us to participate in and celebrate this new dawn as humankind turns toward a transformative era of global healing.

Revolutionary Conservation

For millennia, human beings have been on a trajectory of development that has increasingly contaminated our emerald planet. "The most remarkable feature of this historical moment on Earth," writes ecopsychologist Joanna Macy, "is that we are beginning to wake up, as from a millennia-long sleep, to a whole new relationship to our world, to ourselves, and to each other." Conservation is an act of peace.

We generally protect and conserve that which we care about. Former vice president Al Gore is a member of planet earth's growing community of eco-warriors who released the film An *Inconvenient Truth* in 2006. In this Academy Award–winning documentary, Gore translated scientific data and predictions about climate change to general audiences. In his recent book, *The Future: Six Drivers of Global Change*, Gore articulates his optimism that we'll rise to challenges presented by current global crises.

Eco-conservationists serve for the sake of global goodness. Ways to live more simply so that others can simply live, free of systemic hunger, injustice, violence, and poverty, are priorities. Helen K. Nearing was an early advocate of living more simply with a rich appreciation of what is sufficient. Among her books, written with her husband, Scott, is *Living the Good Life: How to Live Simply and Sanely in a Troubled World*. Regardless of the amount of money spent, *doing* things makes people happier than buying things because meaningful experiences fill us with energy and a sense of being alive. A study conducted at the University of British Columbia reported that personal spending had no link to a person's happiness, while giving to others was significantly related to a boost in happiness.

Chief Seattle wrote, "Humans did not weave the web of life; we are merely a strand in it. Whatever we do to the web, we do to ourselves." It's clear that we need to stop putting 90 million tons of global warming pollution into the atmosphere every day. We need to generate renewable, healthful resources and energy. We need new social and business models that don't subjugate anyone or heedlessly suck away finite resources. We need an evolved paradigm that creates true wealth, the mutually beneficial kind that can be passed on to others and uplifts communities in life-affirming ways.

The natural world is rich with examples of life-affirming transformations. One particularly magnificent whole-system change is evident in the life cycle of a butterfly. At some point in its life, the wormlike caterpillar becomes a ravenous consumer, eating up to 100 times its body weight. Fortunately, within its engorged body are imaginal cells that wake up. These imaginal cells cluster together and become the caterpillar's genetic director. At this point, the other cells dissolve within the pupae, disintegrating into a nutritive soup as the new beauty and delicate wings of the butterfly-to-be take form within a protective chrysalis. Biomimicry is the practice of borrowing nature's design principles to create more sustainable products and processes. May we be biomimics as we seek beautiful, whole-system transformation.

Integral Power and Leadership

The imaginal cells of twenty-first century leaderships will need to reconcile power with service. True power is derived from service and is used only for service. Only one who truly serves can truly command. As tyrants throughout history have revealed, it's a tremendous challenge to develop the harmony between service and the power that is necessary for the exercise of principled leadership. Gandhi reminded us that values-based service to any particular person, group, or issue is always in the context of benefiting all of humanity. He believed in the oneness of humanity and honored nonviolent integral service that merged into universal service.

In *Power vs. Force*, David R. Hawkins, M.D., Ph.D., examines the distinctions between life-affirming power and judgmental, polarizing force: "Power arises from *meaning*. It has to do with motive, and it has to do with principle. Power is always associated with that which supports the significance of life itself. It appeals to that part of human nature that we call *noble*. ... Power is associated with compassion and makes us feel positively about ourselves," he writes.

Dr. Hawkins goes on to distinguish the nobility of true power from force. "Force is associated with the partial, power with the whole. ... Because force automatically creates counter-force, its effect is limited by definition. Power, on the other hand, is still. ... Gravity's power moves all objects within its field, but the gravity field itself does not move." The source of the metaparadigm of *We* is the same source of creative power that gives us life and energy. The organizing principles of this benevolent power emanate from consciousness itself. We're not only connected with this power, we are one with its source.

The blessed unrest of interdependence revolutionaries insists that media speak truth to those who wield force. The protection of a free, unfettered press and other sources of investigative journalism, accurate news, and informed perspectives is essential to democratic governance. Virtually every form of governing structure requires checks and balances of power. Citizens need to be informed by reports that are as unbiased as possible, not misled and manipulated by distorted perspectives that poison trust and harm mutual respect. Ignorance is not bliss.

Representatives of agencies such as the United Nations and investigative reporters from every country do their best to bring light to all sides of a story. Their efforts have revealed, for example, that during the years of Syria's civil war, both sides forced children to become soldiers and committed other human rights atrocities. Reporters are maimed and killed in the line of duty on a regular basis. We owe debts of gratitude to these courageous social artists, as well as to academics, volunteers, and others who contribute their creative intelligence to the emerging interdependence revolution.

History professor Howard Zinn was as well known for honoring the imaginal cells within the human psyche as for his challenges of injustice. Zinn was a World War II bombardier who later devoted his life to peace advocacy and giving voice to the people's history of America until his death on January 27, 2010. In the 1970s, Zinn protested the Vietnam War with his friend Daniel Ellsberg who made available the deceptive secrets contained in the Pentagon Papers about U.S. involvement in Vietnam, contributing to the war's end.

In his 1980 revolutionary book, *A People's History of the United States*, Zinn made the perspectives of minorities and the disenfranchised accessible to our understanding of U.S. history. His writings shattered the myth that history is a series of facts that can be interpreted objectively through a single lens. Zinn also challenged the assumption that those in power are motivated consistently to act in ways that serve their fellow countrymen.

Leaders, like any human being, can fall asleep at the wheel, allow themselves to be seduced by the perks of their position, or abandon their responsibilities. Democracy is government by the people. Despite the 2013 groundswell of American public support for background checks and other gun control measures, most of the members of Congress ignored the voice of the people. Many feel that Congress is bought and sold by special interest groups and that significant reform in urgently required.

As the people's historian, Howard Zinn called attention to the "moments when courage prevailed, when the unpredictable nature of human affairs worked in favor of freedom and fairness." In a collection of writings entitled *The Impossible Will Take a Little While*, an essay by Zinn reminds us, "We forget how often in this century we have been astonished by the sudden crumbling of institutions, by extraordinary changes in people's thoughts, by unexpected eruptions of rebellion against tyrannies, by the quick collapse of systems of power that seemed invincible." The fall of the Berlin Wall and other examples of creative destruction are integral elements of evolutionary social processes.

On the other hand, many harmful social processes are increasingly destructive. Current power structures in the United States are stunting economic growth and assaulting hopes for job security, home ownership, and healthcare benefits. Pulitzer Prize winner Hedrick Smith's recent book *Who Stole the American Dream?* reveals how political and economic decisions made over the past forty years have resulted in extreme income disparity and dismantled a model of shared prosperity. Even before the collapse of the economic bubble in 2008, the middle class lost $6 trillion in transfers to banks and millions of citizens are losing the struggle to stay afloat financially.

Thankfully, we're also learning what does work to create sustainable systems of economic integrity. Decades of research by the McKinsey Global Institute find that competition within business sectors inspires economic dynamism. Governments can build dynamic economies from the ground up through (1) efficient physical and communications infrastructures; (2) quality education; (3) enforceable rules of law; (3) access to financial credit; (4) opening markets to trade; (5) repealing subsidies; (6) breaking up monopolies, (7) creating transparency in heavily regulated sectors; and (8) keeping graft in check, especially in the most fraud-ridden sectors, such as banking, real estate, energy, and infrastructure. When these supports are in place, the goodness, creativity, and innovation of citizens is unimpeded.

Our Metaparadigm of *We*

Buckminster Fuller was a visionary who articulated the metaparadigm of *you and me together* and knew integrity to be the source of everything successful. Repeatedly, he reminded us that under our big dome of sky, we are all in this together. Our interdependence is multilevel, including physical, psychological, and economic. We cannot exist otherwise.

There is wired into our genes a neurobiology of we, of empathy, compassion, and relatedness. The firing of mirror neurons stimulates our emotional reaction to another's pain in a finely tuned feedback system. For thirty years, the physicist Fritz-Albert Popp and dozens of other scientists around the globe researched faint currents of light within our DNA called biophoton emissions. Popp recognized that this light is the primary communication channel among living organisms. One study revealed that these light emissions were capable of instantaneous, or nonlocal, global signaling between cells. The magnificent interrelatedness of life is nonlinear. We create a quantum bond with our world, writes Jean McTaggart, as we take in the light of life around us. Light is particle *and* wave. Humans are unique *and* everyone is everyone. The human and the universal come together.

The paradigm of *we* recognizes this bond of life and calls for "servant," or service-based, leadership. As an interconnected web of leaders, we shine our light as we reflect and amplify the light of others. Many teachers have served as living examples of the kind of leadership that encourages everyone to live as an example to others; we have this responsibility to our own life and to the entire world. Whether we're a single mother, leader of a gang or a country, commander of an army, a rural vaccination worker, the director of a corporation or a United Nations commissioner, each one of us sets an example for someone else.

True leadership exemplifies the Golden Rule and, at times, transcends the subtle dualism inherent in it. Mahatma Gandhi emphasized that service-based leaders focus on responsibilities to the whole as well as its constituents; their essential duty is to treat others as themselves. It's been said that the next wise leader will be an engaged community of awake individuals. We're past the time of waiting passively for some

419

"great" person to play the role of leader, rescuer, or savior. Committed to manifesting the enduring spirit of service as a way of life, we engage our leadership. We all have the responsibility to contribute to a sustainable future for life on earth.

There is a world that is "now but not yet." The largest peace lobby in Washington, D.C., called the Friends Committee on National Legislation (FCNL), uses this phrase. FCNL has a seventy-year record of nonpartisan accomplishments using multifaceted approaches to creating strategies that sustain lasting peace. Within the paradigm of we is the transformative power of collective action. Mairead Corrigan Maguire, a former prime minister of Ireland, has expressed that "we are on the edge of a quantum leap into a whole new way of organizing and living as a human family." Rather than retreating from the challenges of our time, may we manifest a world that is now but not yet.

Our inherent goodness is always present and is accessed most easily when inner and outer environments are healthy. Maya Angelou, Nobel Prize winner in literature, trusts the natural goodness of the human heart. In spite of the abominable abuses and enslavement of her African ancestors, Angelou writes: "We would all be more compassionate if we knew more. If we knew more, we would do more." This doing may be a subtle intentional direction, not an overdoing or effortful struggle. Open gently and listen with a clear mind and compassionate heart: as you know more about yourself and the needs of the world, what are you called to do?

Pause, Reflect, and Record

- How might you practice *being the best that you can be* in your home, workplace, community, or place of worship?

- What might you light with your light? In what ways could you uplift the human spirit?

- Describe a time in your life when "blessed unrest" or "creative destruction" moved you into a time of metamorphosis.

- How could you *live the future* now?

40

Volunteerism—
You Are the World

Volunteering is an act of heroism on a grand scale.
And it matters profoundly.
It does more than help people beat the odds;
it changes the odds.

—Bill Clinton

Volunteerism is a meaningful element of the legacy that many people create. Goodness to go is expressed through both professional vocations and volunteer avocations; one reason that volunteering our energy and abilities is *heroic* relates to its spirit of generosity and citizenship. Sometimes slogans like "Volunteerism changes the odds," "Be the difference," and "You are the world" light the fire of inspiration and intention to serve. Tending our sparks of inspiration with regular self-care prevents exhaustion or disillusionment that may dampen that fire of even the most ardent global citizen.

Volunteers open themselves to callings larger than themselves. Offering integral service on behalf of "some clearly seen and deeply felt good," as anthropologist Ruth Benedict wrote, brings experiences of great happiness. Very naturally, gratitude for life's gifts finds expression in giving. Several studies have confirmed the long-term benefits of philanthropic and civic engagement both for the individual as well as society.

Stepping onto the path of volunteerism is a decision to move compassion into action. Columbia University professor Elke Weber's life work is dedicated to understanding how and why people make the decisions they do. She analyzes psychological processes of attention, memory, and emotion as well as policy makers' strategies to implement social and economic ideas. Although Weber's research suggests that human nature has a "finite pool of worry," volunteering increases our capacity to expand our circle of caring. The heart of compassion is ever new and its caring is much more resourced than mind's worrying. In Sanskrit, the word for heart means "mainstay" or "resting place"; when we take refuge in the serenity of the heart, our compassion in action is rejuvenated.

Everything we want is beyond fear. Worry is fear-based and our reptilian brains are wired to automatically react to perceived threats. Anxiety often keeps us focused on future threats, feeling agitated and overwhelmed or paralyzed and numb. Weber suggests that our primitive brain moves one fear out as another moves in. Anxiety about ongoing environmental devastation is replaced by economic fears as a recession begins. While our brains aren't wired to maintain ever-increasing reservoirs of fear, our consciousness is sourced by infinite compassion living in the eternal present. Love is mightier than fear.

As we learn more about ourselves and working skillfully with emotions, our volunteerism is resilient, meaningful, and joyful. "Find out where joy resides, and give it a voice far beyond singing. For to miss the joy is to miss all," wrote Robert Louis Stevenson. From our vantage point early in the twenty-first century, with its pressing problems and converging catastrophes, it's easy to miss the tremendous innovation and joy that are also present.

Maintaining inspiration and enthusiasm for integral service is challenging, especially during difficult and dangerous times. It's often tempting to protest, minimize, or ignore problems and hide our head in the sands of consumerism and mindless entertainment. Aldous Huxley's *Brave New World* takes on a chilling, prophetic note in which disengaged citizens pass their time with drug-induced escapism and other distractions. However, what good will it do to do nothing? Volunteers and other global citizens discover what they can do for their world.

One way to support volunteerism is by donating air miles. In a program called Beyond Miles, airlines such as Air Canada fly relief workers to war-ravaged and disaster-stricken areas on donated air miles. The airlines fly War Child Canada workers to help young people affected by wars and civil unrest and other humanitarians to battle HIV/AIDS in developing nations. Other programs fly sick children in remote regions to medical centers that provide care not available close to home. Engineers Without Borders, Veterinarians Without Borders, and Schools Without Borders also benefit communities globally with the help of donated air miles.

Several government administrations around the world encourage volunteerism with various public service initiatives. President Barack Obama developed United We Serve in order to promote volunteerism and community civic responsibility. Ideas about paying off college loans by volunteering in community service are being considered as one way to reduce the educational debt burden of young people.

The United Way is a well-known volunteer organization that supports lasting positive community change. Their advertisements suggest ways to live united: "Join hands. Open your heart. Lend your muscle. Find your voice. Plan for the future. Think of *we* before *me*. Give. Advocate. Volunteer." The power of kindness through the committed hearts, heads, and hands of volunteers ripples through communities and uplifts lives.

Thriving Together

It literally feels good to do good, and giving sustains happiness more than getting. Meaningful social connections support states of happiness, whereas consumerism does not. In his book *Thrive*, Dan Buettner wrote about his years of research on *thrivers*, people who consistently report the highest levels of well-being. Buettner found that the happiest people volunteer. Altruism affects the brain's dopamine reward centers and feedback loops, which may be the cause of the delightful "helper's high." Wellness is multi-dimensional: by directing time and attention to serving others, volunteers are also physically healthier, tending to weigh less and suffer fewer heart attacks.

Meaningful service is one of the most effective ways to combat the growing loneliness that was reported in a recent U.S. study. A social neuroscientist at the University of Chicago, John Cacioppo, found that nearly 25 percent of the people in his study experience frequent loneliness. The isolation associated with loneliness can compromise the immune system and is linked to serious health problems, such as depression and anxiety, chronic pain, substance abuse, sleep disorders, and dementia. The World Health Organization has rated loneliness as a higher risk to health than smoking, which is the number one factor of leading causes of early death.

When young students study abroad or volunteer in communities with few material resources, global citizenship grows naturally. A neighbor described how her worldview changed in her late teens as a result of living in Nepal for an extended semester of university study. Three insights especially stayed with her throughout her life: (1) She deeply understood that happiness does not depend on material things; (2) she did not want to take anything for granted; and (3) she recognized that gratitude was an essential practice for living a meaningful, happy life.

These days, Peace Corps volunteers are not only young adults. After midlife careers, many are beginning new chapters in their lives and living a legacy of volunteerism. In 2003, two former Peace Corps volunteers returned to Ghana, West Africa to found Women in Progress, which assists hundreds of women entrepreneurs with everything from creating a business plan to managing daily operations and developing international sales. They also launched an online marketplace, Global Mamas, to help female entrepreneurs analyze their business challenges, identify growth opportunities, and implement their ideas.

A pioneering African American leader, Shirley Ann Jackson, Ph.D., has delved into many facets of power. As a university president and theoretical physicist who chaired the U.S. Nuclear Regulatory Commission, Dr. Jackson has explored ways that decisions and resolutions are manifested. She teaches that power is enhanced by passion, preparation, persistence, and commitment to one's ideas. It is also increased by our compassion as well as our ability to network effectively.

Old societal paradigms have often been driven by fear and greed. The zero-sum belief model insists that for one side to get ahead, another must lose. If *they* win, *we* lose, and the sum stays at zero. Yet often we've experienced that the sum of the elements is greater than its parts. During a visit to the Asia Pacific near the end of 2009, President Obama shared this vision of a new world paradigm: "In an interconnected world, power does not need to be a zero-sum game, and nations need not fear the success of another. ... With great power comes great responsibility. Cultivating spheres of cooperation—not competing spheres of influence—will lead to progress."

"Every choice we make can be a celebration of the world we want," writes Frances Moore Lappé. Integral service is a choice, an act of love, an unconditional offering from our compassion and gratitude that has the potential to be selfless. We may sense a call to serve nearby in our neighborhood or 10,000 miles away. In our global age, everywhere is our backyard.

We Are the World

In Berlin in 2008, President Obama was welcomed by 200,000 hopeful citizens. He called the world community to service, saying: "This is the moment when we must come together to save this planet. Let us resolve that we will not leave our children a world where the oceans rise and famine spreads and terrible storms devastate our lands. ... This is the moment to give our children back their future. This is the moment to stand as one."

Two of the United Nations' Millennium Development Goals are to eradicate extreme poverty and hunger and to achieve universal primary education. Decades ago, Dr. Martin Luther King, Jr. wrote, "I have the audacity to believe that people everywhere can have three meals a day for their bodies, education and culture for their minds, and dignity, equality and freedom for their spirits." Thousands of volunteers are committed to creating a healthier world for people everywhere.

The ability to achieve our goals is often affected by the number and strength of our connections. Nevertheless, in our increasingly interconnected world, starvation continues to kill a human being every six seconds. As you read this short sentence, a child has died of a preventable cause. Recent economic recessions revealed how globalization interconnects our world's financial markets and profoundly impacts the lives of those most vulnerable. Living the values of global citizenship is a deeply rooted need and radical responsibility of our time.

Parents and communities are supporting the natural impulse of young children to be global citizens. "Nobody is born a racist," writes Pulitzer Prize–winning novelist Toni Morrison. As we cultivate nondual awareness, we free ourselves of prejudice and create an inclusive world respectful of ethnic and racial differences. A girl born at the bottom of India's oppressive caste system more than eighty years ago broke free of caste and class restrictions to respond to her inner imperative to do something good for her world. Krishnammal Jagannathan had received the life-changing opportunity of education from friends and family and vowed to donate her life to serve peasant "untouchables." She joined Mahatma Gandhi's movement to help solve social problems of the caste system, saying, "Someone must be there to liberate these people." Jagannathan went on to found the Land for Tillers' Freedom that has expanded rural Indian economic development.

Her epic journey exemplifies *prasad*, the cycle of mutual blessings that flows from giving and receiving. Jagannathan's outstanding vision and work on behalf of our planet and its people were honored with the Right Livelihood Award, the world's premier award for personal courage and social transformation, which has been presented by the

Swedish parliament since 1980. Who would you nominate for the Right Livelihood Award?

While some people are called to volunteer in their local community, others are drawn to distant lands. A woman living in Colorado visited Tibetan refugees residing in Dharamsala in northern India. She was deeply moved by their plight and asked herself what she could offer as a massage therapist with few financial resources. Gradually, what emerged was to share her knowledge and skills of massage to several Tibetans, a social venture that has continued to grow.

International volunteerism is increasing at a rapid rate. Travelers are taking volunteer vacations that combine service with travel. Their community work encompasses many fields, and the cross-cultural exchanges and new friends made are regarded as the most valuable part of these programs. Volunteers have said that the experience touches their soul in ways they could not have imagined. Not infrequently, they ask themselves when they return from their transformative service adventure, "What do I want to do with the rest of my life?"

Several years ago, a busy psychotherapist came to a point where she needed time away from her full-time practice. Growing wearing of crisis management and the dualism she experienced in the client-therapist relationship, she suggested to her husband that they enroll in a volunteer vacation. Soon they found themselves with a small community of social artists from different walks of life on a Native American reservation.

Together with guidance from the indigenous people, the volunteer team created a large vegetable garden and organized several social service initiatives. The therapist deeply appreciated the creative collaboration between equals and realized that she wanted more of this in her work life. After a reflective period of inquiry, the couple left on an extended international service adventure and created work more meaningfully aligned with their needs and values when they returned.

Growing numbers of people who appreciate immersion travel enrich their cultural learning and travel adventures with volunteer service. Some families decide to home-school their children for several months while travelling internationally, staying with local families, and volunteering in a wide variety of community projects. Expeditions at home and abroad include social service, environmental, scientific, and educational opportunities. A few of the many reputable organizations offering travel with purpose are Global Volunteers, Cross-Cultural Solutions, Wiser World Travel, and Global Works. A useful book is

Volunteer Vacations: Short-Term Adventures That Will Benefit You and Others by Bill McMillon.

Volunteers are the heroes we need for the twenty-first century. They serve the greater good in the face of suffering as well as joyful abundance and learn to remain open to everyone and everything. Although some will experience distress as a result of serving traumatized people, psychological trauma and distress can be mitigated to a large extent through therapeutic modalities. We can create a world that supports volunteer heroes on many levels.

Care. Connect. Serve. For the most part, human beings act in the service of needs and values. When we engage in self-inquiry about our needs, values, and motives for volunteering, we're clearer about our reasons for engaging in community service. Self-knowledge is key. As you respond to the following five service inquiries, listen with openness and empathy to your needs, core values, and aspirations. Honor yourself and the interconnectedness of life as you engage in this process of self inquiry.

Five Service Inquiries

1. With what *attitude* do I volunteer my service?

2. What is my *intention* motivating this offering?

3. As I give, am I *free of expectations* about outcomes?

4. Am I willing to *offer without reward* of recognition, gratitude, compensation, or success?

5. Can I *give my best—and let it go*?

Global Citizenship

Global citizenship is a way of thinking and behaving. It is recognition of our interconnectedness and an impulse to treat all people with respect as our extended family. Global citizenship values the earth as precious and unique and safeguards the future for those coming after us. The International School of Global Citizenship offers international experiential learning opportunities through its *Shoulder-to-Shoulder* programs. One student wrote, "I learned what it meant to be a global citizen—a person who is patient, humble, and persistent, who treats every person with the same amount of dignity and respect; a person who not only takes the initiative to fix problems of social injustice but also inspires others to help."

The volunteerism of global citizens of all ages makes a difference. There is a tale of a young boy walking along a seashore who wanted to help some of the countless stranded starfish. When he was told that one child tossing starfish back into the sea wasn't going to make much of a difference, he was neither disappointed nor deterred. Nor did he succumb to cynical or cowardly fatalism. After reflecting for a moment, the boy reached down to pick up another starfish, tossed it out into the ocean, saying, "I sure made a difference for that one." This resilient volunteer served a remarkably resilient lifeform: starfish can regenerate limbs over time.

An independent filmmaker from Portland, Oregon didn't consider herself an activist. However, Lisa Shannon's goodness to go was galvanized by a televised documentary about "Africa's world war" and the rape and torture of women in eastern Congo by marauding militia and army forces. "Immediately, I decided I wanted to help," she said. After training to run long distances, Shannon founded Run for Congo Women, and their fundraising events have spread around the globe. "The Congolese women are living in a war zone, yet they haven't lost their spirit," Shannon marvels. "I don't know what's more inspirational than that."

Innumerable global volunteers feel it is a privilege to have the opportunity to offer integral service. With its stance of deep democracy, global citizenship includes and respects each voice as equally important. Its roots can be traced to ancient Greece where Diogenes declared that he was a citizen of the world. Centuries later, Albert Einstein described nationalism as an infantile disease. A curriculum for global citizenship published by a branch of the United Nations describes global citizenship as understanding the need to tackle injustice and inequality, and having the desire and ability to work actively to do so. It includes the confidence that we can make a difference in our world.

One of many organizations that demonstrates global citizenship is Deepak Chopra's Alliance for New Humanity, whose mission is to connect people dedicated to building a just, peaceful, and sustainable world. Through personal and social transformation, these global citizens hold the awareness of the unity of all humanity and volunteer their service to change social, political, and economic structures on behalf of the greater good. Global works conducts service-learning trips internationally for teenagers. Youth for Global Sustainability, Matter-we-Matter, ¡Empathize, and Project YES, programs are communities of engaged members of Generation We.

Volunteerism is one form of inclusive cooperation that contributes to innovative, evolutionary change. Parent volunteers help students create colorful elementary school murals that declare, "We are one beautiful garden made up of many radiant flowers. We will not tolerate the weeds of discrimination!" Volunteerism, service learning, and global citizenship are strong values in growing numbers of schools around the world. Students find that volunteering doesn't just change their lives: their lives started to take on shape and dimension through meaningful formative experiences. It's empowering and transformational when we realize that we truly can have a positive impact in the world. What was a moment in your life on which your story pivoted from what is to what could be?

Social justice for all includes freedom from political and militaristic harm. One of the greatest legacies we can leave to coming generations is the reduction of military budgets around the world and the complete eradication of all nuclear weapons. It isn't viable for *any* nation to have arsenals of nuclear weapons if the global family is to embrace and practice peace. What we dream, envision, and co-create together can become a reality. We can speak up, act up, get in the way of injustice, and make the way of peace. Justice and peace go hand in hand with global citizenship. In her practical guide to peace-making entitled *The Peace Book*, Louise Diamond wrote: "Peace is more than the absence of war, violence, or conflict. Peace is a presence—the presence of connection."

Life is also the presence of connection and the resources and energies that support life flow in many ways. In nature, underground tuber root systems that move horizontally as well as vertically are called rhizomes. Technology has made it possible for communities of cooperation to be globally connected in ways barely imagined a generation ago. Through webs of social networking, individuals and cultures engage in virtual cross-fertilization. World music is infused with polyrhythms from every continent. Projects of translation and collaboration in contemporary literary communities are rich with this cross-cultural pollination.

Many of us have hybrid identities capable of moving in multiple directions simultaneously, like aspen groves connected by rhizomes. Software applications streamline volunteering in our spare moments, and micro-volunteering is expanding. One pilot program is the Extraordinaries, an enterprise that envisions what thousands of people with a few minutes can accomplish; tutoring students and reporting municipal problems are some of the numerous volunteer opportunities.

For millennia, *know thyself* have been resounding words of wisdom; more recently, we've been encouraged to *think globally and act locally*. Many people are extending this invitation to *think universally and act globally*. The social activism organization Make Poverty History is connecting nodes of global concern to end poverty through an online campaign. Canadian governments have promised to give 0.7 percent of their national income to help eliminate global poverty, and Make Poverty History mobilizes citizens to remind governments of their promise.

On the path of volunteerism and global citizenship, recognize that there is no separation of "us" and "them." The web of life is affected when an evacuation order for an unsafe garment factory is ignored and its collapse kills more than five hundred people in Bangladesh. Learn how corruption and human rights abuses can be eradicated. Celebrate sufficiency, acquire few needs, and engage in regular self-care. Don't confuse comfort with safety. Notice the workings of power and privilege in your culture, knowing that no one has a right to take others' resources or limit their opportunities. Defy corporate domination. Shed light on corruption and cronyism. Reform Congress and pledge allegiance to democracy and the earth. Know where your wastes go and where your bank banks. Don't confuse wellness with lack of disease or money with wealth. Know that many are not heard and work to change this. You are the world.

Global wisdom traditions have made it clear that what we give is what we'll receive. What we plant here and now, we harvest later. With this in mind, let's plant seeds of goodness that benefit everyone. Giving our integral service is a harmonious act of love giving of itself. Together, with our global community of humanitarians, we'll be catalysts of positive change. Imagine what could be if we mobilized our intellect, creative imagination, heart, and hands in service of goodness to go.

Pause, Reflect, and Record

- Recall a time when you volunteered your time, energy, and skills. Look at your offering through the lens of the five service inquires listed in this chapter.

- Recall or imagine an offering of integral service that you've given or would like to give. What difference have you made or would like to make in another's life?

- *Happiness doesn't depend on money. Don't take anything for granted. Gratitude is key to a happy, meaningful life.* These insights gleaned from a semester of international study shaped a woman's life. In what ways do they apply to your life?

- Are you interested in a travel adventure that includes national or international volunteerism? If so, what types of community service might be of potential interest and in which country or culture?

41

Youth Engagement

*You don't have to be a big person
to make a difference.
One child can do a world of good
just by lending a helping hand.*

—Fifth grader Sydney Koffman

The largest generation the world has ever known is alive now. Humans continue to multiply exponentially, with nearly half of the population being under the age of twenty-five. Our creativity and aspirations to serve the public good now and in the future are affecting the design of cities and parks, transportation and information systems, affordable housing, and public spaces as well as the restoration of environmental health. Today's children and their children's children will live with the legacy that we're creating today.

Following World War II, the increased birth rate in high-income countries between 1946 and 1964 created a baby boom. The children of baby boomers, called the "echo baby boomers," or millennial generation, have lived in a culture of conspicuous consumption that has spread to many parts of the world. Undoubtedly, there are many factors contributing to findings of nearly epidemic increases of narcissism and entitlement in segments of recent generations, especially in the West. Excessive egocentrism and preoccupation with personal desires stifles the expression of compassion in action.

Jean Twenge, Ph.D., in her book *Generation Me*, states that 25 percent of American college students in 2006 agreed with most items on standard measures of narcissistic traits. Nevertheless, there is growing global evidence that many of the youth from the millennial generation have moved away from unrestrained self-preoccupation and excessive materialism. This is the dawning of Generation We.

Goodness To Go

One of the important tasks of families and societies is to provide environments and guidance that support the development of resilient, resourced youth. Each child develops his or her integrity and resilience from the inside out. Easy praise and few challenges frequently lead to a sense of narcissistic entitlement or fragile resiliency, which serves no one. The grit and grace of character develop through ongoing efforts to acquire knowledge or mastery of a skill set. Very little of what is valuable in life comes easily.

In 2002, Elizabeth Catlett, a celebratory American artist, addressed the National Visionary Leadership Project when she was eighty-seven years old. This wise woman's words to young people about doing something constructive to help others were archived by the Library of Congress. Catlett encouraged the altruism of young humanitarians. "Think about other people. Base what you are doing on something that has to do with all of us," she said. "Make your life important. Give of yourself."

Throughout human development, the dynamic interweave of freedom and responsibility is ongoing. While young people in modern societies often aren't as involved in their communities, the meaningful engagement of youth in agricultural communities can result in higher levels of accountability and responsibility. Although tending to farm animals and crops in many countries still requires the involvement of every family member, some children, especially girls, are regarded as a source of free labor and are denied basic rights to education. Young people are persons not property, and adults need to be mindful of the distinction between useful contributions to families and abuse or neglect of the needs of children in their community.

How do we cultivate leadership qualities and inspire young minds to reach their full potential, value kindness and generosity, and become positive examples to others. There are many ways that global humanitarians, social justice movements, human rights legislation, and community programs are serving and mentoring young people. With the encouragement of her parents, one young adoptee founded a philanthropy to aid an orphanage in her country of birth. Family and community members pool resources so that a child is able to attend school. Head Start and school lunch programs are effective in supporting under-resourced children to achieve their potential and providing healthy nutrition for their growing brains and bodies.

Young People's Health and Wellness

Vibrant health allows us to reach our full potential and sustains our goodness to go, yet health care remains a pressing need for children the world over. Every day, nearly 20,000 children die from preventable causes because they lack sufficient nutrition, access to clean drinking water, sufficient protein, basic medical attention, and immunizations. Take a moment to acknowledge this nearly unfathomable suffering. Severe diarrhea from rotavirus kills half a million children annually, usually due to lack of access to safe drinking water. Unsafe cooking stoves and traffic infrastructure in developing countries cause the deaths of many more children from indoor air pollution and motor vehicle accidents. A child dies every thirty seconds from malaria for lack of a mosquito net. Although malaria deaths have decreased by 50 percent in many countries, it still kills nearly one million children annually in Africa alone; that is 2,800 deaths every day.

The World Health Organization estimates that more than two million children worldwide under age five die every year from diseases that could be prevented by vaccinations that are routine in other parts of the world. The leading cause of death in children younger than five is pneumonia, and the majority of these 1.7 million deaths could be prevented with adequate nutrition, sanitation, and the pneumococcal vaccine. Every day, more than 1,000 children die because they didn't get a fifteen-cent measles vaccine. Pertussis, or whooping cough, and neonatal tetanus are also in the top five preventable causes of children's deaths due to vaccine-preventable infectious diseases.

In Sierra Leone, an infant has more than a 25 percent chance of not living to five years of age, and many of those deaths are caused by tetanus. The tetanus toxin from environmental spores also kills 30,000 women in developing countries every year. Through the "1 Pack = 1 Vaccine" campaign between UNICEF and Proctor & Gamble, the goal to eradicate tetanus worldwide is well under way.

Another of UNICEF's goals is to prevent childhood mortality around the globe. The organization's "Believe in Zero" campaign is designed to illumine and mobilize human creativity, resolve, and resourcefulness. "Man took to flight when we believed," the advertisements say. "Children will stop dying from preventable causes when you believe. Every day, 19,000 children die of causes we can prevent. We believe that number should be ZERO."

Goodness To Go

Large-scale partnerships are required to increase global health and to decrease childhood deaths and poverty. In collaboration with philanthropic organizations, the Bill & Melinda Gates Foundation invests tremendous resources to address poverty, global health, and opportunity, believing that every person deserves the chance to lead healthy, productive lives. Poverty often leads to malnutrition, stunted educational opportunities, violence, and the breakdown of family and cultural values. When life-affirming values are disregarded, genocidal atrocities and brutal injustices devastate millions of lives. True human security is not possible in these situations.

Every child's life is equally valuable, and increased global investment in vaccinations is key to making major improvements in health. Currently, the United States invests only 0.2 percent of its gross domestic product in global health. Yet the long-term security of every country is affected by global health conditions. For example, it's crucial to address the population explosion with effective, humanitarian strategies. When impoverished mothers know that the children they bear will thrive past their fifth birthday, the birth rate naturally goes down. When mothers are educated to at least the seventh grade, they bear 2.2 fewer children.

There is a large body of evidence showing that education of girls contributes directly to the expansion of health, educational, and economic possibilities for her children and community as well as for herself. Even providing iodized salt can enhance a child's intelligence. Fetal brains, particularly those of females, do not develop properly without enough iodine, and they lose ten to fifteen IQ points as a result. Many pregnant women living in poverty don't get enough iodine, which costs only a couple of pennies per person per year.

Children's achievements are enhanced when their brains have had adequate nutrition during critical brain development periods, particularly during pregnancy and the first three years of life. Children are also more likely to reach their potential when parents read to them regularly and provide environments that encourage learning and enrichment activities, especially in the arts. High-quality preschooling does more for a child's chances in school and life than any other educational intervention. Limiting media exposure, teaching media as well as reading literacy, encouraging regular physical exercise, and developing a relationship with the natural environment are crucial elements of human development.

Music education is particularly valuable in brain development, and the importance of the "practice effect" is well documented. The effort and regular practice required to gain proficiency with a musical instrument develops perseverance, character, and the confidence to move from uncertainty to mastery. In addition to increasing psychological capacity, playing in ensembles, bands, and orchestras is fun and nurtures harmonious, collaborative social skills.

The wellness of our children affects us all, and growing networks of humanitarians are working to end child exploitation and trafficking. Government services in many countries provide free immunizations and public education. Coaches challenge athletes' perceived limits, and teachers sharpen critical thinking skills, strengthen resilience, and address bullying. Courageous truth-tellers speak up and shake up compliance with the status quo, reminding people of all ages that there is no such thing as an innocent bystander. Leaders enact laws upholding human rights and equitable justice. Student exchange programs, civic engagement, and service learning curricula as well as church missions provide opportunities for young people to experience other cultures and work together for the common good. This is the wellness we all need in the twenty-first century.

Gender Equity Is Essential

A prime directive for the twenty-first century is the establishment of full and equal human rights for girls and women. In many countries, females are dehumanized and their lives regarded as expendable. Many young girls are still being sold into bonded servitude, abused, beaten, and forced to work every waking hour. In societies around the world, the bodies of girls are regarded as resources that can be used for profit or pleasure by men. Every year, more than 14 million girls less than eighteen years of age are forced into child marriage; this means that thirteen girls in the past thirty seconds were entrapped in early marriage. Many of these girls die from complications of early pregnancies.

Although the education of girls has the highest investment return of all social or economic interventions, millions of girls are marginalized or excluded from receiving an education, India's gross domestic product (GDP) would increase by $5.5 billion per year if one percent more girls enrolled in secondary school. For conditions that perpetuate poverty and injustice to be transformed, humanity needs to fully awaken to the recognition of gender equity and to end all forms of oppression and violence toward girls and women.

Goodness To Go

Although women and their daughters hold up half the sky, domestic violence, female genital mutilation, bride burning, sexual harassment in the workplace, rape as a weapon of war, decreased educational and economic opportunities, and less pay for equal work continue. When a girl in a developing country receives seven or more years of education, she marries four years later, has at least two fewer children, and is twice as likely to educate her children. Every element of society benefits when the creative intelligence of half of its population is utilized and celebrated equally.

In 1995 at a women's world conference in Beijing, Hillary Rodham Clinton stated that human rights are women's rights and women's rights are human rights. Yet half a million girls are trafficked into the sex slave industry every year. These girls are victims, not criminals, and prostitution is dehumanizing to everyone involved. Prostitution does not end when criminal justice systems go after prostitutes or even their pimps. Several countries are enacting laws that charge the men who solicit sex in the flesh trade. Soon after these laws start to be enforced, the number of transactions involving prostitution drops substantially.

Worldwide, 100 million girls are involved in child labor. Due to multiple, anti-female practices in cultures across the globe, more girls died in the twentieth century than in all the wars combined. Aborting of female fetuses determined by ultrasound, selective infanticide, genocidal rape and torture, relationship violence, nutritional and educational neglect, and longer delays in seeking medical help for daughters than sons resulted in the untimely deaths of at least 100 million girls.

Gender inequity remains rampant in education and food distribution. Although some girls from impoverished families complete government-supported primary school education, most cannot afford the tuition or books for high school. For want of sanitary napkins, thousands of adolescent girls stop attending school.

The labor of girls, including gathering fuel and water and tending crops and children, is expected in millions of homes. If families can afford to send only one child to high school, a son is usually chosen. The best that the family can provide is frequently not given to the girl child. Numerous families around the world continue to believe that daughters were sent to support the family, not for their unique potential to be cultivated.

Girls and women do most of the world's work, and yet a disproportionate percentage of the world's poor are mothers and their daughters. An eleven-year-old girl from the United States visited Tanzania and was struck as much by the joy and generosity of the Tanzanian children as she was by their poverty. At sixteen, Ashley Schuler founded Africaid, which supports the secondary school education of girls in Tanzania as well as digital storytelling over the Internet of many voices that would otherwise not be heard. Through the assistance of organizations like Africaid, more girls are attending secondary school, and the first Masi girl to be accepted at medical school is now studying in Tanzania.

Research conducted by the London School of Economics determined that the greatest return on investments to reduce humans' carbon footprint had nothing to do with improved engineering or technological advances. There was a fivefold reduction for every dollar spent on educating young people about family planning. Educated girls marry later, have fewer children, and uplift the lives of their entire family. Positive effects ripple out into their community, too.

Recognition of the important impact that girls make—especially if they're educated and respected—is growing, and social movements are empowering young people around the world. The Girl Effect uses creative video animation to communicate that educating girls and including them in community development provides countless win-win economic solutions.

The education of girls everywhere is the revolution that we need now. Educating girls in developing nations will change the world by reducing poverty and disease and changing conditions that foster corruption and terrorism. A global social action campaign known as 10 x 10 Fund for Girls' Education invites us to invest in the education of adolescent girls in developing countries. The vision of 10 x 10 is "Educate Girls, Change the World." In 2013, their groundbreaking documentary titled *Girl Rising* showed the remarkable impact that education made in the lives of nine vulnerable, heroic girls from nine developing nations.

One of the girls in *Girl Rising* lives in Cambodia where the Khmer Rouge destroyed most advances in literacy, medical care, and civic life in the 1970s. Sohka was an orphan who survived by picking through garbage. Through miraculous good fortune, she eventually attended school and has risen from the ashes of the dump to being a star student on the brink of a brilliant future. *Girl Rising* champions the truth that *one girl with courage is a revolution.* One of the girls who was freed from bonded domestic slavery now works to free others. Actress Meryl Streep believes that this profound documentary delivers measurable, tangible hope that the education of girls helps to heal the world and create a better future for us all. Change is a song, a breath of hope, flowing through our lives.

Human development research emphasizes the importance of quality education, positive mentoring, and authentic social engagement. Virtual Facebook "friends" are real only when they've been met face-to-face; all Internet users need to be aware that on-line predatory and bullying behaviors have had deadly consequences. Healthy social interactions for young people include team sports, camps, and community service. Not only does the ongoing presence of meaningful, face-to-face relationships decrease risk behaviors such as drug use, driving under the influence of alcohol,and early sexual encounters, it enhances decision-making abilities and the likelihood that the young person will stay in school. The dissatisfaction of people of any age who feel socially isolated, on the other hand, can become dangerous to the safety of their communities as well as themselves.

Education—The Power to Transform

It is the birthright of every child to be educated. "Education is a human right with the immense power to transform," states the Global Education Fund. "On its foundation rest the cornerstones of freedom, democracy and sustainable human development." The word *education* comes from the Latin root *educare* meaning "to call forth." Education calls forth our inner goodness and wisdom, and includes training our ability to think critically and ethically as well as to read and write. We cannot afford to allow the purpose and power of education to be diminished. Educated, engaged citizens are vital to free, democratic nations. As Thomas Jefferson wrote, "If a nation expects to be ignorant and free, it expects something that never was, and never will be."

College tuition is prohibitive to most young people on earth, and students' minds have different learning capacities whose needs are not always met in traditional classrooms. A young Bengali American entrepreneur, Salman Kahn, created a free online education platform to reinvent ways young people can access learning opportunities. Deeply committed to making education available to people who want to take agency for their learning, Kahn wrote *The One World Schoolhouse*. His nonprofit Kahn Academy provides high-quality courses for students of all ages who have Internet access.

As part of the eight United Nations Millennium Development Goals, 189 countries pledged to ensure that children everywhere would have access to primary education by 2015. We have a long way to go. More than 61 million primary school aged children are not in school. Two-thirds of children in Guatemala do not graduate from sixth grade. One-third of Afghani children, mostly girls, are not in school, and most Afghani women are illiterate. The violence of the Taliban closed 600 schools in Afghanistan in 2008, targeting girls and disregarding the Islamic verse that states that education is the obligation of *every* person, male or female. Terrorists threatened by young students' potential power as independent thinkers throw acid in the faces of school girls to disfigure them and mutilate their fortitude. The profoundly resilient courage of these girls will endure and the power of their resolve will prevail.

In Brazil, the poorest children complete only four years of school on average, and two-thirds of all children drop out by the eighth grade. Stipends to families whose children stay in school are beginning to change some of these trends. Even in wealthier countries like Germany and the United States, the quality of education is declining substantially. In parts of the United States, fewer than half of all students graduate from high school, and only ten percent are actually prepared to start college without remediation.

Many educators emphasize that young people need to know not just *what* to think but *how* to think, and on what principles ethical behavior is based. The Nazi SS officer Adolf Eichmann dutifully murdered millions of innocent people in concentration camps, regarding himself as an educated, disciplined man who was proud of doing a "good" job: trains ran on time and quotas were met efficiently. He also ordered the deceptive, temporary transformation of the Terezin concentration camp into the facade of a Jewish-run "town" to fool representatives from the International Red Cross. Repeatedly, history has shown us that inculcating blind obedience is extremely harmful.

One of several organizations offering curricula that engage young global citizens in humanitarian service is Heifer International. Its online service learning program, *Get It!* (Global Education to Improve Tomorrow), provides standards-based academic units to learn about sustainable solutions to end world hunger and poverty. Other acclaimed educational programs of Heifer International, including *Read to Feed* and *Chores for Change*, give students ways to initiate chain reactions of positive change around the world. Heifer International's most widely known programs provide impoverished families with a renewable source of food: "living loans" of goats, chickens, and other animals include the training to take care of them and the agreement to pass on those animals' off-spring to other families in need. Heifer also works in creative partner-ships to combat world hunger and improve global health. One program offers veterinary student opportunities in public health, increasing vol-unteerism and research projects in developing nations.

Nearly 50 percent of the African population is under the age of eigh-teen, and many face tremendous problems of disease, poverty, and en-vironmental degradation. To address these problems with sustainable solutions, programs that develop new generations of African leaders is necessary. In 2002, Educate! was founded in Uganda by Eric Glustrom, a young American whose activist mother was one of his mentors. Educate! has received numerous international awards for its innovative model that's been embraced by the government of Uganda and can be replicat-ed across Africa. It includes a proven mix of a leadership and social en-trepreneurship courses, long-term mentoring, practical experience solv-ing problems in communities, and an alumni program that helps high school students launch social business enterprises.

Integral Education

A leading innovator in higher education, Liz Coleman, Ph.D., became the president of Bennington College in 1987. Her integral vision for the liberal arts and their role and reinvigoration in society has led to many of her vanguard educational missions. One of these is the Center for the Advancement of Public Action, which invites students to put the world's most pressing problems at the center of their education. To her students and to audiences around the world, Dr. Coleman emphasizes the impor-tant connections between the development of our heart and mind with our civic values and engagement. She states: "We've scarcely begun to tap into our intellectual, imaginative, and ethical resources. Imagine what will happen if we do? Imagine what will happen if we do not?"

Nearly every one of us has benefitted from the experience and practical knowledge of teachers and mentors who believed in us. Recall some of the teachers who have impacted your life in beneficial ways. A collection of inspirational stories from educators is entitled *Today I Made a Difference.* Although mentoring young people can be very challenging at times, it leads to the maturation and growth of the teacher as well as the student.

In many countries, poverty and the increasing violence of fundamen-talist extremists have had serious negative effects on the educational opportunities of children. When Saeed Malik returned to Pakistan after decades of working with the United Nations' World Food Program, he was disheartened by the state of elementary education. Few public schools had libraries and children were not being introduced to other worlds of learning. "In what way can we bring these kids back to the beauty of life, to the beauty of the future?" Malik asked. Feeling that books were the way to broaden children's minds, he founded the Bright Star Mobile Library, which serves thousands of Pakistani children.

Developing an inner moral code and learning to act with integrity are key developmental tasks of all young people. Bullying is a pervasive problem and renowned educational consultant Barbara Coloroso has addressed this serious issue for decades. Coloroso inspires communities around the world to empower their children to handle conflict nonviolently and to do what is right. She encourages parents and teachers to provide supportive consistency and structure. "Take the weapons out of the hearts, minds, and hands of our kids," Coloroso teaches, and "give them the tools to stand up for their own rights while respecting the rights of others."

Educators are empowering young people to speak up in the present moment against bullying and other injustices. Although effective interventions that prevent children from resorting to bullying behavior may take decades, some useful tools have been developed that break cycles of violence that begin with bullying. These tools and resources include having a strong sense of self, critical thinking and social skills, support systems, and developing the disciplines of restitution, resolution, and reconciliation. Bullying manifests a dehumanizing contempt for another that has led to murder and suicide. Many young people who've experienced this form of violence have joined the Teen Angels movement and share their insights to empower other students.

Mass media are elements of young peoples' education and it's instructive to note what citizens will tolerate in the media influencing the minds of both children and adults. Accurate information is offered through high quality public television and radio broadcasts that educate us and mobilize our concern. One PBS program challenged viewers to consider the source of the refined sugar that they enjoy on a daily basis. Video footage of children wielding machetes in Guatemalan sugarcane fields included an interview with an exhausted young boy. His growth was stunted from malnutrition, his workday started at 3 a.m., and he was not able to attend school. Recent import treaties seek to address some of these social issues and improve the working conditions and wages of people struggling to survive. Citizens around the globe are insisting that fair trade laws and business practices be equitable and humane.

The quality of young people's education has a huge impact, not only on their personal lives but on the health of their communities and the planet. Rather than the rote learning of old paradigms, indoctrinating children with fundamentalism and extremism, blind obedience, or offering only job training, an optimal education enriches and calls forth the unique gifts and inner light of each learner. With our compassion, wisdom, and resolve, the roadblocks and restraints that prevent children from shining their light in this world will be removed.

The Courage of Youth Is a Revolution

Although there are many points of light and songs of hope, children in every corner of the world continue to be abused, exploited, and oppressed. Frustrated, uneducated, unemployed youth are easy targets for recruitment by violent gangs, terrorist groups, and militia. To empower new generations of leaders as social agents for beneficial change, it's most efficacious to do *with*, not *for*, young people.

The goodness to go of many young people is changing beliefs and behavior that entrench generation after generation in poverty. As a boy, Teju Ravilochan asked a question that changed his life. Born in Colorado to physician parents, Teju first visited relatives in India when he was about ten years of age. While shopping for clothes in a market with his father, a young boy in rags begged for money, and Teju's father gave the boy some rupees. Bewildered, Teju asked why the boy was begging. Not fully satisfied with the gentle explanation his father gave, Teju said: "You and Mother are doctors that help bodies to heal. Is there a doctor for poverty?" At that moment, he vowed to devote his life to empowering people to lift themselves out of poverty. After university training in international affairs, Ravilochan joined the Unreasonable Institute, which gives wings to social entrepreneurs, many of whom are from impoverished communities around the world.

Is there a doctor for poverty? Investment in young people gives great returns. If you could change the world, what would you do first? Central questions that may shape your response are: Is what I want to do truly good? Is it good for the earth and my community as well as for my family and myself? Our intent *to be good* may have the clearest integrity when we're fully committed to being present with things as they are. Very naturally, the next best step will present itself.

The enthusiasm and empathy of young children flows into their communities. A ten-year-old girl, Katie Stagliano, donated a forty-pound cabbage that she'd grown to a homeless shelter. Two days later, Katie returned to help serve the 275 meals to which she'd contributed. Never feeling so good in her life, Katie thought: "Wow, with one cabbage I helped feed that many people? I could do much more." A year later, she had a crew of volunteers and numerous gardens that donated thousands of pounds of vegetables to feed the hungry.

Parents, teachers, and community members catalyze and nurture young people's motivation to transform inequity, strengthen habits of empathy, learn about social issues, and develop tools for informed action. Apathy becomes empathy. The despair of abused, oppressed girls is galvanized into resolve. Fear becomes will. Empowered voices and the song of change are the beginning of a new story of equity in Afghanistan, India, Africa, and beyond. The transformative power of young people's integral service will uplift lives for generations to come.

Most of us have experienced that a kind mentor is invaluable in our personal development and in the early engagement of our goodness to go. A lawyer who has volunteered legal aid and international service for decades has early memories of helping her mother at a local orphanage. A five-year-old girl in Canada was upset after seeing a homeless person foraging in an alley garbage can and asked her mother about his plight. With her parents' support, Hannah Taylor went on to become a community organizer, spokesperson, and fundraising founder of the Ladybug Foundation, raising millions to fund shelters and programs for the homeless.

A delightful tale familiar to millions of young people is Winnie the Pooh written by A. A. Milne. About Piglet, one of the gentle bear's friends, he observed, "Piglet was so excited at the idea of being Useful that he forgot to be frightened any more." The moment when fear dissolves into love and the generous willingness to be of service is one to honor with joy. At every age, we can learn to trust the flow of goodness, even when our external resources seem less abundant. Fresh and timeless stories of informed, integral service exemplify how virtually everyone can participate in the natural cycles of giving and receiving.

Goodness To Go

The Millennial Generation Is Mobilizing

Generation We, also known as the millennial generation or Gen Y, typically refers to people born in the mid-1970s through the early 2000s. This group has grown up with the World Wide Web, collaborative models, and awareness of the importance of transparency. They've seen the waste of time and resources inherent in narcissism marked by rampant materialism, entitlement, and self-absorption.

The virtues of simple living, free of obsessive acquisition of material goods, are striking a chord with this environmentally aware, socially conscious generation. Creating community, serving globally, and making a positive impact are important to Generation We. Students who volunteer with Engineers Without Borders and other humanitarian organizations partner with communities in developing nations to develop sustainable solutions that improve the quality of life while respecting local culture. On campuses, the Peace Corps recruits students of all ages, asking, "Life is calling. How far will you go?"

Across the globe, many university students engage in philanthropic endeavors. Numerous college campuses have chapters of Global Medical Brigades, the world's largest student-led international relief organization. A bioengineering graduate launched a nonprofit business to train unemployed, nonviolent offenders and homeless people in construction techniques to rebuild New Orleans. Teen activists are connecting through social networks of student action groups, current environmental issues, eco-careers, funding opportunities, and green college curricula.

Reverence for nature and awareness of the interconnected web of life are awakening in the hearts and minds of people young and old. Ecologists using advanced computer computations predict the extinction of one million species by 2050. The National Environmental Education Foundation sponsors the Apprentice Ecologist Initiative, one of several scholarship and award programs that engages youth in environmental cleanup projects. Environmental stewardship and conservation are natural facets of world custodianship. *As above, so below.* As the health and beauty of the biosphere is replenished, the human spirit is resuscitated.

One of many organizations supporting youth engagement in urgent social and planetary issues is PeaceJam, founded in 1996. Members of PeaceJam's board of directors include Nobel laureates who serve as mentors and partners for socially engaged young people. A PeaceJam kindergarten-through-college peace curriculum has been developed, and the high school curriculum emphasizes geopolitical and systemic thinking that addresses the root causes of poverty and inequity.

PeaceJam's Global Call to Action that was launched in 2006 hopes to inspire one billion acts of service related to racism, extreme poverty, and environmental degradation over the next ten years. This inspiring initiative dovetails with the United Nations Millennium Development Goals supporting genuine human security, which cannot be accomplished through military force. PeaceJam's Global Call to Action is impacting communities one by one. In New Mexico, young volunteers started an after-school literacy program and distributed donated books throughout their community to offices and organizations serving children.

The PeaceJam club at a Colorado middle school filled 100 donated backpacks in time for Christmas with gifts for teenagers living in a local homeless shelter. Young social entrepreneurs are sharing their positive ideas and sending their creativity along the "holy river" of the Internet. Project YES (Youth Envisioning Social Change) has developed videos on teen pregnancy, public bus art focused on gun violence, and posters about recycling to hang in bus stands. Global Response helps to protect human and environmental rights through letter-writing campaigns to government and corporate representatives. Global Response has found that the action alert letters written by young people are especially able to touch the hearts of the recipients.

Letter writing is an example of the first level of youth engagement, termed *youth voice*. The next level is *youth influence*, where deep listening to concerns and ideas suggested by young people affects policy makers. The most challenging, powerful, and beneficial level is *youth decision making*, where young people have an equal vote with the involved adults. Young people have a right to be involved in decisions that will affect them. The United Nations Convention on the Rights of the Child has declared that youth decision-making is a social justice issue.

Young people, as well as those young at heart, yearn for meaningful, authentic engagement in issues that affect their lives and their world. Parents, teachers, community workers, and health-care providers will continue to serve the next generation by inspiring, mentoring, and supporting the natural altruism of young people to make a difference. We can't afford not to support the next generation to develop effective ways to tackle the world's problems. Consider what concrete resources, roles, or actions you could offer to young people as we create our shared legacy of peace and prosperity.

Light tomorrow with today. "Our children are our only hope for the future, but we are their only hope for their present and their future," wrote Zig Ziglar, a World War II veteran who nurtured optimism for decades after that war through his speeches and books. *Hope sings the tune and never stops.* Commitment to personal transformation catalyzes social and environmental metamorphosis. Enthusiastic change-makers of all ages are summoning their courage to connect, inspire, and collaborate on numerous global issues, from environment and education to community media and social justice. The world may be in a dire state but our ship need not sink. With the life-affirming impact of our goodness to go, we'll co-create our shared future. This is a time when we truly need all hands on deck, including the enthusiastic spirits and compassionate hearts of our youth. Let's all live in ways that show young people everywhere that their future matters.

Pause, Reflect, and Record

- Regardless of our age, each of us can find our purpose and bring more light into the world. How might you shine as a beacon of inspiration? In what ways could you share your gifts with those around you?

- If you're a member of the millennial generation, what social issue especially affects or calls you? What do you sense is the purpose of your life? How could you reimagine the world you're inheriting for twenty-first-century living?

- If you're over thirty, how might you inspire possibility in the life of a young person and in yourself?

- Political activist Emma Goldman has said that the most violent element in society is ignorance. In what circumstances have you noticed attitudes or behaviors that reflect this notion?

- How do we nurture a generation of global citizens committed to mutual respect, ethical justice, generosity, and sustainability?

42

Mother Activism

*We live in a world that does not prioritize or protect
our children's well being. ... This will not change
without each of us finding the courage and commitment
to speak out on their behalf. ...We will protect our children
with our personal and political strength,
wherever they live on earth!*

—Mothers Acting Up

The mothers of the world have enormous power to mobilize goodness to go. We'll define a mother as anyone who advocates for or exercises protective care of children. Regardless of our gender or whether our body physically birthed a child, we can all be mother activists. Caring for young members of the human family is often transformational, awakening our empathy in compelling calls to action. The feminine principle in both women and men is especially involved in the caring protection and nurturance of children and the earth. Our gifts of love, time, and energy are fresh drops of rain in a monsoon of compassion that can support the blossoming of every child on earth.

Individual mothers have vastly different challenges and resources available in their lives. Some pray for relief from dire poverty. Millions struggle to survive in the midst of civil wars and refugee camps. The bodies and lives of young girls forced into child marriage are literally split; after brief, wretched lives, many girl children die giving birth. Girls and women around the globe suffer from the trauma of violence and rape, are oppressed by racial and gender inequity or are illiterate due to lack of educational opportunities. A mother may be financially secure but have a severely handicapped child. Some mothers, driven to provide the best possible of everything for their children, are drained and debilitated by "mother guilt" that they're not doing enough.

It's likely that if you're a mother, you've felt so tired at the end of the day that you can't imagine how to summon the energy to serve outside the demands of your immediate family. On any given day, only you know what you're capable of in the moment. It's not helpful to compare or judge or allow guilt to stifle your spirit, uselessly wasting precious life energy.

Bringing light to our shadow places is important inner work for humanitarians. To move from emotional turmoil to clarity, it's helpful to engage in regular self-care and therapeutic inquiry that frees us from toxic attachment to perfectionistic expectations. The mobilization of our goodness is possible when we give ourselves permission to let go of the snares and shadows of impossible demands.

Hardwired for Web Thinking

Mothers' brains often think differently, and sleep deprivation and hormone changes are not the only reasons. Male and female brains have neurological, hormonal, and anatomic differences. Human brains have gone through periods of intense evolutionary pressure over millennia. A significant shift occurred when human agriculture began. Instead of moving with the seasons to gather food, humans began to experience the increased food security that accompanies a surplus of grain. The illusion that humans could control nature beguiled us. Women and mothers were associated with the natural world, and gradually a patriarchal system became dominant. Through evolutionary advantage, women's brains became particularly adept at emotional connectivity, nonlinear holistic thinking, and community building.

Both linear and nonlinear styles of thinking have merit, and together the ability to address global issues is exponentially increased. Men often like to focus on what they consider relevant, which is a useful propensity developed thousands of years ago as they hunted game. They "get to the point" in a more linear progression called "step thinking" by biological anthropologist Helen Fisher. This logical, linear thinking occurs more often in the left hemisphere. Of course, this is a simplification of complex neurologic processes, and there are many women who are left-brain dominant. "Right brained thinking" is regarded as an almost holographic kind of intelligence that includes creativity, imagination, emotion, and intuition. Fisher describes a familiar way that women process information as "web thinking," an integrative approach that collects and assembles more data into more complex patterns and weighs more options as decisions are made.

The natural aptitude of web thinkers, female and male, for social networking, collaboration, and creative long-term planning is crucial at this global crossroad. Communication through the World Wide Web is one manifestation of humanity's calling forth of divergent thinking, integrative skills, and interconnectivity. The social commentator Harriet Rubin coined the term *mamisma* as the mature, nurturing qualities of the feminine principle. It's available to anyone, willing to choose empathy, inclusion, and caring protection over exclusion and aggression. Third millennial leadership calls for the integration of both step and web thinking as well as both masculine and feminine principles.

Mothers everywhere are extending their care giving beyond hearth and home. As mentioned in Section Three, women in more than 190 countries are using internet cafes and cell phones to speak out from urban streets to rural villages. The action media network World Pulse connects women worldwide in an online community that empowers vocal uprisings, increases global awareness, and inspires social actions that are transforming the world.

More than 15 million baby boomer women are experiencing radical changes as they navigate their midlife transitions. A study by Ronald Lee, a demographer at the University of California at Berkeley, found that natural selection has a basis to favor genes that promote post-reproductive longevity. The protection of grandmothers has been essential for generations of dependent children during their extended developmental stages. This "grandmother effect" is recognized as a source of power and sway in our evolutionary heritage. The wisdom and *mamisma* of today's grandmothers is a great resource around the globe.

Women's Rights Are Human Rights

Female human beings are the biological mothers of us all. The shadow side of patriarchy has enforced many systemic injustices that oppress, discriminate against, and degrade the dignity of women and their children. Globally, there are 150 million victims of sexual violence each year and half of all sexual assaults are against girls less than fifteen years of age. Due to entrenched cultural expectations, almost half of Indian girls are married before their eighteenth birthday; policies prohibiting child marriage have been in place since 1973 but national and international human rights agreements are not being enforced. Other factors that contribute to the oppression of girls and women are political and religious repression, corporate greed, institutionalized poverty, environmental plunder, militarization, and media dehumanization.

The practice of child marriage must end; it crushes girls' opportunities and usually burdens their children with malnutrition, ongoing poverty, and poor health. In the Middle East, sub-Saharan Africa, South Asia, and in many other developing regions, 14 million girls under the age of eighteen are forced into child marriages every year. Dangerous, early pregnancies and cultural oppression deprive them of educational opportunities to fulfill their potential. Young mothers in India are 100 times more likely to die during childbirth than women in Europe and the United States.

To protect their children and their children's children, mothers must have power in the world as well as their homes. Empowerment is particularly effective if it begins in childhood. Women's contributions strengthen economies and thereby reduce poverty for millions. Labor export policies and lack of access to start-up business microloans often crush the potential of women entrepreneurs in developing nations. Yet it's been recognized for years that the rising tide of a dynamic, sustainable economy that includes women equitably lifts all boats in beneficial ways.

Many brilliant minds collaborated to write the U.S. Constitution in 1787, a model of cooperative statesmanship declaring that all people are created equal and are endowed with inalienable rights; liberty is the keystone. In the 1860s, the revolutionary thinker John Stuart Mill wrote about the importance of women's full political engagement. It's astonishing to recall that the suffragette movement in the democratic United States fought tirelessly for decades to legalize the basic freedom of women's right to vote. Early in the twentieth century, a powerful letter from the mother of one male politician inspired him to vote in favor of the Nineteenth Amendment to the U.S. Constitution, which granted women the right to vote. His was the single vote that succeeded in breaking the tie on August 26, 1920. This landmark date continues to be recognized as Women's Equality Day in the United States, although the social movement ensuring equal rights for women is not finished.

Susan B. Anthony and many other formidable, often scorned suffragettes worked for many years to increase the possibilities for all women, recognizing that many lives would be changed by this victory. "Pass on and go on with the work" were Anthony's final words. Just a few years later, a devoted mother and public servant did just that. Although she has slipped into historical oblivion, Mrs. Frances Perkins changed the landscape of American business and society by designing President Franklin D. Roosevelt's New Deal.

In the wealthiest nation on earth, the simple justice of gender equity is long overdue. In 1923, Alice Paul and the National Women's Party introduced the Equal Rights Amendment (ERA) proposing that equality of rights under the law shall not be denied on account of sex. The ERA is not yet in the U.S. Constitution. Another basic human rights issue is that women and their children are not the property of men. Not until the publication of Gloria Steinem's Ms. magazine in the 1970s did the issue of domestic or relationship violence receive widespread recognition.

In March of 2013, the Violence Against Women Act (VAWA), championed for years by Illinois senator Richard Durbin, was signed into U.S. law. Language was included that prioritized the ending of child marriage around the world. The VAWA provides a comprehensive approach for the issues of domestic violence, including protections for the abused women and holding perpetrators accountable for their crimes.

Social and medical researchers investigate "the burdens of being female." The bodies of girls and women belong to them; they're not commodities to be sold by men for profit or to abuse for "pleasure" or feelings of "power." At least one in four women has been raped. The horrendous practice of female genital mutilation continues. In the past, women's feet have been broken and painfully bound into nearly dysfunctional mutilation. Young brides are maimed or murdered by members of their husband's families, and women are still being publicly tortured to death due to false accusations by "dishonored" egos of male family members.

For centuries, trafficking of girls and women has continued to be an inhumane and pandemic injustice. Nearly half of trafficked victims are used for forced commercial sexual exploitation. An estimated 1.2 million children are trafficked each year from 127 countries to be exploited in 137 countries. Every continent and every type of economy in affected. Silence and lack of advocacy are grievous errors of omission, making abused victims feel trapped and alone. The negative cultural impact of pervasive media violence and degradation of women is a toxic environmental hazard. We're all called to join the global movement to end violence against our mothers and grandmothers, daughters, sisters, spouses, and friends.

One Billion Rising is the largest mass global action in the history of humankind to end violence against women and girls. Through media exposure, discourse, and advocacy, these warriors of compassion are creating global solidarity and strength as they cut across borders, races, classes, genders, sexual orientations, and religions. One Billion Rising also has been a catalyst for millions of women to become social media journalists with small cameras recording their narratives of abuse, humiliation, and rising sense of empowerment, community support, and restorative justice.

In 2009, Nobel Peace laureate Shirin Ebadi, J.D. gave the keynote speech at a conference held in Boulder, Colorado on women's leadership in the Muslim world. Dr. Ebadi is a lawyer who founded the Center for the Defense of Human Rights in Iran, working for the rights of women, children, and refugees, as well as those of persecuted religious minorities in Iran.

Dr. Ebadi reminded conference participants that nearly one-sixth of the world's population is Muslim and that their civilization is based on principles of peace and tranquility. The traditional Muslim greeting (Assalamu alaykum) means "May peace be upon you." Ebadi described how she has managed to overcome the fear inherent to activism in Iran. "I cannot get tired or lose hope. I cannot afford to do that. I have learned how to control fear and not allow it to affect my work."

According to Dr. Ebadi and others, the Islamic religion is not opposed to human rights. However, distorted interpretations of its teachings are used by fundamentalists and several nondemocratic Muslim states to justify severe discrimination against women. Dictators interpret Islam in self-serving ways that brutally oppress their subjects. Since many Islamic dictators refuse to give citizenship to women, it's nearly impossible for half of their population to get basic human rights, or even to be regarded as citizens.

Economic independence is a freedom that has inestimable value to individuals and countries. Societies today cannot rebuild strong economies without strong women. How many have been forced to remain in abusive marriages because they were denied opportunities for educational empowerment and economic independence? In countries torn apart by war, violence destroys trust and silences women's voices. Yet it is women who are essential in the behind-the-scenes delivery of peace as well as in more public leadership roles. In 2005, Ellen Johnson Sirleaf became Liberia's president and Africa's only female head of state after years of civil war. Under her leadership, Liberia has been rebuilt and reborn with its debt reduced, industries thriving, and school enrollment increased by 40 percent.

A young Iraqi woman, Zainab Salbi, is the daughter of the personal pilot who worked for Saddam Hussein when he controlled Iraq. Salibi's mother strongly encouraged her daughter's education so that she would not "become a prisoner" in the traditional female role in Iraqi society. Salibi went on to found the Washington-based group Women for Women International, which helps female victims of war reclaim their voices and receive microcredit loans as well as direct aid.

Gender Equality and Socialization

Abject poverty is the absence of all human rights. Research has shown repeatedly that a child's chances of success in school and life depend more on family circumstances than on any other factor. Although economic recessions, corrupt governments, and dwindling middle classes strain families further, educating all children will change the world. Cultural customs and expectations about the value of educating girls can change, resulting in increased shared prosperity for families, communities, and nations.

Gender inequity is one of the most crucial human rights issues of our time, and economic equity is implicit within the vision for global gender equity. In their Pulitzer Prize–winning book, *Half the Sky: Turning Oppression into Opportunity for Women Worldwide*, Nicholas Kristof and Sheryl WuDunn challenge readers to act on behalf of gender equality. Women make up 51 percent of the world's population, perform 66 percent of the world's work, earn 19 percent of the world's income, and own only one percent of the world's property.

At this point in the human story, why does the labor of people doing most of the world's work usually go unpaid? In many countries, women and children are still at the bottom of economic and social pyramids, with few opportunities and many significant barriers to self-determination. Global gender inequities in economic as well as social and political realms must change in order to create a just, sustainable world for our children's children.

In *The Invisible Heart*, Nancy Folbre, Ph.D., wrote about the contribution of women's unpaid labor to global economies. Although the book's title is a play on the term "the invisible hand" used in old economic theory, we live in a time when a person's contributions should not be forced to be invisible, unrecognized, or unpaid because of gender. The good news is that gender equality is growing in many areas of the world and the underutilized resource of women's economic, spiritual, and cognitive contributions is beginning to blossom.

Corporate monopolies that own media sources control vast sums of money and power to influence society's gender socialization. It's almost a marketing "given" that action heroes are boys or, at times, voluptuous girls scantily clad. Women's body parts are used to sell billions of dollars of consumer products, extending far beyond the familiar markets of automobile and beer sales. The vast majority of CEOs, board members, and owners of print media, film studios, and television, cable, and radio networks are men.

Women advocates and supportive male allies are increasing societal awareness about gender socialization that is harming both boys and girls. Many hours a day, media influence young people's values and perceptions of themselves and their culture; unregulated violence and dehumanizing objectification of women are potent elements in the toxic socialization of our children. The documentary film *Miss Representation* explores how the disparaging portrayals of women circulated by mainstream media contribute to women's under-representation in influential positions.

Mothers are taking a stand for increasing the media literacy of their children and all citizens. They're watching programs, movies, and advertisements with their children and asking probing questions: Why is the young woman wearing such a revealing outfit when she's rescuing someone? How would having more female protagonists alter this story? What subliminal message does this commercial give when it only shows the woman's buttocks and not her face? Could the gender violence of this video game exploit, objectify, and dehumanize the girls and women? Might that affect your thoughts and behaviors involving girls and women? The media will reflect new, life-affirming messages when we awaken our discernment, align our purchasing power with our core values, and consciously choose what we allow into our minds, heart, and bodies.

Empowered Women Are Empowered Citizens

The twenty-first century has been called the Century of Women. "The future of the world depends on women," declared Kofi Annan who was the secretary-general of the United Nations from 1997 to 2006. In a research report in 2007, Goldman Sachs wrote that more women entering the workforce had been the "single biggest driver" of the Eurozone's labor market success. Unfortunately, the following year saw the near collapse of global economies driven by dubious policies of over-leveraged financial institutions.

Although social equity and women's movements continue to make gradual progress after periods of backlash and stagnation, there is still a dearth of women in positions of power. Women have not made true progress in corporate America over the past decade: only 14 percent of executive officers, 18 percent of elected congressional officials, and twenty-two of 197 heads of state are women. In Sheryl Sandberg's book, *Lean In: Women, Work, and the Will to Lead,* the chief operating officer of Facebook aims to empower women with some of the tools and guidance they need to keep moving forward in the workforce.

Many cultures continue to imprint a sense of limits on girls and women. The illumination and expansion of actual possibilities is our marvelous task as we nurture and advocate for one another. Basic social support structures can make all the difference in a woman's life. For example, affordable quality childcare is an important safety net that needs to be more accessible to mothers who work outside the home, especially those earning minimum wage.

Growing numbers of mothers who advocate on behalf of all the world's children are attuning to the Native American adage to "live with the future of seven generations in mind." Most wisdom traditions recognize our responsibility to generations coming after us. It's imperative that young people receive healthy, nutritious food, protection, and ongoing educational opportunities that will prepare them for life as empowered citizens and wise role models for their children and grandchildren.

Being marginalized due to gender inequality as well as inadequate resources doubly challenges mothers living in poverty. In many cultures, girl children are taught to feel like worthless burdens to society. However, their voices are key in the creation of equitable societies, sustainable solutions to domestic violence, child marriage, illness and injury caused by lack of safe, efficient cook stoves, and political injustice are needed. Vocal empowerment workshops, alternative global media, and other programs are increasing women's opportunities and confidence to speak their truth. The wave of uprisings in Arab countries in the past few years have revealed their desire for more democratic governance and a revolution in women's leadership.

Extreme poverty and gender inequity are inextricably linked, and the combination is particularly disempowering. One of many organizations working for change serves in the Kibera slum of Nairobi, Kenya.

Shining Hope for Communities is funded by actor Paul Newman's philanthropic foundation and uplifts over 30,000 people living in miserable conditions. The organization's free school for girls provides education, discipline, and food for children living on slum streets and involves the entire community in the fight for gender equity. Shining Hope for Communities' programs provide many local jobs and include a health clinic, water, hygiene, and gender violence support programs, microloans, and community gardens.

For decades, UN consultants, nongovernmental organizations, and international aid efforts have worked in developing countries, and much has been learned about which poverty-eradication strategies are effective and sustainable. One tangible issue being addressed is access to clean water and the declaration that it's time for *head carrying* to end. Resource-poor girls and women around the world spend hours every day to search for safe water and sticks of wood for fuel. Valuable time that could be spent on education or business ventures is used to carry heavy loads on their heads. Girls and women are not beasts of burden.

These time-consuming, exhausting excursions prevent girls from attending school and are fraught with the fear of sexual assault. Countless rapes of young girls occur in the bush as they seek fuel and safe water for their families. We can bring the era of mandatory head carrying to an end. When affordable safe water and renewable energy sources are available, many options open to families; their daughters can be educated and change the world. Deforestation can be reversed. Clean water delivery systems and affordable, safe energy lead to the end of head carrying, increased opportunities for economic development, and the empowerment of millions of girls and women.

Development programs supported by Women for Women International recognize that "regardless of where they come from or what their circumstances may be, mothers everywhere share the same hopes and dreams: to have the means to take care of themselves and their families, to live with dignity and self-respect, and to leave the world a better place than they found it." When Oprah Winfrey's television audience learned about the opportunities provided by Women for Women International for women in war-torn areas, thousands of contributors immediately acted to support its programs and help women rebuild their lives.

Advocating for the World's Children

"There is no trust more sacred than the one the world holds with children," wrote the former UN secretary-general Kofi Annan. "There is no duty more important than ensuring that their rights are respected, that their welfare is protected, and that their lives are free from fear and want and that they grow up in peace."

In this new millennium, we're all asked to respond to the challenge of caring for future generations and creating environments that foster dignity and respect for all beings. In 1989, the United Nations Convention on the Rights of the Child declared the fundamental dignity of every child. Although human rights apply to all age groups, children have additional rights that recognize their particular vulnerability and special needs for protection from discrimination, neglect, and abuse. Children are not the property of families and they have the right to develop their full potential, free from hunger and want, neglect, and abuse.

All children need the assurance that playing or working in a field won't set off a land mine that tears off limbs or kills them. Recent estimates of war casualties inform us that 90 percent are civilians, and that 70 percent of these civilian casualties are women and children. In many areas of oppression and violence, women have had enough fear, enough of not knowing what has happened to "disappeared" family members, and more than enough recruitment of their children as soldiers. Mothers are learning that promises of job opportunities in the city are lies: their daughters are being trafficked as sex slaves. Illiterate mothers who were child brides themselves want more opportunities for their daughters, and they're desperate to nourish their children with enough calories, protein, and clean water.

Mothers especially recognize the imperative of our needs for multiple securities. Recognizing that "security" is a fluid, holistic dynamic and not a permanent guarantee, some of the needs for security that all people share are economic, food, water, health care, educational, environmental, personal, community, and political security. Effective control of violent gangs and government corruption is as important as having sufficient calories or access to health care.

Mother leadership that advocates for children worldwide is imperative to the healing of communities suffering from multiple systemic injustices. Initiatives to eradicate child exploitation, sex slavery, and all forms of forced labor are developing effective strategies and gaining momentum in social and political realms. How might you participate in the global movement for the right of every human being to be free?

Global Go-Givers

Mothers long for an equitable peace for all. Once activated and mobilized, mother advocates contribute a huge global impact that is unstoppable. A Central American indigenous grandmother, Flordemayo, resounds, "Prophecy states that women will walk with the power." The Dalai Lama has spoken directly about the importance of women in the revitalization of the world. Mothers yearning for peace and protesting social problems take stands and start movements that benefit generations to come.

On March 8, 1857, garment workers in New York City staged a protest against inhumane working conditions and low wages, eventually creating the first women's labor union. With the slogan "Bread and Roses," 15,000 women marched in New York City on March 8, 1908, for the end of child labor, shorter work hours, better pay, and voting rights. "Bread" symbolized economic security and "roses" represented better living conditions. Since 1911, March 8 has been recognized as International Women's Day, celebrated by rallies and gatherings around the globe. Women's rights are human rights and every human being deserves to live and work in humane conditions.

After the horrors of prolonged civil war, a young woman named Leymah Gbowee decided that enough was enough and founded Women of Liberia Mass Action for Peace. Through years of determination and daily service, the influence of this nonviolent movement resulted in the removal of military dictator Charles Taylor from power and the signing of a comprehensive peace treaty in 2003. In 2011, this resolute mother became a Nobel Peace laureate before she turned forty.

The vision and remarkable courage of another young mother, Wangari Maathai, led her to found the Green Belt Movement, resulting in the planting of 35 million trees in deforested Kenya. Ravaged forests resulted in loss of topsoil and depleted waterways. Hunger and poverty led to violent conflicts over dwindling natural resources. Maathai endured beatings from Kenya's corrupt dictatorship and risked the safety of her three children as she empowered her people through community gatherings and the Green Belt Movement; she also fought the good fight against abuses of civil rights and degradation of the natural environment. Maathai had attended a Catholic boarding school for twelve years, and said, "I wanted to do good, like the Catholic nuns," she said.

460

Maathai's leadership expanded the possibilities for Kenyan women and their families for generations to come. In 2004, she was awarded the Nobel Peace Prize for the enduring social and environmental legacy that she gave the world. In her Nobel acceptance speech, Maathai said: "As the first African woman to receive this prize, I accept it on behalf of the people of Kenya and Africa, and indeed the world. I am especially mindful of women and the girl child. I hope it will encourage them to raise their voices and take more space for their leadership." There is a powerful documentary about Wangari Maathai's life work entitled *Taking Root*.

Julie Shaw, a co-founder of the Urgent Action Fund for Women's Human Rights, declares, "I'm the undying optimist, the unabashed believer in the strength and capacity of women's movements." The Urgent Action Fund is known for its rapid response grants defending human rights. One of the organization's publications, *What's the Point of Revolution if We Can't Dance?*, is rich with personal experiences of more than 100 activists from around the world, and calls for a revolution within activism that will ensure strong, passionate sustainability for activists and humanitarian movements.

Humanitarian citizens around the globe make the interdependence revolution possible. After visiting rural Mali in 2002, Karen Cunningham Marx founded the Mali Assistance Project in response to the dire lack of food remaining for the village that had hosted her. Some of her story is included in Chapter 5 of *Goodness To Go*. In 2003, Marx negotiated with many of the factions involved in the actualization of the dream to drill 300-foot wells reaching deep aquifers that were desperately needed by Malian villagers.

Drought had dried up surface wells. Many mothers' breast milk had also dried up and their infants were dying. These hospitable, hardworking women respected and appreciated their new benefactor who was the mother of two grown daughters. Thrusting their infants into her arms, desperate mothers begged Marx to breastfeed their children. In her anguish, Marx had a visceral experience of combined, powerful realities: the acknowledgment that she could not save the life of the child in her arms, and that every child is our responsibility.

No one is free until everyone is free. To be alive and free, human beings require many kinds of energy, including fuel for cooking and transportation needs. Energy justice issues affect billions of impoverished families. In October of 2009, the Center for Energy and Environmental Security hosted a conference at the University of Colorado in Boulder. Conference speakers addressed the critical needs of the energy-oppressed poor through long-term, interdisciplinary action, information sharing, and deployment of appropriate, sustainable energy technologies.

Beth Osnes, Ph.D. is a theater professor who presented at this energy justice conference. As a mother, author, energy justice activist, and performer, Osnes inspired university students to create Performers Without Borders, which offers vocal empowerment workshops internationally so that women, mothers, and girls can give voice to their ideas and needs. One need that was articulated by the impoverished women was for clean burning, low-cost alternatives to their inefficient, dangerous cooking stoves.

Through decades of integral service and advocacy for participatory development using community theater, Dr. Osnes has experienced how powerfully community theater involves the poor, giving them voice and dignity. Our voices are expressive tools that can be used in empowering transformative ways. For people around the world, the experiences of respect and dignity are among the greatest gifts of all.

In India in 1972, Bunker Roy founded a voluntary organization known as the Barefoot College that serves in the fields of rural women's empowerment and skill development as well as health, irrigation, and safe drinking water programs. The programs of Barefoot College are influenced by the Gandhian philosophy of each village being sustainably self-reliant.

From villages in Fiji, Peru, Rwanda, India, and beyond, largely unschooled women continue to arrive at the Barefoot College to learn needed skills, such as building, installing, and repairing solar lamps and water pumps. Empowered with new confidence, these women return home after six months as leaders and role models, lighting up their communities with solar lanterns and enthusiasm for the empowerment of girls and women.

In 1968, the American poet and political activist Muriel Rukeyser asked: "What would happen if one woman told the truth about her life? The world would split open." We need to hear these stories. Despite being the majority of humanity, women and children continue to lack resources, social power, and an equal voice. Participatory development projects and media production companies, including Her Many Voices, are enhancing global visibility and empowering transformation for women who are creating a new world.

Although women's contributions have been largely unrecognized and excluded for millennia, opportunities to include themselves in the human story are increasing. How will we create an environment and culture in which all people prosper? For participatory development and popular participation in social change to be effective, an ethic of deep democracy is essential. Deep democracy is committed to respectfully bringing forth and including the voice of every participant, regardless of how young, inexperienced, or oppressed they may be. Disentangle from the sorrow, Irish poet John O'Donohue reminds us gently. Rest, replenish, and awaken the young soul for the new tomorrow.

Pause, Reflect, and Record

- How might mothers create more space for their leadership?

- In what ways does the future of the world depend on women?

- Name three women who have supported or motivated you in some way. Describe their contributions to your life. How might you express your gratitude?

- How will we create an environment and a culture in which all women and girls prosper? Consider what concrete offering, role, or actions you could make.

43

Elder Engagement

It is for us, the living ... to be dedicated here
to the unfinished work
which they who fought here
have thus far so nobly advanced.

—Abraham Lincoln

If we want to leave a living legacy, we have to create one. For a renaissance of the human spirit, for the metamorphosis of unjust societies, and for the Great Turning of destructive currents toward the conscious creation of new paradigms, the wisdom and engagement of our elders is essential.

"It takes a very long time to become young," observed Pablo Picasso who made innovative art into his nineties. Like many wise elders, he discovered that one of the best ways to lift people up is to show them what is fresh and beautiful and good in life. Life's experiences include times rich with creative productivity and thriving relationships as well as times of difficulty marked by illness, divorce, grief, or unanticipated change of career or loss of employment. With mindfulness and compassion, we learn to welcome it all, for each moment carries a gift or learning of some kind. This inner process reduces the sorrow of leaving life unlived.

Corita Kent was an artist, educator, and former nun who devoted her life to making art with messages of love and peace. She wrote, "Life is a succession of moments. To live each one is to succeed." When we've grown up with experiences of the beauty, safety, and goodness of the world, it's easier to know what is out of place when we witness things that are not so good. Core values that developed as we gardened with our father or went fishing with our grandmother tell us that corruption, cruelty, apathy, and environmental degradation don't belong here. Innumerable people survive life's challenges with resilience and often experience insights, personal growth, and even epiphanies. Many human beings who've had the great opportunity to grow old evolve and contribute until their last breath.

Goodness To Go

Two-thirds of all people who have ever reached sixty-five years of age are alive today. By the year 2025, nearly 60 percent of the U.S. population will be fifty-five years old or older, and in another generation the majority in many nations will be over fifty. Depending on the prescription of our glasses, this fact could be seen as a catastrophic success of modern medicine creating societal burdens or a time to celebrate a world of opportunity. Even if we live to be 100, our lives are brief flashes in the vastness of eternity. What matters is what we do with our time.

Millions of productive seniors are "saging," not merely aging. They're growing wiser throughout the phase of life coming to be known as elderhood, or our second adulthood. Many elders and people of all ages who cultivate wisdom come to a place where their spirituality and daily life are inseparable. Unwilling to conform to convention, they contribute mightily to the evolution of society. Although living to a ripe old age has great potential and provides many opportunities, longevity alone does not guarantee maturity or wisdom. Intention and attention are required for the processes involved in psychological and spiritual maturation. These are some of the deepest forms of consciousness transformation that humans undergo, and wise elders are often awash in a sea of compassion, creativity, and gratitude.

The beauty of a wise elder is a work of art. The pioneering feminist writer Betty Friedan wrote *The Fountain of Age* when she was seventy-two years young. She celebrated: "We have barely even considered the possibilities in age for new kinds of ... purposeful work and activity, learning and knowing, community and care. ... For to see age as continued human development involves a revolutionary paradigm shift."

Longevity in most developed nations was extended thirty years in the twentieth century. We've changed the shape and meaning of a lifetime in ways we do not fully understand, according to Mary Catherine Bateson, Ph.D., the daughter of renowned anthropologist Margaret Mead. Bateson is the cultural anthropologist and former English professor who wrote *Overlapping Lives: Culture and Generation in Transition* and *Composing a Further Life: The Age of Active Wisdom*, among other books. Dr. Bateson and others call our first adulthood of child rearing and building careers as Adulthood I. The age of active wisdom, which may extend from forty to eighty years of age and beyond, is referred to as Adulthood II.

The analogy of adding a room to a home is used by Dr. Bateson to understand the impact of adding decades to a lifetime. Creating new space brings new opportunities that change the way we live. We use our time and energy differently when we add a woodshop with a table saw or a studio with new art supplies or digital technologies. As a result of the extension of our lifespans, we're evolving into a rather different species, inhabiting new niches, and challenged to adapt as we integrate the expectation of extended time and space into our current life design. Bateson writes: "We have not added decades to life expectancy by simply extending old age; instead, we have opened up a new space part-way through the life course, a second and different kind of adulthood that precedes old age, and as a result every stage of life is undergoing change." Beyond financial implications, our longer lives hold tremendous opportunity for fulfillment and integral service.

Metanoia—Personal Metamorphosis

Throughout our lifetimes, we encounter countless opportunities to grow and deepen our social involvement. The inner work and personal evolution to which we commit benefits others across space and time. Sometimes a "simple" change of heart seems innocuous. At other times, its metamorphosis leads to a proclamation that emancipates slaves and lifts fervent ideals into a moral sky.

More words have been written about President Abraham Lincoln than nearly any other human being. Lincoln endured at least two failed business endeavors, a "nervous breakdown," a mentally unstable wife, the death of a son, and decades of failed bids to political office. As a new president of a divided nation, it took tremendous self-reflection for Lincoln to fully commit to the emancipation of slaves. His personal *metanoia* transformation joined the rising abolitionist tide that led to the Thirteenth Amendment, freeing all citizens of the United States from slavery for all time.

Maggie Kuhn founded the Gray Panthers in 1970 as an intergenerational movement working for social and economic justice and peace for all people. Kuhn wrote: "We are the risk-takers; we are the innovators; we are the developers of new models. We are trying the future on for size. That is our role." Emphasizing civic participation and responsibility, the Gray Panthers continues to celebrate the intelligence and vital contributions of elders.

"Everyone is the age of their heart," states a Guatemalan proverb. Our inner child can thrive in happiness as our laugh lines deepen. Over two millennia ago, the Chinese philosopher Mencius wrote, "Great is the man who hasn't lost his childlike heart." *It takes a long time to become young.*

Goodness To Go

For centuries, spiritual aspirants have vigorously pursued and integrated spiritual practices that strengthen and purify hearts and minds while engaging with gratitude and happiness in their daily responsibilities.

You're only as young as you think. Often we feel the way we think, and what we think is what we get. The pioneering artist Georgia O'Keeffe painted and worked with clay into her nineties. Anne Spoerry, M.D. offered integral service as a physician-pilot until she was no longer physically capable of doing so. At eighty years of age, Dr. Spoerry was still flying medical missions to reach people who did not have access to medical care. This humanitarian elder dedicated her entire life to helping people, expecting nothing in return.

Wisdom traditions teach that as we think, so we become. In *Counterclockwise*, Ellen J. Langer presents research on the health of elders and the power of possibility. She found that elders' thoughts and beliefs about aging significantly affected their experience of it. Those who were mindful about not succumbing to fatalism were much more likely to remain vital and contributing into their old age. The playwright George Bernard Shaw wrote, "We don't stop playing because we grow old; we grow old because we stop playing."

Personal transformation can continue throughout our later years; the choice is ours in every moment. Many elders are questioning the old notion of "retiring" from one's life work, especially since feelings of isolation and loneliness are on the rise. In 2000, a survey by the American Association of Retired Persons (AARP) reported that a fifth of people over age forty-five experienced chronic loneliness; by 2010, this had increased to a third of people in the second half of life. As mentioned earlier in the chapter on volunteerism, loneliness is linked to serious health problems. One of the best prescriptions for preventing loneliness is ongoing community engagement in which beneficial service is offered to a meaningful cause.

The experience of seasoned professionals contains considerable economic and political clout. The longevity revolution in many countries demands that economists develop new economic indicators in order to make intelligent predictions. The historian Theodore Roszak, author of *The Making of an Elder Culture*, stated that the best measure of a society's wellness is the national life expectancy. A society may be productive in material terms, but if longevity is not increasing, there is something fundamentally problematic.

Today in developed nations, 95 percent of people over sixty are in relatively good health and expect to live at least another twenty-five years.

Gradually, cultural cues and clichés about old age that negatively impact self-concepts and behavior are decreasing. Mindful elders refuse to be victims of stereotypes about aging and health. By doing so, they open to possibilities of being more productive and healthy into old age, and creatively designing their second adulthood. What do you want to do with the rest of your life?

Mature elders are usually less interested in superficial relationships, entitlement, or fifteen minutes of fame. Much of Western culture has swung toward self-absorption, grandiosity, and narcissism. We try to justify thoughts that we *deserve* endless cosmetic surgeries or a vacation and new car every year. Elders often move beyond the whining insistence of *I deserve*. They let go of, often out of necessity, compulsivity about maintaining a youthful appearance. Although many regard the body as a temple of the soul that is to be respected with healthy nutrition and exercise, they know their body does not define them. Their focus shifts from this external package of persona to the integrity and vitality of their heart and mind. While it's futile to try to *look* forever young, we can *be* forever young.

A habit that many elders want to be free of is acquiring more "stuff." "We move among the things we thought we wanted: now they want us," wrote poet Linda Pastan. As we let go, we lighten up. Materialism can become an addiction that fuels hedonistic obsessions with appearances, status, and symbols of wealth. Many lives are strangled by desires, suffocating under too many things that they thought they wanted or deserved. Stuff does not make us happy and it drains our life's energy. He who dies with the most "toys" does not win. Relatively free of a hyper-drive to consume, accumulate, and continuously upgrade, wise elders create life-enhancing legacies through their energy, intelligence, and compassion.

The enhanced freedom of elderhood includes freedom *from* and freedom *for*. Many elders in industrialized nations are relatively free from child rearing and career responsibilities as well as from old beliefs, stereotypes, and habits of consumerism. "Downsizing" is an example of decreased attachment to the size of one's home. Many elders are choosing smaller homes, valuing quality, beauty, and function over accumulating stuff and the space to store it.

This *less is more* movement reflects the words of William Morris, a leader in the nineteenth-century Arts and Crafts movement: "Have nothing in your house that you do not know to be useful or believe to be beautiful." As people free themselves from materialism, more resources such as money, energy, and time are freed up for supporting causes important to them, for developing new vocations, and for creating their legacies of goodness to go.

Making the World More Beautiful

What can you do to make the world more beautiful? This is a soulful inquiry, and the nurturing and crafting of our soul extends throughout our lifetimes. The understanding of many wise beings is that we do not possess a soul: soul possesses us in such a way that we're in communion with the inner Self. The writer Willa Cather described the soul as an essential spirit, an expressive and inviolable self. She felt that the task of each person is to create a life that would "free the expressive self." Consider ways to manifest your goodness to go as you free your expressive self.

An ancient Indian text describes the soul as a lamp whose light is steady; fortunately, this kind of lamp does not depend on fossil fuels. Blind reliance on resource depletion of forests, coal, and oil has devastated many earth ecologies, and people of all ages are wakening to new behavioral and economic paradigms. Elders who mentor young visionaries are needed in this time of transformation that aspires to making the world more beautiful on many levels. Harry Smith was an avant-garde artist whose varied projects included filmmaking and painting in the context of new paradigm thinking. When his multi-volume *Anthology of American Folk Music* was reissued in 1997, it garnered two Grammy awards. One of the young people that Smith's holistic creativity inspired was Warren Karlenzig, who wrote *How Green is Your City?* "I plan metro systems," Karlenzig says, "that include transportation, land use, energy, water, food, buildings, people, and how these systems can reduce risk, energy, and resource use, thus increasing resilience."

The wisdom of sages makes the world more beautiful. Aging is being redefined and perceived anew. Attitudes toward aging are becoming more positive as the generative concerns, potentials, and contributions of elders are understood as assets, not liabilities. Stereotypes that render the elderly as passive and dependent are fading as recognition that we can grow old with grace and wisdom increases. The gathering of elders in community and wisdom circles is increasing. For many years, the author of *From Aging to Saging*, Rabbi Zalman Schachter-Shalomi, mentored individuals and facilitated regular meetings that integrated spiritual perspectives into everyday life.

470

The guidance and integral service of a generation of sages will benefit the world in untold ways. Gerontology conferences held around the world support elders on their path to becoming sages. Some elements of these gatherings include reflection on images of aging, life review, life repair, accepting mortality, mentoring, and clarifying what legacy they want to leave. These contemplations help elders weave the threads of their years into an integrated tapestry that benefits others as well as themselves.

Robert Atchley, Ph.D. is a distinguished professor emeritus in gerontology who's been awarded for his research on spirituality and aging. Atchley recognizes that a goal of spiritual traditions is to move from a fear-driven to a love-motivated life. He finds many ways to make the world more loving and beautiful, and writes "You know something worth knowing if you know that you are loved." This love inspires us to serve. In one of his songs, Atchley sings, "The light from within is our illumination / We are drawn to be love and to serve."

"Social capital" refers to the value of social networks and communities. Elders increase the beauty and depth of social networks by mentoring younger people and sharing their experience, compassion, and creativity. Like most people, elders value the trust, reciprocity, and cooperation that enliven genuine communities. This connectivity, in turn, facilitates the exchange of information, skills, and mutual support that make possible civic engagement, collective action, and community service.

The civic engagement of every generation is the foundation of democracy, and new ways to be involved politically are emerging. Recent elections in the United States made clear the effectiveness of integrating "on the ground" campaign strategies with sophisticated technology and targeted demographic information. Although social movements and technological changes, including radio, television, mobile devices, and expanding Internet connectivity, transform the way people interact, wise elders remind us not to isolate but to nurture face-to-face interconnectivity.

It has long been the role of elders, as well as an honored pursuit of adolescents, to raise the great questions of meaning and purpose. We're reminded that anyone of any age can die at any time. Elders help younger generations consider what they want their legacy to be and to accept that it can take many years to discover what path or destiny is calling. It's possible to cultivate and apply our talents until the day we leave our physical forms. Wise elders are mindful of the present moment as they cultivate compassion and resiliency, learn from setbacks, and face the future with integral optimism.

Many elders deepen along their path of spirituality as the days and years go by. Eugene C. Bianchi, religion professor emeritus at Emory University in Atlanta, Georgia and author of *Elder Wisdom: Crafting Your Own Elderhood* and *Aging as a Spiritual Journey*, has noted that many creative elders work against the cultural expectations of old paradigms by embracing social and environmental causes. Their pursuits enrich their later years as well as the world. By resisting the pressures of "conventional reality," the vocations and legacies of vital elders leave the world a better place for future generations.

One example is former president Jimmy Carter. Since leaving the White House in 1981, Carter has been instrumental in humanitarian service, including his involvement with Habitat for Humanity, disease eradication in developing nations, and assistance in resolving international conflicts. Growing numbers of elders embrace their role as mentors for future generations and recognize that their participation is needed to solve community and global problems.

Eugene Odum is referred to as the father of modern ecology, and spoke widely about environmental responsibility until his death in 2002. A new breed of eco-theologians was inspired by the Catholic priest and "geologian" Thomas Berry. Until his death at ninety-four in 2009, Berry advocated for a return to earth-based spirituality. Many elders in every nation are committed to causes great and small, far and near, that make the world a more beautiful place.

Empowered Elders Create Vital Legacies

Medical studies have found repeatedly that physical and mental health is enhanced for those with purpose and meaningful involvements. The world needs elders who are able to emerge from cocoons they may have spun, to refresh their courageous compassion, and to share their wisdom and service. This is not a time to space out, practice ignorance, feed greed, or fade into the sunset. Our world needs mature, engaged optimists right now.

"I came to live out loud," wrote Emile Zola, a political activist who was France's most prominent novelist in the late nineteenth century. Some people acquiesce to belonging to the "silent majority," and many others have little choice but to live day in and day out with their voices "chained in their throats," as poet Maggie Anderson wrote. When we have the good fortune to live in environments that are not repressive or violent, whether domestic or national, we might take freedom of speech for granted. However, every freedom requires mindful vigilance.

Around the world, older citizens are overcoming silences imposed by their cultures and families and are speaking up in diverse and compelling ways. Many elders continue their human rights activities until their bodies let go of life. Appreciating that libraries are vital common grounds for communities to meet and educate themselves, an elder in San Francisco who was partially blinded by small strokes campaigned to keep local libraries open when they were threatened by budget cuts.

More nuns are choosing to be free from fear of expressing their conscientious convictions and willing to accept Vatican criticism of their work for reproductive rights and social justice. Sister Simone Campbell, leader of the "Nuns on the Bus" tour in 2012, denounced Republican budget proposals that included tax cuts for America's richest two percent and gutted social services that would result in increased suffering for many citizens living in poverty.

Economic empowerment is a vital issue at every age. The recession that began in 2008 resulting from unregulated financial schemes seriously damaged prospects for millions of people at home and abroad, especially those for people over forty-five years of age. Many businesses have closed, including more than 40,000 factories in the United States alone. Most jobs lost have not been recovered. Many people whose homes were foreclosed are in dire straits, and foreclosure fraud continues.

Those over fifty-five have seen their retirement savings cut nearly in half and age discrimination definitely exists among employers. With working days numbered and prolonged rates of unemployment in older age groups, many realize that these losses can't be recouped. However, with resiliency, health, and creative thinking, opportunities exist to reinvent our lives and develop new ways to contribute to the common good.

Of the 78 million members of the post–World War II generation known as baby boomers, the nearly 40 million women boomers are the first cohort of women to have easier access to education, reproductive choice, and financial independence. With longer life spans, they've had the opportunity to begin navigating the unchartered waters of their second adulthood. Postmenopausal vitality and creativity are evolutionary forces. The energy that the entire boomer generation can generate in second adulthood is capable of being an agent of another era of social transformation.

Goodness To Go

Many of the boomer generation were affected by both the positive ideals of the 1960s social movements and by some shadow elements of reactive rebellion and narcissism. The mature compassion and global concern of boomers and their coming gerontocracy have the potential to create a social sea change, shifting human consciousness on an unprecedented scale.

Theodore Roszak published *The Making of a Counter Culture* in 1969. He believed that the counterculture of the 1960s was a very special population because the formative years of its members were a particularly potent historical experience. This generation's significant, often radical challenges of the status quo acquainted them with the willingness and ability to make big changes. The Vietnam War ended, the civil rights of women and African Americans moved forward, and the Environmental Protection Agency was founded. What is the awakening and social revolution needed now?

The counterculture generation already has a place in history, but its most powerful contribution to human civilization may be its members' roles as elders at this pivotal time. They're going to be older for a much longer time than they were young. Just as the potential and possibilities of youth can be wasted on the young, age can be wasted on the old. Hopefully, the tremendous potential of resourced elders will be activated because we need their integral service and genuine wisdom more than ever before.

Being the Change

As we've discussed, the present generation of elders has witnessed dramatic societal and technological changes in their lifetimes and can be a vital force for global healing. Developing meaningful purposes and contributions is an important motif for wise aging. Our callings never retire. Taking a stand for elder engagement, the Gray Panthers' Maggie Kuhn has declared, "My aches and pains are less important than my agenda."

An older businessman, Bill Hansbury, had his lower leg amputated due to serious infection. Soon thereafter, he started a foundation to help amputees buy prosthetic limbs. Through his integral service, Hansbury befriended a young boy who'd also required an amputation, offering ongoing mentoring and inspiration.

After her husband died, a Japanese professor escaped the violent conflict in Syria in 2011, where she'd lived for decades. Eventually, she found ways to raise funds in Japan to support her former students' humanitarian efforts. The young people had emailed their respected teacher about their goal to create a safe underground school for some of the thousands of children who weren't able to attend school due to Syria's civil war.

People in their seventies, eighties, and nineties are unlike any grandparents in human history, and millions continue to work. Vocations in elderhood may be paid or unpaid. In her eighties, former Senator Dorothy Rupert teaches a civic engagement course at the University of Colorado, challenging students to consider how moral courage vitalizes democratic social change. Older entrepreneurs and innovators in education, business, design, governance, and technology are catalyzing cultural and economic renewal around the globe.

Every day, new life-affirming stories celebrate ways that elders contribute to the planet, to younger people, and to their cultures. Pioneering social entrepreneur, inventor, and former psychiatrist Paul Polak, M.D. founded the International Development Enterprise in 1981 to manufacture and distribute water recovery solutions, such as drip-irrigation systems and treadle pumps for the developing world. He's written more than a hundred papers in the fields of mental health, agriculture, design, and development, focusing on affordability, simple design, and mobilizing our humanitarian spirit. Like many generative elders, Dr. Polak knows that excellence is not an act but a habit.

In 2007, Dr. Polak founded Windhorse International as part of his revolution to benefit the 2.6 billion people living on $2 a day. The mission of this social venture is to lead a revolution in how companies design, price, market, and distribute products to benefit billions of people living in poverty. Its first division is Spring Health Water, which sells affordable safe drinking water to rural Indians through village kiosk owners using simple electro-chlorination technology. Disease rates plummet and girls who formerly spent hours finding water are able to attend school.

In Dr. Polak's first book, *Out of Poverty: What Works When Traditional Approaches Fail*, he wrote, "Working to alleviate poverty is a lively, exciting field capable of generating new hope and inspiration." The unconventional thinking and disruptive innovation of his enterprises, including D-Rev (Development Revolution), has created many practical solutions to address community health and global poverty. His newsletter spreads the word about how revolutions in design and big business can end poverty.

Elders encourage us to think in novel ways and expand our circle of caring. In 2009, Paul Polak was named one of the world's "Brave Thinkers" by *Atlantic Monthly*. Along with President Barack Obama and Apple's game changer Steve Jobs, these new-paradigm thinkers were recognized for their creative courage and for being willing to "risk careers, reputations, and fortunes to advance ideas that upend an established order."

In a world that honored deep democracy and equity, every human being would have the choice to live by design, not default or assault. Designing our lives includes preparing for a graceful exit; elders are especially aware that physical death is inevitable and perhaps imminent. Learning to navigate change well during our lives greatly assists the peacefulness and ease with which we meet the great change of death.

"Of all mindfulness meditations," the Buddha experienced, "that on death is supreme." Although we know that death is inevitable, most of us would rather not think about, accept, or embrace it. Many wisdom traditions teach that death is like a mirror in which the true meaning of life is reflected, and encourage us to hold its reality in our consciousness on a daily basis. Obviously, if we wait until we're on our deathbed to wake up, it's far too late. It's been said that when we die, we take only the love in our hearts. Regardless of the amount of money we've amassed or consumer goods we've accumulated, they stay here.

"All that is not given is lost," said Hasari Pal, the peasant farmer featured in *City of Joy*, a novel set in Calcutta, India. Pal was forced by flood and famine to leave his ancestral home and eke out a living as a rickshaw puller in the "black hole of Calcutta." As we consider our legacy, we might ask ourselves what we've given, if we've been kind, what good deeds we've offered, and how engaged we were in manifesting the purpose of our lives.

As we design our lives of integral service, we include time to explore our creativity and spirituality, to travel, have fun, and be with our families. It's helpful to retreat from the world and its disturbing news for sacred rest and spiritual regeneration. The in-breath of self-care is essential to the out-breath of service, and we recognize that many people are too unwell to substantially contribute to others.

"Every second is of infinite value," wrote Goethe. As you consider your legacy, practice self-inquiry: How well have you lived? How well have you loved? What changes would you like to make at this point? Ask yourself probing questions on a regular basis. Few of us want to have worries or regrets on our deathbeds. If we remember this throughout our lives, we'll understand the importance of living our lives in such a way that we can simply let go of the physical body in a state of deep peace and happiness when the time comes. There is freedom and peace in the recognition that we've done enough.

Our later years have been called the Age of Integrity. Periodic life review and revisiting the questions of how well we're living, loving, and learning to let go are valuable aids throughout life's journey. When we let go of less-than-optimal habits, it's possible to resurrect ourselves in unforeseen new forms. Since people are taking longer to grow up and much longer to grow old, re-creating ourselves is an ongoing task. Every stage of life is more meaningful if we take time for reflection and integration. Until our last breath, we can live our lives to the fullest, committed to our highest values and expressing our deepest integrity.

Pause, Reflect, and Record

- Philosopher Yasuhiko Kimura states that the purpose of life is to evolve, to live our lives in integrity with life's creative vision, and to participate in the evolutionary thrust for optimization. What thoughts and questions arise from reflecting on these ideas?

- What do you want your legacy to be? How can you make the world more just and beautiful, healthy or wise?

- What creative resources will you bring to bear on the last season of your life?

- "All that is not given is lost." At this point in your life, what does this phrase mean to you?

44

We're Good to Go

When you serve, you see life as whole.
The impulse to serve emerges naturally
and inevitably from this way of seeing.

—Rachel Naomi Remen, M.D.

The profound gift of human life is rare and precious. In this vast universe, there may be life nowhere else but on the emerald jewel of planet earth. Our lives are brief chapters in a multimillion-year arc of evolutionary development, and they're precious because a great gift has been bequeathed. That gift is the capacity to be conscious of Consciousness and to have the awareness and agency to choose, not just react to stimuli. "Everything you want is on the other side of fear," wrote George Addair, founder of the Omega Vector human potential seminars. "Integrity is our destiny, it is the light that guides your way."

Humans have the liberating ability to choose where we'll place our attention and how harmoniously we'll create our shared future together. This human opportunity to determine where we'll take a stand and to what values we'll commit offers tremendous freedom and responsibility. In so many ways, we are each other's business. We are also each other's harvest, wrote poet Gwendolyn Brooks, the first African American to be awarded the Pulitzer Prize. We are each other's "magnitude and bond," not only now but through eternity.

"We may have all come on different ships, but we are in the same boat now," Dr. Martin Luther King, Jr. noted. During the writing of this chapter, my twelve-year-old daughter shared a story she'd been working on. "They say it's always darkest just before the dawn," Grace Shanti wrote. "For every darkness, there is a hero who carries the torch. We are all torch-bearers on the earth. And every single being is a protector, a guardian, a hero rising." In the Bhagavad Gita, an ancient spiritual text from Grace's home country of India, it says, "The soul is a lamp whose light is steady, for it burns in a shelter where no winds come."

Goodness To Go

The Buddha encouraged us to train ourselves in doing good that lasts and bring happiness. We're invited to expand our circle of caring and engage ourselves in meaningful labors of love. When we do, it is love that does the labor. Although the concerns we face are immediate and urgent, it is not so much our goals that motivate us but the sense of direction that they provide. Plant your vision. Water your dreams. Follow your North Star.

"Begin anywhere," advised John Cage, one of the most influential and pioneering experimental composers of the twentieth century. The contribution of your creativity and integral service is essential to the design and meaning of the whole. "The best thing about the future," remarked Abraham Lincoln, "is that it comes only one day at a time." Day by day, the flow of life provides countless opportunities to extend our capacity to be of benefit.

Breathe gently and fully as you consider that the future of democracy in the Arab world and around the globe is uncertain. Tens of thousands of citizens are dying in civil wars. American mainstream political institutions are breaking down. European finances are in crises and some analysts predict that austerity measures under stagnation are bound to make things worse. More African Americans are imprisoned now than were slaves in the past. Serious threats to peace and environmental health are escalating.

Defunding undermines public education systems; universities are being privatized and corporatized, and charter schools are breaking up communities in some regions. Every day in America, truckers obtain sex from a thousand abused girls who are trying to survive as dehumanized "lot lizards." More awareness among truckers is leading to less mutual degradation and increased humanitarianism through Truckers Against Trafficking. Our integral service is needed and the choices we make now ripple around the world. In every moment, the choice is ours.

The nineteenth-century French novelist Honore de Balzac observed, "It is easy to sit up and take notice; what is difficult is getting up and taking action." Eleanor Roosevelt chose to get up and dedicate her life to compassion in action. Through her work with many organizations, including the United Nations, Roosevelt recognized that our choices and actions could lead to the either the upliftment of humanity or its diminution. "When will our consciences grow so tender that we will act to prevent human misery rather than avenge it?" she asked. "We have to face the fact that either all of us are going to die together or we are going to learn to live together and if we are to live together we have to talk."

Meaningful dialogue frequently galvanizes committed action. As we move toward planetization, every culture has something of great value to offer the whole. Community members and leaders around the globe are creating partnerships intended to lead to a more equitable, peaceful, and verdant world and a renaissance of the human spirit. While it's easy to lose faith in our ability to avert irreparable damage to ecological and social systems, we continue to step into the new unknown with courage and trust that small changes add up.

There are many ways to spread the light of beneficial change, social equity, justice, and wise stewardship of planet earth for generations to come. If we reached a 75 percent recycling rate by 2030, we will have destroyed fewer resources for future generations and 2.3 million jobs will be created in the United States alone. Returning materials to production makes sustainable sense. When they're dumped in landfills that leak toxic chemicals and emit methane, seventy-two times more heat and CO^2 is trapped over the short term. The ethic of the growing green economy meets the triple bottom line of people, planet, and profits.

Joanna Macy, Ph.D. is an octogenarian who continues to serve globally as a renowned eco-philosopher and spiritual activist. She writes, "The most remarkable feature of this historical moment on Earth ... is that we are beginning to wake up, as from a millennia-long sleep, to a whole new relationship to our world, to ourselves, and to each other. ... Gratitude is like the seed that contains everything within it so that life can grow. ... It's a privilege to be alive in this time, when we can choose to take part in the self-healing of our world."

Doing All the Good You Can

The eighteenth-century theologian John Wesley wrote, "Do all the good you can. By all the means you can. In all the places you can. At all the times you can. With all the people you can. As long as you ever can." Together we can change the world and move from chaos to renaissance. With our radical goodwill, reverence for life, and compassionate service, a global community that honors the dignity of every living being will be created. The universal Golden Rule proclaims the essential value of doing unto others as we would have them do unto us. At the heart of this code of conduct is the awareness that we are one. There is no other.

Goodness To Go

Awareness is growing that it's what we scatter not what we gather that reveals the life we've lived. Although her brief life was snuffed out by the horrors of World War II, Anne Frank practiced forgiveness and her words cultivated and scattered hope. In her journal, she noted enthusiastically: "How wonderful it is that no one has to wait, but can start right now to gradually change the world! How wonderful it is that everyone, great and small, can immediately help bring about justice by giving of themselves! ... Give whatever there is to give! You can always—always—give something, even if it's a simple act of kindness. If everyone were to give in this way and didn't scrimp on kindly words, there would be much more love and justice in the world!"

With self-compassion and awareness, discern and evaluate what level of challenge you're willing to embrace as you move from concern to action. Every day, ask yourself how you can inspire and bring forward the goodness in yourself and others. Although you may have empathy for numerous crucial issues, tap into what matters most to you so that your energy isn't frazzled and singed like a moth to a flame. Your voice matters—deliver your message so that it ripples through the web of the world, inspires community gatherings, or rings across fields and through halls of power.

Woodrow Wilson, the twenty-eighth president of the United States, galvanized the spirit of his supporters with this understanding: "You are here to enable the world to live more amply, with greater vision, and with a finer spirit of hope and achievement. You are here to enrich the world." Saying yes to your goodness opens your world and galvanizes your spirit of service.

Now is all we have. By recognizing that we are enough and have enough, we loosen the consuming stranglehold of the industrial growth society. No matter what is happening, it's our choice to be grateful for this breath, this moment, this situation. Although it may be tempting, it's limiting to sidestep a challenge in an attempt to avoid discomfort or pain. C. S. Lewis, the twentieth-century Irish writer of *The Chronicles of Narnia*, experienced intense grief in his life. He wrote that pain is the chisel that shapes who we are; it can be a messenger and a great teacher.

Chiseling away is one aspect of letting go. Patient, skillful chiseling removes marble that obscures the angel in the stone. It can be a letting go of dysfunctional delusions that we'll never be "good enough." Most of the time, *good enough* is more than fine. Woody Allen and others have observed that 99 percent of success is just showing up. When we show up with everything we are in the present moment and follow our north star, a compelling thread of calling or meaning or purpose impels our lives. Some call it love, the Way, or knowing their Truth. Others experience it as spirit, creative intelligence, or the energy of inspiration and devotion.

Find your purpose. Challenge yourself to move outside your comfort zone. Nurture support for your voice of yes. Ask yourself what is one action that you can do now. Positive action is the antidote to habits of resistance or despair. Take a stand and allow curiosity to be an antidote for fear. You can do it, one moment at a time. Show your shine and never say never. Don't take anything for granted. With gratitude for the wonder of being alive at this time, strengthen your capacity and follow through on your mind and heart's resolve to share your gifts with the world.

Celebrating Goodness

"The effect of one good-hearted person is incalculable," wrote Oscar Arias, who received the 1987 Nobel Peace Prize for his efforts as the president of Costa Rica in pacifying Central American upheavals. Let's celebrate everyone who is planting and growing seeds of goodness into orchards that nourish us all. Thank goodness they're not delaying their adventure of integral service until some fantasy future when all their ducks might be in a row.

The Swedish statesman Dag Hammarskjold wrote: "For all that has been, thanks. For all that will be, Yes." Justice Louis Brandeis declared that the highest office in a democracy is that of a citizen ready and willing to exercise democratic rights and responsibilities to meet the challenges of the day. As so many generations of wise elders have told us, we hold in our hands the ability to make the world a better place. Mutual healing is in our collective self-interest. Let's remember to take seven generations of ancestors and seven future generations into consideration as we act now.

Helping war veterans assimilate back into society with meaningful work is one example of compassion and gratitude in action. There is growing concern about the long-term social and economic dislocation of thousands of veterans, including 200,000 Vietnam veterans who remain homeless decades after their tours of duty. Veterans from more recent wars are living with disfigurement and traumatic brain injuries; suicide rates are epidemic. Veterans need meaningful engagement as they re-enter society, and a new frontier with a mission that is appealing to many is the growing green economy investing in cutting-edge technology.

Goodness To Go

In response to this need, a Colorado entrepreneur founded Veterans Green Jobs as well as Boulder Nature Corps, which is involved with ecosystem restoration. Since 2008, Veterans Green Jobs has offered training programs and worked with veterans to develop sustainable employment skills in the green economy. Jobs in green construction, energy efficiency, outdoor conservation, environmental remediation, sustainable agriculture, and wildland firefighting help veterans maintain their sense of service and give back to their communities.

Your goodness to go lives in your countless acts of love, kindness, and courage and may receive no recognition. Do them anyway. Now is the time to summon forth your inner courage. Some may laugh or sneer, calling you a naïve fool or zealot. Your informed enthusiasm, ardent zeal, compassion, and commitment to uplift life on this planet are not zealotry. Dive into your heart of service as a responsible revolutionary. We all need you now—your voice, your heart, your resources, your offerings of compassion. All of us are in this together, and together we can do it.

We're good to go. And everything we do makes a difference. In the film *Contact*, Jodi Foster plays the part of an astrophysicist committed to listening for transmissions from extraterrestrial intelligence. Near the film's end, as she courageously prepares for liftoff into the unknown, the young scientist-adventurer acknowledges that she's good to go. At some point, the moment comes when an idea or concern lifts into action.

It's not necessary or advisable to try to take everything with us as we make our first steps into integral service. We only need enough for liftoff. Start anywhere. Consider writing down an action plan of simple, scheduled, specific steps. We're more likely to make progress when our goals are broken into concrete, measurable actions with some kind of structured accountability and positive reinforcement.

As we fulfill and celebrate our goodness, we'll replenish ourselves by practicing self-care, nurturing relationships, strengthening the solidarity of our communities, and encouraging collaboration. Dynamic synergistic effects that benefit all life will result from the weaving together of our integral service.

For All That Will Be—Yes

With each sunrise, life begins anew. Each new dawn offers fresh beginnings, renewed resilience, and untold possibilities. Robert Holden's book *Shift Happens! Live an Inspired Life* emphasizes the joyful vitality that accompanies self-acceptance and living an authentic life moment by moment. With that inspiration, people shift from stagnation to compassion in action. We are all in the same boat under the same dome of sky, and our fates our linked by choices that we make now.

Let a new life begin. Find what supports your experience of the fullness of your heart. Experience your wholeness and give your best to life. The domain of goodness to go is the actualization of our life's purpose, with reverence and justice as essential factors in the choices we make. Within an ecology of maturing wisdom and spirit of service, we recognize the whole world as our country, all life as our family, and doing good as our path. In your caring, may there be no apathy. In your compassion, no expectation. In your generosity, no measure. In your giving, no holding back. Trust that practice makes progress.

In the single step from *no* to *yes*, the journey of a lifetime begins. The author Margaret Shepherd has noted that at times it may seem that the only reliable form of transportation is a leap of faith. If you're willing, make that leap. With gratitude and informed hope, approach community and global challenges with a balanced, authentic sense of optimism. Psychologist and leadership trainer Bert Parlee, Ph.D., calls this positive resilience *integral optimism*. Live inside and beyond optimism as you faithfully peer into darkness with the light of goodness.

What we sow here and now, we will harvest. We receive what we give. Let's tell new stories about the ancient narrative of our inter-being, that we're part of a greater whole. As we embrace this awareness consciously, our definitions of ourselves will transform. Remember that our genetic code is as hardwired for empathy, compassion, and cooperation as it is for competition. Together, we can create peace with justice and equality.

Transform yourself. Transform the world. "Carpenters fashion wood," said the Buddha, "the wise fashion themselves." Recall economist Adam Smith's warning that injustice utterly destroys society; we can close the gap between what we know and what we do. Equitable societies that honor diversity are based on core values such as reverence for life and merciful justice. Our presence and activities on planet Earth need not be harmful, but beneficial to life now and to come. We can create a world where extreme poverty and violence, injustice and involuntary servitude, extinction of species, and environmental degradation do not exist going forward.

"Be a lamp, or a lifeboat, or a ladder," the poet Rumi encouraged. Many hands make light work in our service as global citizens, and we're defined not only by what we create, but also by what we refuse to destroy. We're capable of creating multiracial and multicultural societies with gender equity. These societies will be more than diverse; they'll be inclusive. As beacons of light, we'll illumine the adventure of creative altruism. With resonant empathy and deep commitment to the democratic values of the Golden Rule, we'll be upstanders not bystanders. May we all have ears to hear the song of hope and change that is blowing in the wind; sometimes its gusts are gentle and sometimes it's a mighty roar.

Through engagement with the process of self-inquiry in *Goodness To Go*, you've invested your valuable time and energy. It has been an honor to explore together what makes us come alive, to resource our resilience, and to clarify how our inner spirit of service seeks to manifest. During this renaissance of spirit, may our goodness always be on the go. To future generations, may it be told that we embraced the challenging tasks of our time to deliver the gift of a healthy, just, and sustainable world for us all.

Pause, Reflect, and Record

- Acknowledge yourself for your ongoing engagement with *Goodness To Go*. Look back over the self-inquiries that you addressed in all four sections of this book. What are themes, concerns, and inspirations that recur for you?

- To get the most out of any deep learning, it must be integrated into your life with ongoing support. How might you nurture what you've learned and weave it into an action plan that furthers the mobilization of your integral service?

- What seeds do you want to scatter, to plant and nurture, to share with others?

- Would you be willing to participate in a small Goodness To Go gathering in your community or an online action group? What might be some of the benefits of sharing this creative, compassionate adventure of integral service with companions?

Related Resources

Section One: Summon Your Heart

Chodron, Pema. *Practicing Peace in Times of War*. Boston: Shambhala Publications, Inc., 2007.

Chodron, Pema. *Start Where You Are: A Guide to Compassionate Living*. Boston: Shambhala Publications, Inc., 2003.

Dalai Lama, The. *Healing Anger: the Power of Patience from a Buddhist Perspective*. Ithaca, NY: Snow Lion Publications, 1997.

Dyer, Wayne W. *The Power of Intention: Learning to Co-create Your World Your Way*. Carlsbad, NM: Hay House, Inc., 2004.

Goleman, Daniel. Social Intelligence: The New Science of Human Relationships. New York: Bantam Dell, 2006.

Hanh, Thich Nhat. *The Art of Power*. New York: HarperOne, a division of HarperCollins Publishers, 2007.

Hanh, Thich Nhat. *Being Peace*. Berkeley, CA: Parallax Press, 1987.

Lappe, Frances Moore, and Ann Lappe. *Hope's Edge: The Next Diet for a Small Planet*. New York: Jeremy P. Tarcher/Penguin, 2003.

Levoy, Gregg. *Callings: Finding and Following an Authentic Life*. New York: Three Rivers Press, 1998.

Lowenthal, Martin, and Lar Short. *Opening the Heart of Compassion: Transform Suffering Through Buddhist Psychology and Practice*. Boston: Charles E. Tuttle Company, Inc., 1993.

Seligman, Martin E. P. *Learned Optimism: How to Change Your Mind and Your Life*. New York: Pocket Books, a division of Simon & Schuster, Inc., 1998.

Straub, Gail. *The Rhythm of Compassion: Caring for Self, Connecting with Society*. Boston: Journey Editions, 2000.

Tolle, Eckhart. *The Power of Now: A Guide to Spiritual Enlightenment*. Novato, CA: New World Library, 1999.

Section Two: Empower Your Mind

Castle, Victoria. *The Trance of Scarcity: Stop Holding Your Breath and Start Living Your Life*. San Francisco: Berrett-Koehler Publishers, Inc., 2007.

Enright, M.D., Robert D. *Forgiveness Is a Choice: A Step-by-Step Process of Resolving Anger and Restoring Hope*. Washington, D.C.: APA Life Tools, 2008.

Fisher, Roger, and William Ury. *Getting To Yes: Negotiating Agreement Without Giving In*. Edited by Bruce Patton. New York: Penguin Books, 1991.

Gandhi, Mahatma. 2007. *Peace*. Edited by Cameron Gibb, Annatjie Matthee, and Carolyn Lewis. Boulder: Blue Mountain Arts, Inc.

Greenspan, Miriam. *Healing Through the Dark Emotions: the Wisdom of Grief, Fear, and Despair*. Boston: Shambhala Publications, Inc., 2003.

Hanh, Thich Nhat. *Present Moment Wonderful Moment: Mindfulness Verses for Daily Living*. Berkeley, CA: Parallax Press, 1990.

Hanh, Thich Nhat. *The Art of Power*. New York: HarperOne, a division of HarperCollins Publishers, 2007.

Johnson, Steven. *Mind Wide Open: Your Brain and the Neuroscience of Everyday Life*. New York: Scribner, 2004.

Kegan, Robert, and Lisa Laskow Lahey. *How the Way We Can Talk Can Change the Way We Work: Seven Languages for Transformation*. San Francisco: Jossey-Bass, a Wiley Company, 2001.

LeDoux, Joseph. *The Emotional Brain: the Mysterious Underpinnings of Emotional Life*. New York: a Touchstone Book, published by Simon & Schuster, 1996.

Mitchell, Donald W., and James Wiseman, O.S.B., edit. *Transforming Suffering: Reflections of Finding Peace in Troubled Times*. New York: Doubleday, 2003.

Reivich, Ph.D., Karen, and Andrew Shatte, Ph.D. *The Resilience Factor: 7 Keys to Finding Your Inner Strength and Overcoming Life's Hurdles*. New York: Broadway Books, 2002.

Shafir, M.A. CCC, Rebecca Z. *The Zen of Listening: Mindful Communication in the Age of Distraction*. Wheaton, IL: The Theosophical Publishing House, 2000.

Section Three: Mobilize Integral Service

Brown, Lester R. *Plan B 3.0: Mobilizing the Save Civilization*. New York: W. W. Norton & Company, Inc., 2008.

Burg, Bob, and John David Mann. *The Go-Giver: A Little Story About a Powerful Business Idea*. London: Portfolio, 2007.

Caldicott, M.D., Helen. *If You Love this Planet: A Plan to Heal the Earth*. New York: W. W. Norton & Company, Inc., 1992.

Goleman, Daniel. Social Intelligence: The New Science of Human Relationships. New York: Bantam Dell, 2006.

Hillman, James. *The Soul's Code: In Search of Character and Calling*. New York: Warner Books, 1996.

Jones, D.D., Dennis Merritt. *The Art of Being: 101 Ways to Practice Purpose in Your Life*. New York: Jeremy P. Tarcher/Penguin, 2008.

Keltner, Dacher. *Born to Be Good: The Science of a Meaningful Life*. New York: W. W. Norton & Company, Inc., 2009.

Lowenstein, Frank, Sheryl Lechner, and Erik Bruun, editors. *Voices of Protest: Documents of Courage and Dissent*. New York: Black Dog & Leventhal Publishers, 2007.

Macy, Joanna, and Chris Johnstone. *Active Hope: How to Face the Mess We're in Without Going Crazy*. Novato, CA: New World Library, 2012.

Macy, Joanna. *Widening Circles: A Memoir*. Gabriola Island, BC: New Society Publishers, 2002.

Macy, Joanna. *World As Lover, World As Self*. Berkeley, CA: Parallax Press, 1991.

Skog, Susan. *The Give-Back Solution: Create a Better World With Your Time, Talents, and Travel (whether your have $10 or $10,000)*. Naperville, IL: Sourcebooks, Inc., 2009.

Yamashita, Keith, and Sandra Spataro. *Unstuck: Just How Stuck Are You?* New York: the Penguin Group, 2004.

Zweig, Connie, and Jeremiah Abrams, Ed. *Meeting the Shadow: the Hidden Power of the Dark Side of Human Nature*. New York: Jeremy P. Tarcher/Putnam, a member of Penguin Putnam, Inc., 1991.

Digital Resources

www.350.org

www.afsc.org (American Friends Service Committee)

www.ajws.org (American Jewish World Service)

www.anewstory.org

www.charterforcompassion.org

www.earthday.net

www.girlrising.com

www.GoodnessToGo.org

www.GoodPlanet.org

www.gratefulness.org

www.halfthesky.org

www.jeanhouston.com

www.kiva.org

www.learningtoforgive.com

www.onemother.org

www.parkinsonsyoga.org

www.slaveryfootprint.org

www.thepeacealliance.org

www.thrillionaires.org

www.womenforwomen.org

Index

Index

Y

Z

CPSIA information can be obtained at www.ICGtesting.com
Printed in the USA
BVOW03s0409181113

336581BV00004B/16/P